Complete Automotive Painting

Robert Scharff
Richard J. Paquette

WE ENCOURAGE
PROFESSIONALISM

THROUGH TECHNICIAN
CERTIFICATION

Delmar Publishers Inc.®

NOTICE TO THE READER

For information address Delmar Publishers, Inc.
2 Computer Drive West, Box 15-015,
Albany, New York 12212

Delmar Staff
Editor-in-Chief: Mark W. Huth
Administrative Editor: Joan Gill
Project Editor: Carol Micheli

Printed in the United States of America
Published simultaneously in Canada
by Nelson Canada,
a division of The Thomson Corporation

10 9 8 7 6 5 4 3 2 1

Library of Congress Cataloging-in-Publication Data

Scharff, Robert.
    Complete automotive painting / Robert Scharff, Richard J.
Paquette.
        p.   cm.
    1. Automobiles—Painting.   I. Paquette, Richard J., 1962–
II. Title.
TL154.S33   1990   89-39625
629.28'72—dc20   CIP

511-31
ISBN 0-8273-3582-2

Contents

Preface

The entire automobile industry is changing faster than ever before. This is especially true of the auto body repair and refinishing trade. But before taking a look at the new materials and techniques of vehicle refinishing, Chapter 1 is devoted to shop and personal safety rules and practices. The governmental regulation of OPA, OSHA, and NIOSH that affect body/paint shops are fully covered in this chapter, including the "right-to-know" laws and the proper methods of handling hazardous wastes. This chapter also informs the painters or refinishers how they can receive ASE certification.

Chapters 2, 3, and 4 detail the use of refinishing equipment, spray guns, and compressed air supply equipment. The most up-to-date spray booths are described and they should be maintained. Airless spray gun, electrostatic spraying, and the high-volume, low-pressure (HVLP) systems are covered. While these three "new" systems are required by some state laws, the methods of handling these guns are almost the same as conventional air spray types.

While the work procedures given in Chapters 5 and 6 generally performed by the body shop, the refinisher should know about the materials used so that he/she can properly perform the final refinishing. This is especially true when it comes to methods of handling acid rain difficulties—a major problem to painters in some parts of the country.

Chapters 6 to 11 cover the actual techniques of refinishing, including selection of refinishing materials, preparation of the surface before it is painted, and matching paint colors and the application of paints, including two-coat and tri-coat systems. Chapter 12 is devoted to painting plastic parts and adding special decorative effects. A complete glossary of refinishing terms is given in the Appendix.

A color tinting table and chart appear on page vii and color page i, respectively.

ACKNOWLEDGMENTS

To organize a book requires the help of many companies and people. As noted here are the companies that provided technical data and illustrations for the book. Also, I would like to thank the following for permission to use information from their training programs and manuals.

- Maaco Enterprises, Inc., for the use of text and photographs from the Maaco refinishing training program.
- Toyota Motor Corp. for the use of materials and illustrations from their manual, *Fundamental Painting Procedures*.
- Du Pont Co. for the use of materials from their refinishing handbook.
- PPG Industries, Inc., for information from *Ditzler® Repaint Manual*.
- Binks Mfg. Co. and DeVilbiss Co. for the use of materials from several of their manuals.

In addition, I would like to thank the following for providing the photographs for the color section:

Page i: PPG Industries, Inc.
Page ii: Maaco Enterprises, Inc.
Page iii to vi: America Sikkens, Inc.
Page vii to viii: Sherwin-Williams Co.

And finally, I would like to thank the following persons for reviewing the manuscript and for their helpful comments:

Mr. Joseph Kroeger
Antelope Valley College
3041 West Avenue K
Lancaster, California 93536

Mr. Donald M. Pendergrass
Utah Technical College
1395 North 150 East
Post Office Box 1609
Provo, Utah 84603

Mr. James E. Phillips
Hawkeye Institute of Technology
1501 East Orange Road
Post Office Box 8015
Waterloo, Iowa 50704

Mr. Roger Michael
Northwest Tech BOCES
Park Street
Ogdensburg, New York 13669

GENERAL RULES FOR TINTING (See Color Page i)

Base Color	General Usage	Base Color	General Usage
1. Yellow Gold	Use for reddish-yellow tint in solids and metallics. Lightens flop in metallics.	15. Indo Orange	Use an orange tint in pastel solids and metallics.
2. Lt. Chrome Yellow	Use in substantial amounts to give bright greenish yellow hue. Not used in metallics.	16. Moly Orange (Red Shade)	Use as reddish-orange tint in solids only.
3. Oxide Yellow	Use for reddish-yellow tint in solids, has yellow tint with light flop in metallics.	17. Red Oxide	Use for clean red tone in beige solids, not commonly used in metallics.
4. Indo Yellow	Use for greenish-yellow tint in all colors. Lightens flop in metallics.	18. Transparent Red Oxide	Use to give red-gold tint in metallics. Also beige tint in solids.
5. Transparent Yellow Oxide	Use for yellow tint in solids and metallics. Lightens flop in metallics.	19. Deep Violet	Use as purple tint in pastel solids and metallics. Also use in blues and grays for violet tones.
6. Rich Brown	Use to give clean golden tint to metallics and clean beige to solid colors.	20. Quindo Violet	Use as blue-red tint in pastel solids and metallics.
7. Black	Use where small amounts of black are needed. Has brown or yellow undertone.	21. Magenta Maroon	Use as blue-red tint in pastel solids and metallics.
8. Strong Black	Use where a large amount of black is needed. Has brown or yellow undertone.	22. Phthalo Green (Yellow Shade)	Use as green tint in pastel solids and metallic. Has yellow-green tint.
9. Organic Orange (Light)	Use as reddish-orange tint in pastel solid and metallic colors.	23. Phthalo Green	Use as green tint in all colors.
10. Oxide Red	Use for clean red tint in beige colors. Not commonly used in metallics.	24. Scarlet Red	Use in bright red solid colors.
11. Permanent Red	Use for blue-red tint in pastel solids and metallics. Lightens flop in metallics.	25. Perrindo Maroon	Use as rich brown-maroon tint in solids and metallics.
12. Organic Scarlet	Use as red in pastel solids and metallics.	26. Phthalo Blue (Medium)	Use as blue tint in pastels and metallics. Has a clean red-blue tint.
13. Phthalo Blue (Green Shade)	Use as blue tint in pastel and metallics. Has a very green-blue tint.	27. Phthalo	Use as green tint in all colors.
14. Permanent Blue	Use as blue tint in pastel solids and metallics. Has a very red-blue tint.	28. Phthalo Green (Yellow)	Use as yellow-green tint in pastel solids and metallics.

1. Base colors have two tones: mass tone (as appears in can) and tint tone (small amount mixed with white or aluminum).
2. Colors darken as they dry. Always match on the light side.
3. The same color arrived at with two different formulations (using different pigments) might vary in color under different lights and might weather differently.
4. Metallic colors have varying degrees of flop (obligue angle view). Colors with a deep rich flop contain coarse aluminum and tinting colors with greater transparency or depth.
   a. To maintain a rich flop, use coarse aluminum, and if required, tinting colors with greater transparency.
   b. When the flop requires a grayer appearance, use finer aluminum.

This table and color page i are strictly for tinting existing colors and not original formulation work. When tinting colors it is not recommended to add more than 50 parts per pint, 100 parts per quart or 400 parts per gallon.

(Courtesy of PPG Industries, Inc.)

Preface

Through the generosity of the following companies, photographs and other material have been supplied to enhance the text of this book.

Acme Paint Co.
America Sikkens Inc.
Babcox Publications
Badger Air-Brush Co.
BASF Coating and Inks Div.
Binks Mfg. Co.
Black & Decker, Inc.
Campbell Hausfeld Co.
Champion Pneumatic Machinery Co.
Chrysler Corp.
Dedoes Industries, Inc.
DeVilbiss Co.
Du Pont Co.
Dynatron/Bondo Corp.
Eurovac, Inc.
Fibre Glass Evercoat Co., Inc.
Florida Pneumatic Mfg. Co.
Ford Motor Co.
Forward Mfg. Co., Inc.
General Motors Corp.
Graco, Inc.
Herkules Equipment Co.
Hutchins Mfg. Co.

Inter-Industry Conference on Auto Collision Repair (I-CAR)
Maaco Enterprises, Inc.
Majestic Tools Mfg. Co.
Marson Corp.
Martin-Senour Paint Co.
Meguiar's Mirror Glaze
Motor Publications, Inc.
Nilfisk of America Inc.
Nissan Motors Corp.
Oatey Corp.
O'Brien Corp
Paint-Safe Products
Pittway Corp.
PPG Industries, Inc.
Seelye, Inc.
Sherwin-Williams Co.
Sparton Plastics, Inc.
3M Corp.
Toyota Motor Corp.
Urethane Supply Co. Inc.
Willson Safety Products, Inc.

CHAPTER ONE

SAFETY PROCEDURES

Objectives

After reading this chapter, you will be able to:

- describe the various precautions for personal safety that must be followed in a body shop.
- outline several control measures necessary when working with air contaminants and other hazardous substances.
- describe safety practices to avoid fire and explosion.
- list the classifications of fires.

SHOP SAFETY PRACTICES

The most important considerations in any refinishing shop should be accident prevention and safety. Carelessness and the lack of safety habits cause accidents. Accidents have a far-reaching effect, not only on the victim, but on the victim's family and society in general. More importantly, accidents can cause serious injury, temporary or permanent, or even death. Therefore, it is the obligation of all shop employees and the employer to foster and develop a safety program to protect the health and welfare of those involved.

In the following chapters of this book, the text contains special notations labeled **SHOP TALK,** *CAUTION,* and *WARNING.* Each one is there for a specific purpose. **SHOP TALK** gives added information that will help the technician to complete a particular procedure or make a task easier. *CAUTION* is given to prevent the technician from making an error that could damage the vehicle. *WARNING* reminds the technician to be especially careful of those areas where carelessness can cause personal injury. The following text contains some general *WARNINGs* that should be followed when working in a body and paint shop.

MANUFACTURER'S WARNINGS AND GOVERNMENT REGULATIONS

Most of the products used in a body shop carry warning and caution information that must be read and understood by all users before use. Likewise, all federal (including Occupational Safety and Health Administration [OSHA], Mine Safety and Health Administration [MSHA], and National Institute for Occupational Safety and Health [NIOSH]), state, and local safety regulations should not only be *fully* understood, but strictly observed.

In refinishing shops, hazardous wastes are generated. Every employee in the shop is protected by Right-to-Know laws. These laws started with OSHA's Hazard Communication Standard published in 1983. This document was originally intended for chemical companies and manufacturers that require employees to handle potentially hazardous materials in the workplace. Since then, the majority of states have enacted their own Right-to-Know laws and the federal courts have decided that these regulations should apply to all companies, including the auto refinishing profession.

The general intent of the law is for employers to provide their employees with a safe working place as it relates to hazardous materials. Specifically, there are three areas of employer responsibility:

1. **Training/educating employees.** All employees must be trained about their rights under the legislation, the nature of the hazardous chemicals in their workplace, the labeling of chemicals, and the information about each chemical posted on Material Safety Data Sheets (MSDS). These sheets detail product composition and precautionary information for all products, which can present a health or safety haz-

ard. These sheets or forms are generally prepared by the material supplier. Employees must be familiarized about the general uses, characteristics, protective equipment, accident or spill procedures, and so on associated with major groups of chemicals. This training must be given to employees annually and provided to new employees as part of their job orientation.

2. **Labeling/information about potentially hazardous chemicals.** All hazardous materials must be properly labeled, indicating what health, fire, or reactivity hazard it poses and what protective equipment is necessary when handling each chemical. The manufacturer of the hazardous waste materials must provide all warnings and precautionary information, which must be read and understood by the user before application. Attention to all label precautions is essential to the proper use of the coating and for prevention of hazardous conditions.

3. **Record keeping.** Shops must maintain documentation on the hazardous chemicals in the workplace, proof of training programs, records of accidents and/or spill incidents, satisfaction of employee requests for specific chemical information via the MSDSs, and a general Right-to-Know compliance procedure manual utilized within the shop.

PERSONAL SAFETY AND HEALTH PROTECTION

The following are very important personal safety rules that must be heeded.

AIR PASSAGES AND LUNGS

Abrasive dust, vapors from caustic solutions and solvents, spray mist from undercoats and finishes—all present dangers to the air passages and lungs, especially for workers who are among them day in, day out.

Respirators are usually needed in refinishing shops even though adequate ventilation is provided for the work areas. There are three primary types of respirators available to protect refinishing technicians: the hood or air-supplied respirator, cartridge filter respirator, and dust or particle respirator.

Air-Supplied or Hood Respirators. A NIOSH approved air-supplied respirator provides protection from sensitization and other dangers of inhaling isocyanate paint vapors and mists, as well as from hazardous solvent vapors.

Exposure to isocyanates often found in urethanes and other two-pack or two-part materials can lead to a variety of health problems with symptoms that include dizziness, abdominal pain, and vomiting. If a person is allergy-prone or has already suffered from overexposure to isocyanates, a more severe reaction most likely will occur, even at a lower-level concentration.

The air line respirator is comfortable to wear and does not require fit testing (Figure 1–1). It consists of a half mask, full facepiece, hood or helmet, to which clean, breathable air is supplied through a small diameter hose from a separate compressed air source.

The air line respirator should include a self-contained 3/4 horsepower oilless pump (Figure 1–2) to supply air to either one hood or two half mask respirators. The pump's air inlet must be located in a clean air area. Some shops mount the pumps on an outside wall, away from the dust and dirt generated by shop operations. If shop-compressed air must be used, it must be filtered with a trap and carbon filter to remove oil, water, scale, odor, and taste. The air supply must have a valve to match air pressure to respirator equipment and an automatic control to sound an alarm or shut down the compressor in case of overheating. (Overheating frequently causes carbon monoxide contamination of the air supply.)

Remember that the air source for an air line respirator must be located in a clean, fresh air environment, outside of the spray area.

Cartridge Filter Respirators. If the refinishing system that is sprayed contains no isocyanates, an air-purifying, cartridge respirator with organic vapor cartridges and prefilters can be used (Figure 1–3). These respirators protect against vapors and spray mists of nonactivated enamels, lacquers, and other nonisocyanate materials.

This type of respirator consists of a rubber facepiece designed to conform to the face and form an airtight seal. It includes replaceable prefilters and cartridges that remove solvent and other vapors from the air. The paint respirator also has intake and exhaust valves, which ensure that all incoming air flows through the filters.

It is very important with air-purifying cartridge respirators that it fits securely around the edge of the face to prevent contaminated air from leaking into the breathing area. To check this, a quantitative fit test should be done prior to using the respirator, performing both negative and positive pressure checks. To check for negative pressure, the wearer

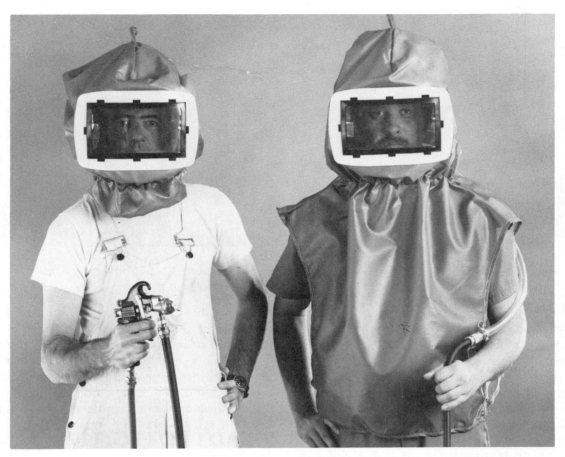

FIGURE 1-1 Air-supplied respirators. (A) Neck-length and (B) waist length *(Courtesy of Binks Mfg. Co.)*

FIGURE 1-2 Typical oilless air pump that moves ambient air from a clean environment and supplies it to air line respirators of hood. The 3/4-horsepower unit shown is suitable for two persons. *(Courtesy of Willson Safety Products, Inc.)*

FIGURE 1-3 Half mask, dual cartridge air purifying respiratory kit *(Courtesy of Paint-Safe Products)*

should place the palms of his hands over the cartridges and inhale. A good fit will be evident if the facepiece collapses onto the wearer's face. To perform a positive pressure check, the wearer covers up the exhalation valve and exhales. A proper fit is evident if the facepiece billows out without air escaping

FIGURE 1-4 (Left) Typical cartridge filters with full facepiece *(Courtesy of Mine Safety Appliance Co.)* and (right) cartridge filters with no faceplate *(Courtesy of Herkules Equipment Co.)*

the mask. Another form of quantitative fit testing consists of exposing amyl acetate (banana oil) near the seal around the face. If no odor is detected, a proper fit is evident.

Cartridge respirators are available in several sizes and might or might not contain a face mask (Figure 1-4). The most common size will provide the best protection. But, wearers of this type of respirator should be aware that facial hair might prevent an airtight seal, presenting a hazard to the wearer's health. Therefore, refinishers with facial hair should use a positive pressure-supplied air respirator system, because hair will prevent a seal of mask to face, eliminating the respirator's effectiveness. Remember that cartridge respirators should be used only in well-ventilated areas. They must not be used in environments containing less than 19.5 percent oxygen.

To maintain the cartridge filter respirator, keep it clean and change the prefilters and cartridges as often as directed by the manufacturer. Here are a few other maintenance tips:

- Replace the prefilters when it becomes difficult to breathe through the respirator.
- Replace the cartridge at least weekly, or earlier, at the first sign of solvent odor.
- Regularly check the mask to make sure it does not have any cracks or dents.
- Store the respirator in an airtight container.
- Follow the manufacturer's instructions provided to ensure proper maintenance and fit.

Dust or Particle Respirators. To protect against dust from sanding, use a dust respirator (Figure 1-5). Sanding operations in the body shop create dust that can cause bronchial irritation and possible long-term lung damage if inhaled. Protec-

tion from this health hazard is necessary; a NIOSH-approved dust respirator should be worn whenever a refinisher or someone working close to him/her is involved in a sanding operation. Follow the instructions provided with the dust respirator to ensure proper maintenance fit. Remember that dust masks do not protect against vapors and spray mists.

HEAD PROTECTION

Be sure to tie long hair securely behind the head before beginning to work on a vehicle. The hair also must be protected against dust and sprays. To keep hair clean (and healthy) wear a cap at all times in the

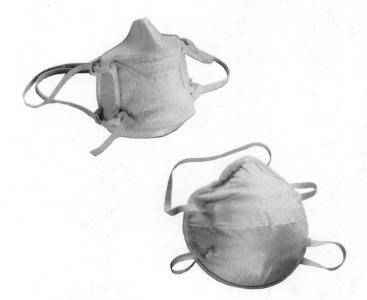

FIGURE 1-5 When power sanding, dust and dirt can get into the lungs without proper protection. Always wear safety glasses and a NIOSH-approved dust particle mask before grinding.

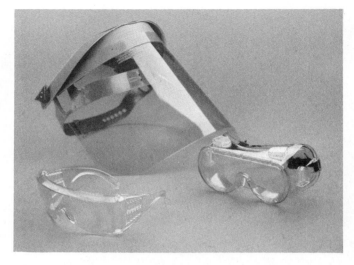

FIGURE 1-6 Eyewear protection *(Courtesy of Paint-Safe Products)*

work area and a protective painter's stretch hood in the spray booth.

Eye and Face Protection

The eyes are sensitive to dust and flying particles from grinding and to mists and vapors from spraying. Such exposure could cause severe pain, and possibly the loss of sight. Whenever such external risks exist, a full-face shield and a good pair of safety glasses or chemical splash goggles should be worn (Figure 1-6). Remember that eyes are irreplaceable.

BODY PROTECTION

Loose clothing, unbuttoned shirt sleeves, dangling ties, loose jewelry, and shirts hanging out are **very** dangerous in a body shop. Instead, wear approved shop coveralls or jumpsuits (Figure 1-7). Pants should be long enough to cover the top of the shoes. Keep them mended and tear free.

A clean jumpsuit or lint-free coveralls should be worn when in the spray area. Dirty, solvent-soaked clothing will hold these chemicals against the skin, causing irritation or a rash. Make sure they are long sleeved for complete protection.

HAND PROTECTION

The harmful effects of liquids, undercoats, and finishes on the hands can be prevented very effectively by wearing proper gloves (Figure 1-8). Impervious gloves, such as the nitrile latex type, should be used when working with solvents or two-pack primers and topcoats. These gloves offer special protection from the materials found in two-component sys-

FIGURE 1-7 Jumpsuits or coveralls are usually in the paint shop. *(Courtesy of Du Pont Co.)*

FIGURE 1-8 Typical gloves worn in a paint shop *(Courtesy of Du Pont Co.)*

tems. See the MSDS for glove recommendations. Thick, strong work gloves should be worn in the prep area to avoid cuts or abrasions. (Table 1-1 gives the advantages and benefits of various glove types.) Always remember to wash hands thoroughly when leaving the shop area. This provides protection from ingesting any harmful elements that may have been touched.

When washing hands, it is usually recommended that the hands be cleaned with a proper hand cleaner. At the end of a day's work, it is wise to oil the skin a little by applying a good silicone-free

TABLE 1-1: GLOVES		
Features	Advantages	Benefits
Synthetic latex material	1. Hazard resistant	1. Helps resist abrasion, cuts, snags, and punctures.
	2. Flexible	2. Excellent dexterity to perform even delicate tasks
17 mils thick, 11 inches long, case hardened	1. Greater wear resistance and tensile strength	1. Longer lasting
Flock lined	1. Soft fit	1. Wearer comfort and absorbs perspiration

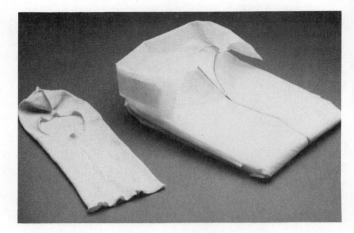

FIGURE 1-10 Disposable protective clothing *(Courtesy of Paint-Safe Products)*

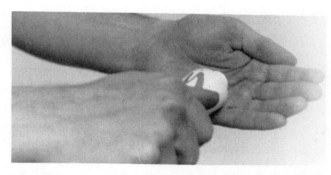
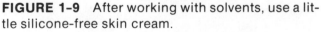

FIGURE 1-9 After working with solvents, use a little silicone-free skin cream.

skin cream (Figure 1-9). Do not use thinner as a hand cleaner.

WARNING: Before using any solvent as a hand cleaner, be sure there is no manufacturer's warning on the label against this practice. Some of the hardeners and additives used in the newer paints can cause skin rashes and dermatitis.

FOOT PROTECTION

Wear safety work shoes that have metal toe inserts and nonslip soles. The inserts protect the toes from falling objects; the soles help to prevent falls. In addition, good work shoes provide support and comfort for someone who is standing for a long time. **Never** wear sneakers, gym shoes, or dress shoes; none of these shoes provide adequate protection in a refinishing shop.

When spraying, many painters wear disposable shoe covers. In fact, disposable garments and hoods are becoming more commonly used by sprayers (Figure 1-10).

DAY-BY-DAY PERSONAL SAFETY GUIDE

The following guidelines are designed to protect the painter while on the job—from the moment he or she determines what steps need to be taken and the products to be used until the time comes to put away the equipment and get ready to head home.

- **Be informed.** Read the warnings on the product labels and in manufacturers' literature. If more information is desired, get copies of the Material Safety Data Sheets for specific products from the shop's office or from the paint suppliers. As previously mentioned, these contain information on hazardous ingredients and protective measures that the painter should use.
- **During power sanding.** When power sanding, dust and dirt fly into the air. These can get into eyes, lungs, and scalp without proper protection. Safety glasses or goggles will protect the eyes. Do not wear contacts when grinding, sanding, or handling solvents. Head covers provide scalp and hair protection. A NIOSH-approved dust particle mask should also be worn to prevent inhaling dust and particles. All masks should fit tightly to your skin.

- **During cleaning with compressed air.** When using a dust gun to clean doorjambs and other hard-to-reach places, eye protection and particle masks should always be worn.
- **During metal conditioning.** Metal conditioners contain phosphoric acid. Breathing these chemicals or allowing them to come in direct contact with the skin, eyes, or clothing may cause irritation. The use of safety glasses (to prevent splashs into the eyes), coveralls, rubber gloves, and a NIOSH-approved organic vapor respirator is recommended when using these products. If the coveralls become soaked for any reason, make sure they are changed to clean ones to avoid irritation to the skin; or soak with water to dilute the chemicals.
- **During mixing and handling.** Mixing and pouring of refinish materials should be done in a well-ventilated location away from areas used to store or apply the products. When opening cans or mixing, materials might splash. To avoid splashes to the eyes, goggles or other protection should be worn.
- **During spraying of undercoats or topcoats.** Application of undercoats and topcoats requires the use of spraying equipment, which can be hazardous if not used properly. Static electricity is generated when using airless or electrostatic spraying methods. Special attention must be paid to grounding and bonding for this equipment to prevent problems. Painters should be fully protected when applying undercoat or topcoat products. Coveralls, rubber gloves, safety shoes, eye protection, and an appropriate respirator and/or protective hood for the product being applied should be worn throughout the process.
- **Storing paint materials.** All refinish products should be stored away from the actual work area. Paint kept in the work area should be limited to a one-day supply. Empty containers should be disposed of daily. All partially used containers should be kept securely closed and should be placed in proper metal (fire-resistant) storage cabinets (Figure 1-11) at the end of the day.
- **Before leaving the shop.** Solvents, chemicals and other materials can contaminate clothing and wind up on the hands when removing personal protective equipment or put away the refinishing tools. They can still enter one's system through the body's digestive tract if the hands were not washed before eating, drinking, smoking, or using toilet facilities.

GENERAL SHOP PROCEDURES

In addition to personal safety, the refinishing technician must be aware of general shop safety procedures. The following are some of the rules and precautions that should be observed to insure a safe and healthful work environment in the paint shop.

ENVIRONMENTAL CONTROLS

Persons working in body/paint shop facilities are often exposed to dangerous amounts of various gases, dusts, and vapors. Because of this exposure, control measures should be established and practiced for the following frequently observed air contaminants and other hazardous substances.

- **Ventilation.** Proper ventilation is very important in areas where caustics, degreasers, undercoats, and finishes are used. In the paint shop and the area where vehicles are prepared, ventilation can be by means of an air-changing system, extraction floors, or central dust extraction for dust from abrasives combined with spraying area walls with good extraction power. For the spray booth (Figure 1-12), adequate air replacement is necessary not only to promote evaporation and drying of the areas sprayed, but also to remove harmful mist and vapors.

FIGURE 1-11 Large metal safety cabinet *(Courtesy of Paint-Safe Products)*

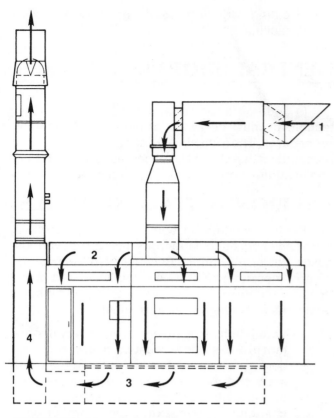

FIGURE 1-12 Modern air replacement unit for a downdraft spray booth that operates like this: (1) the cycle begins with the outside being filtered and conditioned to the proper temperature. The processed air then flows through (2) a ceiling plenum and unique filter system and down into the spray booth. As air flows downward it passes around the car and is drawn through (3) a grating in the floor that contains paint arrester filters. The (4) booth fan exhausts the air from the pit, up a duct, and out the stack on the roof.

- **Carbon monoxide.** Operate the engine only in a well-ventilated area to avoid the danger of carbon monoxide (CO). If the shop is equipped with a tailpipe exhaust system to remove CO from the garage, use it. If not, use the direct piping to the outside method or a mechanical ventilation system.

  Space heaters used in some shops can also be a serious source of CO and therefore should be periodically inspected to make sure they are adequately vented and do not become blocked.

- **Paints, body fillers, and thinners.** Thinners used in most paints have a narcotic effect and long term exposure can eventually cause irreparable damage. In addition to the ventilation in the spray area or paint booth, respi-

rators should be worn. As previously mentioned, rubber or safety gloves should be worn while handling paints and thinners. If any of these materials get on the skin, promptly wash the affected area with soap and water.

- **Dust.** Dust is a problem in paint shops. It is produced during operations such as sanding paints, primers, body fillers, and so forth. When doing this type of work, wear a dust particle respirator or mask.

Many shops are installing so-called "dustless" sanding machine systems. Depending on the system, vacuum pumps, vacuum pullers, brush motors, or turbine motors can be used, all in the quest of sufficient air volume and/or velocity to pull airborne sanding dust through either holes in a special sanding pad or a shroud that entirely surrounds the sanding pad. Some systems run constantly, others are started "on-demand" by plugging a vacuum hose into the vacuum outlet or pushing a button at the sanding tool end of the hose. Figure 1-13 shows a portable vacuum system, while Chapter 2 contains an illustration of central vacuum system.

By using a dustless system, the paint shop can comply with OSHA's airborne dust standards and eliminate costly, nonproductive cleanups. Some dustless system manufacturer's claim that their machines can trap over 99 percent of the toxic dust created by sanding lead- or chrome-based automotive paint and primer, which can contaminate the work area.

VEHICLE HANDLING IN THE SHOP

When handling a vehicle in the shop, keep the following safety precautions in mind:

- Set the parking brake when working on the vehicle. If the car has an automatic transmission, set it in PARK unless instructed otherwise for a specific service operation. If the vehicle has a manual transmission, it should be in REVERSE (engine **off**) or NEUTRAL (engine **on**).
- If for some reason a work procedure requires working under a vehicle, use safety stands.
- To prevent serious burns, avoid contact with hot metal parts such as the radiator, exhaust manifold, tailpipe, catalytic converter, and muffler.
- Keep clothing and oneself clear from moving parts when the engine is running, especially the radiator fan blades and belts.

FIGURE 1-13   Portable vacuum system *(Courtesy of Nilfisk of America, Inc.)*

- Be sure that the ignition switch is always in the **off** position, unless otherwise required by the procedure.
- When moving a vehicle around the shop, be sure to look in all directions and make certain that nothing is in the way.

HORSEPLAY

No horseplay, running, or fooling around should be attempted in any shop. One thing can lead to another and eventually cause an injury. Horseplay is distracting and wastes time.

HANDLING OF SOLVENT AND OTHER FLAMMABLE LIQUIDS

The refinisher will be working with various solvents to clean surfaces and equipment and to thin finishes. These solvents are extremely flammable. Fumes in particular can ignite explosively.

The following safety practices will help avoid fire and explosion:

- Do not light matches or smoke in the spraying and paint area, and make sure that the hands and clothing are free from solvent when lighting matches or smoking in other areas of the shop where smoking or an open flame is permitted.
- All ignition sources should be carefully controlled and monitored to avoid any possible fire hazard where a high concentration of vapor from highly flammable liquids might at times be present.
- A UL (Underwriters Laboratories) approved drum transfer pump/drum pump along with a drum vent should be used when working with drums to transfer chemicals.
- Keep all solvent containers closed, except when pouring.
- Handle all solvents (or any liquids) with care to avoid spillage. Extra caution should also be used when transferring flammable materials from bulk storage. The most important thing to remember is to make sure the drum is grounded (Figure 1-14A) and that a bond wire connects the drum to a safety can (Figure 1-14B). Otherwise, static electricity can build up enough to create a spark that could cause an explosion.

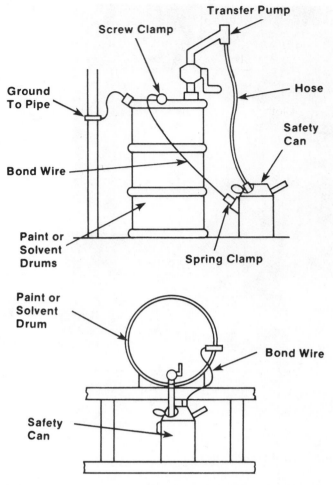

FIGURE 1-14 Two safe methods of moving flammable liquids from a drum to a portable safety can are shown above.

- Discard or clean all empty solvent containers as prescribed by local regulations. Solvent fumes in the bottom of these containers are prime ignition sources. Remember: Never use gasoline as a cleaning solvent.
- Paints, thinners, solvents, and other combustible materials used in the body and paint shop must be stored in approved and designated metal (never wood) storage cabinets or rooms. Storage rooms should have adequate ventilation, which takes harmful fumes and pollutants away from the actual working area. Many paint shops use a separate facility for the bulk storage of flammable material. Never have more than one day's supply of paint outside of approved storage areas.
- The connectors on all drums and pipes of flammable and combustible liquids must be vapor- and liquid-tight.

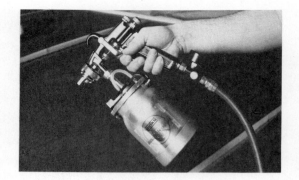

FIGURE 1-15 When spraying paint, keep the safety procedure given in the text. *(Courtesy of Binks Mfg. Co.)*

- When spraying paint (Figure 1-15), follow these procedures:
  —Remove portable lamps before spraying.
  —Ventilation system must be turned on.
  —Spray areas must be free from hot surfaces such as heat lamps.
  —The spray area must be kept clean of combustible residue.
  —Ventilation system must be left on while the paint is drying.

FIRE PROTECTION

Every paint shop requires fire extinguishers (Figure 1-16). Since fires are classified as Class A, B, C, and D type, there are different types of extinguishers specially designed for a particular class of fire. Table 1-2 gives the common classes of fire that are found in paint shops and methods of containing

FIGURE 1-16 All body and paint work require plenty of fire extinguishers capable of fighting type A, B, and C fires. *(Courtesy of Pittway Corp.)*

TABLE 1-2:   GUIDE TO EXTINGUISHER SELECTION

	Class of Fire	Typical Fuel Involved	Type of Extinguisher
Class A Fires (green)	**For Ordinary Combustibles** Put out a class A fire by lowering its temperature or by coating the burning combustibles.	Wood Paper Cloth Rubber Plastics Rubbish Upholstery	Water[*1] Foam[*] Multipurpose dry chemical[4]
Class B Fires (red)	**For Flammable Liquids** Put out a class B fire by smothering it. Use an extinguisher that gives a blanketing, flame-interrupting effect; cover whole flaming liquid surface.	Gasoline Oil Grease Paint Lighter fluid	Foam[*] Carbon dixoide[5] Halogenated agent[6] Standard dry chemical[2] Purple K dry chemical[3] Multipurpose dry chemical[4]
Class C Fires (blue)	**For Electrical Equipment** Put out a class C fire by shutting off power as quickly as possible and by always using a nonconducting extinguishing agent to prevent electric shock.	Motors Appliances Wiring Fuse boxes Switchboards	Carbon dioxide[5] Halogenated agent[6] Standard dry chemical[2] Purple K dry chemical[3] Multipurpose dry chemical[4]
Class D Fires (yellow)	**For Combustible Metals** Put out a class D fire of metal chips, turnings, or shavings by smothering or coating with a specially designed extinguishing agent.	Aluminum Magnesium Potassium Sodium Titanium Zirconium	Dry power extinguishers and agents only

*Cartridge-operated water, foam, and soda-acid types of extinguishers are no longer manufactured. These extinguishers should be removed from service when they become due for their next hydrostatic pressure test.

Notes:
(1) Freeze in low temperatures unless treated with antifreeze solution, usually weighs over 20 pounds, and is heavier than any other extinguisher mentioned.
(2) Also called ordinary or regular dry chemical. (sodium bicarbonate)
(3) Has the greatest initial fire-stopping power of the extinguishers mentioned for class B fires. Be sure to clean residue immediately after using the extinguisher so sprayed surfaces will not be damaged. (potassium bicarbonate)
(4) The only extinguishers that fight A, B, and C classes of fires. However, they should not be used on fires in liquefied fat or oil of appreciable depth. Be sure to clean residue immediately after using the extinguisher so sprayed surfaces will not be damaged. (ammonium phosphates)
(5) Use with caution in unventilated, confined spaces.
(6) May cause injury to the operator if the extinguishing agent (a gas) or the gases produced when the agent is applied to a fire is inhaled.

them. Some extinguishers are capable of fighting more than one type of fire.

However, the mere provision of a fire extinguisher is useless unless those who might come in contact with it know how to use it properly. If a fire breaks out, there is no time to lose figuring out how to use the fire extinguisher effectively. Operating instructions are imprinted on each listed or approved extinguisher. The approval agencies require information on the front of extinguishers indicating their classification, the relative extinguishing effectiveness (the numeral preceding the classification letter), and the methods of use. However, during an emergency there might be no time to read the label. The basic information should be known ahead of time by anyone who might come in contact with and need to use the fire extinguisher.

A fire can be extinguished by depriving it of its essential ingredients, which are heat, fuel, and oxygen. Most extinguishers work by cooling the fire and removing the oxygen. If the fire extinguisher is going to be used effectively, it must be aimed at the base of the flame where the fuel is located. Fire extinguishers should be checked regularly and be placed at strategic shop locations.

GOOD HOUSEKEEPING

Here are some simple good housekeeping precautions that often go unattended:

- Keep aisles and walkways free of tools, creepers, and any material that might cause a person or fellow worker to trip or stumble.
- Keep floors clean. Oil, paint, or other materials that are spilled should be cleaned up immediately. Sand, earth, or absorbents can be used to absorb the liquids. But once they have done their job, they should also be cleaned up. Make sure that these liquids are not discharged through floor drains or other outlets leading to public waterways.
- Any dirty rags or other combustible material must be deposited in a metal container with a suitable metal cover and should be removed to a safe place outside the building. Keep used paper towels and other paper products in a separate, covered container, which should be emptied every day.
- Customers and all nonemployees should never be allowed in any of the paint refinishing shop's work areas.

Personal protective equipment, a properly maintained paint shop environment, and attention to good safety and health practices all play important roles in the refinisher's good health. Taking the time to properly prepare **before** working on a vehicle can avoid many accidents or potentially dangerous chemical exposures. Repetition of careful safety procedures will turn them into habits—good habits that will contribute to a long, healthy life.

ASE CERTIFICATION

Just as doctors, nurses, accountants, electricians, and other professionals are licensed or certified to practice their profession, a painter can also be certified. Certification protects the general public and the practitioner or professional. It assures the general public and the prospective employer that certain minimum standards of performance have been met. Many employers now expect their refinishing technicians to be certified. The certified technician is recognized as a professional by employers, peers, and the public. For this reason, the certified

TABLE 1-3: PAINTING AND REFINISHING	
Content Area	Number of Questions in Test
A. Surface Preparation	10
B. Spray Gun Operation	5
C. Paint Mixing, Matching, and Applying	11
D. Solving Paint Application Problems	7
E. Finish Defects, Causes, and Cures	5
F. Safety Precautions and Miscellaneous	2
Total	40

refinisher usually receives higher pay than the non-certified operator.

Refinishers can get certified in one or more technicial areas by taking and passing a refinisher certification test. The National Institute for Automotive Service Excellence (ASE) offers a voluntary certified program that is recommended by the major vehicle manufacturers in the United States. The Painting and Refinishing Test contains 40 questions in the areas noted in Table 1-3.

FIGURE 1-17 ASE painter's shoulder patch or emblem

Craftsmen passing the written tests are awarded a certificate, shoulder emblem (Figure 1–17), and other credentials attesting to their "know-how." ASE certification is a badge of *proven* professionalism.

To help prepare for the Painting and Refinishing Performance programs, some test questions at the end of each chapter are similar in design and content to those used by the ASE. For further information on the ASE certification program, write: National Institute for Auto Service Excellence, 1920 Association Drive, Reston, Virginia 22091.

REVIEW QUESTIONS

1. Which of the following presents dangers to the air passages and lungs of the auto painter?
   a. dust
   b. vapors from caustic solutions and solvents
   c. spray mists from undercoats and finishes
   d. all of the above
   e. both a and b

2. Which of the following respirators covers the entire head and neck area?
   a. cartridge filter respirator
   b. dust respirator
   c. air-supplied respirator
   d. none of the above

3. Painter A and Painter B are both in the practice of spraying continuously for extended periods of time. Painter A changes the cartridges of the respirator every other day. Painter B changes them once a week. Who is right?
   a. Painter A
   b. Painter B
   c. Both A and B
   d. Neither A nor B

4. Which respirator is to protect against dust from sanding and grinding?
   a. hood respirator
   b. organic vapor-type respirator
   c. air-supplied respirator
   d. none of the above

5. Eye protection should be worn when using
   _____ .
   a. grinders
   b. disc sanders
   c. pneumatic chisels
   d. all of the above

6. Which of the following should not be worn in a paint shop?
   a. jumpsuit
   b. loose clothing
   c. cap
   d. all of the above
   e. both b and c

7. By what means can ventilation be achieved in the paint shop?
   a. extraction floors
   b. central dust extraction
   c. air-changing system
   d. all of the above
   e. both b and c

8. Which of the following is not a safety measure to use when applying a lead filler?
   a. Wear a dust mask.
   b. Vacuum the area after the job is complete.
   c. Do not smoke or eat until the hands have been thoroughly washed.
   d. Work in ventilated area.

9. What is the maximum amount of paint that should be left outside of approved storage areas?
   a. 10 quarts
   b. 20 quarts
   c. one day's supply
   d. a half day's supply

10. Painter A discards all empty solvent containers. Painter B cleans them out to be used again. Who is right?
    a. Painter A
    b. Painter B
    c. Both A and B
    d. Neither A nor B

11. Which of the following is a typical fuel for Class D fires?
    a. plastics
    b. motors
    c. zirconium
    d. wiring

12. Which class of fire can be extinguished with a carbon dioxide extinguisher?
    a. Class A
    b. Class C
    c. Class D
    d. None of the above

13. Which type of extinguisher can be used on all classes of fires?
    a. water
    b. foam
    c. multipurpose dry chemical
    d. none of the above

Complete Automotive Painting

14. Which type of extinguisher can be used to put out a Class B fire?
    a. carbon dioxide
    b. halogenated agent
    c. standard dry chemical
    d. all of the above

15. What is another name for the cartridge filter respirator?
    a. dust mask
    b. organic vapor-type respirator
    c. air-supplied respirator
    d. hood respirator

14

CHAPTER TWO

REFINISHING EQUIPMENT AND ITS USE

Objectives

After studying this chapter, you will be able to:

- explain the operation of spray booths and drying rooms.
- identify air-powered tools in the paint shop.
- name the electric power tools most commonly used in paint shops.
- describe the hydraulic equipment used in paint shops.
- maintain shop power equipment tools.
- name various other tools and materials used in the refinishing shop.

To do a good refinishing job, the proper equipment must be used correctly. But to achieve high-quality finishes on automobiles, good materials, proper equipment, and correct techniques are necessities.

The spray booth, drying room, various air-, electric-, and hydraulic-powered tools, and other paint shop equipment and materials are presented in this chapter. Chapter 3 presents the spray gun and its use. The selection and use of air compressors, air control equipment, and air hose connectors are thoroughly described in Chapter 4.

SPRAY BOOTHS

The body shop, by necessity, is continually generating dust and dirt from the pounding out of metal, grinding of welds and fillers, sanding, and similar dirt creating operations—the very worst kind of environment in which to paint cars. Much of this dust is so fine it can scarcely be controlled.

Providing a clean, safe, well-illuminated healthful enclosure for painting is the primary purpose of a spray booth (Figure 2-1). It isolates the painting operation from the dirt and dust producing activities and confines and exhausts the volatile fumes created by spraying automotive finishes. Modern spray booths are scientifically designed to create the proper air movement, provide necessary lighting, and enclose the painting operation safely. In addition, their construction and performance must conform to federal, state, and even local safety codes, not to mention those of insurance underwriters. In some areas, automatically operated fire extinguish-

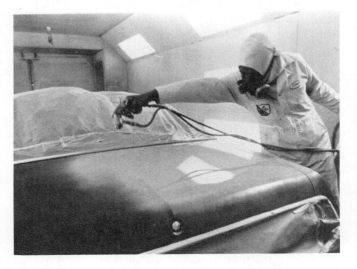

FIGURE 2-1 Inside a well-designed spray booth. *(Courtesy of Sherwin-Williams Co.)*

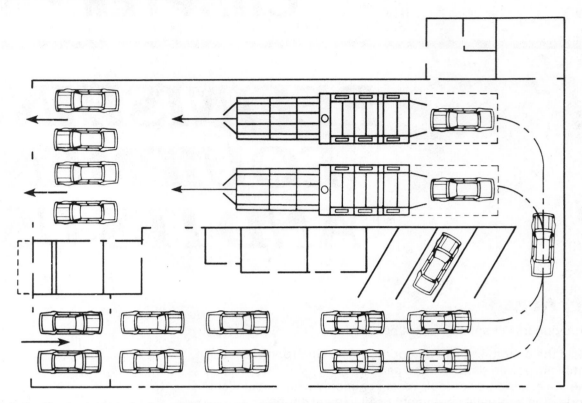

FIGURE 2-2 Typical body/paint shop layout showing straight line work flow finishing operation. The important stops in such an arrangement are: paint preparation, spray booth, and final clean-up. *(Courtesy of Du Pont Co.)*

ers are required because of the highly explosive nature of the refinishing materials.

The spray booth should be located as far removed as possible from the area where dust and dirt are prevalent. Therefore, it should be isolated from the mechanical and metalworking portions of the shop wherever possible. This can be accomplished with partitions, walls, or a separate building arrangement. A workbench should be handy in the spray booth for thinning the paint and filling the gun cup. Paint storage should, however, be outside the booth, but nearby.

When a spray booth must be located in the same room with metalworking stalls or other locations where there is excessive dust, the intake air can be drawn from the outdoors, utilizing an air replacement system. This arrangement greatly reduces the number of filter changes required in the booth doors and reduces the chances of ruined paint jobs.

If the volume of paint work is sufficient, a straight line work flow is recommended (Figure 2-2). Utilizing a drive-thru type spray booth, the layout is designed for maximum efficiency of manpower and equipment. Jobs are started in the metalworking stalls in the normal manner. From this point the work flows in a production line manner through each of the various stages all the way to final cleanup. Cleaning preparation should be done outside the booth area. Steam clean the underbody of the vehicle thoroughly and air dust the entire vehicle before moving it into the spray booth. After the vehicle is in the booth, close the booth doors tightly and tack-rag the entire vehicle again before proceeding with the painting operation. All spray booth doors must be kept tightly closed during painting. If it becomes necessary to open the door, be sure the fan and air supply are turned off. In fact, many spray booths are equipped with door switches that shut off the air supply and fan when the doors are opened. The air compressor should be outside the booth with the air delivery pipes slanting back toward the compressor. The drive-thru principle can be used in a one or two booth arrangement (Figure 2-3).

An air make-up or replacement system is important because of the large volume of air exhausted from spray booths. This exhaust is sufficient to produce two or more complete changes every hour. Under such conditions in winter, the spray area can become cold and uncomfortable, finish problems can arise because of spraying with cold materials on cold products in cold air. An air make-up system will provide even temperatures and clean filtered air as

16

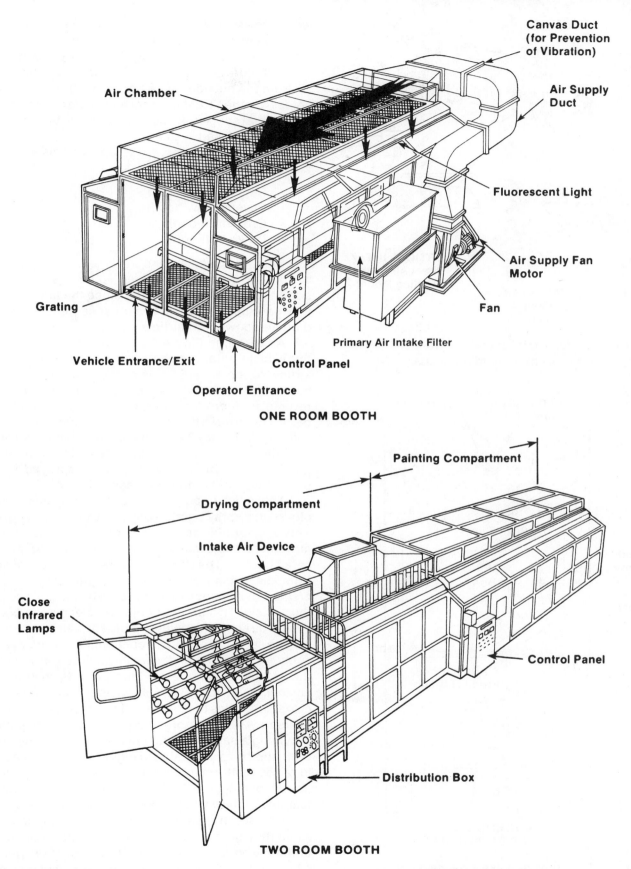

Canvas Duct
(for Prevention
of Vibration)

Air Chamber

Air Supply
Duct

Fluorescent Light

Air Supply Fan
Motor

Fan

Grating

Primary Air Intake Filter

Vehicle Entrance/Exit

Control Panel

Operator Entrance

ONE ROOM BOOTH

Painting Compartment

Drying Compartment

Intake Air Device

Close
Infrared
Lamps

Control Panel

Distribution Box

TWO ROOM BOOTH

FIGURE 2-3 Typical one and two room booths. *(Courtesy of Toyota Motor Corp.)*

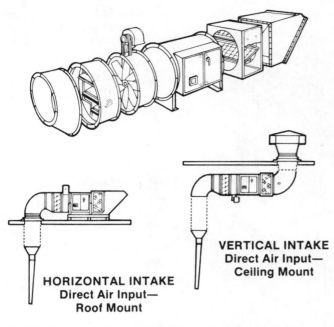

VERTICAL INTAKE
Direct Air Input—
Ceiling Mount

HORIZONTAL INTAKE
Direct Air Input—
Roof Mount

FIGURE 2-4 Air replacement is available in various configurations to fit building needs.

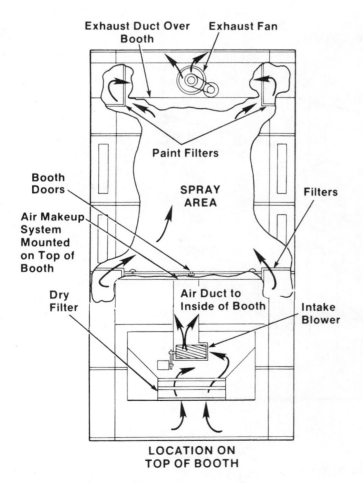

Exhaust Duct Over Booth

Exhaust Fan

Paint Filters

Booth Doors

SPRAY AREA

Filters

Air Makeup System Mounted on Top of Booth

Dry Filter

Air Duct to Inside of Booth

Intake Blower

LOCATION ON TOP OF BOOTH

FIGURE 2-5 A typical make-up air system

well as to assure proper booth performance. Sometimes paint shops employ an independent air replacement system specifically designed for the spray booth (Figure 2-4). This provides clean, dry, filtered air from the outside to the booth, heating the air in colder weather. Replacement air can be delivered to the general shop area or directly into the booth for a completely closed system.

There are four air make-up systems in use today:

- Regular flow booth
- Reverse flow booth
- Crossdraft booth
- Downdraft booth

Both the regular and reverse flow types of booths were once considered standards in spray booth construction. However, since the late 1970s, they have been replaced to a great degree by crossdraft and downdraft airflow types.

As shown in Figure 2-5, in the regular system, the vehicle enters at the air inlet and follows the airflow to the exhaust area at the other end of the booth; that is, the airflow is from back to front. In the reverse flow process, the airflow is from front to back. The reverse flow type of booth generally has a solid back (Figure 2-6), while a regular flow usually is of the drive-thru style. It is interesting to note a good number of vehicles that were sprayed in a reverse type of booth were backed in.

The most popular air movement system employed in a spray booth today is the downdraft type. This system utilizes the downdraft principle of air movement, the same as huge auto production line spray booths. The downward directional flow of air from the ceiling of the booth to the exhaust pit creates an envelope of air passing by the surface of the vehicle. This process of taking clean, tempered air and directing it downward past the surface of the vehicle serves to eliminate contamination and overspray from settling on the freshly painted surface of the vehicle (Figure 2-7). This process insures a cleaner paint job. But just as important, this air movement helps to remove toxic vapors and harmful overspray from the breathing zone of the painter, providing a safer working environment. The downdraft booths as illustrated in Figure 2-8 are available in raised platform models and floor models and are usually of the drive-thru type. Some more important features of this system are shown in Figure 2-9.

Crossdraft systems are less expensive to install since they do not require a raised platform or a pit under the booth. The crossdraft type booth provides a horizontal airflow and many of the advantages of

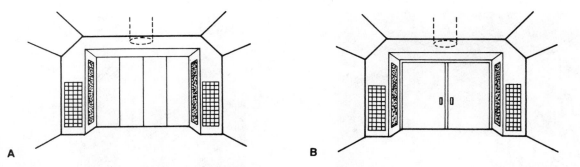

FIGURE 2-6   Two designs of spray booths: (A) solid back and (B) drive-thru. The solid design is generally found in smaller shops.

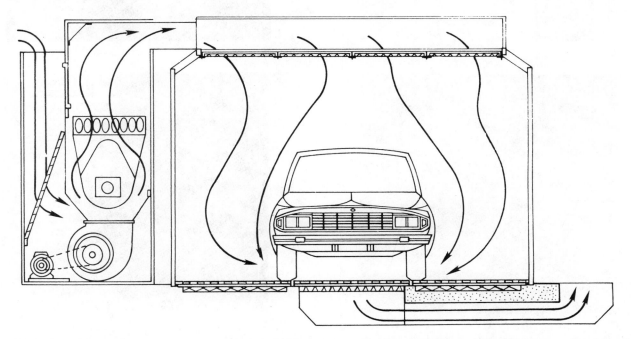

FIGURE 2-7   The airflow pattern of a downdraft spray booth. The location of the intake and exhaust system will depend on the system manufacturer.

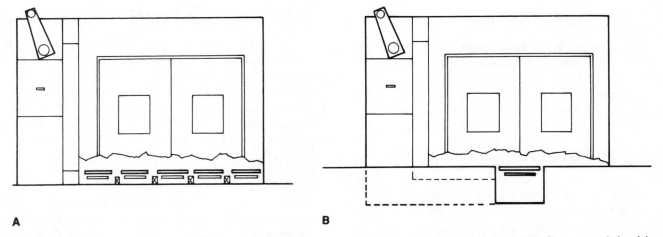

FIGURE 2-8   Two models of downdraft booths: (A) raised platform model and (B) floor model with underfloor pit.

FIGURE 2-9 Important parts of a downdraft refinish system include: (A) spray booth itself; (B) air replacement unit; (C) ceiling plenum and filter system; (D) floor grating and filter. *(Courtesy of DeVilbiss Co.)*

the downdraft system. It is available in solid back and drive-thru models.

Because of the many OSHA, state, and local regulations regarding spray booths, the use of solid concrete or cinder block types have been on a decline. While many are still in use, building a new "do-it-yourself" spray booth is seldom done today.

AIR FILTRATION SYSTEMS

The most important feature of spray booths, as far as the paint specialist's health safety is concerned, is the filtration system. Currently there are two commonly in use (Figure 2-10):

1. Wet filtration system
2. Dry filtration system

WET FILTRATION SYSTEMS

Although wet or wash filtration has a higher initial cost than a dry filter system, it has grown in popularity with downdraft spray booths because water filtration does an excellent job of removing paint particles from exhaust air regardless of the paint viscosity or drying speed. It can handle a variety of spray materials, is capable of high volume production, eliminates the expense and inconvenience of changing exhaust filters, and is accepted by most local fire codes.

The typical downdraft booth with a water filtration system has ducts or an open grate floor under which a layer of water circulates to carry away overspray. The contaminated water is routed through a "compounding" tank where the paint is separated out before the water recirculates through the sys-

Wet or Wash Type

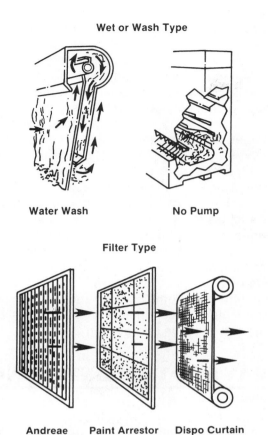

A   Water Wash   No Pump

Filter Type

B   Andreae   Paint Arrestor   Dispo Curtain

FIGURE 2-10 Different methods of spray booth filtration: (A) wet filtration and (B) dry filtration

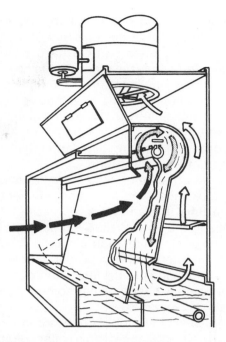

FIGURE 2-11 The air is cleansed by a combination of water spray and centrifugal separation in a typical water wash system. *(Courtesy of Binks Mfg. Co.)*

tem. Exhaust air from the booth is purified by routing it through a water curtain wash system. A continuous spray mist of water scrubs the paint particles from the air, while baffles reverse the direction of the airflow to help separate out the particles by centrifugal action. The air that emerges is as clean or cleaner than that achieved by a quality dry filtration system (Figure 2-11).

There are wide varieties of water wash configurations available, with some offering various advantages over others. There are also "pumpless" wash systems. Instead of using a curtain spray wash to clean the air, the air is pulled through a pan of water and series of baffles by a high-pressure fan. Air velocity pulls the air through the water creating a swirling mixture that washes out the paint particles. The water is treated with an anticoagulant additive so the paint particles settle to the bottom (in pump wash systems, the paint rises to the top). Pumpless wash systems are very sensitive to the water level and air pressure, so proper maintenance is very important.

The paint residue that collects in the water must be removed periodically, and the water kept at the specified level. The rate at which water evaporates from the system will depend on temperature, humidity, the volume of usage, and the design of the system

itself. But it is necessary to add makeup water at least once a week unless the booth has an automatic water makeup feature. Plus water additives must be placed in the water to prevent the growth of bacterial/germ growth and the creation of an unpleasant smell.

The paint residue that is separated from the water hardens and can be disposed of by bagging it and, in most areas, sending it to a landfill. One innovative approach is to "recycle" it by mixing it with undercoating and spraying it under cars. As for water disposal, there is no reason to worry about it because the water is continuously recycled. If the system has to be drained for some reason, the waste water would have to be disposed of in accordance with whatever local sewer restrictions might apply.

DRY FILTRATION SYSTEMS

These spray booth systems come in various configurations and filter media (paper, cotton, fiberglass, polyester, and so on). What is important here is the efficiency of the filtration system and how quickly the filters clog up. Dry filters work like a sieve. They mechanically filter out particles of paint and dirt by trapping the particles as air flows through the filter. Some are also coated with a tacky substance so particles will adhere to the surface of the fibers.

Most filtration systems today can remove virtually 100 percent of the particulates that are of a size large enough to cause a noticeable blemish in a paint job. Anything larger than about 14 microns (.0005 inch, the smallest particle that can be seen by the naked eye) can leave a noticeable speck in the paint. Anything smaller than 14 microns is usually encapsulated in the paint and will not cause problems. Most of the filters that are used in the ceilings of downdraft booths or the doors of crossdraft booths today will stop anything larger than about 10 microns from getting through.

As a filter traps more and more particles, it becomes more dense and thus more efficient. But at the same time, it also offers increasingly greater resistance to the flow of air. Eventually the point is reached where the filter restricts airflow to such an extent that it interferes with proper airflow through the spray booth. Ideally, the filter should be changed before it reaches that point. It is something that has to be watched very closely.

The best way to judge a filter's condition is to measure its air resistance with a water column pressure differential gauge (manometer or magnehelic gauge). Some booths have built-in gauges, others do not (Figure 2-12). Comparing air pressure upstream of the filter to that which is downstream indicates whether or not it is time to replace filters. The amount of restriction that is considered "acceptable" will vary according to filter construction and media, spray booth construction and air volume. Some filters should be changed when there is as little as 0.25 inch difference in the water column side to side while others can handle up to 2-1/2 inch of difference before they have to be replaced.

Because the amount of restriction that is considered acceptable can vary so much from one type of filter to another, it is important to check with the filter supplier before using any replacement filters that are different from those originally supplied with a particular spray booth. The type of filter media used

will also have a significant bearing on maintenance costs, filtration efficiency, and filter longevity. Filters are not a generic product. One type might be much better suited to a particular application than another. That is why spray booth manufacturers typically put such a high emphasis on filter selection.

There are still other considerations that a paint shop operation must keep in mind when selecting a filtration system. In southern California, for example, shops over a certain size are now facing an additional air filtration expense. Neither dry nor wet filtration can remove harmful chemicals and solvents such as isocyanates from the exhaust air, so additional exhaust filtration is now being required. To date, unfortunately, the only "approved" methods of treating exhaust air are with an afterburner system (which is very expensive) or with activated carbon filtration. Some booth manufacturers claim that water filtration can "neutralize" isocyanates, but this has not yet been approved in California.

SPRAY BOOTH MAINTENANCE

Regardless of the type of filtration that a paint shop employs, maintenance is a prime consideration, not only from the standpoint of cost and convenience, but also because it is essential to maintain the quality of the paint job. The best air filtration system in the world will not be able to do its job if it is poorly maintained. The first task in learning how to avoid dirt is to understand where dirt comes from. Anything that is brought into the booth can bring dirt with it. Potential sources of dirt include the air, the vehicle, the painter, the equipment and supplies, and even the paint.

Incoming air is a prime source of dirt. Dirt in the air is generated by dirty filters, imbalanced air pressures, and open doors. Check the intake filters daily and change them as soon as the manometer indicates. When dust and dirt start to clog filters and restrict airflow, the velocity of air passing through the filters begins to climb. Increased velocity increases the likelihood of pulling dirt through the filters. Balance the input air pressure against the exhaust air to provide slightly positive pressure in the booth. This balance constantly changes as filters load up and can change from car to car. Therefore, check and adjust it with each new job.

Enter the downdraft booth only with the fans running. The positive pressure helps keep the dirt out. Once a vehicle is inside, keep traffic flow in and out of the booth to an absolute minimum. Also, make sure that the body shop doors are closed at all times during the painting operation. Opening and closing

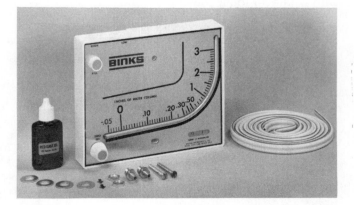

FIGURE 2-12 A typical manometer *(Courtesy of Binks Mfg. Co.)*

these doors can cause the booth balance to fluctuate, creating turbulence and dirt inside the booth.

The booth itself can be a main contributor to dirt problems through air leaks, poor housekeeping habits, exhaust air, and floor coverings. There are proper seals for door frames, light openings, and panel seams that must be installed properly and replaced periodically. Heavy usage and temperature extremes quickly destroy these seals. Use caulking as an inexpensive gap sealant to keep dirt out of the clean air stream.

Whey operating the spray booth, keep the following points in mind:

1. Follow the manufacturer's recommendations for the minimum velocity needed to exhaust spray vapors properly. If that recommendation is exceeded, turbulence cancels out the screening performed by the filters. If the velocity is too low, the air will not move fast enough to remove overspray and airborne dirt before it causes defects.
2. Depending upon the volume of spraying, paint arresters are a high-consumption item requiring frequent changing. Check filter resistance daily on the manometer. When paint accumulation builds up, velocity goes down, and air movement is too slow to the overspray.
3. In a dry filtration system, the filters must be periodically inspected and replaced (Figure 2–13). And when they are replaced, the multistage filters designed for the booth should be used.

WARNING: Clogged filters are a fire hazard, because they could catch fire, under certain conditions.

---

4. Be sure the water level in the wet filtration system is kept at its proper working level and that the correct water additive is used.

In order to get the best results from any type of spray booth, it is important to follow a routine good housekeeping program such as this:

- Periodically wash down the booth walls, floor and any wall-mounted air controls to remove dust and paint particles. Many shops require that floor and walls be wiped down after every job. Always pick up any scrap, paper, rags, and so forth.
- The booth is no place to store parts, paint, trash cans, or work benches because dirt will

FIGURE 2–13 Good paint shop housekeeping includes filter changes in both spray booth and the compressor. *(Courtesy of DeVilbiss Co.)*

accumulate on these things and will eventually land on the vehicle. Keep these items in a sealed, ventilated storage area.

- Be sure that all bodywork and most paint preparation procedures are done outside of the spray booth. Make certain no sanding or grinding operations are performed in or near the spray booth. The dust created will go all over and ruin not only a present job but many future jobs.
- Water is most often used to contain dirt. It is cheap and effective at trapping dirt, but it can splash on the car midway through the job; or, in a heated booth, dry out before the paint job is finished. If water is sprayed on the floor to keep any stray dust down on the floor, be sure to eliminate all puddles to prevent splashes. Water can also rust the walls of the spray booth, resulting in premature deterioration.
- Roofing felt held to the floor with duct tape provides an inexpensive method of containing dirt. It attracts and holds lint, lasts longer than water, is not a hazardous waste, and does not deteriorate in the booth.
- Clay tiles look nice and provide an easy-to-clean smooth surface, but are expensive and make it difficult to load a car in the booth on dollies.
- Concrete sealant provides a smooth, easily cleaned surface that is somewhat inexpensive. It should be noted that any slick surface treatment adds to the turbulence while a textured surface tends to impede the turbulence

or at least scrub the air. There are also strippable spray-on coverings. When the overspray on it becomes too thick, strip and recoat.

The vehicle itself is often the greatest source of dirt in the spray booth. Dirt hides in cracks and crevices, behind bumpers, and in the engine compartment. Even a thoroughly cleaned vehicle collects dirt when left in the general sanding area before being brought into the booth. When the spray gun hits this dirt at 50 psi, it kicks it out of its hiding places and deposits it into the finish. That is why a good prep job is so important.

 **SHOP TALK**

A cotton T-shirt is perhaps the greatest source of contamination and should never be worn in the booth. Lint-free paint suits, rubber form-fitting gloves, a dirt-free head cover, and the appropriate respirator should be worn inside the booth. Remain in the booth between the application of coats rather than risk dragging dirt back into the booth. If this step is not possible, remove the protective suit inside the booth and leave it there. Upon returning, put the suit back on to contain the dirt collected on the clothing worn outside the booth. (Anyone not interested in wearing the proper attire should view the work through an observation window rather than risk contaminating the paint.)

Spray guns and cups should always be kept spotless inside and out. Do not use those dirt-collecting cloth wheel covers. Spray guns, masking paper, paint cans, tape, wheel covers, air transformers, hoses, respirators, coveralls, tack rags, and various other supplies can all collect dirt if stored in a dirty environment. All of these items should be kept in a filtered, ventilated storage/mix room. If any of these items are subject to sanding dust, they will quickly ruin a paint finish.

Unbelievable as it might seem, dirt from compressed air lines often causes blemishes in paint jobs. Air transformers, with properly cleaned and regularly drained filters, keep the air clean and dry. Oil and water separators are absolutely necessary to eliminate dirt and contamination.

A buildup of overspray can collect on the air cap and turn into a kind of fuzz. Clean the gun frequently to prevent fuzz from blowing off and ruining a paint job. Paint will set up in and on the gun. If the dried

paint flakes, it will land on the job and cause a defect. Clean the gun inside and out after every job.

Improper viscosity can cause excessive overspray, higher booth maintenance, runs or sags, pebble-dry finishes and color mismatches. Always mix the paint according to the manufacturer's recommendations and check the viscosity with a Zahn cup and stopwatch (see Chapter 3).

Paints are complex formulations. A combination of two or more brands of ingredients can result in unbalanced viscosity, poor adhesion, dry spray, mottling, low gloss, off-standard soft finish and solvent pop. Until wrinkle finishes become popular, avoid this condition at all times by using the manufacturer's recommended products.

Oil fan pulley and motor bearings regularly, if required; but, always be sure to shut off main fan switch of power supply before oiling the fan.

If the spray booth is not properly maintained, it can cause the finish problems described in Table 2-1.

DRYING ROOM

A dust-free drying room following the spray booth will speed up drying, turn out a cleaner job, and increase the volume of refinishing work that can be handled. The drying rooms of more sophisticated paint shops have permanent infrared or sodium quartz units for the forced drying of paint, particularly enamels. These oven-like units (Figure 2-14) can speed up the dry time of enamels as much as 75 percent. The use of forced drying on putty, prime, and sealer coats will reduce waiting time between operations and can also be used for fast drying spot and panel finish coats.

FIGURE 2-14 An infrared or sodium quartz drying unit in place in a drying room

TABLE 2-1:   TROUBLESHOOTING SPRAY BOOTH PROBLEMS

Fault	Result	Dirty Job	Thin Coats	Poor Opacity	Sags	Overloading	Popping	Softness	Overspray	Uneven Application	Recoat Failure	Fire Hazard	Water Splashes
Dirty filters in a dry filtration system	Vacuum in booth (hot air drawn from oven)	C				B	A	A	C	C,D	A		
	OR Not pressurized (low air movement and dirty air drawn in from preparation area)	A	A	C	B					C,D			
Torn or damaged filter in a dry filtration system	Turbulence	A							B	B,D			
	Over-pressurized				A	A	A	A	B	C,D	A		
Water level in a wet filtration system — Low	Increased extraction					A	A	A		C,D	A		A
High	Restricted extraction		A	C	B				C	C,D			A
Empty	Increased extraction with buildup of dry paint in reservoir	A										A	
Use of incorrect water additive, or incorrect use of water additive in a wet filtration system	Blocked water jets and filters. Formation of dry powder on anti-splash panels. Corrosion of plant. Paint deposits difficult to remove	A										C	A
Rags, masking paper, old cans, and so on in booth.	Dirt accumulation	A										A	
Spraying on walls of booth	Poor light reflection									C,D			
Loose deposits of dirt, dry spray, rust, and so forth on booth walls	Dirt in atmosphere	A											

A   Most likely failure to be associated with the fault
B   Likely failure
C   Failure less likely to be associated with the fault
D   Will affect color of metallics

Infrared or sodium quartz drying equipment is available in portable panels for partial or sectional drying, or in large travelling ovens capable of moving automatically on track over the vehicle to dry a complete overall job. There are two types of infrared drying equipment:

1. **Near drying equipment.** Because drying equipment uses lamps as the heat source, this type of equipment is easy to handle; the radiation angle can be varied easily; and construction, relocation, and assembly are simple, so it is the most common

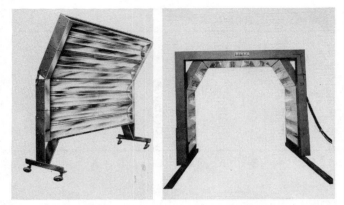

FIGURE 2-15 Typical near drying equipment. The unit on the left has a moveable top and is portable, while the one on the right moves over the vehicle on a track. *(Courtesy of Binks Mfg. Co.)*

type used for automobiles. There are several shapes and sizes of this equipment, depending on what it is used for, but the most common types are illustrated in Figure 2-15.

2. **Far drying equipment.** Far drying or sodium quartz equipment affects paint drying by means of heat radiated from a tubular or plate type heater. The heat source is either gas or electricity. Far drying equipment also comes in various types and sizes depending on what it is used for, but the most common types are shown in Figure 2-16.

Drying can best be accomplished in a separate drying chamber attached to the back of a downdraft system or conventional drive-thru booth (Figure 2-17A) where the travelling oven is housed and operated. In this configuration, the highest production is achieved since both the painting and drying operations can be performed simultaneously.

Drying can also be performed directly in the spray booth after painting. A storage vestibule is used to store the travelling oven until it is needed (Figure 2-17B). After the vehicle is painted, the oven is rolled out of the vestibule and into the spray booth for the drying operation.

When using a drying room, certain precautions must be taken not to destroy the finish. Table 2-2 gives the common difficulties that can be caused in the drying room.

AIR-POWERED TOOLS

The automotive industry was one of the first industries to see the advantages of air-powered tools. Although electric grinders, polishers, and heat guns are found in some refinishing shops, the use of pneumatic (air) tools is a great deal more common. Pneumatic tools have four major advantages over electrically powered equipment in the auto repair/paint shop:

1. **Flexibility.** Air tools run cooler and have the advantage of variable speed and torque; damage from overload or stalling is eliminated. They can fit in tight spaces.

FIGURE 2-16 Examples of portable far drying equipment

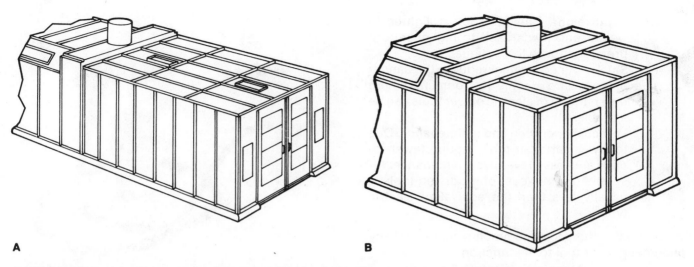

A   B

FIGURE 2-17   (A) Spray booth with drying chamber; (B) spray booth with storage vestibule

TABLE 2-2:   TROUBLESHOOTING DRYING ROOM PROBLEMS

Fault	Result	Popping	Softness	Dirty Job	Overspray	Impaired Durability	Polishing Impaired	Fire and Explosion Hazard	Loss of Gloss	Recoat Failure	Discolorate
Dirty filters	Diminished air velocity	A	A			C	B			A	
	Diminished oven pressure		A	C	B	C	B				
	Spray booth/oven pressure imbalance			B							
Filters damaged or breached	High velocity jet streams and turbulence	A	B	A		C	C				
Thermostat probe not correctly sited in moving airstream and/or insufficiently sensitive.	Excessive high/low temperature modulation	A	A			C	C				
10% Bleed duct closed/ 10% Make-up filter clogged	Foul oven Excessive fumes							B	A	A	A
Failure to remove deposits of rust, dust, and flaking paint from oven surfaces	Excessive dirt circulation			A							
Failure to clean unpainted areas on vehicles. Failure to clean masking or remask. Operators entering oven with dirty overalls	Unnecessary dirt introduced into oven			A							

A   Most likely failure to be associated with the fault   **C**   Failure less likely to be associated with the fault
B   Likely failure

2. **Lightweight.** The air tool is lighter in weight and lends itself to higher rate of production with less fatigue.
3. **Safety.** Air equipment reduces the danger of fire hazard in some environments where the sparking of electric power tools can be a problem.
4. **Low cost operation and maintenance.** Due to fewer parts, air tools require fewer repairs and less preventive maintenance. Also, the original cost of air driven tools is usually less than the equivalent electric type.

Actually, the most common causes for any pneumatic or air tool to malfunction are:

- Lack of proper lubrication
- Excessive air pressure or lack of it
- Excessive moisture or dirt in the air lines

Installation of an air transformer and lubricator (Figure 2-18) will greatly reduce the causes for an air tool malfunction. With these units installed, it is possible to assure clean air, proper lubrication of internal wear parts, and control of air pressure to suit different tool applications.

There are pneumatic equivalents for nearly every electrically powered tool, from sanders to drills, grinders, and screwdrivers. Furthermore, there are some pneumatic tools with no electrical equivalent, in particular: the needle scaler, air blow gun, scraper, and various auto tools.

Jacks and lifts can be used in conjunction with a compressed air system. However, in most cases, these pieces of equipment are hydraulically operated.

PAINT SPRAY GUNS

The spray gun (Figure 2-19) is probably the most used air-powered tool in the paint shop. It is used to do the majority of the refinishing work.

FIGURE 2-19 Paint spray gun air system arrangement

Spray guns are also one of the most efficient of all pneumatic tools.

A conventional air spray gun (Figure 2-20) is a precision tool using compressed air to atomize sprayable material. Air and paint enter the gun through separate passages and are mixed and ejected at the air nozzle to provide a controlled spray pattern.

Pulling back slightly on the trigger opens the air valve to allow use of the gun as a blow gun. In this position the trigger does not actuate the fluid needle and no fluid flows. As the trigger is further retracted, it unseats the needle in the fluid nozzle and the gun begins to spray. The amount of paint leaving the gun is controlled by the pressure on the container, the viscosity of the paint, the size of the fluid orifice, and the fluid needle adjustment. In industrial finishing where pressure tanks or pumps are used, the fluid needle adjustment should normally be fully opened. In suction cup operation, the needle valve controls the flow of paint.

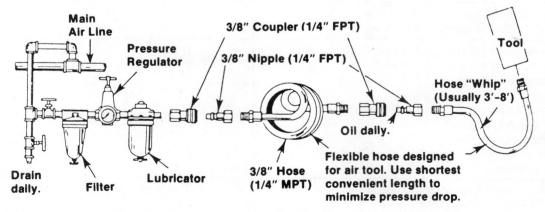

FIGURE 2-18 Typical auto shop air system arrangement for tools

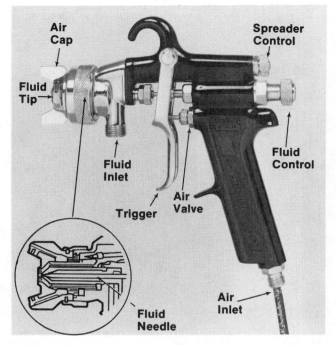

FIGURE 2-20 Components of an air gun. *(Courtesy of Binks Mfg. Co.)*

Complete details on the operation of the various types of spray guns and their use can be found in Chapter 3.

AIR SANDERS

There are two basic types of air sanders: disc and orbital (finishing). Most rough sanding done in automotive work is done with a disc sander (Figure 2-21) or its counterpart, the dual-action (DA) orbital sander (Figure 2-22). The latter oscillates while it is rotating thus creating a buffing pattern rather than the swirls and scratches often caused by the disc sander.

The finishing orbital sanders, also called "pad" or "jitterbug" sanders (Figure 2-23), are designed for fine finish sanding. It is possible to use a wider variety of abrasives with finish sanders than with any

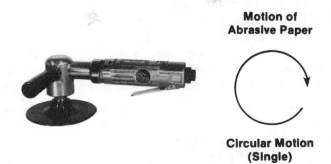

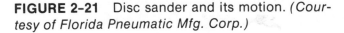

FIGURE 2-21 Disc sander and its motion. *(Courtesy of Florida Pneumatic Mfg. Corp.)*

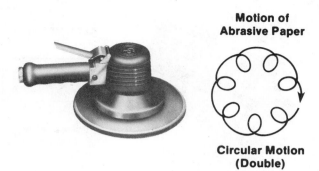

FIGURE 2-22 Dual or double action sander and its motion. *(Courtesy of Chicago Pneumatic Tool Division)*

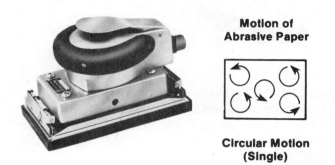

FIGURE 2-23 Pad or jitterbug sander and its motion. *(Courtesy of Chicago Pneumatic Tool Division)*

other type of power sanding, but for the most part, the best work is done with comparatively fine grit abrasive paper. Finish sanders are also especially designed for hard-to-reach places and tight corners.

Another sander found in auto body shops is the long board type sander (Figure 2-24). It operates in either an orbital or straight line motion that will cover about 40 square inches of working area per minute.

Details on operating sanders can be found in Chapter 8.

AIR GRINDERS

The most commonly used portable grinder in body and paint shops is the disc type grinder (Figure 2-25). It is operated like the disc sander.

CAUTION: Avoid grinding too close to the trim, bumper, or any other auto parts projections that might snag or catch the edge of the disc (Figure 2-26). Also do not stop a disc grinder while in contact with the work surface. Start any grinding operation just before the machine makes contact with the work surface.

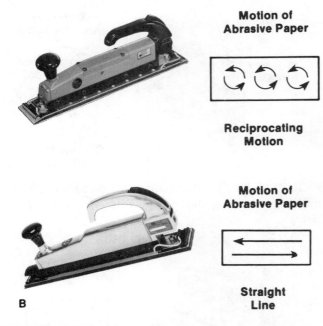

Motion of
Abrasive Paper

Reciprocating
Motion

Motion of
Abrasive Paper

Straight
Line

B

FIGURE 2–24 Two types of board sander: (A) orbital and its motion and (B) straight line and its motion. *(Photo A courtesy of Florida Pneumatic Mfg. Corp; photo B courtesy of Chicago Pneumatic Tool Division)*

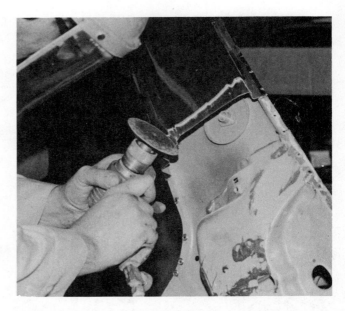

FIGURE 2–26 Take care not to catch projections. *(Courtesy of Marson Corp.)*

FIGURE 2–25 Disc type grinder at work

There are, of course, several other grinders used in the paint/body shop. The more common ones that a painter can use include

- **Horizontal grinder** (Figure 2–27A) is used for heavy-duty grinding.
- **Vertical grinder** (Figure 2–27B) is a larger version of the disc grinder. With a sanding

pad, this grinder can be converted into a disc sander. Most vertical grinders can be used with both straight wheels as well as cup wheels (Figure 2–27C).

- **Angle grinder** (Figure 2–27D) is used primarily for smoothing, deburring, and blending welds.
- **Small wheel grinder** (Figure 2–27E) can be used with cone wheels, wire brushes, or collet chucks and burrs in addition to a straight grind.
- **Die grinder** (Figure 2–27F) is used with mounted points and carbide burrs for a variety of applications such as weld cleaning, deburring, blending, and smoothing. Available in both straight and angle head designs.

POLISHER/BUFFERS

Polisher/buffers (Figure 2–28) are used in compounding, rubbing, and final polishing. Their uses are fully described in Chapter 11.

One of the most important considerations when operating a polisher/buffer is the selection of the proper buffing pad. Here are some points to consider when making a selection:

- Match the pad to the needs of the job. Low pile heights (1 to 1-1/4 inches) work best for the early stages of cutting and compounding. High pile heights (1-1/2 to 2 inches) are better for light compounding and critical

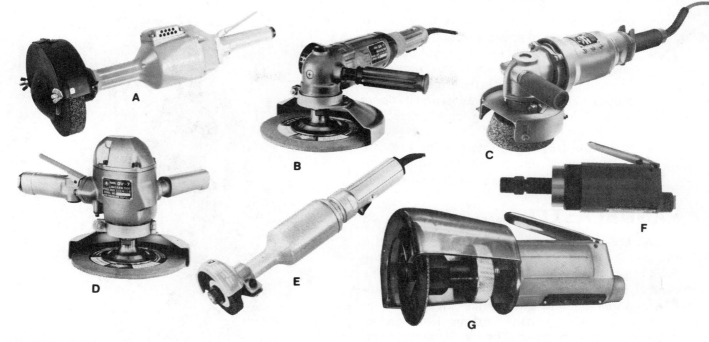

FIGURE 2-27   Various types of grinders found in a body shop: (A) horizontal grinder; (B) vertical grinder; (C) vertical grinder with cup wheel; (D) angle grinder; (E) small wheel grinder; (F) die grinder.

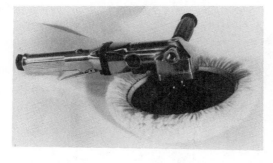

A

FIGURE 2-29   Typical polishing/buffing pads

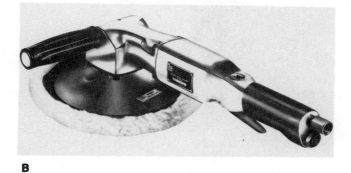

B

FIGURE 2-28   Two types of polisher/buffers: (A) angle and (B) vertical. *(Photo A courtesy of Florida Pneumatic Mfg. Corp; photo B courtesy of Chicago Pneumatic Tool Division)*

jobs, such as touchups and blending (Figure 2-29) where raised body lines demand cushioning. For final finishing and waxing, use a clean lamb's wool bonnet or a final finish disc with long even pile. These will run the coolest and offer the most polishing action. For further protection, consider using pads with rounded-up edges.

- Let the pad do the work. Using the design of a pad to its best advantage means changing pads at the various stages of the job.
- Be sure that the pad does not load up too fast, does not burn (a rounded-up edge helps

prevent edge burns), and is constructed tightly enough to prevent wool flyout.

- Remember that 100 percent wool pads are best for automotive finishes. Wool runs cooler, cushions more, and lasts longer than synthetics, because wool breathes, and its fibers retain their natural spring longer. Most can be washed and reused.
- It is poor practice to intermix the use of a buffer with a grinder. Employ a buffer for buffing only or surface scratches can result.

SANDBLASTERS

Another pneumatic tool that is fully described in Chapter 9 is the sandblaster. Sandblasting is the most effective way to remove all finishes from any vehicle. Sandblasting leaves metal in perfect condition for priming. There is no chance of wax or chemical residue remaining on the bare metal, in crevices, or under chrome stripping. The refinisher has complete control of refinishing methods from the bare metal out. Special care must be taken, however, in shielding all glass and chrome parts.

As shown in Figure 2-30, there are two basic types of sandblasters:

- Standard sandblaster
- "Captive" sandblaster

The standard sandblaster is usually operated outdoors, while the captive units can be used indoors. The indoor sandblasters have a nozzle assembly that confines the blasting action, while a vacuum in the machine sucks the abrasive and debris.

For either blaster, sand grit size number 30 is used for general purpose applications (light rust and paint removal from metal). Aluminum oxide (grid size number 50 to 90) is used for heavy rust removal and rough surface paint removal.

OTHER PNEUMATIC TOOLS

There are several other air tools that can be found in some auto paint shops. They include:

- **Needle Scalers.** Used for derusting and cleaning of metals as well as for peening welded joints (Figure 2-31A).
- **Air Blow Gun.** Possibly the smallest air tool in the shop, it is one of the most worthwhile. It blows away dust and dirt from any small hard-to-reach place (Figure 2-31B).
- **Scaper.** Removing undercoating and other coverings is this accessory's function.

A

B

FIGURE 2-30 Two types of sandblasters: (A) standard pressure and (B) captive

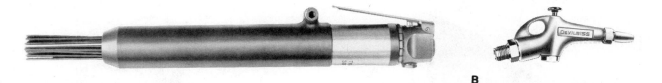

FIGURE 2-31   (A) Needle scalers and (B) air blow gun *(Courtesy of DeVilbiss Co.)*

PNEUMATIC TOOL MAINTENANCE

Air tools require little maintenance but could easily cause big problems if that little maintenance is not performed. For instance, moisture gathers in the air lines and is blown into the tools during use. If a tool is left with water in it, rust will form and the tool will experience reduced efficiency and will wear out much more quickly.

To prevent this from happening, remember that most air tool motors need daily (or as often as used) lubrication with a good grade of air motor oil. If the air line has no line oiler or lubricator, run a teaspoon of oil through the tool. The oil can be squirted into the tool air inlet or into the hose at the nearest connection to the air supply; then run the tool. Most air tool manufacturers recommend the use of their special oil for lubricating tools; however, when this is not available standard automatic transmission fluid may be substituted.

Most air refinishing tools have a recommended air pressure (Table 2-3). If the tool is overworked, it will wear out sooner. If something goes wrong with the tool, fix it. If not, a chain reaction might occur and the other parts will require maintenance also. For example, if the gearing must be replaced and the tool is used anyway, the rotor and end plate might soon wear out as a result. A tool with worn parts will also use more air pressure. The air compressor, in turn, will then become overworked and put out air that is not as clean or dry and is shot right back into the tools.

Full information on pneumatic air system operation is given in Chapter 4.

ELECTRIC-POWERED TOOLS

As mentioned earlier in this chapter, shop tools such as sanders and polishers can also be powered by electric motors. But, for most paint shops, the most important electric only tools are bench grinders, vacuum cleaners, and heat guns.

Other than these specialized electrically driven power tools, electric drills, polishes, sanders, and so

TABLE 2-3: AIR CONSUMPTION CHART†		
Tool	**Scfm***	**Psi***
Air blow gun	1–2.5	40–90
Air brush	1	10–50
Car washer	8.5	40–90
Cut-off grinder	4–8	80–90
Drill 3/8 inch	4–6	70–90
Grinders, vertical	10–16	70–90
Needle scaler	3–4	70–90
Paint sprayer	0.7–5	10–70
Pneumatic garage door	2	90–150
Polisher	2	70–90
Riveter	4.5–5.5	70–90
Sandblast gun	2.2–4	30–90
Sandblast gun/hopper	2–6	40–90
Sander, disc	4–6	60–80
Sander, double action	6–8	60–80
Sander, finish	6–8	60–80
Sander, straight line	6–8	70–90
Screwdriver	2–6	70–90
Shears	5–8	70–90

*SCFM: Standard cubic feet per minute
 PSI: Pounds per square inch
†Always check with the tool manufacturers for the actual air consumption of the tools being used. These figures are based on averages and should not be considered accurate for any particular make of tool.

on perform the same shop tasks as their pneumatic counterparts.

BENCH GRINDER

This electric power tool (Figure 2-32) is generally bolted to one of the shop's workbenches. A bench grinder is classified by wheel size; 6- to 10-inch wheels are the most common in auto repair shops. Three types of wheels are available with this bench tool:

- **Grinding Wheel.** For a wide variety of grinding jobs from sharpening cutting tools to deburring.
- **Wire Wheel Brush.** Used for general cleaning and buffing, removing rust and scale, paint removal, deburring, and so forth.

FIGURE 2-32 Typical bench grinder. *(Courtesy of Snap-On Tools Corp.)*

- **Buffing Wheel.** For general purpose buffing, polishing, light cutting, and finish coloring operations.

When using a bench grinder (these safety rules also apply to portable air grinders), remember to:

- Always use a wheel with a rated speed equal to or greater than the grinder's.
- Always use a wheel guard.
- Inspect wheels for wear or cracks before using them. Use correct wheel for job and mount it properly.
- Always wear safety goggles or face shield and make sure the eye shields of the grinder operator are in position.

VACUUM CLEANER

A must in every body and refinishing shop is a vacuum cleaner (Figure 2-33). Actually, it should be one of the first tools used when a vehicle comes in for refinishing. That is, an incoming vehicle should be completely washed and vacuumed before it is prepared for refinishing. This will greatly reduce the chance of dirt getting into the complete job.

There are two basic types of shop vacuum cleaners: the dry pick-up type and wet/dry unit. The wet/dry unit, in the 20- to 30-gallon capacity, is the one found in most paint shops. For interior vehicle cleaning the portable vacuum cleaner is popular (Figure 2-34).

Power washers can be used in exterior car preparation, engine cleaning, undercarriage cleaning, shop degreasing and cleaning, and snow and salt removal from vehicles. Figure 2-35 shows typical stationary and portable units.

FIGURE 2-33 Typical portable paint shop vacuum cleaner

FIGURE 2-34 Vacuum cleaner suitable for the interior of a vehicle.

To keep dust out of the refinishing shop, some power orbital sanders—both electric and air powered—have a sanding dust pick-up arrangement. Figure 2-36 shows a straight line sander equipped with its own vacuum system and a catching bag while Figure 2-37 illustrates an adapter that connects to a central vacuum cleaner system.

HEAT GUN

Heat guns (Figure 2-38) have a number of uses in the auto paint shop. They can be used in removing woodgrain transfers as well as speeding up drying times. They are also helpful in stretching vinyl roof top corners.

ELECTRIC POWER TOOL SAFETY

To protect the operator from electric shock, most power tools are built with an external ground-

FIGURE 2-35 Typical electric power washer: (A) stationary and (B) portable. *(Courtesy of Graco, Inc.)*

FIGURE 2-36 Sander equipped with dust collecting bag. *(Courtesy of Hutchins Mfg. Co.)*

FIGURE 2-38 Typical heat gun. *(Courtesy of Black & Decker, Inc.)*

FIGURE 2-37 Typical central vacuum system *(Courtesy of Eurovac, Inc.)*

ing system. That is, there is a wire that runs from the motor housing, through the power cord, to a third prong on the power plug. When this third prong is connected to a grounded, three hole electrical outlet, the grounding wire will carry any current that leaks past the electrical insulation of the tool away from the operator and into the ground of the shop's wiring. In most modern electrical systems, the three prong plug fits into a three prong, grounded receptacle. If the tool is operated at less than 150 volts, it has a plug like that shown in Figure 2-39A. If it is for use on 150 or 250 volts, it has a plug like that shown in Figure 2-39B. In either type, the green (or green and

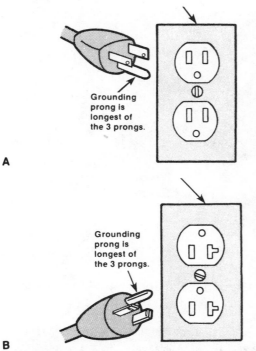

FIGURE 2-39 (A) Approved type of three prong grounding plug and outlet box for 115 volts AC; (B) approved type of three prong grounding plug and outlet box for 230 volts AC.

yellow) conductor in the tool cord is the grounding wire. Never connect the grounding wire to a live terminal.

Some of the new electric power tools are self-insulated and do not require grounding. These tools have only two prongs since they have a nonconducting housing. In shop operations, never use a three prong adapter plug.

Extension Cords

If an extension cord is used, it should be kept as short as possible. Very long or undersized cords will reduce operating voltage and thus reduce operating efficiency, possibly causing motor damage. Actually, an extension cord should be used only as a last resort. But, when an extension cord must be employed, the following wire gauge sizes are recommended for different lengths:

Length	115 Volts	230 Volts
Less than 25 feet	12	14
25 to 50 feet	10	12
50 to 100 feet	8	10

The smaller the gauge number, the heavier the duty cord. These are recommended minimum wire sizes.

Tools with three prong, grounded plugs must only be used with three wire grounded extension cords connected to properly grounded, three wire receptacles (Figure 2–40).

SHOP TALK

Here are some safety tips to keep in mind when using extension cords:

- *Always plug the cord of the tool into the extension cord before the extension cord is inserted into a convenience outlet. Always unplug the extension cord from the receptacle before the cord of the tool is unplugged from the extension cord.*
- *Extension cords should be long enough to make connections without being pulled taut, creating unnecessary strain and wear.*
- *Be sure that the extension cord does not come in contact with sharp objects. The cords should not be allowed to kink, nor should they be dipped in or splattered with oil, grease, hot surfaces, or chemicals.*
- *Before using a cord, inspect it for loose or exposed wires and damaged insulation. If a cord is damaged, it must be replaced. This advice also applies to the tool's power cord.*
- *Extension cords should be checked frequently while in use to detect unusual heating. Any cable that feels more than comfortably warm to the bare hand, which is placed outside the insulation, should be checked immediately for overloading.*
- *See that the extension cord is in a position to prevent tripping or stumbling.*
- *To prevent the accidental separation of a compressor cord from an extension*

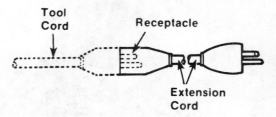

FIGURE 2-40 Typical three wire extension cord with an approved connector cap to ensure continuity of the tool's grounding wire

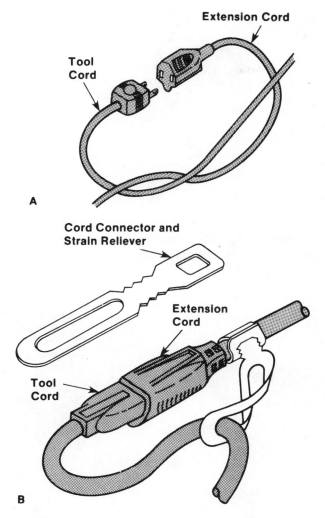

A

B

FIGURE 2-42   Typical cordless tools: (A) drill and (B) sander

FIGURE 2-41   (A) Knot will prevent the extension cord from accidentally pulling apart from the tool cord during operation; (B) cord connector will serve the same purpose effectively.

> *cord during operation, make a knot as shown in Figure 2-41A, or use a cord connector as shown in Figure 2-41B.*
> • *Do not use extension cords inside paint room.*

In recent years a few cordless tools—drills and sanders (Figure 2-42)—have made their way into the body/paint shop. These tools require no air hose or electric cord, but they require recharging.

OTHER PAINT SHOP EQUIPMENT AND TOOLS

There are several pieces of paint shop equipment that can help the refinishing technician perform paint jobs better. These items include:

• **Wet Sanding Stand.** A wet sanding stand (Figure 2-43) is used for wet sanding individual components or small parts. These cabinets are made by individual paint shops with the size and installation location depending on shop requirements and conditions.
• **Paint Hanger.** Paint hangers are used to suspend or secure individual components or small parts for spray painting. As with the wet sanding stands, these are made by the individual shop in accordance with the shape of the item to be painted, the quantity required, and so on. Paint hangers keep the panel from dropping during painting. They must be made of a material that will withstand heat during paint drying. An example is shown in Figure 2-44.
• **Panel Drying Ovens.** These are small ovens used to dry test pieces. There are various types—from a very simple kind using infrared lamps to more complicated kinds with

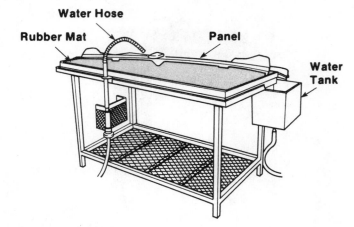

FIGURE 2-43 Typical wet sanding stand

FIGURE 2-45 The paint shaker shown here is compressed air operated. Paint shakers are also available that are electrically driven. *(Courtesy of Broncorp Mfg. Co.)*

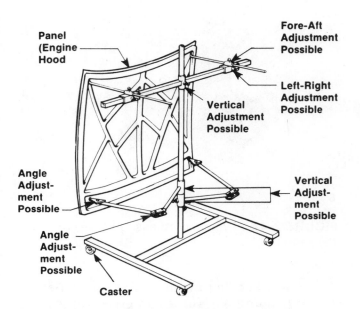

FIGURE 2-44 Typical paint shop hanger stand

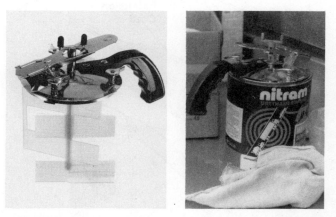

FIGURE 2-46 The blade agitator type mixer unit fits right on the top of paint can. *(Courtesy of Dedoes Industries, Inc.)*

an electric heater, vent fan, and a timer for controlling the temperature and drying time.

• **Paint Shakers and Paddle Agitators.** For a good refinishing job, it is very important that the paint be thoroughly mixed or agitated. In fact, with metallic paint topcoats it is essential. These paints contain metallic particles that are heavier than the paint itself and quickly settle to the bottom of the container. For this reason, metallic paint, as well as most other types, needs a proper mixing job. The quickest method of achieving this is with a paint shaker (Figure 2-45).

Another type of paint mixer is the blade agitator (Figure 2-46). The blades of the agitator are dipped into the paint and the paint

can sealed by the agitator cover. The cover locks over the can opening by spring action. These agitators with a cover usually come in 1 and 4 quart sizes and are the types of mixer used by color mixing centers (Figure 2-47).

• **Churning Knives.** Churning knives are also used to stir paint. The handle tip is designed as a paint can lid opener. Some churning knives have a scale for measuring paint or hardening agents.

• **Color Matching Scales.** Color matching scales are used to match the paint with the original color or tone. There are volume type and weight type scales. The paint is matched against a color formula card. Use of these scales will enable even a relatively inexperienced person to match paint although a final visual check is recommended before

FIGURE 2-47 Most custom color mixing service centers use blade agitator mixers. As shown here, the blades are build right into the shelf units. *(Courtesy of Du Pont Co.)*

using the paint since the scales are not always 100 percent accurate. There are three types of color matching scales:

—**Volume Type Scale.** This type matches the paint according to volume. The container for the paint to be mixed should have smooth walls. To match the paint, first set the color card into the scale, insert the ingredients as specified, and mix them.

—**Weight Type Scale.** This type (Figure 2-48) matches paint according to the weight of the ingredients. Weighing must be accurate, according to specifications on the formula card, in order to obtain a correct color match. First, combine the

ingredients and then mix thoroughly to obtain the desired color.

—**Computer Type Scale.** This type of scale allows very small quantities of paint to be mixed and its accuracy makes ingredients mix easily.

- **Masking Paper Dispenser.** A masking paper dispenser (Figure 2-49) allows dispensing of both masking paper and masking tape at the same time; as the paper is pulled, masking tape automatically adheres to the paper edge. Two or three sizes of roll paper can be set in the dispenser to help upgrade work efficiency.

- **Metal Paint Cabinet.** Paint cabinets are used for storage and stock control of paint, thinner, and putties. These cabinets should be selected in accordance with the amount of paint and thinner normally handled and the conditions of the shop layout.

- **Body Surfacing Tools.** A number of surfacing tools are used to give a repair its final shape and contour. Some are used to shape the repaired metal. Others are used to apply and shape plastic body filler and putty.

FIGURE 2-48 A weight type scale such as the one shown here is used with most color mixing systems. Exact weight scales are available with standard or digital scales. *(Courtesy of Du Pont Co.)*

FIGURE 2-49 A typical masking paper and tape dispenser. The tape is automatically applied to the edge of paper as it is rolled off. *(Courtesy of Marson Corp.)*

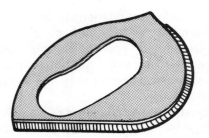

FIGURE 2-50 A reveal file is used to shape tight curves.

—**Metal Files.** After working a damaged panel back to its approximate original contour, a metal file is used to remove any remaining high spots. Two special files are necessary for most bodywork.

—**Reveal File.** The reveal file (Figure 2-50) is a small file that is available in numerous shapes. Generally it is curved to fit tightly crowned areas such as around windshields, wheel openings, and other panel edges. The reveal file is pulled, not pushed, when used. Pushing causes the file to chatter, resulting in nicks and an uneven surface.

—**Body Files.** Body files are used to level large surfaces. After a dent has been

bumped or pulled back into shape, the body file will hone down high spots and reveal any low spots that might require additional bumping.

The blade of the body file is held in a holder. Figure 2-51A shows a flexible holder with a turnbuckle. The turnbuckle can be adjusted to flex the file. The flexible holder allows the shape of the file to fit the contour of the panel.

Fixed file holders (Figure 2-51B) are also available for filing flat or slightly convex shapes.

—**Surform File.** Body filler should be made level to the adjacent panel with a surform file (Figure 2-52). Commonly referred to as

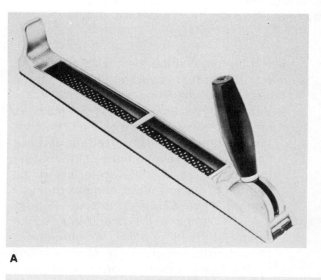

A

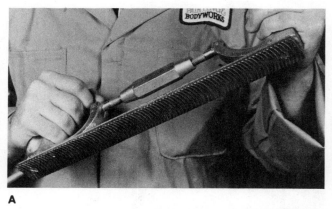

A

B

FIGURE 2-51 A body file (A) in a flexible holder and (B) rigid file holder. *(Photo B courtesy of Snap-on Tools Corp.)*

B

FIGURE 2-52 (A) Surform "cheese grater" and (B) replacement blades. *(Photo A courtesy of Bond-Tite Products; photo B courtesy of Du Pont Co.)*

FIGURE 2-53 Speed files. *(Courtesy of Du Pont Co.)*

a cheese grater, the surform file is used to shape body filler while it is semihard. Shaping the filler before it hardens shortens the waiting period while the filler cures and reduces the sanding effort later in the repair process.

—**Speed File.** Once the body filler has hardened, the repair can be shaped and leveled with a speed file (Figure 2-53). The

speed file is a rigid wooden holder about 17 inches long and 2-3/4 inches wide. Also called a flatboy, the speed file allows a repair area to be sanded quickly with long, level strokes. This eliminates waves and uneven areas.

The lightweight aluminum sander shown in Figure 2-54A is designed to quickly level body filler. The extra long length helps avoid creating a wavy surface. The sander also flexes to match the panel contour. Adhesive-backed sandpaper is applied from a roll (Figure 2-54B). This particular sander can also be attached to a straight-line air sander.

—**Spreaders and Squeegees.** Spreaders and squeegees are two important tools used in auto body resurfacing. Spreaders are used to apply body filler. Spreaders (Figure 2-55) are made of rigid plastic and are available in various sizes. Be sure to use one that is large enough to apply plastic filler over the repair area before the filler begins to set up.

A squeegee (Figure 2-56) is a flexible rubber block approximately 2 inches by 3 inches and 3/16-inch thick. Squeegees are

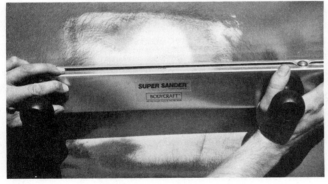

A

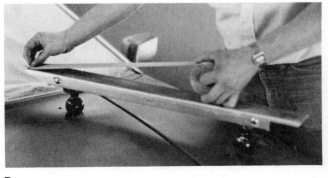

B

FIGURE 2-54 A flexible sander. *(Courtesy of Bodycraft Corp.)*

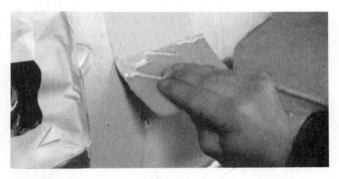

FIGURE 2-55 A body filler spreader. *(Courtesy of Du Pont Co.)*

FIGURE 2-56 A rubber squeegee

used to apply glazing putty and light coats of body filler. They are also used when wet sanding to skim water and sanding grit from the repair area.

- **Respirators.** Spray finishing creates a certain amount of overspray, hazardous vapors, and toxic fumes. This is true even under ideal conditions and there is no way to avoid it entirely. Anyone who is around a spray finishing operation must consider wearing some type of respirator or breathing apparatus (Figure 2-57).

There are two good reasons for wearing a respirator. First, some sort of respiratory protection is dictated by OSHA/NIOSH regulations. And second, even if this were not true, common sense would tell one that inhaling overspray is not healthy. Overspray contains particles of toxic paint pigments, harmful dust, and in some cases vapor fumes, which can be harmful to your health. Depending on design, a respirator can remove some or all of these dangerous components in the air around a spray finishing operator.

There are three primary types of respirators available to protect the operator: the hood respirator, the cartridge filter respirator, and the dust respirator. These are fully discussed in Chapter 1. But, when there is any doubt about the respirator to be worn, always use the air line hood respirator.

FIGURE 2-57 Many painters wear a respirator when mixing paints, especially those containing isocyanates.

WARNING: The precautionary measures mentioned here should prevent overexposure by inhalation, but if any symptoms of overexposure develop such as breathing difficulty, tightness of chest, severe coughing, irritation of the nose or throat, or nausea, leave the area quickly and get fresh air. If breathing continues to be labored, see a physician immediately.

It is important to note that symptoms of inhalation overexposure might not appear until 4 to 8 hours after the exposure. Depending upon the severity of overexposure, symptoms might persist for 3 to 7 days.

Because high concentrations of vapor will irritate the eyes, goggles or sufficient eye protection should be worn at all times during application. If spray residue finds its way to the eyes, they should be flushed immediately with water for at least 15 minutes. If irritation persists, see a physician.

BASIC PAINT SHOP MATERIAL

Paint shop materials differ from refinishing equipment in one key way: Paint shop refinishing materials are expendable. They are used up in the day-to-day operation; whereas, equipment is used over and over.

Popular paint shop materials include:

- Abrasive paper
- Clean cloths or paper towels
- Tack rags
- Paint paddles
- Strainers
- Containers
- Masking paper and tape

ABRASIVE PAPER OR SANDPAPER

The rough side of paper is called the "grit side." Grit sizes vary (Figure 2-58) from coarse to micro fine and are ordered by number. The lower the number, the coarser the grit.

CLEAN CLOTHS OR PAPER TOWELS

It is important that the areas to be painted are clean. Most paint shops provide clean cloths or spe-

FIGURE 2-58 Various grits, sizes, and shapes of abrasive papers. *(Courtesy of Carborundum Abrasives Co.)*

cial disposable paper wipers. Whichever is used, these simple tips will help:

- Use clean, dry cloths folded into a pad.
- When using a cleaning solvent, make sure to pour enough onto the pad being used to thoroughly wet the surface to be cleaned.
- Do not wait for the solvent to dry. Wipe it dry with a second clean cloth.

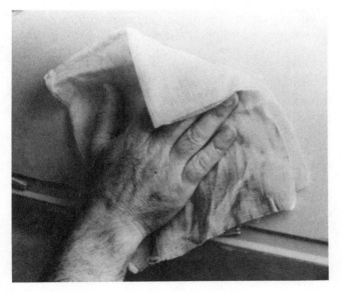

FIGURE 2-59 Tack cloths are used to remove any dirt or sanded particles before actual spraying.

- Refold the cloth often to provide a clean section.
- Change cloths often.
- Once an area is clean, do not touch it with the hands, as it might affect adhesion.

🔫 SHOP TALK _____

Cheesecloth strainers can add as much as a tablespoon of lint to the paint. The wrong mesh size can allow dirt to pass through the strainer that will later show up in the finish. Metallics require the coarsest mesh; clearcoats the finest. Clearcoats can develop small globs in the can that show up like dirt in the finish. Therefore, use only approved paper, or better yet, properly maintained metal strainers. Always strain the paint.

TACK RAGS OR CLOTHS

These are specially treated sticky cloths (varnish-coated cheese cloth) that are used in the make-ready operation to wipe the surface clean just before the paint is applied (Figure 2-59). They should be used on the area to be painted to remove all sanded particles, dirt, old paint chips, and so on. Often the painter will simply blow off the area with an air nozzle or will use an old rag to wipe off the area. These procedures will leave minute impurities on the surface that will detrimentally affect adhesion and performance of the product. A tack cloth will pick up fine particles that are invisible to the naked eye. Tack rags should be stored in an airtight container to conserve their tackiness.

PAINT PADDLES

Made of either wood, metal, or plastic, paint paddles are used to stir the paint material. If the paddle is wood, it is recommended that the end be tapered to a sharp edge like a chisel. This will make it easier to dislodge the pigment and metallic flakes from the bottom of the can.

STRAINERS

Consisting of a cardboard funnel with cotton mesh, a strainer is used when pouring thinned topcoat and other materials into a spray cup (Figure 2-60). This is done to make sure it is free of any dirt or foreign material.

FIGURE 2-60 Straining thinned topcoat into a spray cup through a strainer. *(Courtesy of Du Pont Co.)*

CONTAINERS

Paint shop containers come in six common sizes and/or shapes and contain various materials:

- **Tubes.** Contain putty.
- **Round cans.** Gallon, quart, and pint containers for topcoats and some undercoats, including putty and body filler.
- **Square cans.** Gallon containers for thinners, reducers, primer-surfacers, sealers, and clear topcoats.
- **Pails.** Contain thinners, reducers, undercoats, and topcoats.
- **Drums.** Contain thinners, reducers, and undercoats.
- **Plastic containers.** Metal conditioner, body filler, polish, and buffing compounds.

Lids on round containers of a gallon or less—called "friction lids"—should be carefully opened with a proper opener. After pouring off whatever amount of material is needed from a round can, the lip should be wiped and the lid replaced tightly to form a good seal (Figure 2-61). A pouring spout made of masking tape will keep liquid from collecting in the rim, while a rubber mallet is recommended for tapping the lid around the edge. Proper resealing of the can will keep air out and minimize the formation of the film on the top—called "skinning." It will also prevent the loss of solvents. Screw top cans should be carefully wiped and closed tightly for the same reasons.

FIGURE 2-61 Device for applying lids. *(Courtesy of Dedoes Industries, Inc.)*

 **SHOP TALK** _____

Keep the pouring spouts of the stirring heads clean to avoid a buildup of paint residues around the spout that can ultimately affect the accuracy of pouring. Wiping the spout after every pour is the simplest method. Alternatively, application of masking tape around the spout that can be replaced at regular intervals, removing solidified residues, is fairly effective.

Where there is heavy usage of undercoats, thinners, and reducers, the material can be purchased in drums at a considerable savings. When lacquer undercoats are stocked in large containers, the solvents keep the solids properly mixed, so there is less waste of materials. Drums of undercoats should be fitted with a gate valve for pouring, while drums of thinners and reducers should be fitted with either a faucet or a pump.

 **SHOP TALK** _____

Store clean empty containers upside down to prevent entry of dirt or other forms of contamination.

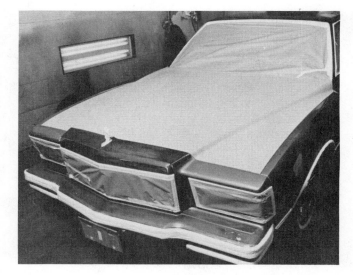

FIGURE 2-62 Masking paper and tape are used to protect areas where paint is unwanted.

Plastic measuring cups are used for matching or thinning paint. Generally, their sizes range from 1 quart to 5 quarts and they are made of easy-to-use and easy-to-clean plastic.

MASKING PAPER AND TAPE

Masking paper is used to cover surrounding areas not to be painted so that paint mist does not settle there (Figure 2-62). It is necessary that the masking paper be capable of preventing solvent in the paint mist from seeping through to the surface of the object. Some paint shops use newspapers for this purpose, but this cannot be recommended because thin fibers from the paper come off and adhere to the freshly painted surface, resulting in dirt. Also, solvent will seep through newspaper or even transfer newsprint onto the area covered.

Masking tape is used to stick the masking paper to the areas to be covered or it can be used by itself. Masking tape is made of different types of materials, such as paper, cloth, and vinyl, so that adhesion performance is assured regardless of the season or weather. The adhesive performance of masking tape does not change when heat is applied and will not leave traces of adhesive when removed. Also, it is easy to cut or tear off.

There are several types of paper masking tape depending on what it is used for, but they can be roughly classified into general masking tape used for air drying and heat-resistant tape used for baking enamel. The proper tape for the job must always be used. Full information on masking paper and tape and how it is used is given in Chapter 9.

REVIEW QUESTIONS

1. Which spray booth provides the safest environment for the painter?
   a. regular flow booth
   b. reverse flow booth
   c. downdraft booth
   d. crossdraft booth

2. Which spray booth is the most popular today?
   a. regular flow booth
   b. reverse flow booth
   c. downdraft booth
   d. crossdraft booth

3. Painter A monitors the manometer readings hourly. Painter B monitors the manometer readings daily. Who is right?
   a. Painter A
   b. Painter B
   c. Both A and B
   d. Neither A nor B

4. Which drying room problem will result in a loss of gloss?
   a. dirty filter
   b. damaged filter
   c. 10 percent bleed duct closed
   d. insufficiently sensitive thermostat probe

5. What causes a pneumatic tool to fail?
   a. lack of lubrication
   b. excessive air pressure
   c. lack of air pressure
   d. all of the above
   e. both a and c

6. Which air sander creates a buffing pattern?
   a. disc sander
   b. dual-action orbital sander
   c. long board type sander
   d. all of the above

7. Which pad should be used on a polisher/buffer to do the early stages of cutting and compounding?
   a. 1/2 to 1 inch pile height
   b. 1 to 1-1/4 inch pile height
   c. 1-1/4 to 1-1/2 inch pile height
   d. 1-1/2 to 2 inch pile height

8. Which type of sandblaster can be used indoors?
   a. standard
   b. captive
   c. both a and b
   d. none of the above

9. What is the recommended air pressure for a disc sander?
   a. 60 to 80 PSI
   b. 70 to 90 PSI
   c. 40 to 90 PSI
   d. 10 to 50 PSI

10. Which type of vacuum cleaner is most often found in shops?
    a. dry pick-up type, 20 to 30-gallon capacity
    b. dry pick-up type, 30 to 40-gallon capacity
    c. wet/dry unit, 20 to 30-gallon capacity
    d. wet/dry unit, 30 to 40-gallon capacity

11. Painter A plugs the electric cord of the tool into the extension cord before the extension cord is inserted into the convenience outlet. Painter B reverses the order. Who is right?
    a. Painter A
    b. Painter B
    c. Both A and B
    d. Neither A nor B

12. What is the probable cause of a spongy effect in hydraulic equipment?
    a. dirt in release valve
    b. reservoir over full
    c. air in system
    d. release valve not fully closed

13. What causes hydraulic equipment to work properly one time but not the next?
    a. air bubble in valve system
    b. dirt in check valve
    c. dirt in release valve
    d. none of the above

14. Which of the following scales is used in color matching?
    a. volume type
    b. weight type
    c. computer type
    d. all of the above

15. Which type of file is used to shape body filler while it is semihard?
    a. reveal file
    b. body file
    c. surform file
    d. speed file

CHAPTER THREE

SPRAY GUN AND ITS USE

Objectives

After reading this chapter, you will be able to:

- identify the spray painting equipment used in auto refinishing.
- explain how a spray gun works.
- identify the basic techniques of good spray painting and recognize variables that influence the quality of the spray finish.
- adjust the spraying equipment to test and develop a good spray pattern.
- implement the stroke technique procedure for single and double coat application and recognize common errors made by apprentice refinishers.
- identify the various types of spray coats.
- determine when and how to make spot repairs.
- clean and properly care for a spray gun.
- identify situations for which airless spray systems or airbrushes are recommended.

The spray gun (Figure 3–1) is the key component in a refinishing system. It is a precision engineered and manufactured tool, and each type and size available is specifically designed to perform a certain number of tasks. Even though all spray guns have many parts and components in common, each gun type or size is suited for only a certain, defined range of jobs. As in most other areas of refinishing work, having the right tool for the job goes a long way toward getting a professional job done right in minimum time.

FIGURE 3–1 The proper use of a spray gun is a must in any refinishing paint shop. *(Courtesy of Maaco Enterprises, Inc.)*

ATOMIZATION AND THE SPRAY GUN

An air spray gun can be defined as a tool that turns a liquid into tiny droplets by means of air pressure. This process is called atomization (Figure 3–2). A thorough understanding of atomization is the key to using a spray gun correctly. Atomization breaks paint into a spray of tiny, uniform droplets. When properly applied to the auto's surface, these tiny droplets will flow together to create an even film thickness with a mirror-like gloss.

FIGURE 3-2 An atomized spray

Atomization takes place in three basic stages (Figure 3-3):

- In the first stage, the paint siphoned from the fluid tip is immediately surrounded by air streaming from the annular ring. This turbulence begins the breakup of the paint.
- The second stage of atomization occurs when the paint stream is hit with jets of air from the containment holes. These air jets keep the paint stream from getting out of control and aid the breakup of the paint.
- In the third phase of atomization, the paint is struck by jets of air from the air cap horns. These air streams hit the paint from opposite sides, causing the paint to form into a fan-shaped spray.

PRINCIPAL PARTS OF A SPRAY GUN

The principal parts or components of a typical air spray gun are illustrated in Figure 3-4. Some guns are equipped with a removable spray head unit containing the air cap, fluid tip, and fluid needle.

- Air cap or nozzle
- Fluid tip or nozzle
- Fluid needle valve
- Trigger
- Fluid control (or spreader) knob
- Air valve
- Pattern (or fan adjustment) control knob
- Gun body (or handle)

The air cap directs the compressed air into the material stream to atomize it and form the spray pattern. There are three types of orifices (holes)

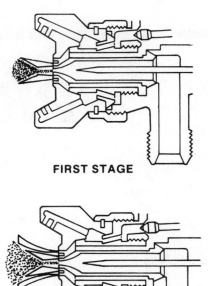

FIRST STAGE

SECOND STAGE

THIRD STAGE

FIGURE 3-3 The three stages of atomization

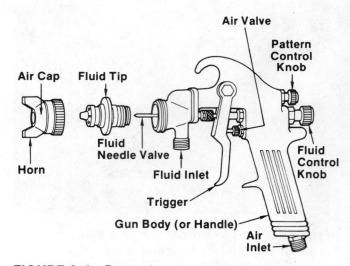

FIGURE 3-4 Parts of a typical air spray gun

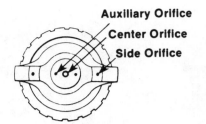

FIGURE 3-5 Nomenclature of air orifices

(Figure 3-5): the center orifice, the side orifices or ports, and the auxiliary orifices. Each of the orifices has a different function. The center orifice located at the nozzle tip creates a vacuum for the discharge of the paint. The side orifices determine the spray pattern by means of air pressure, and the auxiliary orifices promote atomization of the paint. Figure 3-6 illustrates the relationship between the auxiliary orifices and the gun's performance. Large orifices increase the ability to atomize more material for painting large objects with great speed. Fewer or smaller orifices usually require less air, produce smaller spray patterns, and deliver less material to conveniently paint smaller objects or apply coatings at lower speeds.

Air also flows through the two side orifices in horns of the air cap. This flow forms the shape of the spray pattern. When the **pattern control valve** is closed, the spray pattern is round. As the valve is opened, the spray becomes more oblong in shape.

The **fluid needle valve** and the **fluid tip** meter direct the flow of material from the gun into the air stream. The fluid tip forms an internal seat for the fluid needle that shuts off the flow of material. The amount of material that actually leaves the front of the gun depends on the size of the fluid tip opening provided when the needle is unseated from the tip. Fluid tips are available in a variety of sizes to properly handle materials of various types and viscosities and pass the required volume of material to the cap for different speeds of application. The **fluid control knob (valve)** changes the distance the fluid needle valve moves away from its seat in the nozzle when the **trigger** is pulled.

The **air valve,** like the fluid valve, is opened by the trigger. When the trigger is pulled partway, the air valve opens. When it is pulled a little farther, the fluid valve opens.

TYPES OF AIR SPRAY GUNS

As pointed out in Table 3-1, there are three basic methods of paint supply or feed to the air spray gun (Figure 3-7):

FIGURE 3-6 Number of auxiliary holes and gun performance

	TABLE 3-1: TYPES OF AIR SPRAY GUNS		
Type	**Paint Feed Method**	**Advantages**	**Disadvantages**
Suction Feed Type	Paint container is installed below the spray nozzle and paint is supplied by suction force alone.	Stable gun operation. Easy to refill container or make color changes.	Difficult to spray on horizontal surfaces and some variations occur in discharge volume due to variations in viscosity. Has a larger paint container than gravity feed type, but this causes quicker painter fatigue.
Pressure Type	Paint is pressurized by a compressed air tank or pump.	Large surfaces can be painted without stopping to refill container. A paint with a high viscosity can also be used.	Not suitable for small area painting. Color changes and gun cleaning take time.
Gravity Feed Type	As the paint cup is installed above the spray nozzle, paint is supplied by gravity and a suction force at the nozzle tip.	Because there is no change in paint viscosity, there is no variation in the injection volume. The position of the gun can be changed according to the configuration of the the painted item.	Because the cup is installed above the injection nozzle, it adversely affects gun stability. Cup capacity is small so not useful for painting larger surfaces.

Gravity Feed Type

Compressor Feed Type

Suction Feed Type

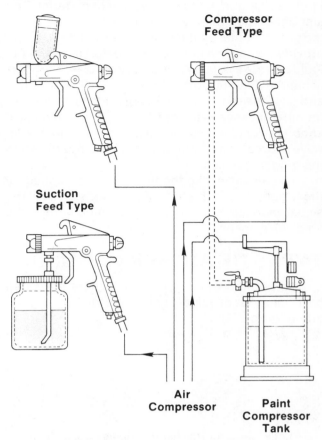

Air Compressor

Paint Compressor Tank

FIGURE 3-7 Paint feed methods to air spray guns

- Suction (or siphon) feed type (Figure 3–8A)
- Compression feed type (Figure 3–8B)
- Gravity feed type (Figure 3–8C)

The suction feed type air spray gun is by far the most used type in auto paint shops. The paint material is held in a 1-quart cup attached to the gun. When the spray gun trigger is partially depressed, the air valve opens and air rushes through the gun. As the air passes through the openings in the air cap, a partial vacuum is created at the fluid tip (Figure 3-9A). Further squeezing of the trigger withdraws the fluid needle from the fluid tip. The vacuum sucks paint from the cup, up the fluid inlet, and out through the open fluid tip. Air enters through the air hole and replaces the siphoned paint (Figure 3-9B). The inlet air vent holes in the cup lid **must** be open.

The suction feed equipment (Figure 3-10) is hooked up for operation as follows:

- Connect air line from the compressor outlet to the air control device inlet.
- Connect air hose leading from the air outlet on the air control device to the air inlet on the spray gun.

A

B

C

FIGURE 3-8 Use of three types of air spray guns: (A) suction, (B) pressure, and (C) gravity

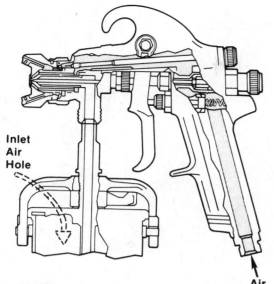

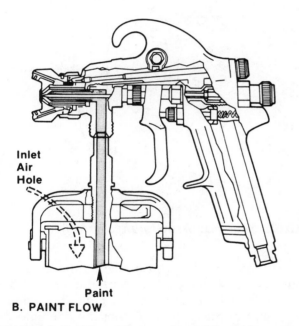

Inlet
Air
Hole

A. AIRFLOW

Air

Inlet
Air
Hole

Paint

B. PAINT FLOW

FIGURE 3-9   The airflow and paint flow of pressure feed gun

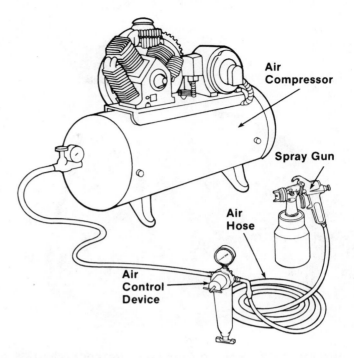

Air
Compressor

Spray Gun

Air
Hose

Air
Control
Device

FIGURE 3-10   The suction feed equipment hook-up

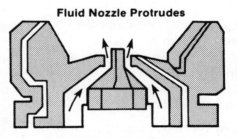

Fluid Nozzle Protrudes

A. SUCTION AIR NOZZLE

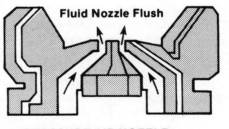

Fluid Nozzle Flush

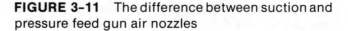

B. PRESSURE AIR NOZZLE

FIGURE 3-11   The difference between suction and pressure feed gun air nozzles

- After the material has been reduced to proper consistency, thoroughly mixed, and strained into the cup, attach the gun to the cup.

In the gravity feed system, the paint is supplied by gravity and the material is suction forced at the nozzle tip. This system is ideal for heavier material such as lightweight body filler. The handling of the gun is the same as a suction feed type gun.

It is easy to identify a suction feed gun by its fluid tip that extends slightly beyond the face of the air cap, as shown in Figure 3-11A.

In the design of an air pressure feed gun, the fluid tip is flush with the face of the air cap (Figure 3-11B) and no vacuum is created. The fluid is forced to the air cap by pressure kept on the material in the system: a separate cup, tank, or pump.

Figure 3-12 illustrates how the regulated pressure cup is hooked up for spraying:

FIGURE 3–12 Hook-up for pressure cup. *(Courtesy of Binks Mfg. Co.)*

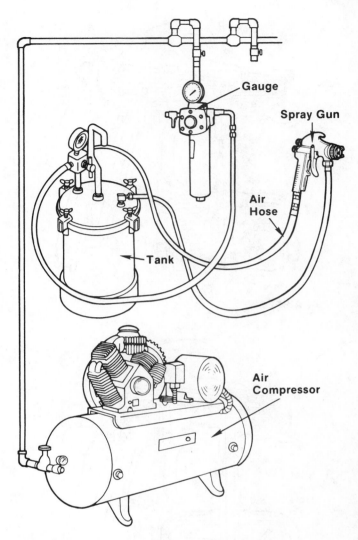

FIGURE 3–13 Hook-up for pressure tank

- Connect air hose from air control device to air regulator on cup.
- Connect air hose or tank air regulator to air inlet on gun.
- Connect fluid hose from fluid outlet on cup to fluid inlet on gun.

Figure 3–13 illustrates how the equipment of the pressure tank spraying system is hooked up:

- Connect regulated air hose from air control device on tank to air inlet on gun.
- Connect mainline air hose from main regulating device to air regulator inlet on tank.
- Connect fluid hose from fluid outlet on tank to fluid inlet on gun.

Paint pressure tanks are available in sizes from 2 quarts to 10 gallons. They are available in dual, single, or nonregulated models (Figure 3–14). Dual air regulators control both material and atomization air pressure; single models regulate material pressure only. Some tanks have an agitation paddle system to keep the pigments and solids thoroughly mixed at all times, assuring color uniformity. Some siphon gun cups also have an agitator system (Figure 3–15). These cups provide constant mixing of all automotive finishes and primers; they even keep metal flakes and metallics in total suspension and complete dispersion.

The gravity feed gun preceded the present—and now more widely used—pressure feed method of material delivery to the spray gun. The main requirement of gravity feed is that the container be vented so that atmospheric air can replace the material as it is being sprayed.

The gravity feed equipment is relatively inexpensive in initial cost and in operation. The container can be refilled without interrupting the spraying operation because it is at atmospheric pressure. However, this method does have some limitations. Viscosity and flow characteristics of the material directly affect rate of flow to the gun, as does hose size and hose length. Flow is also affected by changes in pressure head, which will vary with vertical position of the gun and with material in the container.

The container can be of any convenient size with 1/2 and 1 pint the most common in auto shops.

FIGURE 3-14 Pressure tanks (A) dual regulated, (B) single regulated, and (C) nonregulated. *(Courtesy of Binks Mfg. Co.)*

FIGURE 3-15 Agitator type paint cup. *(Courtesy of Binks Mfg. Co.)*

Its location should suit the material supply requirements of the gun, taking into account that resistance to material flow increases with length of hose and with additional valves and fittings. Its location should also make filling convenient. The container material should be compatible with the contents to avoid corrosion and chemical reaction. It should be covered with a lid that has a vent hole.

The suction feed gun is by far the most popular type of gun in auto refinishing shops for all types of work (spot, panel, and overall). The pressure feed gun is mainly used for overall painting of vehicles (including trucks and vans), for spraying some heavier refinishing materials that are too heavy to be siphoned from a container, or where volume painting is required. Although gravity feed guns can be used for basecoat/clear coat work, they are employed to spray undercoat refinishing materials such as primers and sealers, as well as some lighter body putties and fillers. Gravity feed guns are especially good for those European and Japanese finishes that are formulated for these types of guns.

SPRAYING TECHNIQUES

Spraying a vehicle is a skilled job and calls for considerably more experience and knowledge than just holding down the trigger and hoping that the gun will put the paint where it is supposed to be and in the right amount. There are several variables contributing to the quality of the spray finish including spraying material viscosity, spray booth temperature, film thickness, and spray practice.

SPRAYING MATERIAL VISCOSITY

Using an incorrect viscosity paint will result in various paint finish defects. The paint must be thoroughly mixed and be properly thinned or reduced (Figure 3-16) or a good-quality paint finish cannot be attained. Therefore, the paint viscosity is measured by means of a viscometer. The two types of viscometers used for automobile painting are the Ford cup and the Zahn cup. Although the Ford cup is very accurate, because of its high cost it is not used as much as the Zahn cup, which is less accurate but less expensive.

The viscosity of a spray material is an indication of its ability to **resist** flow. The flow characteristics of liquids relate directly to the degree of **internal friction;** therefore anything that will influence the internal friction (such as solvents, thinners, or temperature change) will influence flow. Similarly, it is the flow characteristics that determine how well a material will atomize, how well it will "flow out" on the work, and the type of equipment needed to move it.

When preparing material for spraying, thin to the proper viscosity according to the directions on the can, using the thinner or reducer best suited for the shop temperature and conditions. It can be demonstrated that at a given temperature, a 3-second difference in spraying viscosity will have a distinct influence on the flow of the material being sprayed. It can therefore be seen that exact reduction is essential if the painter is going to spray at the

FIGURE 3-17 Robots are used by most car manufacturers for the application of the finishing system. *(Courtesy of Sherwin-Williams Co.)*

viscosity at which the paint will spray the easiest and the best results can be obtained. In auto factory operations (Figure 3-17), where new cars are sprayed, spraying viscosity is held within a tolerance of 1 second at a given temperature.

No method other than measurement of the thinner or reducer does the job adequately. Because appearance is affected by the temperature, the way the paint runs off the stirring paddle is not a reliable method of determining viscosity.

The amount of reduction should be the same regardless of temperature. At a higher temperature the viscosity of the reduced material is actually slightly lower, but this is offset by the faster evaporation of the thinner as it travels between the gun and the surface being painted. The result is that the paint reaches the surface at the correct viscosity. The reverse is true in a cold shop. The reduced paint is a little thicker, but evaporation in the air is less so that

FIGURE 3-16 To achieve correct atomization, the paint must be reduced with the proper solvent. *(Courtesy of Maaco Enterprises, Inc.)*

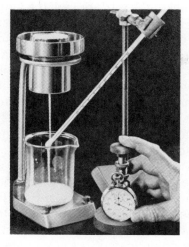

FIGURE 3–18 Ford viscosity cup with thermometer and stopwatch for testing paint viscosity. In practice, the thermometer is immersed in the paint. *(Courtesy of PPG Industries, Inc.)*

the paint reaches the surface being sprayed at the proper viscosity.

Various automotive finishes are manufactured to spray at ideal viscosities. For instance, lacquer primer-surfacer sprays best at 15 seconds viscosity, acrylic lacquer at 12 seconds, and alkyd enamel colors, lacquer colors, and synthetic primer-surfacers all at 19 seconds.

Ford Cup

The Ford cup (Figure 3–18) used for automobile painting comes in two sizes: #3 and #4. It has a cylindrical container, made of either aluminum or stainless steel, with a capacity of 6.1 cubic inches. The bottom of the cup is conical shaped with an orifice in the center. The #3 and #4 cups are distinguished by the diameter of this orifice. Ford cups are precision-made and care should be taken to prevent any damage or deformation of the inner surface of the cup or to the orifice. To measure the viscosity of a paint material with a Ford cup, proceed as follows:

1. Keep the temperature of the paint and Ford cup at about 68 degrees Fahrenheit.
2. Secure the cup with the set bolt and place the glass plate on top.
3. Place the level on top of the glass plate, and adjust the level of the frame with the level adjusting bolts. Then, place a container below the cup.
4. While supporting the bottom of the cup with one hand, place a piece of thick rubber in between to prevent transmission of body heat to the orifice and pour in the paint, being careful that no air bubbles enter.
5. Slide the glass plate horizontally over the top of the cup to remove any excess paint and set it aside.
6. Release the rubber plate supporting the orifice and at the same time begin measuring the time of the continuous downward drain of the paint with a stopwatch. Measure until the continuous paint flow stops. This time is used as an indicator of the paint viscosity. For example, if it takes 15.4 seconds, the viscosity of the paint is said to be 15.4 seconds at 68 degrees Fahrenheit.

Zahn Cup

The #2 Zahn cup is very popular in auto refinishing shops. It is cylindrical in shape and has an orifice (hole) at the bottom. To determine viscosity with a #2 Zahn cup (Figure 3–19), proceed as follows:

1. Prepare the material to be tested. Mix, strain, and reduce as directed by the manufacturer.
2. Fill the cup by submerging it in the material.

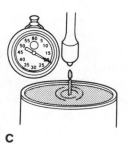

FIGURE 3–19 (A) Dip cup into paint until it is full. (B) Remove cup, and as it clears the surface of the paint, begin timing the flow of paint from the small hole in the bottom of the cup. (A stopwatch is preferred for this step.) (C) Stop the timer when the stream of paint breaks. *(Courtesy of Du Pont Co.)*

TABLE 3-2: SPRAYING VISCOSITIES USING THE #2 ZAHN CUP

Material	Reduction	Viscosity
Acrylic enamel	33-1/3%	19 seconds
Acrylic enamel	50%	18 seconds
Acrylic enamel with hardener	75%	16 seconds
Acrylic lacquer	150%	15 seconds
Polyurethane enamel	per manufacturer's instructions	20 to 22 seconds

3. Release the flow of the material and trigger the stopwatch. Keep all eyes on the flow, not on the watch.
4. When the solid stream of material "breaks" (indicating air passing through the orifice), stop the watch.
5. The result is expressed in seconds. Table 3-2 gives typical desired results of the #2 Zahn cup.

 SHOP TALK ———————

A stopwatch is necessary for measuring paint viscosity with either viscometer system. Most painters prefer a digital stopwatch to the standard type because it is easily read.

TEMPERATURE

The temperature at which material is sprayed and dried has a great influence on the smoothness of the finish. This involves not only the air temperatures of the shop, but the temperature of the work as well. A job should be brought into the shop long enough ahead of spraying time to arrive at approximately the same temperature as the shop. Spraying warm paint on a cold surface or spraying cool material on a hot surface will completely upset flow characteristics. The rate of evaporation on a hot summer day is approximately 50 percent faster than it is on an average day with a shop temperature of 70 degrees. Appropriate thinners or reducers should be used for warm and cold weather applications.

FILM THICKNESS

As noted in Chapter 7, acrylic lacquers dry by evaporation only. Alkyd and acrylic enamels dry by both evaporation and oxidation. Urethanes dry by evaporation and chemical cross-linking reaction.

The thicker the film applied, the longer the drying time. The difference in film thickness shows up plainly in primer-surfacer and in enamel colors. A lacquer primer-surfacer that can be sanded in 30 minutes at 70 degrees will take over an hour to dry if sprayed twice as heavily. Alkyd enamel of normal film thickness should dry tack free in 4 to 6 hours at 70 degrees and be hard enough for careful unmasking and handling in 16 hours. If sprayed twice the normal thickness, it will take 2 to 3 times longer for handling. The reason is that the thicker the film, the greater the depth of paint from which the thinner or reducer must work its way out, and, in enamels, the greater the distance the oxygen from the air must penetrate in order to dry or oxidize the finish. This process is complicated in thick coats by surface skins or crusts as the paint dries.

The painter or paint technician should develop a technique so that the coat sprayed on a surface will remain wet long enough for proper flow-out, and no longer. Heavier coats are not necessary, and they might produce sags, curtains, or wrinkles, as well as strongly influence metallic color where matching is required.

The amount of material sprayed on a surface with one stroke of the gun will depend on width of fan, distance from gun, air pressure at the gun, amount of reduction, speed of stroke, and selection of thinner or reducer. Many paint shops have a paint thickness measuring meter such as the one shown in Figure 3-20. This instrument is able to determine the

FIGURE 3-20 A meter for measuring paint thickness. *(Courtesy of PPG Industries, Inc.)*

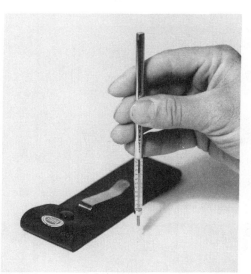

FIGURE 3-21 The Tinsley gauge is a paint thickness gauge. *(Courtesy of Biddle Instruments)*

thickness of the paint on a vehicle. Working on a magnetic principle, it measures the thickness of paint and any body filler by sensing the magnetic pull of the metal under the paint and filler. If the paint and filler are too thick, the magnetic pull will be less than if they are thin. The meter then converts this "pull" to read the approximate thickness of the filler/paint base.

Another popular and less expensive paint thickness gauge is the Tinsley gauge (Figure 3-21). This gauge consists of a special lightweight magnet attached to a spring and contained within a pencil-like tube. To take a measurement, the exploring head or magnet is placed on the surface and the body of the gauge is drawn away, thus extending the spring. The spring extension, the amount of which is observed on the scale, is proportional to the force required to detach the magnet from the surface. The reading is taken at the point when the magnet breaks away from the surface, and the thickness is read directly from the scale.

ADJUSTING THE SPRAY

A good spray pattern depends on the proper mixture of air and paint droplets much like a fine-tuned engine depends on the proper mixture of air and gasoline. The sprayed material should go on smoothly in a medium to wet coat without sagging or running. There are three basic adjustments, which under normal conditions will give the proper spray pattern, degree of wetness, and air pressure for suction feed guns.

1. Adjust the pressure (Figure 3-22). Air pressure, as described in Chapter 5, gen-erally is set at the separator-regulator (or transformer). But due to friction as air passes from the regulator through the hose to the gun, pressure will be lost. The difference between the reading at the regulator and the reading at the gun will vary depending upon the length and diameter of the hose. (For example, a 50-foot, 1/4-inch diameter hose will yield a lower reading than a 15-foot, 5/16-inch diameter hose.) For this reason, pressure should be measured at the gun and all recommended pressures in this test are for readings at the gun.

The surest method to measure this pressure drop is with an air gauge, which is inserted between the hose coupler and the gun. [Some guns are equipped with regulators that allow for checking and setting pressure at the gun (Figure 3-23), while others have optional accessories to do the same thing.] Another method is to consult Table 3-3.

2. Set the size of the spray pattern using the fan adjustment or pattern control knob. To adjust the fan pattern, turn the pattern control knob all the way in to create a small, round pattern (Figure 3-24A). Backing the

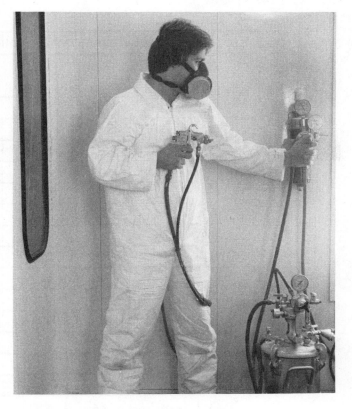

FIGURE 3-22 Setting air pressure

FIGURE 3-23 A gauge installed at the spray gun will give accurate readings of pressure at the gun. *(Courtesy of Binks Company)*

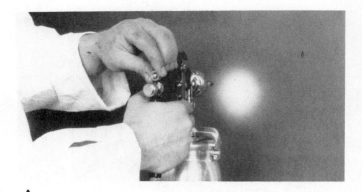

A

B

FIGURE 3-24 (A) Turning in fan valve and (B) backing out fan valve. *(Courtesy of Maaco Enterprises, Inc.)*

pattern control all the way out will produce a wide spray pattern (Figure 3-24B). Use narrower patterns for spot repairs and wider patterns for panel repairs or overall painting. Figure 3-25 represents the evolution of spray pattern from all the way in to all the way out.

3. Set the fluid control knob (Figure 3-26) to regulate the amount of paint according to the selected pattern size; backing the knob out increases the paint flow and turning the knob in decreases paint flow (Figure 3-27).

	Pressure Reading (lbs.) at Gauge	Pressure at the Gun for Various Hose Lengths					
		5 feet	**10 feet**	**15 feet**	**20 feet**	**25 feet**	**50 feet**
1/4-Inch Hose	30	26	24	23	22	21	9
	40	34	32	31	29	27	17
	50	43	40	38	36	34	22
	60	51	48	46	43	41	29
	70	59	56	53	51	48	36
	80	68	64	61	58	55	43
	90	76	71	68	65	61	51
5/16-Inch Hose	30	29	28-1/2	28	27-1/2	27	23
	40	38	37	37	37	36	32
	50	48	47	46	46	45	40
	60	57	56	55	55	54	49
	70	66	65	64	63	63	57
	80	75	74	73	72	71	66
	90	84	83	82	81	80	74

TABLE 3-3: ESTIMATED AIR PRESSURES AT THE GUN

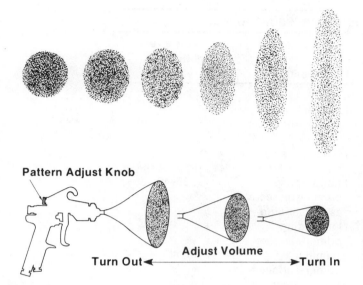

FIGURE 3-25   Pattern width adjustment

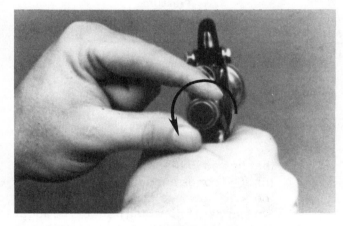

FIGURE 3-26   Adjusting fluid control valve

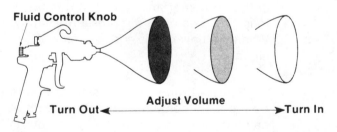

FIGURE 3-27   Paint fluid volume adjustment

SHOP TALK ─────────

*In most cases the fluid control knob is left set in the full **open** position. The full **open** position is attained when two or three threads are showing on the adjusting valve.*

The optimum spraying pressure is the lowest needed to obtain proper atomization, emission rate, and fan width. A pressure that is **too high** results in excessive paint loss through overspray (and therefore high usage), and poor flow, due to high solvent evaporation before the paint reaches the surface being sprayed.

A pressure that is **too low** gives a paint film poor drying characteristics, due to high solvent retention, and makes it prone to bubbling and sagging. The recommended pounds of air pressure vary with the kind of material to be sprayed. The typical ranges are given in Table 3-4.

BALANCING PRESSURE FEED GUN SYSTEM

To balance the pressure tank (Figure 3-28) or cup for spraying the procedure is as follows:

1. After paint is poured in the container (Figure 3-29), open the pattern control knob for maximum pattern size and open the fluid control knob until the first thread is visible.
2. Shut off the atomization air to the gun. Set the fluid flow rate by adjusting the air pressure in the paint container. Use about 6 psi

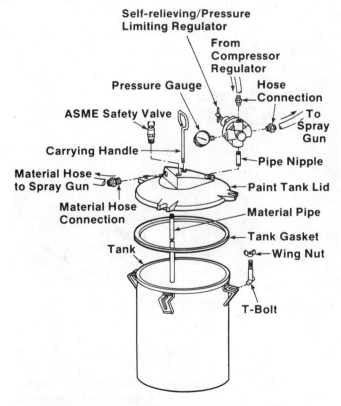

FIGURE 3-28   Major parts of pressure tank

TABLE 3-4: RECOMMENDED AIR PRESSURE RANGES

Topcoats	Pressure at the Gun (psi)	Undercoats	Pressure at the Gun (psi)
Polyurethane enamel	50–55 (solids) 60–65 (metallic)	Lacquer primer-surfacers	25–30 (spot) 35–45 (panel)
Acrylic lacquer	20–45	Multipurpose primer-surfacers	30–40 as primer-surfacer
Acrylic enamel	50–60	Multipurpose primer-surfacers as nonsanding	35–40
Alkyd enamel	50–60	Nonsanding primer-sanders	45
Flexible finishes	35–40	Enamel primer-surfacers	45
		Epoxy primer	45
		Zinc chromate primer	45

Sealers	Pressure at the Gun (psi)	Miscellaneous	Pressure at the Gun (psi)
Acrylic lacquer	25–30	Uniforming finishes	15–20
Universal sealer	35–45		
Bleederseal	35–40		

NOTE: Spot repairs should be made at the low end of the air pressure range.

FIGURE 3-29 Pouring paint into tank

for a remote cup and about 15 psi for a 2-gallon or larger container. Adjust the fluid flow in **either** of the following ways:

Remove the air cap, aim the gun into a clean container, and pull the trigger for 10 seconds. Measure the amount of material that flowed in that time and multiply by 6 (or 30 seconds and multiply by 2). This is the fluid flow rate in ounces per minute. For standard refinishing it should be about 14 to 16 ounces per minute. If the flow rate is less than this, increase the air pressure in the container and repeat. If it is faster than this, decrease the pressure slightly. When the flow rate is correct, reinstall the air cap.

OR

Pull the trigger and adjust the pressure on the paint container until the stream of paint discharging from the gun squirts about 3 to 4 feet before it starts to drop. This indicates a fluid flow of about 14 to 16 ounces per minute.

3. Turn on the atomization air to about 50 **at the gun.** Then spray a fast test pattern.

TESTING THE SPRAY PATTERN

After setting the air pressure, the fan size, and the fluid flow, test the spray pattern on a piece of

FIGURE 3-30 The best way to learn the effects of gun movement and gun adjustments is to experiment on a test surface.

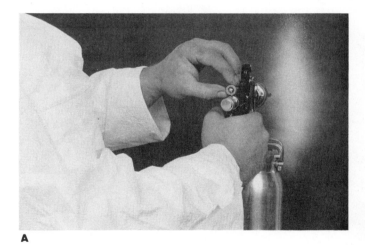

A

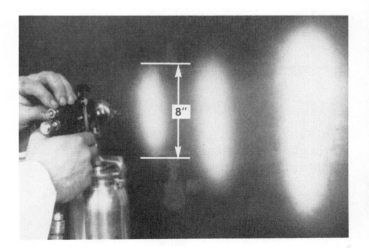

FIGURE 3-31 Test patterns

masking paper or newspaper (Figure 3-30). Hold the gun 6 to 8 inches away from the paper if spraying lacquer and 8 to 10 inches for enamel. Pull the trigger all the way back and release it immediately. This burst of paint should leave a long, slender pattern on the test paper (Figure 3-31A). Spraying primer-surfacer usually requires a small spray pattern. Turn the pattern control knob in until the spray pattern is 6 to 8 inches wide (Figure 3-31B).

For spot repair, the pattern should be about 5 to 6 inches from top to bottom. For panel or overall repair, the length of the pattern should be about 9 inches from top to bottom. A larger pattern can be obtained by opening the pattern control knob.

Carefully inspect the texture of the spray pattern (Figure 3-32). If the paint droplets are coarse and large, turn the fluid control knob in about 1/2 turn or increase the air pressure 5 pounds. If the spray is too fine or too dry, either open the fluid control knob about 1/2 turn or decrease the air pressure 5 pounds.

SHOP TALK

Remember the objective of spraying on a test surface is twofold. First, make sure all atomized paint particles are of uniform size. Second, make sure this size is fine enough to achieve proper flow out (Figure 3-33).

Next, test the spray pattern for uniformity of paint distribution. Loosen the air cap retaining ring and rotate the air cap (Figure 3-34) so that the horns

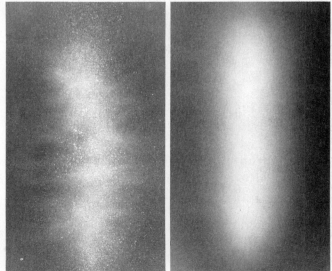

FIGURE 3-32 Inspect the texture of the spray pattern.

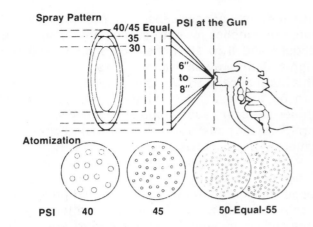

FIGURE 3-33 As shown here, the correct spraying pressure is, therefore, 50 psi.

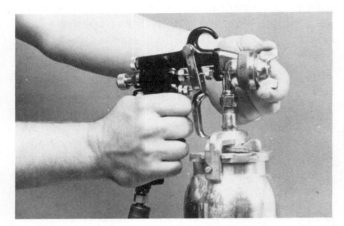

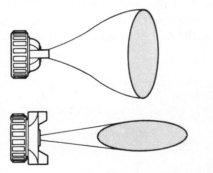

FIGURE 3-34 How rotating the air caps affects the pattern.

are straight up and down. The air cap in this position will produce a horizontal spray pattern rather than a vertical one. Spray again, but this time hold the trigger down until the paint begins to run. This is called **flooding** the pattern. Inspect the lengths of the runs. If all adjustments are correct, the runs will be approximately equal in length (Figure 3–35).

The uneven runs in the split pattern shown in Figure 3–36 are a result of setting the spray pattern

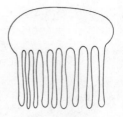

FIGURE 3-35 Balanced spray pattern

FIGURE 3-36 Split pattern

FIGURE 3-37 Heavy center pattern

too wide or the air pressure too high. Turn the pattern control knob in 1/2 turn or raise the air pressure 5 pounds. Alternate between these two adjustments until the runs are even in length.

If paint runs are longer in the middle than on the edges (Figure 3–37), too much paint is being discharged. Turn the fluid control knob in until the runs are even in length.

WARNING: Always wear a suitable air respirator (Figure 3–38) when spraying test patterns.

THE APPLICATION STROKE

The proper stroke is most important in obtaining a good refinishing job. To obtain a good stroke technique, proceed as follows:

 1. Hold the spray gun at the proper distance from the surface—6 to 8 inches for lacquer, 8 to 10 inches for enamel (Figure 3–39). If the humidity is high, a shorter distance

might be necessary. But remember that if the spraying is done from a shorter distance, the high velocity of the spraying air tends to ripple the wet film. If the distance is increased beyond that, there will be a greater percent of thinner evaporated, resulting in orange peel or dry film, and adversely affecting color where matching is required. A slower evaporating thinner will permit more variation in the distance of the spray gun from the job but will produce

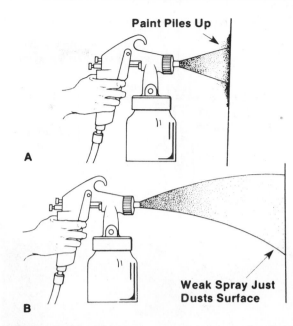

FIGURE 3-40   The correct gun-to-work distance is important. If the gun is too close, (A) the finish material piles up and causes runs and sags. When the gun is too far away, (B) material tends to dry into dust before it reaches the surface. Adjust distance accordingly.

FIGURE 3-38   Be sure to wear an air respirator when spraying. *(Courtesy of Maaco Enterprises, Inc.)*

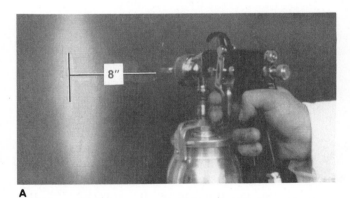

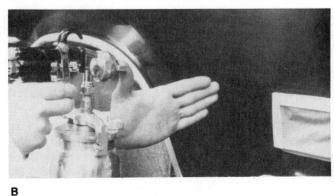

FIGURE 3-39   (A) Proper spray distance; (B) easy method of checking spray distance. *(Courtesy of Maaco Enterprises, Inc.)*

runs if the gun gets too close (Figure 3-40). Excessive spraying distance also causes a loss in materials due to overspray.

2. Hold the gun level and perpendicular to the surface (Figure 3-41). If the spray gun is not kept at a right angle even at curves in the body, an uneven paint film will result (Figure 3-42). This might not always be physically possible, but it is the ideal that should always be strived for. On flat surfaces such as the hood or roof, the gun should be pointed straight down (Figure 3-43).

3. The gun should be in motion before the trigger is pulled, and the trigger (fluid) should be released before the gun motion stops. This technique gives a fade in and fade out effect, which prevents overloading where one series of strokes is joined to the next by overlapping the stroke ends.

4. Do not fan the gun and do not use wrist motions if a uniform film is desired. The only time it is permissible to fan the gun is on a small spot spray where the paint film at the edges of the spot should be thinner than the center portion.

5. Move the gun with a steady deliberate pass, about 1 foot per second. Moving the

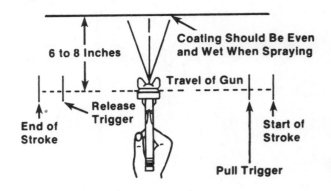

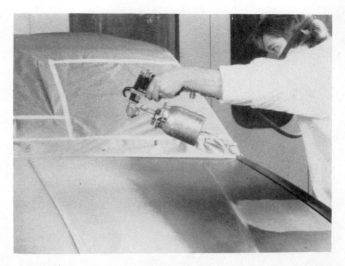

FIGURE 3-43 Proper spraying technique for flat surfaces. *(Courtesy of Maaco Enterprises, Inc.)*

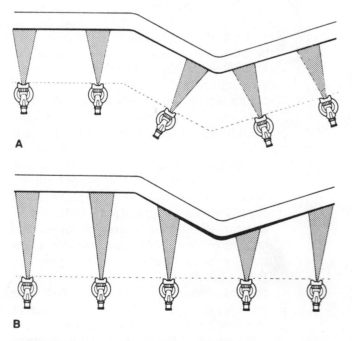

FIGURE 3-41 Proper parallel motion

FIGURE 3-42 (A) Proper spray gun movement. (B) If the spray gun is not kept at a right angle even at curves in the body, an uneven paint film will result.

gun too fast will produce a thin film, while moving it too slowly will result in the paint running. The speed must be consistent or it will result in an uneven paint film. Never stop in one place or the sprayed coat will drip and run!

6. Release the trigger at the end of each pass. Then pull back the trigger when beginning the pass in the opposite direction. In other words: "trigger" the gun and turn off the gun at the end of each sweep. This avoids runs, minimizes overspray, and saves paint. Proper triggering involves four steps (Figure 3-44): (A) Begin the stroke over the masking paper, triggering the gun halfway to release only air; (B) when the starting edge of the panel is reached, squeeze the trigger all the way to release the paint; (C) release the trigger halfway to stop the paint flow when directly over the finishing edge; and (D) continue the stroke several more inches before reversing the direction and repeating the sequence.

7. Difficult areas such as corners and edges should be sprayed first. Aim directly at the area so that half of the spray covers each side of the edge or corner. Hold the gun an inch or two closer than usual, or screw the pattern control knob in a few turns. Either technique will reduce the pattern size. If the gun is just held closer, the stroke will have to be faster to compensate for a normal amount of material being applied to the smaller areas. After all of the edges and

A

B

C

D

FIGURE 3-44 Proper triggering involves four steps: (A) begin the stroke over the masking paper and as the gun is moved, trigger halfway to release only air; (B) when reaching the starting edge of the panel, squeeze the trigger all the way to release the paint; (C) release the trigger halfway to stop the paint flow when directly over the finishing edge; and (D) continue the stroke several more inches before reversing the direction and repeating the sequence. *(Courtesy of Maaco Enterprises, Inc.)*

corners have been sprayed, the flat or nearly flat surfaces should be sprayed.

8. For painting very narrow surfaces, switch guns or caps with a smaller spray pattern to avoid having to readjust the full size pattern gun. The smaller pattern guns are easier to handle in critical areas. As an alternate, a full size gun can be used by reducing the air pressure and fluid delivery and triggering properly.

9. Generally, start at the top of an upright surface such as a door panel. The spray gun nozzle should be level with the top of the surface. This means that the upper half of the spray pattern will hit the masking.

10. The second pass is made in the opposite direction with the nozzle level at the lower edge of the previous pass. Thus one half (50 percent) of the pattern overlaps the previous pass and the other half is sprayed on the unpainted area (Figure 3–45).

11. Always blend into "the wet edge" of the previous section sprayed (Figure 3–46). Proper triggering technique at the area where the sections are joined will avoid the danger of a double coat at this point and the possibility of getting a sag (Figure 3–47).

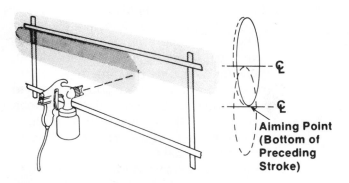

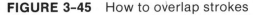

FIGURE 3-45 How to overlap strokes

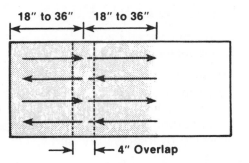

FIGURE 3-46 Always blend into the wet edge.

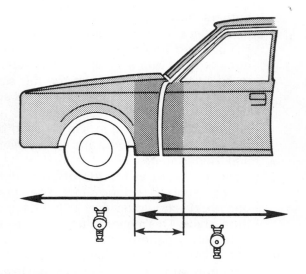

FIGURE 3-47 Gun overlap area where runs occur easily in overall painting jobs.

12. Continue back and forth passes, triggering the gun at the end of each pass, and lowering each successive pass one half the top-to-bottom width of the spray gun pattern.
13. The last pass should be made with the lower half of the spray pattern below the surface being painted. If it is a door, the pattern would shoot off into space below it.
14. The procedure just followed is called a **single coat.** For a **double coat,** repeat the single coat procedure immediately. Generally, two or more double coats are required to properly apply a lacquer topcoat. Allow for flash time (the time required for the solvents to evaporate and the finish to dull slightly) or several minutes between coats. This can be observed as a slight dulling of the coat's appearance. Two or three single coats are normally required for enamel topcoats. Allow the first coat to set up (become tacky) before applying additional coats.

GUN HANDLING PROBLEMS

The inexperienced painter is prone to several spraying errors including:

- **Heeling.** This occurs when the painter allows the gun to tilt (Figure 3-48). Because the gun is no longer perpendicular to the surface, the spray produces an uneven layer of paint, excessive overspray, dry spray, and orange peel.
- **Arcing.** This occurs when the gun is not moved parallel with the surface (Figure

FIGURE 3-48 Heeling is a common gun handling error.

FIGURE 3-49 Another common gun handling error is arcing.

3-49). At the outer edges of the arced stroke, the gun is farther away from the surface than at the middle of the stroke. The result is uneven film buildup, dry spray, excessive overspray, and orange peel.

- **Speed of stroke.** If the stroke is made too quickly, the paint will not cover the surface evenly (Figure 3-50). If the stroke is made too

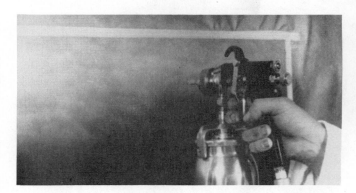

FIGURE 3-50 Gun movement too fast

FIGURE 3-51   Gun movement too slow

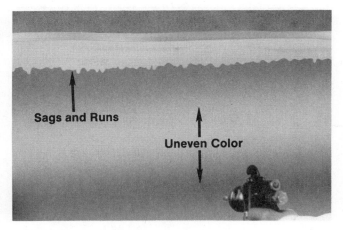

FIGURE 3-52   Improper overlapping can cause problems.

slowly, sags and runs will develop (Figure 3-51). The proper stroking speed is something that comes with experience.

- **Improper overlap.** Improper overlapping results in uneven film thickness, contrasting color hues, and sags and runs as shown in Figure 3-52.
- **Wasteful overspray.** Failure to trigger the gun before and after each stroke results in wasteful overspray and excessive buildup of paint at the beginning and end of each stroke (Figure 3-53).
- **Improper coverage.** Triggering at the wrong time is another common error. Failure to trigger exactly over the edge of the panel results in uneven coverage and film thickness (Figure 3-54).

TYPES OF SPRAY COATS

There are varying degrees of thickness for a sprayed coat. Generally, they are referred to as light, medium, or heavy. The easiest way to control this degree of thickness is by the speed with which the gun is moved. That is, the slower the speed, the heavier the coat.

There are also six other terms to describe spray coats:

- Tack
- Full wet coat
- Mist
- Dust
- Shading or blending
- Banding

The **tack coat** allows the application of heavier wet coats without sagging or runs. This is a light covering coat applied to the surface and then al-

FIGURE 3-53   An example of wasteful overspray

FIGURE 3-54   An example of improper coverage

lowed to **flash** until it is just tacky, which usually takes only a few minutes. The finish wet coats are then sprayed over the tack coat.

TABLE 3-5: SUMMARY OF VARIABLE CONTROLLING QUALITY IN SPRAY FINISHING

Atomization	1. Fluid viscosity 2. Air pressure 3. Fan pattern width 4. Fluid velocity or fluid pressure 5. Fluid flow rate 6. Distance of spray gun from work
Evaporation Stages	1. Between spray gun and part 2. From sprayed part
Evaporation Variables Between Spray Gun and Sprayed Part	1. Type of reducing thinner 2. Atomization pressure 3. Amount of thinner 4. Temperature in spray area 5. Degree of atomization

Evaporation Variables Affecting	1. Physical properties of solvents (i.e., fast or slow evaporation)
	2. Temperature
	   a. Fluid
	   b. Work
	   c. Air
	3. Exposed area of the surface sprayed

Evaporation Variables from the Sprayed Part	1. Surface temperature 2. Room air temperature 3. Air pressure velocity 4. Flash time between coats 5. Flash time after final coats 6. Physical properties of the solvents (i.e., fast or slow evaporation)

Operator Variables	1. Distance of spray gun from the work surface
	2. Stroking speed over the work surface
	3. Pattern overlap
	4. Spray gun attitude
	   a. Heeling
	   b. Arcing
	   c. Fanning
	5. Triggering

A **full wet coat** is a heavy, glossy coat that is applied in a thickness almost heavy enough to run. It requires skill and practice to spray such a coat.

The **mist coat** is an application of slower drying thinners over a color coat. It helps to level the final coat, melt in the overspray, and control mottling of metallics. Uniforming finishes or blenders are applied as mist coats in spot and panel repairing of acrylic lacquers and acrylic enamels.

A **dust coat** is a light, dry coat of finish. It is accomplished by holding the gun a little from the surface being sprayed.

Shading or blending coats are applications of paint on the boundary of spot repair areas so that a color difference between the new paint and surrounding original paint is not noticeable. It is applied in two coats and the second coat is thinner and sprayed over a wider area than the first. Finally a mist coat is applied. Shading can also be done when repainting a panel so that a color difference is not noticeable between adjacent panels.

Banding is a single coat applied in a small spray pattern to the frame in an area to be sprayed. This technique assures the painter of coverage at the edges without spraying beyond the spray area and reduces overspray. Banding is often used in spraying panel repairs with a primer-surfacer.

Sometimes a banding coat is thinned more than the normal application that follows. This is especially true when the paint to be sprayed is of high viscosity. The additional thinning of the paint used for banding allows it to fully enter cracks and seams. A good example is the application of textured vinyl finish. Table 3-5 summarizes the variables that control quality when spray painting.

CLEANING THE SPRAY GUN

Neglect and carelessness are responsible for the majority of spray gun difficulties. Proper care of a gun requires little time and effort. Thorough cleaning of gun and accessory equipment **immediately after use,** lubrication of bearing surfaces and packings at recommended intervals, and proper care in handling (do not drop or throw gun) are important factors in the care of a spray gun.

To clean a suction feed gun, first loosen the cup from the gun (Figure 3-55A). Keep the fluid tube in the cup. Next, unscrew the air cap two or three turns. Hold a folded cloth over the air cap and pull the trigger (Figure 3-55B). This will force the paint in the gun back into the cup.

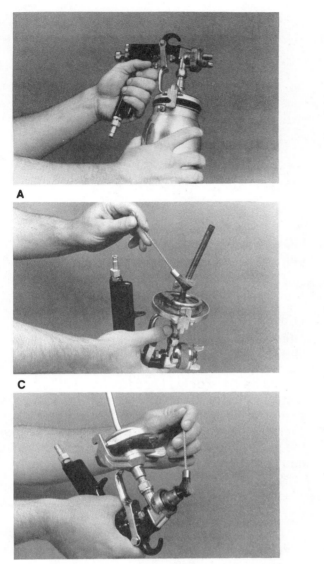

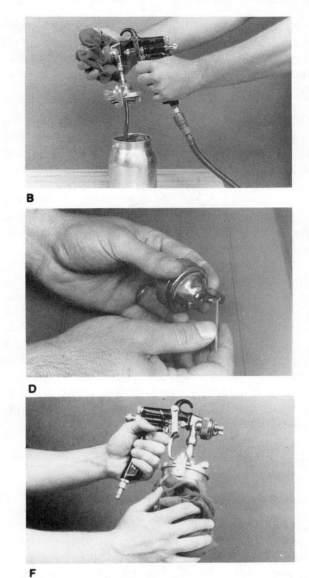

FIGURE 3-55   Steps in cleaning spray gun: (A) loosen cup; (B) discharge paint; (C) clean cup cover; (D) clean fluid tip; (E) clean outside of gun and; (F) clean clogged holes. *(Courtesy of Maaco Enterprises, Inc.)*

 SHOP TALK ⎯⎯⎯⎯⎯⎯

Use very low pressure (5 pounds). Do not attempt when paint cup is loaded, because paint could be splashed from the container.

Retighten the air nozzle and pour the paint in the cup back into the original container. Clean the cup and the cup cover with solvent and a thin bristle brush (Figure 3-55C). Wipe up residue with a clean rag soaked with solvent. Then, pour 1 inch of clean solvent in the cup. Spray the solvent through the gun to clean out the fluid passages.

On pressure feed air guns, release the pressure in the cup, loosen the air nozzle and force the material in to the cup by triggering the gun. Take the air nozzle off. Empty the contents into a suitable container and refill the cup with a clean compatible solvent. The air nozzle can be left off. Spray solvent from the gun and repeat this process until clean solvent is flowing from the gun. If a tank is used, clean as directed by the manufacturer and reassemble for future use.

With either type of gun, remove the air cap and soak it in thinner or solvent. Clean out clogged holes with a soft item such as a round type toothpick or a broom straw (Figure 3-55D). Remember, **never** use wires or nails to clean the precision-drilled openings. Clean the fluid tip with a gun brush and solvent (Figure 3–55E). With a clean rag soaked in thinner, wipe the outside of the gun to remove all traces of paint (Figure 3–55F).

Areas in the United States with air pollution problems, such as southern California, require the use of enclosed spray gun cleaning equipment. The paint spraying equipment—guns, cups, stirrers, and strainers—is placed in the larger tub of the gun washer/recycler (Figure 3–56), the lid is closed, then the air-operated pump recirculates the thinner into the upper portion of the tub, cleaning inside and outside of the paint gun, etc. In less than 60 seconds, the equipment is clean and ready for use.

The gun washer/recycler saves the painter time. Compared with traditional manual gun-cleaning methods, the automatic gun washer/recycler machine saves 10 minutes on each color change. The cleaning system offers increased safety for the painter, because the skin no longer is exposed to the drying effects of solvent. The system is designed so sludge from the cleaning action settles to the bottom for easy drainage and disposal with other shop wastes. Check the owner's manual for complete operational details and proper solvents to use.

 SHOP TALK _____

If the gun is not cleaned soon after use, the nozzle might clog, completely or partially, causing the gun to spit (eject pieces of dried paint) or form the wrong spray pattern. For enamel paints with additives, this is of particular importance because the enamel paint might harden right in the gun lining if not properly cleaned after use.

FIGURE 3–56 A typical gun waster/recycler *(Courtesy of Herkules Equipment Co.)*

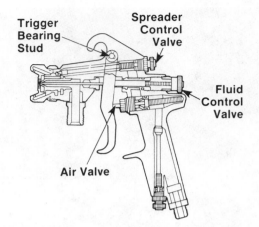

FIGURE 3–57 Parts to lubricate in an air spray gun

Most spray gun manufacturers recommend lubricating, at the end of each day, the parts shown in Figure 3–57 with light machine oil. Packings and springs plus needles and nozzles must periodically be replaced due to normal wear and tear. This should be done only in accordance with the manufacturer's instructions. Extreme care should be taken not to overlubricate since the excess oil could overflow into the paint and oil passages, mixing with the paint and resulting in a defective paint film. Oil and paint do not mix to produce a good finish.

 **SHOP TALK** _____

Never soak the entire gun in cleaning solvent. Doing this will dry out the packings and remove lubrication.

For best results in refinishing, use separate guns for topcoats and undercoats. In fact, in any shop where there are sufficient jobs going through to justify it, there should be at least three guns. One gun to be used primarily for spraying undercoats like primer-surfacers, another for spraying lacquers and acrylic lacquers, and a third gun for spraying enamels. If these guns are kept clean and in good working order, much time will be saved over trying to make one gun serve and having to adjust it each time that the operation is changed.

SPRAY GUN TROUBLESHOOTING

If the air spray gun is not adjusted, manipulated, and cleaned properly, it will apply a defective coat-

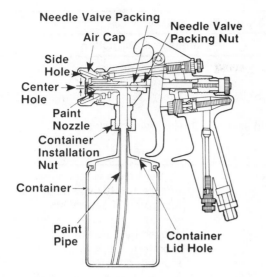

Needle Valve Packing
Air Cap
Needle Valve Packing Nut
Side Hole
Center Hole
Paint Nozzle
Container Installation Nut
Container
Paint Pipe
Container Lid Hole

FIGURE 3-58 Possible trouble spots of an air spray gun

ing to the surface. Fortunately, defects from incorrect handling and improper cleaning can be tracked down quite readily, and then corrected without much difficulty. The most common spray gun application problems, with their possible causes and suggested remedies, are given in Chapter 11.

If not properly maintained, the air spray gun itself (Figure 3-58) can also create some problems. Table 3-6 contains the cause and possible solutions to some of more common spray gun difficulties.

Failure of the compressed air supply system to perform properly can cause the paint problems as shown in Table 3-7.

OTHER TYPES OF SPRAY GUNS

There are three other types of spray guns that can be found in some auto body shops. They are the airless spray gun, the electrostatic system, HVLP system, and the airbrush.

AIRLESS SPRAY GUN SYSTEM

Airless spraying equipment (Figure 3-59) uses hydraulic pressure to atomize paint rather than air pressure. With the airless spray method, pressure is applied directly to the paint, which is injected at high speed through small holes in the nozzle and formed into a mist. Unlike the air spray method, there is less mixing of air in the paint and, consequently, less mist dispersion. Also, since the paint is pressurized directly, less energy is used for atomization so that

Chapter Three   Spray Gun and Its Use

with the same amount of power, a degree of atomization is accomplished that is several times that for air spraying. In fact, the pressure developed in airless equipment ranges from 1,500 to 3,000 psi. Actual pressure depends on the pump ratio of the equipment.

The airless system reduces overspray and rebound to a minimum, and application of the finish is much faster than with conventional atomized air. Because of higher pressures involved, the airless system can be used with paints and other materials that have a higher viscosity. However, this system of application can only be used where a fine finish is **not** required. It is often employed to apply the finishing coating in the truck fleet commercial vehicle refinishing business. It also has found a place for

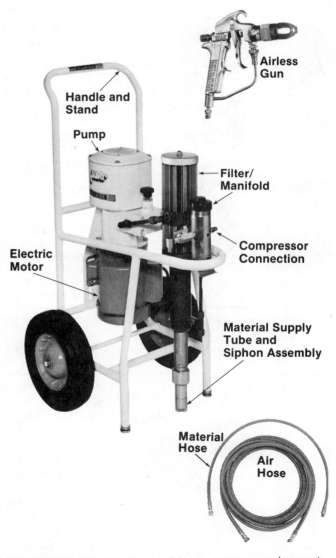

FIGURE 3-59 Typical airless spray equipment. *(Courtesy of DeVilbiss Company)*

71

TABLE 3-6: TROUBLESHOOTING AN AIR SPRAY GUN

Trouble	Possible Cause	Suggested Correction
Spray pattern top heavy or bottom heavy	1. Horn holes partially plugged (external mix). 2. Fluid tip clogged, damaged, or not installed properly. 3. Dirt on air cap seat or fluid tip seat.	1. Remove air cap and clean. 2. Clean, replace, or reinstall fluid tip. 3. Remove and clean seat.
Spray pattern heavy to right or to left	1. Air cap dirty or orifice partially clogged. 2. Air cap damaged. 3. Paint nozzle clogged or damaged. 4. Too low a setting of the pattern control knob.	1. To determine where buildup occurs, rotate cap 180 degrees and test spray. If pattern shape stays in same position, the condition is caused by fluid buildup on fluid tip. If pattern changes with cap movement, the condition is in the air cap. Clean air cap, orifice, and fluid tip accordingly. 2. Replace air cap. 3. Clean or replace paint nozzle. 4. Adjust setting.
Spray pattern heavy at center	1. Atomizing pressure too low. 2. Fluid of too great viscosity. 3. Fluid pressure too high for air cap's normal capacity (pressure feed). 4. Caliber of paint nozzle enlarged due to wear. 5. Center hole enlarged.	1. Increase pressure. 2. Thin fluid with suitable thinner. 3. Reduce fluid pressure. 4. Replace paint nozzle. 5. Replace air cap and paint nozzle.
Spray pattern split	1. Not enough fluid. 2. Air cap or fluid tip dirty. 3. Air pressure too high. 4. Fluid viscosity too thin.	1. Reduce air pressure or increase fluid flow. 2. Remove and clean. 3. Lower air pressure. 4. Thicken fluid viscosity.
Pinholes	1. Gun too close to surface. 2. Fluid pressure too high. 3. Fluid too heavy.	1. Stroke 6 to 8 inches from surface. 2. Reduce pressure. 3. Thin fluid with thinner.
Blushing or a whitish coat of lacquer.	1. Absorption of moisture. 2. Too quick drying of lacquer.	1. Avoid spraying in damp, humid, or too cool weather. 2. Correct by adding retarder to lacquer.
Orange peel (surface looks like orange peel)	1. Too high or too low an atomization pressure. 2. Gun too far or too close to work. 3. Fluid not thinned. 4. Improperly prepared surface. 5. Gun stroke too rapid. 6. Using wrong air cap. 7. Overspray striking a previously sprayed surface. 8. Fluid not thoroughly dissolved. 9. Drafts (synthetics and lacquers). 10. Humidity too low (synthetics).	1. Correct as needed. 2. Stroke 6 to 8 inches from surface. 3. Use proper thinning process. 4. Surface must be prepared. 5. Take deliberate, slow stroke. 6. Select correct air cap for the fluid and feed. 7. Select proper spraying procedure. 8. Mix fluid thoroughly. 9. Eliminate excessive drafts. 10. Raise humidity of room.

TABLE 3-6: TROUBLESHOOTING AN AIR SPRAY GUN (Continued)

Trouble	Possible Cause	Suggested Correction
Excessive spray fog or overspray	1. Atomizing air pressure too high or fluid pressure too low.	1. Correct as needed.
	2. Spraying past surface of the product.	2. Release trigger when gun passes target.
	3. Wrong air cap or fluid tip.	3. Ascertain and use correct combination.
	4. Gun stroked too far from surface.	4. Stroke 6 to 8 inches from surface.
	5. Fluid thinned out too much.	5. Add correct amount of thinner.
No control over size of pattern	1. Air cap seal is damaged.	1. Check for damage, replace if necessary.
	2. Foreign particles are lodged under the seal.	2. Make sure surface that this sets on is clean.
Sags or runs	1. Dirty air cap and fluid tip.	1. Clean cap and fluid tip.
	2. Gun manipulated too close to surface.	2. Hold the gun 6 to 8 inches from surface.
	3. Not releasing trigger at end of stroke (when stroke does not go beyond object).	3. Release trigger after every stroke.
	4. Gun manipulated at wrong angle to surface.	4. Work gun at right angles to surface.
	5. Fluid piled on too heavy.	5. Learn to calculate depth of wet film of fluid.
	6. Fluid thinned out too much.	6. Add correct amount of fluid by measure.
	7. Fluid pressure too high.	7. Reduce fluid pressure with fluid control knob.
	8. Operation too slow.	8. Speed up movement of gun across surface.
	9. Improper atomization.	9. Check air and fluid flow; clean cap and fluid tip.
Streaks	1. Dirty or damaged air cap and/or fluid tip.	1. Same as for sags.
	2. Not overlapping strokes correctly or sufficiently.	2. Follow previous stroke accurately.
	3. Gun moved too fast across surface.	3. Take deliberate, slow strokes.
	4. Gun held at wrong angle to surface.	4. Same as for sags.
	5. Gun held too far from surface.	5. Stroke 6 to 8 inches from surface.
	6. Air pressure too high.	6. Use least air pressure necessary.
	7. Split spray.	7. Reduce air adjustment or change air cap and/or fluid tip.
	8. Pattern and fluid control not adjusted properly.	8. Readjust.
Gun sputters constantly	1. Connections, fittings, and seals loose or missing.	1. Tighten and/or replace as per owner's manual.
	2. Leaky connection on fluid tube or fluid needle packing (suction gun).	2. Tighten connections; lubricate packing.
	3. Lack of sufficient fluid in container.	3. Refill container with fluid.
	4. Tipping container at an acute angle.	4. If container must be tipped, change position of fluid tube and keep container full of fluid.
	5. Obstructed fluid passageway.	5. Remove fluid tip, needle, and fluid tube and clean.

TABLE 3-6: TROUBLESHOOTING AN AIR SPRAY GUN (Continued)

Trouble	Possible Cause	Suggested Correction
	6. Fluid too heavy (suction feed).	6. Thin fluid.
	7. Clogged air vent in canister top (suction feed).	7. Clean.
	8. Dirty or damaged coupling nut on canister top (suction feed).	8. Clean or replace.
	9. Fluid pipe not tightened to pressure tank lid or pressure cup cover.	9. Tighten; check for defective threads.
	10. Strainer is clogged up.	10. Clean strainer.
	11. Packing nut is loose.	11. Make sure packing nut is tight.
	12. Fluid tip is loose.	12. Tighten fluid tip. Torque to manufacturer's specifications.
	13. O-ring on tip is worn or dirty.	13. Replace O-ring if necessary.
	14. Fluid hose from paint tank loose.	14. Tighten.
	15. Jam nut gasket installed improperly or jam nut loose.	15. Inspect and correctly install or tighten nut.
Uneven spray pattern	1. Damaged or clogged air cap.	1. Inspect air cap and clean or replace.
	2. Damaged or clogged fluid tip.	2. Inspect fluid tip and clean or replace.
Fluid leaks from spray gun **Nozzle Drip**	1. Fluid needle packing not too tight.	1. Loosen nut; lubricate packing.
	2. Fluid needle packing dry.	2. Lubricate needle and packing frequently.
	3. Foreign particle blocking fluid tip.	3. Remove tip and clean.
	4. Damaged fluid tip or fluid needle.	4. Replace both tip and needle.
	5. Wrong fluid needle size.	5. Replace fluid needle with correct size for fluid tip being used.
	6. Broken fluid needle spring.	6. Remove and replace.
Fluid leaks from packing nut **Packing Nut Leak**	1. Loose packing nut.	1. Tighten packing nut.
	2. Packing is worn out.	2. Replace packing.
	3. Dry packing.	3. Remove and soften packing with a few drops of light oil.
Fluid leaks through fluid tip when trigger is released	1. Foreign particles lodged in the fluid tip.	1. Clean out tip and strain paint.
	2. Fluid needle has paint stuck on it.	2. Remove all dried paint.
	3. Fluid needle is damaged.	3. Check for damage; replace if necessary.
	4. Fluid tip has been damaged.	4. Check for nicks; replace if necessary.
	5. Spring left off fluid needle.	5. Make sure spring is replaced on needle.
Excessive fluid	1. Not triggering the gun at each stroke.	1. It should be a habit to release trigger after every stroke.
	2. Gun at wrong angle to surface.	2. Hold gun at right angles to surface.
	3. Gun held too far from surface.	3. Stroke 6 to 8 inches from surface.
	4. Wrong air cap or fluid tip.	4. Use correct combination.
	5. Depositing fluid film of irregular thickness.	5. Learn to calculate depth of wet film of finish.
	6. Air pressure too high.	6. Use least amount of air necessary.
	7. Fluid pressure too high.	7. Reduce pressure.
	8. Fluid control knob not adjusted properly.	8. Readjust.

TABLE 3-6: TROUBLESHOOTING AN AIR SPRAY GUN (Continued)

Trouble	Possible Cause	Suggested Correction
Fluid will not come from spray gun	1. Out of fluid. 2. Grit, dirt, paint skin, etc., blocking air gap, fluid tip, fluid needle, or strainer. 3. No air supply. 4. Internal mix cap using suction feed.	1. Add more spray fluid. 2. Clean spray gun thoroughly and strain spray fluid; always strain fluid before using it. 3. Check regulator. 4. Change cap or feed.
Fluid will not come from fluid tank or canister	1. Lack of proper air pressure in fluid tank or canister. 2. Air intake opening inside fluid tank or canister clogged by dried-up finish fluid. 3. Leaking gasket on fluid tank cover or canister top. 4. Gun not converted correctly between canister and fluid tank. 5. Blocked fluid hose. 6. Connections with regulator not correct.	1. Check for air leaks or leak of air entry; adjust air pressure for sufficient flow. 2. This is a common trouble; clean opening periodically. 3. Replace with new gasket. 4. Correct per owner's manual. 5. Clear. 6. Correct as per owner's manual.
Sprayed coat short of liquid material	1. Air pressure too high. 2. Fluid not reduced or thinned correctly. (Suction feed only) 3. Gun too far from work or out of adjustment.	1. Decrease air pressure. 2. Reduce or thin according to directions; use proper thinner or reducer. 3. Adjust distance to work; clean and adjust gun fluid and spray pattern controls.
Spotty, uneven pattern, slow to build	1. Inadequate fluid flow. 2. Low atomization air pressure. (Suction feed only) 3. Too fast gun motion.	1. Back fluid control knob to first thread. 2. Increase air pressure, rebalance gun. 3. Move at moderate pace.
Unable to get round spray	1. Pattern control knob not seating properly.	1. Clean or replace.
Dripping from fluid tip	1. Dry packing. 2. Sluggish needle. 3. Tight packing nut. 4. Spray head misaligned on type MBC guns causing needle to bind.	1. Lubricate packing. 2. Lubricate. 3. Adjust. 4. Tap all around spray head with wood and rawhide mallet and retighten locking bolt.
Excessive overspray	1. Too much atomization air pressure. 2. Gun too far from surface. 3. Improper stroking, i.e. arcing, moving too fast.	1. Reduce. 2. Check distance. 3. Move at moderate pace, parallel to work surface.
Excessive fog	1. Too much or quick drying thinner. 2. Too much atomization air pressure.	1. Remix. 2. Reduce.
Will not spray on pressure feed	1. Control knob on canister cover not open. 2. Canister is not sealing. 3. Spray fluid has not been strained. 4. Spray fluid in canister top threads.	1. Set this knob for pressure spraying. 2. Make sure canister is on tightly. 3. Always strain before using. 4. Clean threads and wipe with grease.

TABLE 3-6: TROUBLESHOOTING AN AIR SPRAY GUN (Continued)

Trouble	Possible Cause	Suggested Correction
	5. Gasket in canister top worn or left out.	5. Inspect and replace if necessary.
	6. No air supply.	6. Check regulator.
	7. Fluid too thick.	7. Thin fluid with proper thinner.
	8. Clogged strainer.	8. Clean or replace strainer.
Will not spray on suction feed	1. Spray fluid is too thick.	1. Thin fluid with thinner.
	2. Internal mix nozzle used.	2. Install external mix nozzle.
	3. Spray fluid has not been strained.	3. Always strain before use.
	4. Hole in canister cover clogged.	4. Make sure this hole is open.
	5. Gasket in canister top worn or left out.	5. Inspect and replace if necessary.
	6. Plug or clogged strainer.	6. Clean or replace strainer.
	7. Fluid control knob adjusted incorrectly.	7. Correct adjustment.
	8. No air supply.	8. Check regulator.
Air continues to flow through gun when trigger has been released (on nonbleeder guns only)	1. Air valve leaks.	1. Remove valve, inspect for damage, clean valve, and replace if necessary.
	2. Needle is binding.	2. Clean or straighten needle.
	3. Piston is sticking.	3. Clean piston, check O-ring, and replace if necessary.
	4. Packing nut too tight.	4. Adjust packing nuts.
	5. Control valve spring left out.	5. Make sure to replace this spring.
Air leak at canister gasket	1. Canister not sealing on canister cover.	1. Check gasket, clean threads, and tighten canister.
Leak at setscrew in canister top	1. Screw not tight.	1. Clean threads and tighten screw.
	2. Damaged threads on setscrew.	2. Inspect and replace if necessary.
Leak between top of canister cover and gun body	1. Retainer nut is not tight enough.	1. Check nut to make sure it is tight.
	2. Gasket or gasket seat damaged.	2. Inspect, clean, and replace if necessary.
Pressure Fluid Tank Problems		
Leaks air at the top of the tank lid	1. Gasket not seating properly or damaged.	1. Drain off all of the air from fluid tank thus allowing the gasket to seat. Retighten wing nuts, and fill with air again. Lid will seat tightly.
	2. Wing screws not tight enough.	2. Make sure all wing screws are tight. By following remedy #1 (above), wing screws can be pulled down even tighter.
	3. Fittings leak.	3. Check all fittings and apply pipe dope if necessary.
	4. Air pressure too high.	4. Maximum 60 psi. Normal w.p. 25–30 psi.
No fluid comes through the spray gun	1. Not enough pressure in tank.	1. Increase regulator setting until fluid flows; do not exceed 60 psi.
	2. Out of fluid.	2. Check fluid supply.
	3. Fluid passages clogged.	3. Check tube, fittings, hose, and spray gun. Clean out fittings, hose, tube, and spray gun making sure all residual fluid is removed.

TABLE 3-7: TROUBLESHOOTING A COMPRESSED AIR SUPPLY

Fault	Result	Blistering	Nondrying	Poor Adhesion	Contamination	Poor Atomization	Poor Flow	Overloading	Sags	Popping	Slow Application	Off-shade Metallic	Uneven Application	Dry Spray	Dirt	Remedy
Oil/water not adequately condensed out.	Oil/water at spray gun	A	C	A	C											Ensure regular drainage of air receiver, separator, and transformer. Site transformers of adequate capacity in cool places. Lubricate compressors with recommended grade of mineral oil of good emulsifying properties.
Long air line; inadequate internal bore of air line; connectors, fittings, compressor, air transformers, and regulators of inadequate capacity.	Pressure drop					B	C	C	A	A	C	A				Ensure adequate air supply with 30 feet 5/16 inch (8mm) internal bore air line with appropriate fittings. NOTE: Reduction of viscosity to give improvement may produce other defects.
Inadequate compressor capacity. No pressure regulator. Regulator diaphragm broken.	Pressure fluctuation							A	A	A		A	A	A		
Compressed air intake filter breached. Transformer filter not properly maintained. Compressor sited in dusty area.	Dirt in compressed air														A	

A   Most likely failure to be associated with the fault
B   Likely failure
C   Failure less likely to be associated with the fault
D   Will affect color of metallics
E   Health hazard

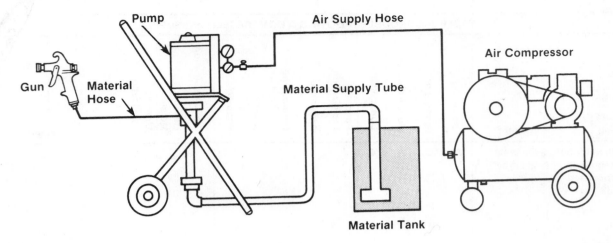

FIGURE 3–60 Typical airless spray equipment setup

auto underbody and corrosion work (see Chapter 6). The so-called air-assisted airless system that uses some air to assist in the spraying operation tends to give a better finish.

Figure 3–60 shows a typical assembly of an airless system. The gun is connected to the pump with a single hose. When the gun is spraying, the pump delivers fluid under pressure adjusted by the air pressure to the pump. When the gun is not spraying, the fluid pressure and air pressure are balanced and the pump stops. The quality and economy of the finish is dependent upon operator skill, fluid preparation, and nozzle size. There are six ways that a painter can control the operation of this system. They are as follows:

- **Orifice size.** This determines the amount of paint sprayed through the gun. The range for automotive coatings is 7/64 inch to 1/64 inch. More paint will be applied through the gun with a larger orifice.
- **Paint viscosity.** This is controlled by the amount of reduction. Viscosity ranges can be from 24 to 36 seconds on a #2 Zahn cup (18 to 28 seconds on a #4 Ford cup).
- **Speed of the reducer.** Generally, use the fastest reducer consistent with flow and sagging. Airless equipment sprays much wetter than conventional air-atomized equipment.
- **Speed of gun movement.** Because of the wetter spray with airless, the painter will generally have to move faster than with conventional spray equipment.
- **Gun distance.** Because of wetter spray patterns, the gun distance to the work should be around 14 inches.
- **Coating material.** Prepare the coating material and use the air pressure as recommended in the manufacturer's instruction manual.

The basic operating techniques of an airless spray gun are the same as those for conventional guns. That is, the gun should be held **perpendicular** and moved **parallel** to the surface in order to obtain a uniform coating of fluid. The wrist, elbow, and shoulder must all be used. Once the best working distance (10 to 15 inches) is determined, the spray gun should be moved across the work at this optimum distance throughout the stroke.

Some object shapes do not allow this practice, but it should be used whenever possible. The proper speed allows a full wet coat application with each stroke. If the desired film thickness cannot be obtained with a single stroke or pass because of sagging, then two or more coats can be applied with a flash-off period between each coat. The spray movement should be at a comfortable rate. If the spray gun movement is excessive in order to avoid flooding the work, then the fluid nozzle orifice is too large or the fluid pressure is too high. If the stroke speed is very slow in order to apply full wet coats, then the fluid pressure should be increased slightly or a larger tip is required.

WARNING: An airless system maintains pressure after the system is shut down. High pressure can cause a serious injury. Before attempting any disassembly of the gun, system pressure must be relieved.

ELECTROSTATIC SPRAYING SYSTEM

Electrostatic spraying utilizes the principle that positive(+) and negative(–) electricity mutually attract each other but oppose a like charge. Therefore,

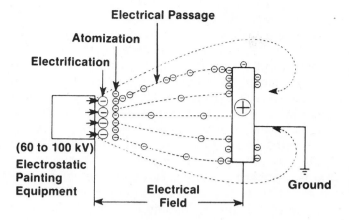

FIGURE 3-61   Principle of electrostatic painting

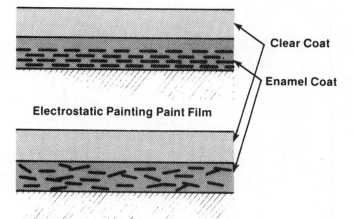

FIGURE 3-62   Electrostatic painting film and spray paint film

when paint particles are given a negative charge by a high-voltage generator (Figure 3-61), the particles oppose each other, causing them to become atomized. On the other hand, because the adherend is grounded, it is under a positive electrical charge. In this manner, when high voltage is applied between the adherend and the electrostatic painting equipment, an electrical field is formed and the air in the field allows the electricity to pass through easily. In other words, electrical passages are formed and the atomized paint passing through these passages is sent to and adheres to the object that is being painted.

Advantages and disadvantages of electrostatic painting are as follows:

- Because the paint particles are drawn to the adherend by electrical attraction, there is less paint loss compared to normal spray painting.
- Because atomization is promoted by opposing electrical forces, a very good quality paint finish can be attained. This is particularly true for metallic painting because the metallic paint particles are formed into rows by the opposing electrical forces, providing an appearance that cannot be attained with the usual air spray gun (Figure 3-62).
- Paint adhesion efficiency is very good and, as a result, painting operations are fast. The reverse side of cylindrical objects, lattice work, and linear objects can be painted simultaneously with the front surface.
- Because the electrical potential in depressed areas is low, the adhesion is not as good, necessitating touchup.
- Unless nonconductors such as plastic, glass, and rubber are made conductive, painting is not possible.

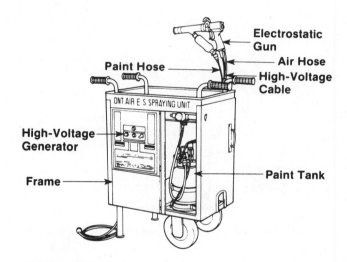

FIGURE 3-63   Air type electrostatic painting equipment

As for portable electrostatic painting equipment, there are both the air-assisted spray type (Figure 3-63) and the airless spray type (Figure 3-64).

As with normal air spray painting, an air spray gun is also used for air spray type electrostatic painting and the paint is atomized by the force of compressed air (Figure 3-65). However, atomization is further promoted by the application of a negative electrical charge. Therefore, the paint is sprayed onto the adherend by both the force of the compressed air and electrical attraction. Adhesion efficiency is not as good as with airless electrostatic spraying (Figure 3-66A), but because the air spray gun is easy to use, this method is suitable when delicate spray gun manipulation is required. The

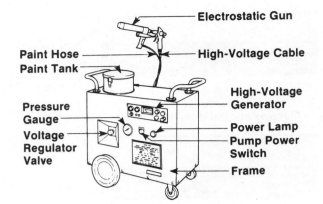

FIGURE 3-64 Airless type electrostatic painting equipment

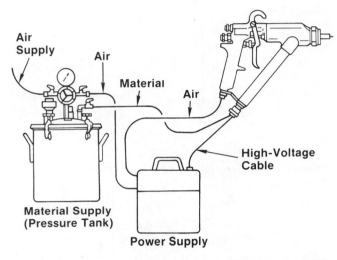

FIGURE 3-65 Atomization electrostatic equipment layout

air-assisted airless electrostatic equipment overcomes this problem in some degree (Figure 3-66B).

Like the normal airless spray method, airless electrostatic spraying utilizes high pressure to atomize the paint by injecting it through small holes in the nozzle, but it also gives the paint a negative electrical charge to further promote atomization. Paint is adhered by means of both injection pressure and electrical attraction. This method provides a very good adhesion efficiency and work is faster due to the large discharge volume. However, because compressed air is not used, injection energy is not as strong and air spray prepainting of depressed areas like the underside of the hood and inner side of the doors is necessary.

WARNING: Because of the high voltage involved in electrostatic spraying it is very important to follow the manufacturer's instructions on the use of the equipment and all safety procedures. It is important that the vehicle be grounded. It is a good idea to always ground the car's body (or frame) to a good ground source (such as a water pipe) as soon as it enters any spray booth (Figure 3-67). Grounding the car will help prevent dust and dirt from being attracted to the new paint by static electricity.

Table 3-8 details some of the features of the six types of spray painting systems. Although at the present, airless, air type electrostatic, and airless

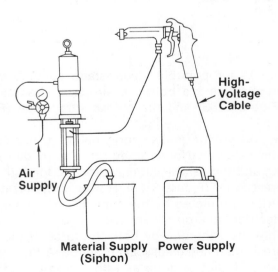

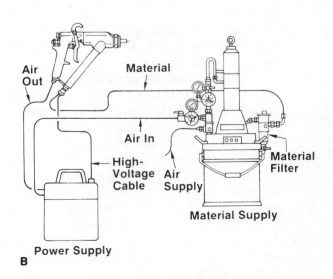

FIGURE 3-66 (A) Airless electrostatic equipment layout; (B) air-assisted airless electrostatic equipment

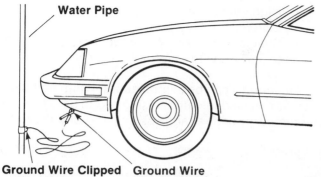

**Ground Wire Clipped
to Water Pipe**   **Ground Wire
Clipped to Frame**

FIGURE 3-67   Grounding a vehicle in spray booth before spraying.

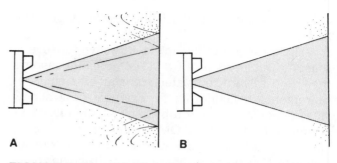

A   B

FIGURE 3-68   (A) High pressure spray results in overspray, particle bounce, and blow back. (B) Low pressure spray has less of these.

type electrostatic are used primarily in commercial vehicles, the environment consideration in some states is toward a 65 percent adhesion efficiency. The only way this seems possible is by using electrostatic and air-assisted airless, and airless techniques. Spray equipment manufacturers are hard at work attempting to improve the quality of finishes obtained from these methods. In the foreseeable future, it is possible that electrostatic and airless spray equipment might be used on topcoat finishes.

HVLP SYSTEMS

The HVLP (high volume, low pressure) spray system (also known as the "high solids" system)

uses a high volume of air, delivered at low pressure, to atomize the paint into a pattern of low-speed particles. The most important way it differs from conventional spray is its high transfer efficiency.

The high pressure air of conventional sprays tends to "blast" the material into small particles. In the process, it creates a fair amount of overspray. The transfer efficiency of high-pressure systems suffers as a result of overspray, particle "bounce," and blow back. In contrast, HVLP relies on air delivered at 10 psi or less to break the material into small particles (Figure 3-68). As the material flows into the air stream, far less is lost in overspray, bounce, and blow back, hence the dramatic improvement in transfer efficiency. HVLP will work with any medium solids material that can be atomized by the gun. These include two-component paints, urethanes,

	Normal Air Spraying	Airless Spraying	Air-Assisted Airless Spraying	Air-Assisted Electrostatic Spraying	Airless Type Electrostatic Spraying	HVLP Spraying
Adhesion of Spray Efficiency	20 to 40%	50 to 60%	40 to 60%	60 to 70%	70 to 80%	65 to 90%
Quality of Finished Surface	Excellent	Poor	Fair to Good	Good	Fair	Good to Excellent
Work Environment (paint mist dispersion)	Poor	Good	Good	Excellent	Excellent	Excellent
Paint Speed	Slow	Fast	Fast	Very fast	Very fast	Slow
Paint of Depressed Areas	Excellent	Poor	Fair	Good	Fair	Excellent
Gun Handling (partial repainting and touch up)	Excellent	Fair	Fair	Fair	Good	Excellent

TABLE 3-8:   COMPARISON OF VARIOUS SPRAYING SYSTEMS

acrylics, epoxies, enamels, lacquers, stains, primers, and so on.

High transfer efficiency is attractive for several reasons. But, perhaps the most compelling reason is the trend toward legislated transfer efficiency requirements. In California, for example, several new rules enacted by the South Coast Air Quality Management District (SCAQMD) require the use of spray methods, which are at least 65 percent transfer efficient. Low pressure spray (up to 10 psi) has been approved, along with electrostatic spray methods. Similar legislation is pending or under consideration in many of the industrial states. The forecast is that soon high transfer efficiency will be a requirement of doing business.

The purpose of this legislation is to protect the environment, but there are other good reasons for looking into HVLP, too. Higher transfer efficiency improves the quality of the workplace and the quality of the finished products. Overspray not only makes painting work less desirable, it also cuts visibility, which contributes to mistakes and low productivity. Overspray is one of the main causes of paint operation maintenance, so cutting overspray cuts downtime. All paint spraying equipment can be affected by overspray, but the booth and its filters get it the worst.

To illustrate how much of a difference transfer efficiency makes in booth maintenance, consider that HVLP can be two to three times as efficient as conventional air spray. Depending on how it is used, conventional air spray might be as little as 20 to 30 percent efficient. That means for every 3 gallons of paint sprayed, more than 2 gallons are wasted. With HVLP typically between 65 and 90 percent efficient, as little as 1 pint of paint would be wasted for every gallon applied. That is how a 3:1 difference in transfer efficiency becomes a 16:1 advantage in terms of overspray.

Booth maintenance and material costs will drop accordingly. But one of the most troublesome problems high transfer efficiency can solve for some companies is waste disposal. In air spray systems where overspray volume meant using a water wash booth, the easy-to-handle dry filter media may now be sufficient, completely eliminating the hazardous waste that is often the by-product of these systems.

High transfer efficiency can make existing water wash filtration systems virtually maintenance-free, particularly when using the new sludge removal techniques. Conventional air spray productivity usually does not suffer, either. Since more paint is applied per pass, fewer passes are often needed to build up the same film thickness.

HVLP systems (Figure 3–69) are basically simple, consisting of the following:

- High volume air source
- Material supply system
- Special HVLP spray guns that are designed to operate with a high volume of low pressure air

Air sources can be centralized, serving multiple guns, or can be dedicated to single-gun use. These sources will provide a range of delivery volumes and

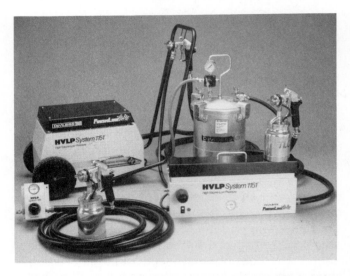

FIGURE 3–69 The basic components of a portable HVLP system *(Courtesy of DeVilbiss Co.)*

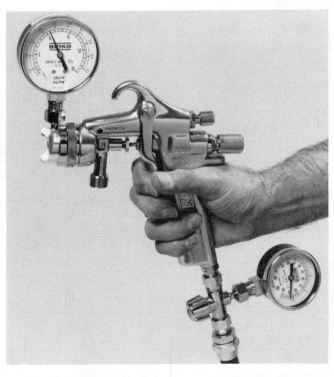

FIGURE 3–70 Modified conventional air spray gun in an applied HVLP system. As you will note there are gauges on both the gun's input and output. *(Courtesy of Binks Mfg. Co.)*

pressures. As a general rule, maximum pressure is best but should be limited to 10 psi. It is pressure, not volume, that atomizes the paint.

Material can be supplied through pressure pots, quart cups, or other conventional supply systems. Flow requirements are usually lower than air spray systems for similar applications because of higher transfer efficiency.

Special guns (Figure 3-70) are used; they have no obstructions that could restrict the flow and increase the pressure drop. In many designs, the airflow through the gun is continuous; the trigger opens the material flow valve. Special caps and tips are also needed to assure proper atomization. Because use of heated air is common, a few HVLP guns feature insulated grips.

There are two basic air supply designs. One generates airflow from a turbine generator, the other converts 80 to 100 psi shop air to a lower 2 to 10 psi. Each of these approaches has pros and cons.

- **Turbine Generators.** The turbine approach offers portability (Figure 3-71) that generally is not available when connecting to shop air lines. Additionally, in some cases, existing shop air sources offer insufficient volume. For example, in a body shop with its existing air compressor already working at full capacity, a turbine unit would work well as it would not use the existing shop air. Due to friction, the turbine generates enough heat to provide moderate air temperatures. However, the temperature of the air depends on turbine design, distance from the gun, and the insulating values of the air conduit. It is not always controllable. Assuming the air intake system and its filter are well designed and maintained, turbine air generators provide relatively clean, oil-free, and dry air. For turbine systems to be used inside the spray booth, they must be of costly, explosion-proof design.

- **Air Conversion Units.** A standard shop air compressor such as described in Chapter 4 and air conversion unit provide more control over the variable that affect application performance. Heat and pressure are the two most important HVLP variables.

    When fitted with air heaters (Figure 3-72), they offer controlled air temperature. The heat can be varied or turned off completely. Furthermore, they can deliver a consistent 10 psi or be regulated to provide somewhat less pressure. Air conversion units eliminate turbine maintenance and reliability problems.

The shortcomings of air conversion units primarily revolve around its relationship with the air supply. The shop air lines must be capable of delivering a sufficient volume of clean, dry, oil-free air. If the system is adequate for conventional air spray systems, however, the same volume of air will suffice with HVLP. Additional equipment and maintenance procedures could be required to assure that the air is clean, dry, and oil-free. Otherwise contaminated air could spoil the paint job. Again, if the air supply system is currently maintained for conventional air spray finishing, existing equipment and procedures will do the job.

Except for certain subtle differences, the HVLP and conventional air spray gun operate in basically the same manner as described earlier in the chapter. For instance, the HVLP gun should be held closer to

FIGURE 3-71   A typical portable HVLP turbine generator *(Courtesy of DeVilbiss Co.)*

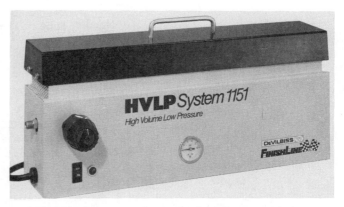

FIGURE 3-72   A typical HVLP air heater *(Courtesy of DeVilbiss Co.)*

FIGURE 3-73 The airbrush can be used for simple touch-up jobs. *(Courtesy of Binks Mfg. Co.)*

FIGURE 3-74 The airbrush can also be used in custom finishes. *(Courtesy of PPG Industries, Inc.)*

the surface of the workpiece because of the lower speed of the particles. A rule of thumb would be to hold the gun 6 to 8 inches when spraying from the part with HVLP, compared to 8 to 10 inches for enamel. Greater distances result in excessive dry spray and lack of film buildup.

Many first time HVLP users get the impression that HVLP is slower than conventional air spray. This is not always the case. Film thickness is often greater than air spray systems. This results in fewer total passes for the desired build. Sometimes the application **is** slower, but this is generally because the air source is not delivering sufficient air pressure. Remember that not all systems deliver their rated pressure under actual conditions. To many people, HVLP sounds ineffective. Unlike conventional air spray systems, which sound like a leaking tire when airflow is present, HVLP is very quiet.

AIRBRUSHES

Airbrushes range from simple types used for touch-up work (Figure 3-73) to complex and exacting tools used in custom finishing (Figure 3-74). The latter, of course, is generally found only in paint shops that do custom auto finishes.

It is important to select the correct airbrush for the type of work to be performed. Consider the size and type of the work to be done, the fineness of the line desired, and the fluids to be sprayed. Airbrushes used for custom auto finishing are generally in two categories: double-action and single-action types (Figure 3-75). The double-action brushes are more

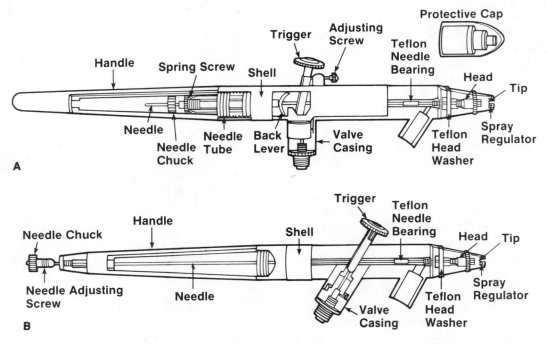

FIGURE 3-75 (A) Double-action and (B) single-action airbrush. *(Courtesy of Badger Air-Brush Co.)*

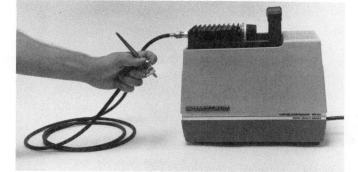

FIGURE 3-76 A typical airbrush operated with a diaphragm type compressor

versatile than are the ones found in most custom paint shops. They are available with a choice of tips to further increase their versatility. The double-action airbrush is usually recommended for projects that require very fine detailing. They produce a variable spray that works by depressing the finger-controlled front lever for air and pulling back on the same lever for the proper amount of color to be sprayed.

With single-action airbrushes, air is released by depressing the finger lever, while the amount of color desired is controlled by rotating the rear needle adjusting screw. While working, it is not possible to change the amount of color being sprayed because the operator must stop spraying to rotate the needle adjusting screw in the rear.

Airbrushes operate on a range of 5 to 50 psi pressure, with the normal operating pressure being approximately 30 psi. A scfm rating of about 0.7 is sufficient for most airbrushes. Compact compressors (Figure 3-76) are very popular with custom auto painters.

REVIEW QUESTIONS

1. Which of the following is located at the nozzle tip of the spray gun and creates a vacuum for the discharge of the paint?
   a. center orifice
   b. side orifices
   c. auxiliary orifices
   d. none of the above

2. Which of the following promotes atomization of the paint?
   a. center orifices
   b. side orifices
   c. ports
   d. none of the above

3. Which of the following controls the amount of material that actually leaves the front of the gun?
   a. amount of air flow through the two side orifices
   b. size of the auxiliary orifices
   c. size of the fluid tip opening
   d. all of the above

4. Which type of spray gun has the disadvantage of having a small cup capacity?
   a. suction feed type
   b. pressure type
   c. gravity feed type
   d. both a and b

5. Which type of spray gun can be used with a high-viscosity paint?
   a. suction feed type
   b. pressure type
   c. gravity feed type
   d. none of the above

6. Which sprays best at 19 seconds viscosity?
   a. lacquer colors
   b. alkyd enamel colors
   c. synthetic primer-surfacers
   d. all of the above

7. A spraying pressure that is too high results in which of the following?
   a. poor flow
   b. poor drying characteristics
   c. bubbling
   d. sagging

8. What happens when testing the spray pattern for uniformity of paint distribution?
   a. A vertical spray pattern is used.
   b. The trigger is pulled all the way back and released immediately.
   c. The pattern is flooded.
   d. None of the above
   e. Both a and b

9. What distance should the spray gun be held from the surface when spraying an enamel?
   a. 6 to 8 inches
   b. 8 to 10 inches
   c. 10 to 12 inches
   d. 8 to 12 inches

10. Which coat helps to level the final cost, melt in the overspray, and control mottling of metallics?
    a. banding coat
    b. dust coat
    c. mist coat
    d. blending coat

11. Pinholes appear in the finished surface. Painter A says this condition might have been caused

by holding the gun too close to the surface. Painter B says that the fluid might have been too heavy. Who is right?
a. Painter A
b. Painter B
c. Both A and B
d. Neither A nor B

12. Fluid leaks from the packing nut of the spray gun. Painter A says the gun has the wrong size fluid needle. Painter B says the fluid needle spring is broken. Who is right?
a. Painter A
b. Painter B
c. Both A and B
d. Neither A nor B

13. There is an excessive amount of overspray. Painter A reduces the atomization air pressure. Painter B increases the atomization air pressure. Who is right?
a. Painter A
b. Painter B
c. Both A and B
d. Neither A nor B

14. When the regulator diaphragm of a compressor is broken, what could be the result?
a. dry spray
b. uneven application
c. slow application
d. all of the above
e. both a and b

15. Which type of spray gun provides a very good adhesion efficiency?
a. airless spray gun
b. electrostatic spray gun
c. airbrush
d. none of the above

CHAPTER FOUR

COMPRESSED AIR SUPPLY EQUIPMENT

Objectives

After reading this chapter, you will be able to:

* explain the operation of an air compressor.
* identify the different types of filters.
* describe the function of air and fluid control equipment.
* properly maintain an air supply system.

The compressed air supply system is designed to provide an adequate supply of compressed air at a predetermined pressure to insure efficient operation of all air-operated equipment in the paint shop. The system can vary in size from small portable units (Figure 4-1) to large in-shop installations (Figure 4-2). The following basic requirements and considerations for these systems are the same (Figure 4-3):

* An air compressor, sometimes referred to as a **pump,** can be one compressor or a series of compressors.
* The power source is generally an electric motor. (Portable gasoline driven compressors are available for work outside the shop.)
* A control or set of controls to regulate the operation of the compressor and motor.
* Air intake filters/silencers are designed to muffle intake noises as well as filter out dust and dirt.
* The air tank or receiver must be properly sized. It cannot be too small or it will cause the compressor to cycle too often thus causing excessive load on the motor. It should not be too large because of space problems and also unnecessary capacity.
* The distribution system is the key link in the compressed air system. This is the hose or piping, or arrangement of hose and piping, from the air receiver to distribution points requiring compressed air. This distribution system consists of the proper sizes of hose or pipe, fittings, valves, air filters, oil and water extractors, regulators, gauges, lubricators and other air and fluid control equipment that will provide for the effective and efficient operation of specific air devices, tools, and spraying equipment.

FIGURE 4-1   Portable air compressor unit

Complete Automotive Painting

AIR COMPRESSOR

The compressor—the heart of any air system—is designed to raise the pressure of air from normal atmospheric to some higher pressure, as measured in pounds per square inch (psi). While normal atmospheric pressure is about 14.7 pounds per square inch, a compressor will typically deliver air at pressures up to 200 psi.

FIGURE 4-2 Multicompressor setup from large body shops. *(Courtesy of Binks Mfg. Co.)*

There are three basic types of air compressors:

- Diaphragm type
- Piston type
- Air screw (or rotary) type

DIAPHRAGM TYPE COMPRESSOR

In this type of compressor (Figure 4-4), a durable diaphragm is stretched across the bore of a very shallow compression chamber. A connecting plate, operated by an eccentric mounted on the motor shaft, alternately pulls the diaphragm down and thrusts it upward. As the diaphragm is pulled down (Figure 4-5A), air is drawn into the small space above the diaphragm. When the diaphragm is thrust upward (Figure 4-5B), the air trapped in the compression chamber is squeezed and forced out into the delivery chamber and supply lines. Although only a very small amount of air—in the 30 to 35 psi range—is compressed during each cycle, the action is very rapid—in excess of 1500 strokes per minute.

Because most body and refinishing operations consume large quantities of compressed air at relatively higher pressures, the diaphragm compressor is seldom found in the average shop. The exception to this is a refinishing shop that specializes in custom painting and airbrush work.

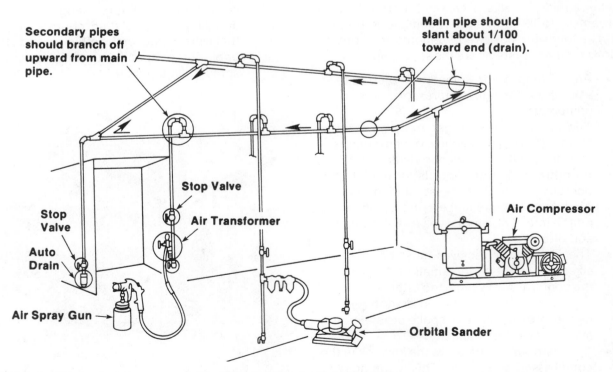

FIGURE 4-3 Typical piping arrangement found in a body/paint shop

FIGURE 4-4   Typical diaphragm type compressor

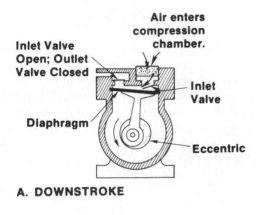

A. DOWNSTROKE

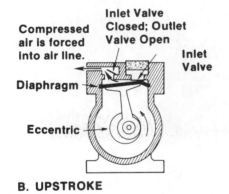

B. UPSTROKE

FIGURE 4-5   The operation of a diaphragm compressor

PISTON RECIPROCATING TYPE COMPRESSOR

The piston type air compressor pump develops compressed air pressure through the action of a reciprocating piston. As shown in Figure 4-6, a piston, which is actuated by a crankshaft, moves up and down inside a cylinder, very much like a piston in an automobile engine. On the downstroke (Figure 4-6A), air is drawn into the compression chamber

through a one-way valve. On the upstroke (Figure 4-6B), as the air is compressed by the rising piston, a second one-way valve opens and the air is forced into a pressure tank or receiver. As more and more air is forced into the tank, the pressure inside the tank rises.

Piston compressor pumps are available in single or multiple cylinder and single- or two-stage models, depending on the volume and pressure required. When the air is drawn from the atmosphere and compressed to its final pressure in a single stroke, the compressor is referred to as a **single stage** compressor. Single-stage units normally are used in pressure ranges up to 125 psi for intermittent service. Most single-stage compressors are rated at 50 percent duty cycle (1/2 the time ON, 1/2 the time OFF). They are available in single- or multicylinder compressors (Figure 4-7). The principal parts of a typical piston type compressor are shown in Figure 4-8.

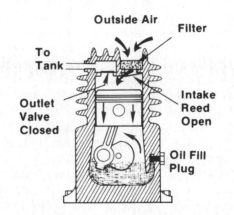

A. DOWNSTROKE—AIR BEING DRAWN INTO COMPRESSION CHAMBER

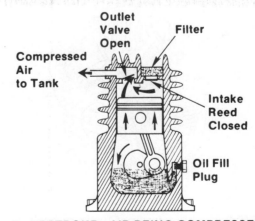

B. UPSTROKE—AIR BEING COMPRESSED AND FORCED TO TANK

FIGURE 4-6   The operation of a piston type compressor

FIGURE 4-7 Single-stage compressor pumps (left to right): single cylinder, angled V-cylinders, and two cylinders

When the air drawn from the atmosphere is compressed first to an intermediate pressure and then further compressed to a higher pressure, it is done in a **two-stage** compressor (Figure 4-9). Such a compressor has cylinders of unequal bore. The first stage of compression takes place in the large bore cylinder. In the second stage, the air is compressed for a second time to a higher pressure in the smaller bore cylinder (Figure 4-10) after passing through an intercooler. Two-stage compressors are usually more efficient, run cooler, and deliver more air for the power consumed, particularly in the 100 to 200 psi pressure range; this range of pressure is enough for most body or finishing applications.

The advantage of the piston compressor is that it is generally more durable and has a greater capacity than diaphragm types, which are more suitable for heavier duty work. However, since the piston rides in a cylinder, lubrication is necessary.

In recent years, an oilless or oil-free piston compression system has been introduced that employs self-lubricating materials that do not require an oil lubricant. Until recently, most oilless compressors, like the diaphragm type, were considered

FIGURE 4-9 Typical two-stage compressor. *(Courtesy of Binks Mfg. Co.)*

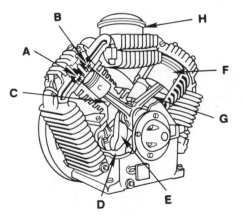

FIGURE 4-8 The principal parts of a piston type compressor: (A) intake and (B) exhaust valves; (C) cylinder; (D) crankcase; (E) crankshaft; (F) piston; (G) connecting rod assembly; and (H) air intake filter

compacts and limited in both output and pressure. However, there are oilless compressors (Figure 4–11) now on the market of up to approximately 5 horsepower that will nearly equal, in output and pressure, oil-lubricated compressors of the same horsepower. All oilless compressors produce a clean air output. But, they should never be used as a part of a fresh air supplied respirator system because they lack the necessary safety filters and controls.

ROTARY SCREW AIR COMPRESSOR

Rotary screw type air compressors (Figure 4–12) have been a standard in industry, but because an oil output problem, it was never accepted by the automotive refinishing profession. Recent innovations have greatly or completely eliminated the oil problem but, except in certain areas of the country,

the rotary air compressor is not overly used in auto paint shops. The rotary screw air compressor is a highly efficient and dependable machine.

HOW COMPRESSORS ARE RATED

The following terms are used to measure the performance of a compressor.

- **Horsepower (hp).** Horsepower is the measure of the work capacity of the motor or engine that drives the compressor. Compressors found in body and paint shops usually range from 3 to 25 hp. As a general rule, the greater the horsepower, the more powerful the compressor.

- **Cubic feet per minute (cfm).** Cubic feet per minute is the volume of the air being delivered by the compressor to the spray gun or

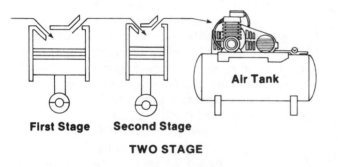

First Stage   **Second Stage**
TWO STAGE

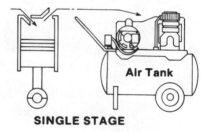

SINGLE STAGE

FIGURE 4-10   Comparison of a single- and two-stage compressor

FIGURE 4-11   Three mountings for oilless compressors

FIGURE 4-12 Typical rotary screw air compressor *(Courtesy of Champion Pneumatic Machinery Co., Inc.)*

A

B

FIGURE 4-13 (A) Horizontal- and (B) vertical-mounted piston compressors

air tool and is used as a measure of the compressor's capabilities. Compressors with higher cfm ratings provide more air through the hose to the tool, thus making higher cfm outfits more practical for larger jobs. Actually, compressors have two cfm ratings:

—**Displacement cfm.** This is the theoretical amount of air in cubic feet that the compressor can pump in 1 minute. It is a relatively simple matter to calculate the air displacement of a compressor if the piston diameter, length of stroke, and rpm are known. For example, the area of the piston multiplied by the length of the stroke and the shaft revolutions per minute equals the displacement volume. The formula for computing it is as follows:

$$\frac{\text{Area of piston} \times \text{stroke} \times \text{rpm} \times \text{number of pistons}}{1,728}$$

$$= \text{Displacement in cfm}$$

—**Free air cfm.** This is the actual amount of free air in cubic feet that the compressor can pump in 1 minute at working pressure. The free air delivery at working pressure, not the displacement or the horsepower, is the true rating of a compressor and should be the only cfm rating considered when selecting an air compressor. Keep in mind that compressor units are frequently rated in standard cubic feet per minute (scfm), which is really cfm corrected for a given barometric pressure and temperature.

It should be remembered that free air delivery is always less than the displacement rating since no compressor is 100 percent efficient. The volumetric efficiency of a compressor is the ratio of free air delivery to the displacement rating, expressed in percent. For example, if a compressor unit for 100 pounds service has a displacement of 8 cfm and its volumetric efficiency is 75 percent, at this pressure the free air delivery will be: 8 cfm × 75 percent, or 6 cfm.

 SHOP TALK _____

The displacement of a two-stage compressor is always given for that of the first stage cylinder or cylinders only. This is because the second stage merely rehandles the same air the first stage draws in and cannot increase the amount of air discharged.

- **Pressure (psi).** Pounds per square inch (psi) is the measure of air pressure or force delivered by the compressor to the air tool. This is usually expressed in two figures:
  —Normal or continuous working pressure
  —Maximum pressure
Average psi and free air delivery requirements for various air tools and accessories are given in Chapter 2.

TANK SIZE

As previously mentioned, with most piston types of compressor pumps, air is forced into a tank or receiver. Working pressure is not available until the tank pressure is above the required psi of the air tool. The compressor puts more into the tank than is required for application. Thus, the larger the tank, the longer a job can be done at the required pressure before a pause is necessary to rebuild pressure in the tank. Since the air tank acts as a reservoir, the unit may for a short time exceed the normal capacity of the compressor. This reservoir action of the tank also reduces the running time of the compressor, thereby decreasing compressor wear and maintenance.

Air tanks or receivers usually have a cylindrical shape, and the compressor motor and pump are usually mounted on top of it. Tanks can be purchased with either horizontal (Figure 4-13A) or vertical stationary mountings (Figure 4-13B) or can be mounted horizontally on wheels for portability (Figure 4-14).

COMPRESSOR OUTFITS

As already illustrated, there are two types of compressor outfits used in paint shops: portable and stationary. A portable outfit is designed for easy movement. It is equipped with handles, wheels, or casters and usually a small air receiver or pulsation chamber.

A stationary outfit is one that is permanently installed. It is usually equipped with a larger air receiver than the portable type and might have a pressure switch as found on service station compressors or an automatic unloader as found on larger industrial units. Larger stationary models are generally equipped with a centrifugal pressure release.

As shown in Figure 4-15, the typical parts of a stationary compressor are:

- Air compressor pump
- Electric or gasoline engine (powers the compressor)
- Air receiver or storage tank (holds the compressed air)

FIGURE 4-14   Typical portable piston compressor mounted on wheels. *(Courtesy of DeVilbiss Co.)*

- Check valve (prevents leakage of the stored air)
- Pressure switch (automatically controls the air pressure)

On Large Models

- Centrifugal pressure release (relieves the motor of starting against a load)
- Safety valve (protects air lines and equipment against excessive pressure)
- Drain valve at the bottom of the air receiver (drains condensation)

Because of the importance of the system's safety controls, it is wise to know how they operate to protect excessive pressure and electrical problems. The most common of these are:

- **Automatic unloader** is a device designed to maintain a supply of air within given pressure limits on gasoline and electrically driven compressors when it is not practical to start and stop the motor during operations. When the demand for air is relatively constant at a volume approaching the main capacity of the compressor, an unloader is recommended.

  When maximum pressure in the air receiver is reached, the unloader pilot valve (Figure 4-16A) opens to let air travel through a small tube to the unloader mechanism (Figure 4-16B) and holds open the intake valve on the compressor, allowing it to run idle. When pressure drops to a minimum setting, the spring loaded pilot automatically closes, air to the unloader is shut off causing the intake valve to close, and the compressor resumes normal operation. Maximum and minimum pressures can be varied by reset-

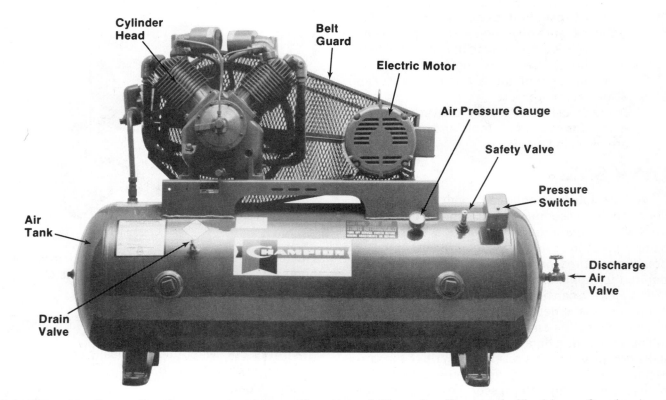

FIGURE 4-15 Parts of stationary compressor. *(Courtesy of Champion Pneumatic Machinery Co., Inc.)*

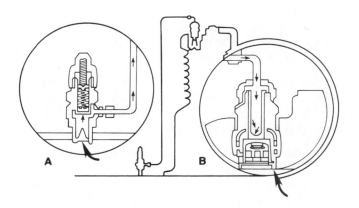

FIGURE 4-16 Automatic "pop-off" unloader. *(Courtesy of DeVilbiss Co.)*

ting the pressure adjusting screw on the pilot.

- **Pressure switch** is a pneumatically controlled electric switch for starting and stopping electric motors at present minimum and maximum pressures. That is, this switch maintains a "cut-in" low pressure point; for example, 80 psi. When the pressure in the air receiver drops to this low point, the motor will start and the compressor will then pump up to its cut-off high pressure point, which might be 100 psi, thus breaking contact and

stopping the motor; when the pressure drops to its low point, the cycle is repeated. The time to pump as shown in Table 4-1 varies by compressor size and type and cut-in/cut-out pressure.

- **Motor starter** is an electrical switch designed to provide overload protection or other necessary electrical control for starting motors of various types. The design of the switch varies with different motor sizes and current characteristics.

- **Overload protection** is usually provided on small units by fuses and on larger ones by thermal overload relays on the starting device. Relays are recommended with time delay features so that circuits will not be opened by overloads of short duration not harmful enough to injure the motor. Overload protection should be employed on all compressor installations, except the smaller types that are designed to operate from the standard wall socket.

- **Centrifugal pressure release** is a device that allows the motor to start up and gain momentum before engaging the load of pumping air against pressure. When the compressor slows down to stop, rotating the crankshaft more slowly, steel balls (Figure 4-17A) move

TABLE 4-1: TYPICAL CUT-IN/CUT-OUT COMPRESSION TIMES

Outfit	HP	Cut-in pounds pressure	Cut-out pounds pressure	Time to pump from Cut-in to Cut-out (in seconds)	Tank Size
Single Stage	1	80	100	83	30 gal.
Single Stage	2	80	100	69	60 gal.
Single Stage	3	80	100	51	60 gal.
Two Stage	1	140	175	284	60 gal.
Two Stage	3	140	175	115	80 gal.
Two Stage	5	140	175	75	80 gal.
Two Stage	10	140	175	56	120 gal.
Two Stage	15	140	175	42	120 gal.
Two Stage	20	140	175	36	200 gal.
Two Stage	25	140	175	30	200 gal.

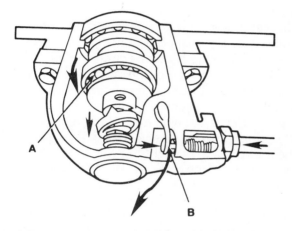

FIGURE 4-17 Centrifugal pressure release. *(Courtesy of DeVilbiss Co.)*

toward the center where they wedge against a cam surface forcing the cam outward. This opens a valve (Figure 4-17B) "bleeding" air from the line connecting to the check valve. With air pressure bled from the pump and aftercooler, the compressor can start up free of back pressure until it gets up speed. When normal speed is reached, balls move out by centrifugal force, releasing the cam, closing the valve, and allowing air to again be pumped into the air receiver.

- **Fused disconnect switch** is a knife type, OFF/ON switch, containing the proper size fuse. This should be used at or near the compressor unit with the line going from the fused disconnect to the starter. Fuses should be large enough to handle 2-1/2 times the current rating stamped on the motor. A qualified electrician should always make the electrical hookup of an air compressor.

AIR AND FLUID CONTROL EQUIPMENT

The control of the amount, pressure, and cleanness of the air going to the pneumatic tools, especially spray guns, is of critical importance in the system. The intake air filter located on the compressor is very important as all the air going into the compressor must pass through this filter. The filter element must be made of fine mesh or felt material to insure that small particles of grit and abrasive dust do not pass into the cylinders, thus preventing excessive wear on cylinder walls, piston rings, and valves.

Once the air leaves the compressor, any equipment installed between the air pump and the point of use modifies the nature of the air stream. This modification could be a change in pressure, in volume, in cleanliness, or some combination of them. It must be remembered that raw air piped directly from a compressor is of little use to the refinishing shop. The air contains small but harmful quantities of water, oil, dirt, and other contaminants that will lessen the quality of the sprayed finish. And the air will likely vary in pressure during the job. Furthermore, there will probably be a need for multiple air outlets for compressed air to run various pieces of equipment. Any type of item installed in the air line that performs one or more of these functions is a piece of air control equipment.

DISTRIBUTION SYSTEM

The interconnecting piping, that is, the piping from the compressor to the tool input, can be copper tubing, or galvanized or black iron pipe. Table 4-2 shows the correct pipe size in relation to compressor size and air volume.

TABLE 4-2: MINIMUM PIPE SIZE RECOMMENDATIONS*

Compressing Outfit		Main Air Line	
Size	Capacity	Length	Size
1-1/2 and 2 HP	6 to 9 CFM	Over 50 feet	3/4"
3 and 5 HP	12 to 20 CFM	Up to 200 feet	3/4"
		Over 200 feet	1"
5 to 10 HP	20 to 40 CFM	Up to 100 feet	3/4"
		Over 100 to 200 feet	1"
		Over 200 feet	1-1/4"
10 to 15 HP	40 to 60 CFM	Up to 100 feet	1"
		Over 100 to 200 feet	1-1/4"
		Over 200 feet	1-1/2"

*Piping should be as direct as possible. If a large number of fittings are used, large size pipe should be installed to help overcome excessive pressure drop.

The location of the compressor unit is important. If possible, the compressor should be placed where it can receive an ample supply of clean, cool, dry air. In most areas of the country, it is recommended that the compressor be installed inside the shop and draw inside clean filtered air. The compressor area or room should be well ventilated and the moisture condensation should be kept to a minimum. With cold ambient winter temperatures, the outside air could damage the compressor.

In shops that use an outside intake, the distance between it and the compressor should be as short as possible for best efficiency and the outside intake should be protected from the elements with a hood or suitable weatherproof shield. The compressor air intake should not be located near steam outlets or other moisture-producing areas.

The pump unit itself should be at least 1 foot from any wall or obstruction so that air can circulate around the compressor to aid in proper cooling. The compressor must be level. Mounting pads or vibration dampeners are generally used under the feet of the compressor. These absorb the vibration, eliminating excessive wear in the area where the feet are welded to the tank. Normally the air compressor is mounted with the fly wheel facing the wall for additional safety.

The compressor should be located as near as possible to operations requiring compressed air. This cuts down lengthy air lines that cause needless pressure drop. It is good practice if the shop is long and narrow to install an extra air receiver at the far end to act as a cushion and help reduce pressure drop when peak loads are placed on the compressed air supply.

Pressure drops, to a great extent, can be avoided by encircling the shop or looping the distribution system. This is accomplished by running the piping in a full circle or loop from the air receiver around the shop and back to the air receiver. A double loop or circle is accomplished by installing a tee in the line and then running a loop or circle in both directions back to the air tank. For this type of installation, it is recommended that an extra air tank (Figure 4-18) be installed at the far end to balance out peak loads. All piping should be installed so that it slopes toward the compressor air receiver or a drain leg installed at the end of each branch, to provide for drainage of moisture from the main air line. This line should not run adjacent to steam or hot-water piping.

In the air distribution or supply system, there should be a shut-off valve on the main line, close to the storage receiver tank. This valve is used to shut off the air at the air receiver. Keeping the air shut off at the storage tank overnight insures a full tank of air when the shop is opened each day.

Other air control devices come in a very wide variety of types, but they basically all perform one or more of the following functions: air filtering and cleaning; air pressure regulation and indication of pressure; and air distribution through multiple outlets. Some typical devices to perform these functions are called air transformers, air condensers, air regulators, and in some circumstances, air lubricators.

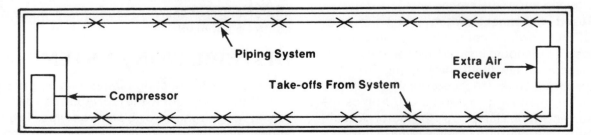

FIGURE 4-18 Some body/paint shop layouts require an extra air receiver.

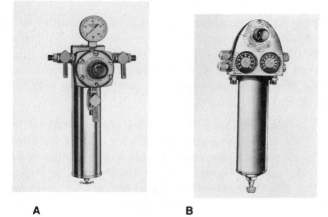

A   B

FIGURE 4-19   Two types of air transformers. *(Courtesy of DeVilbiss Co.)*

AIR TRANSFORMER

An air transformer, sometimes called a moisture **separator/regulator,** is a multipurpose device that removes oil, dirt, and moisture from the compressed air; filters and regulates the air; indicates by gauge the regulated air pressure; and provides multiple air outlets for spray guns, dusters, air-operated tools, and so on. Figure 4-19A illustrates a typical air transformer. Some air transfers (Figure 4-19B) are equipped with a second gauge that indicates main line pressure.

Air transformers are used in all spray finishing operations that require a supply of clean, dry, regulated air. They remove entrained dirt, oil, and moisture by a series of baffles, centrifugal force, expansion chambers, impingement plates and filters,

FIGURE 4-20   Typical air filter. *(Courtesy of De-Vilbiss Co.)*

FIGURE 4-21   Simple air regulator

allowing only clean, dry air to emerge from the outlets. The air regulating valve provides positive control insuring uniformly constant air pressure. Gauges indicate regulated air pressure, and in some cases, main line pressure as well. Outlets with valves allow compressed air to be distributed where it is needed. The drain valve provides for elimination of sludge consisting of oil, dirt, and moisture. The air transformer should be installed at least 25 feet from the compressing unit.

AIR CONDENSER OR FILTER

An air condenser is basically a filter that is installed in the air line between the compressor and the point of use. It separates solid particles such as oil, water, and dirt out of the compressed air. No pressure regulation capability is supplied by this device. A typical air condenser is illustrated in Figure 4-20.

AIR PRESSURE REGULATOR

An air pressure regulator is a device for reducing the main line air pressure as it comes from the compressor. It automatically maintains the required air pressure with minimum fluctuations. Regulators (Figure 4-21) are used in lines already equipped with an air condenser or other type of air filtration device. Air regulators are available in a wide range of cfm and psi capacities, with and without pressure gauges, and in different degrees of sensitivity and accuracy. They have main line air inlets and regulated air outlets (Figure 4-22).

LUBRICATOR

Certain types of air-operated tools and equipment described in Chapter 2 require a very small amount of oil mixed in the air supply that powers them. An automatic air line lubricator (Figure 4-23)

FIGURE 4-22   Typical filter/air regulator

FIGURE 4-23   Typical air line lubricator. *(Courtesy of DeVilbiss Co.)*

should be installed on leg or branch line furnishing air to pneumatic tools. (Never install a lubricator on a leg or branch air line used for paint spraying since the small oil supplied by it could damage the finish.) Lubricators are often combined with air filters and regulators in a single unit. Figure 4-24 shows a lubricator/filter/regulator unit with a built-in sight glass for determining reserve oil level.

THERMAL CONDITIONING AND PURIFICATION EQUIPMENT

While the air control devices already described in this chapter will remove contaminants from the compressed air most satisfactorily, there are some special problems in some shops in the country with heat, dampness, and dirt that require special thermal conditioning and purification equipment. This equipment is usually installed between the compressor and the air storage receiver tank (Figure 4-25). It includes the following:

- **Aftercooler.** The primary purpose of this device is to reduce the temperature of compressed air. Heat, as well as some impurities, can be removed by installing an aftercooler in the system (Figure 4-26). Aftercoolers are very efficient in lowering air temperature and removing most of the oil and water; the residue of oil and water will be removed before it enters the air receiver. A "fish eye" condition is common in shops that do not remove the oil from their lines. There are several different designs or types of aftercoolers available. The most common is the water-cooled "air tube" design in which air passes through small tubes and recirculating water is directed back and forth across the tubes by means of baffles and moves in a direction counter to the flow of air. This cross-flow principle is accepted as the most efficient means of heat transfer.
- **Automatic dump trap.** This trap, installed at the lowest point below the air receiver, will

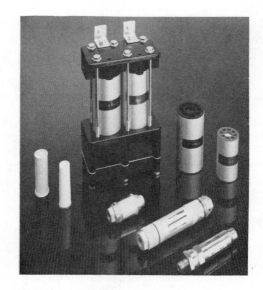

FIGURE 4-24   There are several types of extractor/dryers, filters, and lubricating units that provide clean, dry air to spray guns, tools and other compressed air applications. The lubricating units supply the correct amount of oil to air tools to help keep them running smoother and longer. *(Courtesy of DeVilbiss Co.)*

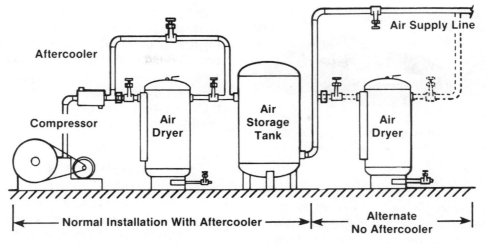

Air Supply Line

Aftercooler

Compressor

Air Dryer

Air Storage Tank

Air Dryer

Normal Installation With Aftercooler

Alternate No Aftercooler

FIGURE 4-25 Arrangement where dry air supply is required.

FIGURE 4-26 Air-cooled aftercooler for system requiring drier air. It is installed between the two compressor stages. *(Courtesy of Hankison Corp.)*

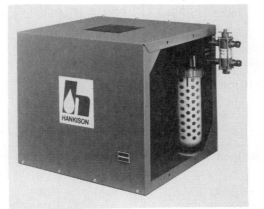

FIGURE 4-27 Typical air dryer used in paint shops. *(Courtesy of Hankison Corp.)*

collect condensed moisture. It is so designed that the trap opens automatically to discharge a predetermined volume. Due to the air pressure behind the water, the trap opens and closes with a snap action that insures proper seating of the closing valve. A small line strainer should be installed ahead of any automatic device to keep foreign particles from clogging the working parts. If this unit is properly installed, with a line strainer, it will give long and satisfactory service with minimum maintenance.

• **Air dryers.** Good aftercoolers will remove the greatest percentage of water vapor, but the residue can still cause problems. To prevent such problems an air dryer (Figure 4-27) is used. There are many designs of air dryers available; among these the most common are chemical, desiccant (a drying agent), and refrigeration types. All dryers are designed to remove moisture from the compressed air supply so that no condensation will take place in the distribution system under normal working conditions.

HOSE AND CONNECTIONS

The various types of hose used to carry compressed air and fluid to the spray gun are important parts of the system. Improperly selected or maintained hose can create a number of problems.

HOSE TYPES

There are two types of hoses in a compressed air system: air hose and a fluid or material hose (Figure 4-28). The air hose in most compressed sys-

FIGURE 4-28 Two types of hoses used in most compressed air systems. *(Courtesy of Binks Mfg. Co.)*

tems is usually covered in red rubber, although in smaller, low pressure systems it might be covered with a black and orange braided fabric. The fluid or material hose is normally black or brown rubber.

SHOP TALK _____

*The air hose is **not** to be used for solvent-based paints.*

The air hose is usually a simple braid-covered hose that consists of rubber tubing (1) reinforced and covered by a woven braid (2), as shown in Figure 4-29A. The single braid, rubber-covered hose (Figure 4-29B) consists of an inner tube (1), a braid (2), and an outside cover (3), all vulcanized into a single unit. The double braid hose, illustrated in Figure

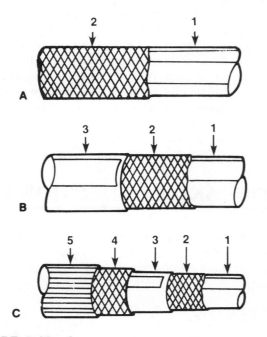

FIGURE 4-29 Construction of hoses used in compressed air system: (A) braid-covered hose; (B) single braid hose; and (C) double braid hose

4-29C, consists of an inner tube (1), a braid (2), a separator or friction layer (3), a second layer of braid (4), and an outer rubber cover (5), all vulcanized into one. Double braid hose has a higher working pressure than single braid hose. The inside diameter of some synthetic hoses are checked by a small ball of the I.D. size through it and these are described as "ball-tested" hose.

SHOP TALK _____

Since the solvents in some coatings used in refinishing would readily attack and destroy ordinary rubber compounds, fluid hose is lined with special solvent-resistant material that is impervious to all common solvents.

HOSE SIZE

With both the air and fluid (material) hoses, it is important to use the proper size and type to deliver the air from the compressor and the material from its source to the air tools and guns. When compressed, air must travel a long distance; its pressure begins to drop. However, for a distance of up to 100 feet, this air pressure drop can be considered minimal when the proper hose is used. That is, make certain to employ only the hose constructed for compressed air use and with a rating of at least four times that of the maximum psi being used.

Table 4-3 indicates just how much pressure drop can be expected at different pressures with

TABLE 4-3: AIR PRESSURE DROP				
	Air Pressure Drop			
Size of Air Hose (ID)*	5-Foot Length	15-Foot Length	25-Foot Length	50-Foot Length
1/4 Inch	PSIG	PSIG	PSIG	PSIG
@ 40 PSIG†	0.4	7.5	10.5	16.0
@ 60 PSIG	4.5	9.5	13.0	20.5
@ 80 PSIG	5.5	11.5	16.0	25.0
5/16 Inch				
@ 40 PSIG	0.5	1.5	2.5	4.0
@ 60 PSIG	1.0	3.0	4.0	6.0
@ 80 PSIG	1.5	3.0	4.0	8.0
3/8 Inch				
@ 40 PSIG	1.0	1.0	2.0	3.5
@ 60 PSIG	1.5	2.0	3.0	5.0
@ 80 PSIG	2.5	3.0	4.0	6.0

*ID: Inner diameter
†PSIG: Pounds per square inch gauge

hoses of varying length and internal diameters. At low pressure and with short lengths of hose this drop is not particularly significant, but as the pressure is increased and the hose lengthened, the pressure drop rapidly becomes very large and must be compensated for. Too often a tool is blamed for malfunctioning when the real cause is an inadequate supply of compressed air resulting from using too small an inner diameter (ID) hose.

MAINTENANCE OF HOSES

A hose will last a long time if it is properly cared for and maintained. Caution should be taken when it is dragged across the floor. It should never be pulled around sharp objects, run over by vehicles, kinked, or otherwise abused. Hose that ruptures in the middle of a job can ruin or delay the work.

The fluid hose can be cleaned using a hose cleaner, a device that forces a mixture of solvent and air through the fluid hose and spray guns, ridding them of paint residue. A valve stops the flow of solvent and allows air to dry the equipment. Clean the fluid hose internally with the proper solvent when the gun is cleaned.

The outside of both the air and fluid hose should be wiped down with solvent at the end of every job, then stored by hanging up in coils.

CONNECTORS

Connections are necessary among the compressor, the ends of hoses, and the air tools. Of the many different types used, the most common are the threaded and quick-connect types. The former is a screw type fitting and is usually tightened with a wrench, while the quick-connect is readily attached and detached by hand (Figure 4-30).

Both types of connections use the compression ring system to mount the fittings to the air or fluid hose. The system employs a ring that is slipped over the end of the hose. The stem on the fitting is in-

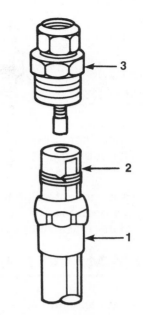

FIGURE 4-31 Compression ring connection installation

serted into the hose, and then a sleeve is slipped on and tightened. It forms a perfect seal against the ridges of the stem. The compression ring fitting has a number of advantages. It is economical, in that all of the parts are reusable, it forms a perfect seal free of leaks, and there is no pinching or distortion of the hose cover. The fittings are easily removed and reattached without special tools.

To install a compression ring connection, slip the sleeve (1) and the compression ring (2) over the end of the hose as shown in Figure 4-31. Hold the body (3) of the connection in a vise, and push the hose into the body as far as it will go. Slide the compression ring up to the body and bring the sleeve over the ring and thread it on by hand. Tighten it with a wrench.

Most paint spray guns require either 1/4- or 5/8-inch hoses; air hoses for pneumatic tools usually have 5/8 to 3/8-inch inside diameters. A few of the air tools described in Chapter 2 require hoses of specified inside diameters, which the tool manufacturers usually supply.

ADAPTERS AND COUPLINGS

An adapter is a type of connection, shown in Figure 4-32A, which is male on one end and female on the other. It is used to convert the connections on the hose and other equipment from one thread size to another. Adapters are available in a very wide variety of sizes and threads.

A coupling is a type of connection, illustrated in Figure 4-32B, that is male on both ends. It is used to

FIGURE 4-30 Quick-connect coupler kit

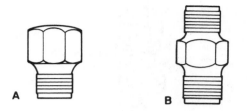

FIGURE 4-32 Typical compressed air hose line (A) adapter and (B) coupling

couple two pieces of hose or pipe together or to convert a female connection of one size thread to a male connection of another size thread.

AIR SYSTEM MAINTENANCE

The manufacturer's specific maintenance schedule given in the owner's manual should be followed exactly. In general, however, all air systems require the following periodic maintenance:

DAILY

- Drain the air receiver and drain the moisture separator/regulator or air transformer. If the weather is humid, drain them several times a day.
- Check the level of the oil in the crankcase. While it should be kept at full level, do not overfill. Overfilling causes excessive oil usage.
- SAE 10W-30, a multigrade oil, can be used as a substitute when SAE 10 or 20 weight oil is not readily available. Multigrade oils do contain additives that can cause harmful carbon residue and varnish. Detergent type oils are satisfactory if used before hard carbon deposits have developed. Before changing to a detergent type oil, pistons, rings, valves, and cylinder head should be cleaned since the detergent oil can loosen hard carbon deposits that can plug passages and damage cylinders and bearings.

WEEKLY

- Pull the ring on the safety valve and unseat it. If the valve is working properly, it will release air as follows:
  —Valves located on the air receiver or check valve release air when the tank contains compressed air.
  —Valves located on the compressor inner cooler release air only during compressor operation.

Repeat the safety valve by pushing down the stem with a finger. If the valve malfunctions, repair or replace immediately.

- Clean air strainers. Felt and foam air strainers should be washed in nonexplosive solvent, allowed to dry, and reinstalled. A dirty air strainer decreases compressor efficiency and will increase oil usage.
- Clean or blow off fins on cylinders, heads, intercoolers, aftercoolers, and any other parts of the compressor or outfit that collect dust or dirt. A clean compressor runs cooler and provides longer service.
- Check the oil filter in the air line and change the filter element if necessary.

MONTHLY

- Add or change the compressor crankcase oil. Under **clean** operating conditions, the oil should be changed at the end of 500 running hours or every six months, whichever occurs first. If operating conditions are **not clean**, change oil more frequently.
- Adjust the pressure switch cut-in and cut-out settings.
- Check relief valve or CPR for exhausting head pressure each time the motor stops.
- Tighten belts to prevent slippage. A heated motor pulley is a sign of loose belts. Overtightening of belts can cause motor overload or premature failure of motor and compressor bearings.
- Check and align a loose motor pulley or compressor flywheel. It will be necessary to remove the front section of the enclosed belt guard.
- Tighten all valve plugs and covers on the compressor head to insure that each valve does not become loose and damage the valve or piston.
- Check for air leaks on the compressor outfit and air piping system.
- Check compressor pump up time when the air receiver outlet valve is closed.
- Listen for unusual noises.
- Check and correct oil leaks.
- Perform weekly maintenance.

AIR SYSTEM SAFETY

An air compressor system is a very **safe** arrangement to operate. Accidents seldom happen, but the few that do occur can usually be traced to **human error.** To lessen the chance of human error, keep in mind the following safety precautions that should always be observed:

 SHOP TALK _____

- **Read the instructions.** *Learn what each part of the compressor does by carefully reading the owner's manual that comes with the unit.*
- **Inspect before each use.** *Carefully check the hoses, fittings, air control equipment, and overall appearance of the compressor before each use. Never operate a damaged unit.*
- **Proper electrical outlets.** *Electrical damage often results from using improperly grounded outlets. Use only a properly grounded outlet that will accept a three-prong plug.*
- **Always run the compressor on a dry surface.** *The compressor should be located where there is a circulation of clean, dry air. Avoid getting dust, dirt, and paint spray on the unit.*
- **Starts and stops.** *Most compressors start and stop automatically. Never attempt to service a unit that is connected to a power supply.*
- **Keep hands away.** *Fast moving parts will cause injury. Keep fingers away from the compressor while it is running.* **Do not** *wear loose clothing that will get caught in the moving parts.* **Unplug** *the compressor before working on it.*
- **Keep the belt guard on.** *Use all the safety devices available and keep them in operating condition. Also, remember that compressors become hot during operation. Exercise caution before touching the unit.*
- **Release air slowly.** *Fast moving air will stir dust and debris.* **Be safe!** *Release air slowly by using a pressure regulator to reduce pressure to that recommended for the tool.*
- **Keep air hose untangled.** *Keep the air, power, and extension cords away from sharp objects, chemical spills, oil spills, and wet floors. All of these can cause injury.*
- **Depressurize the tank.** *Be sure the pressure regulator gauge reads zero before removing the hose or changing the air tools. The quick release of high pressure air can cause injury.*

REVIEW QUESTIONS

1. Which type of compressor is seldom found in a paint shop?
   a. piston reciprocating type compressor
   b. diaphragm compressor
   c. one-stage compressor
   d. two-stage compressor

2. The piston compressor is _____ .
   a. less durable than the diaphragm compressor
   b. more durable than the diaphragm compressor
   c. one that requires lubrication
   d. both b and c

3. This is the actual amount of free air in cubic feet that the compressor can pump in 1 minute at working pressure.
   a. cfm
   b. displacement cfm
   c. free air cfm
   d. psi

4. What does the displacement of a two-stage compressor equal?
   a. the sum of the two stages
   b. the difference between the stages
   c. that given for the first stage
   d. none of the above

5. Air tanks have _____ .
   a. horizontal mountings
   b. vertical mountings
   c. horizontal mounted wheels
   d. all of the above
   e. both a and c

6. Which safety control is designed to maintain a supply of air within given pressure limits on gasoline and electrically driven compressors when it is not practical to start and stop the motor?
   a. pressure switch
   b. automatic unloader
   c. centrifugal pressure release
   d. overload protection

7. What is the recommended fuse rating for a fused disconnect switch?
   a. equal to the current rating stamped on the meter
   b. twice the current rating stamped on the motor
   c. three times the current rating stamped on the motor
   d. none of the above

8. The intake air filter must be made of
   _____ .
   a. fiberglass
   b. fine mesh
   c. felt material
   d. all of the above
   e. both b and c

9. How far away from the compressor unit should an air transformer be installed?
   a. at least 5 feet
   b. at least 15 feet
   c. at least 25 feet
   d. at least 35 feet

10. Which of the following is often combined with a lubricator in a single unit?
    a. thermal conditioning equipment
    b. air condenser
    c. air pressure regulator
    d. both b and c
    e. none of the above

11. How much pressure is dropped at 60 PSIG when using a 50-foot length 1/4-inch (ID) air hose?
    a. 20.5
    b. 6.0
    c. 4.5
    d. 1.5

12. Painter A wipes down the outside of both the air and fluid hoses with a solvent after every job. Painter B wipes down only the fluid hoses. Who is right?
    a. Painter A
    b. Painter B
    c. Both A and B
    d. Neither A nor B

13. Painter A checks the level of the oil in the crankcase on a monthly basis. Painter B checks it daily. Who is right?
    a. Painter A
    b. Painter B
    c. Both A and B
    d. Neither A nor B

14. How often should the air transformer be drained in humid weather?
    a. several times a day
    b. daily
    c. every other day
    d. weekly

15. How often should the compressor crankcase oil be changed under normal circumstances?
    a. monthly
    b. every six months
    c. every 2,000 running hours
    d. every 1,000 running hours

CHAPTER FIVE

MINOR AUTO BODY REPAIRS

Objectives

After reading this chapter, you will be able to:

- list the different types of body fillers and glazes.
- choose the correct plastic body filler for a particular repair job.
- identify the correct way to mix filler and hardener.
- explain how to repair scratches, nicks, dings, surface rust, and rustouts with plastic filler and glazing putty.
- understand the basics of lead filling.

Plastic body filler is the finishing touch to most sheet metal repairs. Restoring bent and stretched metal to its exact original shape and dimension would be very time consuming and almost impossible in many instances. But after the basic shape and soundness of the damaged panel has been restored (to within 1/4 inch of its original contour) with proper metalworking techniques, the remaining minor blemishes can be quickly and easily masked with a thin coat of body filler. However, very careful attention must be given to preparation and application of plastic fillers. The permanence of the repair and the quality of the final finish is adversely affected by filler improperly mixed and applied. While most body repairs, including minor ones, are done by the body shop, the refinisher should have a knowledge of the materials and the basic procedures.

BODY FILLERS

Most auto body repairs require some application of plastic body filler. Plastic body filler is a fast, inexpensive way to restore the final contour of a damaged panel. But many body shops tend to skimp on the sheet metal repairs and simply hide the damage under a thick layer of filler. Body fillers were never meant to replace proper metalworking techniques. Before any fillers are applied, the damaged

panel should be returned to its correct shape and dimension by bumping, picking, and pulling. Stretched metal should be shrunk and high spots should be lowered. After the panel has been filed to locate low spots, low areas should be bumped or picked up so that no area is more than 1/4 inch below the original contour of the panel.

Before any filler is applied, all holes, cracks, and joint gaps must be welded or brazed. Conventional body fillers are very hygroscopic, which means they absorb moisture like a sponge when exposed to humid conditions. Unless filled with a waterproof pigment, the filler will absorb moisture through holes or cracks in the metal. The moisture will penetrate to the metal where rust will begin to form. Eventually, the rust will destroy the bond between the filler and the metal.

Body fillers and putties can also be used to repair minor defects, such as dings, nicks, surface rust, and rustouts. Procedures for making these minor auto body repairs are given in this chapter. Be aware, though, that plastic body fillers have limitations. Large panels such as hoods, deck lids, and door panels tend to vibrate violently under normal road conditions. Vibrations can crack and dislodge filler that is applied over an area that is too large or applied too thickly.

Care must also be taken when applying filler to semi-structural panels in unibody frames. Panels such as quarter panels and roofs absorb road shocks and torque flexing. Excessive fillers applied in these areas can be popped off by stresses in the panels. Plastic filler should also be used sparingly on rocker panels, lower rear wheel openings, and other areas subject to flying stones and rock chips. Nor should protruding body lines, fender or door edges, or other edges and corners that are subject to scrapes and bumps be shaped with filler.

CAUTION: Plastic body fillers are hazardous materials. Always wear an approved dust mask when sanding filler. Filler dust can damage the eyes, throat, lungs, and liver.

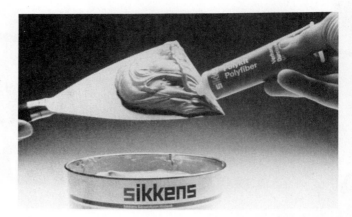

FIGURE 5-1 Chemical catalyst, called hardener, is mixed with body filler. *(Courtesy of America Sikkens, Inc.)*

GENERAL DESCRIPTION

Plastic body filler is very similar to paint in composition. Both are made of resins, pigments, and solvents. Most plastic body fillers have a polyester resin that acts as a binder. When the filler is applied and the solvents evaporate, the binders hold the pigments together in a tough, durable film. The basic pigment or filler in conventional fillers is talc. Talc, also used in baby powders, absorbs moisture. That is good for the baby but bad for the car if proper steps are not taken to shield the filler from moisture. If holes in the metal or cracks in the paint expose the filler to the atmosphere, the talc in the filler absorbs moisture, which attacks the metal substrate and forms rust. The rust destroys the filler-to-metal bond, causing the filler to fall off. Waterproof fillers are available. Fiberglass strands or metal particles are used instead of talc as pigments.

Like enamel paints, plastic fillers harden by chemical action. Hardening, or curing, produces a molecular structure that will not shrink or soften. The chemical reaction is set off by oxygen. If the container of plastic filler is open and left exposed to the oxygen in the atmosphere, it will slowly harden. To speed up the process, a chemical catalyst is provided by the manufacturer. The catalyst, in liquid or cream form, is called **hardener** (Figure 5-1). Hardener is basically a chemical compound called peroxide. The oxygen in the peroxide drastically speeds up the curing process. As Table 5-1 shows, the filler will soon become too stiff to work in just a few minutes after adding hardener, depending on the ambient air temperature.

As the filler cures and hardens, the chemical reaction produces a tremendous amount of heat. For this reason, unused filler should not be dis-

carded in trash cans containing solvent-wet paper or cloths.

Curing fillers also produce a waxy coating, or paraffins, on the surface. The purpose of the paraffins in the filler is to form a film that prevents oxygen absorption from the atmosphere. The paraffins are suspended in the filler solvent and are carried to the surface when the solvents evaporate. The paraffins must be either removed with a wax and grease remover before being sanded or else filed off with a surform cheese grater.

TYPES OF BODY FILLERS

During the first 50 years of auto body repair, blemishes in sheet metal panels were corrected by applying lead filler. Lead filler or solder is an alloy of lead and tin. A welding torch is used to soften the solder and bond it to the body sheet metal. Before World War II, automobiles were made with heavy gauge steel panels that were unaffected by the heat used in the "tinning" operation. But changes began to take place in automotive construction in the late 1940s and early 1950s. In the economic boom following World War II, Americans began demanding larger and fancier cars. So, manufacturers re-

TABLE 5-1: EFFECT OF TEMPERATURE ON WORKING TIME	
Temperature	**Working Times**
100° F	3 to 4 minutes
85° F	4 to 5 minutes
77° F	6 to 7 minutes
70° F	8 to 9 minutes

sponded with vehicles made with thinner, larger, and more complex body panels. The thinner metals, however, made the old lead repair methods almost obsolete. The heat required for the lead filler warped the thin panels, and hammer-and-dolly work stretched metals too thin for filing. There was a real need for an inexpensive, time saving substitute.

In the early 1950s, epoxy-based fillers were developed. Usually mixed with aluminum powder, epoxy fillers cured very slowly and did not harden at all if applied too thickly.

In the middle 1950s the first polyester resin-based body fillers were developed. These fillers were made from the same resin used to make fiberglass boats and required mixing with a liquid hardener and accelerator. Since the fiberglass resin is very brittle when cured and depends on cloth or matte for flexibility, the early polyester body fillers were also very brittle and hard.

The early fillers were composed of approximately 40 percent (by weight) polyester resin and 60 percent talc. Because the thin resin was difficult to work with and cured hard and brittle, many applications eventually cracked and fell off the vehicle.

Early fillers had other problems, too. Plastic filler technology had still to develop the inhibitors used today to promote stability. Therefore, shelf life of the early fillers was very short. The original products were sold in quart cans only; yet, a very high percentage of the product hardened in the can before it could be used. Early fillers also used a clear liquid hardener that made it difficult to determine when the filler and hardener were thoroughly mixed. Incomplete mixing often resulted in soft spots in the repair area.

When the filler and hardener were properly mixed together, the filler dried very hard. Early fillers were difficult to file and had to be leveled with a grinder, resulting in choking clouds of dust that blanketed the shop. Low dust, straight-line air fillers had not been developed yet.

Finally, a product was developed that utilized more flexible polyester resins and benzoyl peroxide as a cream hardener. Black pigment was added to the resin and talc mixture and white pigment was added to the cream hardener. The contrasting colors provided a reference to ensure proper mixing of the two ingredients.

As the technology developed, body fillers became softer, easier to apply, and easier to shape. Fillers soon appeared in black, red, gray, white, and yellow. Cream hardeners in contrasting colors—red, white, green, and blue—were also developed to provide a mixing reference for the various colored polyester fillers. The softer fillers could also be grated while still semicured, thus reducing the amount of sanding required. Note that the addition of color does not affect the working characteristics of the filler.

Conventional body fillers have over 30 years of development backing them today. The premium heavyweights use very fine grain talc to provide superior workability, sandability, and featheredging. High-quality resins ensure excellent adhesion and quick curing properties. Most heavyweights can be grated in 10 to 15 minutes.

Table 5–2 summarizes the ingredients, characteristics, and applications of body fillers and putties.

Fiberglass Fillers

As thinner gauge sheet metal replaced the heavy gauge steel used on vehicles of the 1940s and 1950s, rust became a problem, especially in areas of the country where road salts are used in winter. A product was needed to repair rustouts. Because talc-filled body fillers absorb moisture readily, the available heavyweight fillers did not provide long lasting protection when used to repair rustouts.

To meet this demand for a waterproof filler, fiberglass-reinforced fillers were developed. Fiberglass fillers use fiberglass strands rather than talc as a bulking agent. These fillers are more flexible and stronger than conventional fillers. Because they are also waterproof, they can be used to bridge holes, tears, and rustouts.

Fiberglass fillers are available in two basic forms. One is formulated with short strands of fiberglass. The other is made with long strands. Short strand fiberglass fillers are generally used to repair small holes (approximately 1 to 1-1/2 inches in size). When used to repair larger holes, a fiberglass cloth or screen should be used as a back support. The short strand fillers can be sanded and finished as any conventional filler.

Long strand fiberglass products are designed to fill holes larger than 1-1/2 inches in size. The longer strands interlock and provide a much stronger patch. The long strand filler might also be used with fiberglass cloths or mattes to bridge even larger rustouts. The long strand fillers, however, are used only as a base. Smoother fillers, either short strand fiberglass fillers or conventional fillers, must be used for the final fill. Chopped fiberglass fibers are also available to be added to fillers to increase their strength.

Aluminum Fillers

Some manufacturers attempted to improve water resistance of their products by replacing part of the talc with aluminum powder. This small quantity

Filler	Composition	Characteristics	Application
TABLE 5-2: COMPARING FILLERS AND PUTTIES			
Conventional Fillers			
Heavyweight Fillers	Polyester resins and talc particles	Smooth sanding; fine feather-edging; nonsagging; less pinholing than lightweight fillers	Dents, dings, and gouges in metal panels
Lightweight Fillers	Microsphere glass bubbles; fine grain talc; polyester resins	Spreads easily; nonshrinking; homogenous; no settling	Dings, dents, and gouges in metal panels
Premium Fillers	Microspheres; talc; polyester resins; special chemical additives	Sands fast and easy; spreads creamy and moist; spreads smooth without pinholes; dries tack-free; will not sag	Dings, dents, and gouges in metal panels
Fiberglass-Reinforced Fillers			
Short Strand	Small fiberglass strands; polyester resins	Waterproof; stronger than regular fillers	Fills small rustouts and holes. Used with fiberglass cloth to bridge larger rustouts.
Long Strand	Long fiberglass strands; polyester resins	Waterproof; stronger than short strand fiberglass fillers; bridges small holes without matte or cloth	Cracked or shattered fiberglass. Repairing rustouts, holes, and tears.
Specialty Fillers			
Aluminum Filler	Aluminum flakes and powders; polyester resins	Waterproof; spreads smoothly; high level of quality and durability	Restoring classic and exotic vehicles
Finishing Filler/ Polyester Putty	High-resin content; fine talc particles; microsphere glass bubbles	Ultra-smooth and creamy; tack-free; nonshrinking; eliminates need for air dry type glazing putty	Fills pinholes and sand scratches in metal, filler, fiberglass, and old finishes.
Sprayable Filler/ Polyester Primer-Surfacer	High-viscosity polyester resins; talc particles; liquid hardener	Virtually nonshrinking; prevents bleed-through; eliminates primer/glazing/ primer procedure	Fills file marks, sand scratches, mildly cracked or crazed paint films, and pinholes. Seals fillers and old finishes against bleed-through.

of aluminum powder did not stop moisture failures because of the talc still remaining in the formula. Another complaint was the short shelf life of the aluminized products since aluminum is, itself, a catalyst for polyester resin.

The first talc-free, 100 percent aluminum auto body filler was developed in England and was introduced into the United States under the name "Alum A Lead." The shelf life problem was solved by packaging the resin and powder separately; mixing was done by the refinisher.

The first premixed, 100 percent aluminum auto body fillers were introduced in 1965. This product was waterproof, used a red-tinted liquid hardener, and had a fairly good shelf life. Due to their very high relative costs, the 100 percent aluminum-filled body fillers are used sparingly on special applications, such as restoring antique cars. Today there are several similar 100 percent aluminum products available. Metal fillers are nonshrinking, waterproof, and very smooth. When cured, they are harder than talc or fiberglass-filled plastic fillers.

Lightweight Fillers

Until the middle 1970s only minor improvements were made to conventional heavyweight fillers. With the invention of microsphere glass bubbles by 3M came the technology to produce the modern, lightweight auto body fillers of the 1980s (Figure 5-2). Lightweight fillers were formulated by replacing about 50 percent of the talc in the filler with tiny glass spheres. The resulting higher resin content dramatically improved the filing and sanding characteristics of the filler as well as improved the filler's adhesion and water resistance. Most lightweight fillers are homogenous. The glass bubbles remain suspended in the resin and do not settle to the bottom of the can. This homogenous composition allows lightweight fillers to be packaged in plastic bags or cans and dispensed with rollers or compressed air or squeezed out with a plastic spreader (Figures 5-3, 5-4, and 5-5). The plastic bags keep the filler fresh and eliminate much of the wasted filler sometimes associated with canned fillers.

By the middle 1980s lightweight body filler technology was shared by most manufacturers, and major brands again became very similar to each

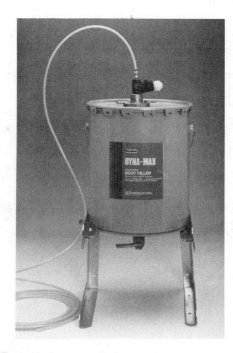

FIGURE 5-4 5-gallon pneumatic cans or roller dispenser. *(Courtesy of Dynatron/Bondo Corp.)*

FIGURE 5-2 Lightweight fillers with microsphere glass beads

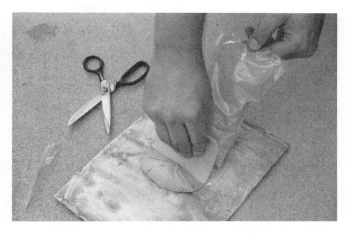

FIGURE 5-5 Lightweight fillers in a plastic pack.

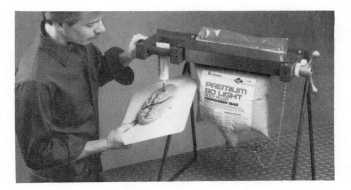

FIGURE 5-3 Roller dispensers for lightweight fillers. *(Courtesy of Oatey Corporation)*

other in working characteristics. Lightweight fillers quickly became the most popular filler used. Nationally, lightweight fillers represent more than 80 percent of the total filler used in paint shops.

Premium Fillers

Filler manufacturers in the mid 1980s have taken advantage of new technology to produce premium quality fillers. Premium fillers have superior performance qualities that go beyond the capabilities of conventional lightweight fillers. Premium fillers are moist and creamy. They spread easily yet will not sag on vertical surfaces. They dry tack-free without

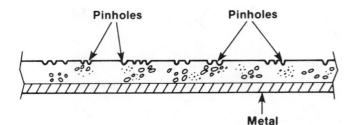

Pinholes   Pinholes

Metal

Glazing Putty (Before Sanding)

Metal

After Sanding,
Pinholes Filled
With Putty

Metal

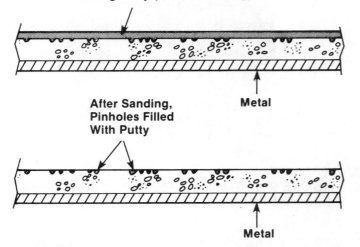

FIGURE 5-6 Glazing putty fills pinholes.

pinholing. Best of all, premium fillers are easy to sand. The smooth finish and ease of sandability reduce the time and labor involved in filling and shaping the repair.

Spot and Glazing Putties

Because mixing, applying, and shaping of body fillers usually creates tiny pinholes and sand scratches, glazing putties have been developed to fill the minor surface imperfections and produce a perfectly smooth surface. Until the mid 1980s a nitrocellulose glazing putty was used for this purpose almost exclusively. Nitrocellulose glazing putties are actually very thick lacquer paints. They have a high concentration of solids and, like lacquer paints, cure by solvent evaporation. Glazing putties should be used only to fill very shallow sand scratches and pinholes (Figure 5-6). Maximum filling depth is only 1/32 inch. Although glazing putties featheredge very nicely, they do not develop the hardness of a body filler. When coated with primer or paint, putties absorb paint solvents and swell. Sufficient time must be allowed for the putty to fully cure again before finish sanding of the finish coats. Because if the putty is sanded too soon, sand scratches will appear in the finish as the putty dries completely and shrinks below the sanded surface.

Polyester Glazing Putty

In the 1980s, the European basecoat/clear coat paint system became popular in the United States. The new basecoat/clear coat paint systems stirred up a problem that had occurred occasionally since the inception of the candy and mother-of-pearl colors in the late 1960s. The rich solvents and multicoats required for these "trick" paint jobs caused the pigment from the cream hardener in the body filler to "bleed" and stain the finish on light colors, usually after several days of exposure to sunlight. The widespread use of basecoat/clear coat products and other multicoat systems has made this staining problem a more frequent occurrence.

Developing a body filler that will not stain results in either extremely high cost or working prop-

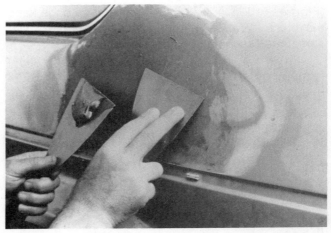

FIGURE 5-7 Applying polyester putty

FIGURE 5-8 Sprayable polyester primer-filler. *(Courtesy of America Sikkens, Inc.)*

erties not acceptable to most body technicians. At present, the only absolutely stain-free fillers are liquid hardener-catalyzed aluminum fillers.

To solve the staining problem, body filler manufacturers have developed a fine-grained, catalyzed polyester glazing putty (Figure 5-7). Polyester glazing putty does not shrink, has excellent dimensional stability, and resists solvent penetration (the cause of bleed-through). When applied over traditional body fillers, polyester glazing putties effectively solve the bleed-through problem. Bleed-through problems can also be avoided by using a sprayable polyester filler (Figure 5-8). This type of primer-surfacer has polyester resins and talc fillers and must be catalyzed with a liquid hardener. Sprayed from a gravity feed gun (Figure 5-9), polyester primers fill minor imperfections and seal both fillers and old paint finishes.

REPAIRING SCRATCHES

Most vehicles brought to the refinishing shop for damage repair and/or refinishing have a variety of minor imperfections in the paint. Some defects, such as chalking or scuff marks, can be removed with rubbing compound. The abrasive compound removes the damaged surface paint and brings out the luster in the paint beneath. Compounding is discussed at length in Chapter 11. Other defects, such as a scratch, are too deep to buff out with rubbing compound. If the scratch penetrates through the primer and exposes the metal underneath, the scratch must be repaired using the technique for repairing nicks and chips discussed later in this chapter. On the other hand, shallow scratches that are too deep to be buffed out, but do not reach the metal underneath the paint, can be filled with putty or a polyester primer-surfacer. An example of such a scratch is shown in Figure 5-10.

PREPARING THE SURFACE

Wash and clean the repair area with a wax and grease removing solvent; then lightly sand the scratched areas. Use a sanding block when sanding large areas, but a 9 inch by 11 inch sheet of #240 grit paper folded three ways is fine for small areas. A light sanding will rough up the finish coat so the glazing putty and new primer will adhere to the old finish. Do not press hard on the sandpaper. Excessive pressure can result in low spots or a wavy surface that will require additional filling and sanding. After the rough sanding is complete, clean the sanded area with compressed air or a soft cotton cloth and wipe with a tack cloth.

APPLYING GLAZING PUTTY

If the scratch is part of a larger panel being refinished, try filling the repair area with the primer-surfacer. Some sprayable polyester primers will provide up to 15 mils of fill. Another solution is to fill the scratch with glazing putty.

Following the instructions on the tube of putty, apply a daub on the edge of a clean rubber contour squeegee. A little bit of putty goes a long way. When filling only scratches and low spots, do not squeeze too much putty onto the spreader.

FIGURE 5-9 Applying sprayable filler with a gravity feed gun

FIGURE 5-10 A shallow scratch

FIGURE 5-11 Applying glazing putty to scratch

FIGURE 5-12 Sanding repair area

Using moderate pressure, spread putty over the repair area. Apply it with the rubber squeegee (Figure 5-11) and use a fast scraping motion. Apply in one direction only. Do not pass the squeegee over the same area more than once. Multiple passes can pull the putty away from the body.

Allow the putty to dry completely. Drying time varies with the putty's thickness, but it usually takes between 20 and 60 minutes. For best results, allow the putty to dry overnight before sanding. Sanding the putty before it completely cures will result in sand scratches in the finish.

SANDING THE GLAZING PUTTY

After the putty dries, sand the repair area with #240 grit sandpaper. Wet sand to prevent putty from clogging the paper and creating more scratches in the finish. Use a sanding block to avoid making low spots with finger pressure.

When sanding, rub the palm of the hand over the puttied area to feel for high spots on the surface. When finished, rinse the sludge away and wipe the surface dry. Clean the repair area with a tack cloth.

Inspect the scratch for low spots and voids in the putty. If the scratch requires additional putty, repeat the above procedure. When the surface of the previously scratched area is free of imperfections, it is ready for priming and refinishing.

PRIMING THE GLAZING PUTTY

Once the scratched surface is filled with putty and sanded level with the surrounding panel, the repair area must be sanded to a smooth finish and then primed.

Use water, a sanding block, and #400 grit sandpaper to finish sanding the puttied scratch (Figure 5-12). Wet sanding prevents the paper from clogging and creating additional scratches. The sanding block helps avoid creating low spots in the finish. Sand with light pressure and long strokes across the face of the repair. Do not concentrate or bear down on any one spot; doing so will almost guarantee a low spot. Low spots created by finish sanding must be filled with additional glazing putty.

When satisfied with the smoothness of the repair, rinse away sanding sludge and wipe the surface dry. Clean the area with a tack cloth. When it is dry and free of dust, spray a medium coat of primer over the entire repair area (Figure 5-13). Allow the primer to flash or surface dry for about 5 minutes; then wet sand the primer with #400 grit sandpaper. Repeat this process until the repair area is glassy smooth. When glassy smoothness is achieved, the surface is ready for painting.

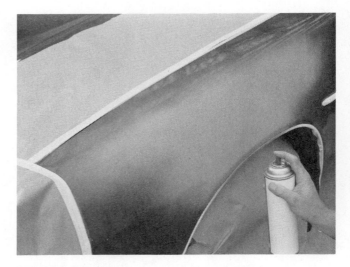

FIGURE 5-13 The primed repair area

REPAIRING NICKS

Minor bumps and scrapes often leave nicks and scratches in a car's finish. A stone thrown up by a passing vehicle can chip the paint, exposing the sheet metal beneath. Side swipe collisions result in scrapes and gouges. Anytime bare metal is exposed to the air, rust formation must be inhibited with primer before the new finish is applied. A large nick is shown in Figure 5-14.

FEATHEREDGING THE OLD FINISH

After cleaning and dewaxing the repair area, the first step in repairing a nick or deep scratch is sanding the ragged edges of the chipped paint to a smooth surface. This is commonly referred to as featheredging. Featheredging tapers the edges of the paint so that it gradually blends in with the metal surface.

Featheredging chips and nicks is quickly done with a #80 grit disc and a DA. In tight spots, use a sanding block (Figure 5-15). Sand the edges of the

FIGURE 5-14   A sizeable nick in the finish

FIGURE 5-15   Featheredging the nick

old finish to a fine taper. When the sanded area is smooth to the touch, switch to #180 or #240 grit sandpaper and sand any sandpaper scratches away.

APPLYING PRIMER AND PUTTY

After the nicked paint edges are sanded to a smooth surface, clean the metal with a metal conditioner. Metal conditioner is an acid compound that neutralizes microscopic rust particles. The acid also etches the metal to improve the bond between metal and primer. Metal conditioners are discussed fully in Chapter 9. Never leave bare metal surfaces exposed to air. Moisture in the air quickly encourages rust to form on the metal. The slightest film of rust will prevent the paint from properly adhering to the metal. Subsequent lifting and blistering will eventually ruin the paint, and the area will have to be sanded down and refinished again. Priming the bare metal areas with a zinc chromate base primer inhibits rust formation and ensures good bonding of the finish paint.

Blow away any sanding dust and wipe the area with a tack cloth. Then, apply a coat of primer-filler to build up the area and fill any uneven featheredging. After the primer has dried, apply a mist coat of gray primer, block sand the area to identify low spots, and apply glazing putty to fill the low spots (Figure 5-16).

APPLYING FINISHING PRIMER

Final sanding and priming are necessary to achieve a super smooth surface. Wet sand with #400 grit sandpaper and a sanding block. Sand in long, straight strokes to avoid creating low spots. When

FIGURE 5-16   Applying glazing putty

sanding curved surfaces, sand very lightly holding the paper with the palm of the hand or use a flexible sander.

Clean, dry, and wipe the sanded surface with a tack cloth. Then, spray the repair area with primer. Completely cover the puttied area and several inches of the old finish around it. Allow the primer to flash (surface dry) for 5 minutes; then sand lightly with water and #240 grit sandpaper.

Clean and prime once or twice more. Between coats, wet sand lightly with #400 or #600 grit sandpaper to achieve an extremely smooth surface. The surface is now ready to be painted.

REVIEW QUESTIONS

1. Which of the following is contained in plastic body filler?
   a. resins
   b. pigments
   c. solvents
   d. all of the above

2. Which of the following substances is used in body fillers to prevent oxygen absorption from the atmosphere?
   a. hardener
   b. peroxide
   c. paraffins
   d. both a and b
   e. none of the above

3. Fiberglass fillers are _____ .
   a. waterproof
   b. available in three basic forms
   c. never used to bridge rustouts
   d. all of the above

4. Lightweight fillers have improved
   _____ .
   a. filing characteristics
   b. sanding characteristics
   c. water resistance
   d. all of the above
   e. both a and b

5. A body filler that does not bleed through a basecoat/clear coat paint _____ .
   a. is very expensive
   b. is liquid hardener-catalyzed aluminum filler
   c. has excellent working properties
   d. all of the above
   e. both a and b

6. If too little hardener is used, the filler
   _____ .
   a. will not adhere to the metal
   b. will be subject to rampant pinholing
   c. will be easier to handle
   d. none of the above

7. Wiping over the repaired area with solvents before applying the mixed filler
   _____ .
   a. improves adhesion
   b. illuminates pinholes
   c. is a mistake
   d. both a and b

8. The first step in repairing nicks is
   _____ .
   a. sanding the ragged edges of the paint to a smooth surface
   b. featheredging
   c. dewaxing
   d. both a and b
   e. none of the above

9. Once a ding has been properly filled and leveled, Painter A uses a dual-action sander to featheredge the surrounding paint edges. Painter B uses a block sander. Who is right?
   a. Painter A
   b. Painter B
   c. Both A and B
   d. Neither A nor B

10. Metal conditioner is _____ .
    a. an acid compound
    b. used to etch the metal surface
    c. used to neutralized rust
    d. all of the above
    e. both a and b

CHAPTER SIX

RESTORING CORROSION PROTECTION

Objectives

After reading this chapter, you will be able to:

- define corrosion and describe the common factors involved in rust formation.
- describe the anticorrosive materials used to prevent and retard rust formation.
- explain the conditions and events that lead to corrosion on the auto body.
- choose the correct anticorrosive application equipment for specific applications.
- outline the correct corrosion treatment procedures for each of the four general corrosion treatment areas.
- list the four types of seam sealers and explain where each should be used.

Corrosion is a problem that has always concerned paint shop technicians and refinishers. It requires either repair work (see Chapter 5) or special treatment when refinishing (see Chapter 9). But, with the following recent developments in the automotive industry, **corrosion prevention** has taken on new meaning to paint shop personnel:

- Once an auto body has been repaired after a collision, the rustproofing, undercoating, and sound deadening should be restored. Rustproofing, undercoating, and sound deadening had suggested a one-time application to the new vehicle by car dealerships and rustproofing franchises.
- Car manufacturers are including in their owner's manual instructions recommendations for sheet metal repair or replacement. They suggest that the paint shop should apply an anticorrosive material to the part repaired or replaced so that corrosion protection is restored.
- In affiliation with the Inter-Industry Conference on Auto Collision Repair (I-CAR), the insurance companies are promoting corrosion prevention repair to the paint shops.

- The increased usage of replacement panels in the paint shops requires widespread corrosion prevention treatment.
- Possibly the major reason, however, is the advent of the unibody car.

In unibody construction, the car's body panels are no longer cosmetic sheet metal. They now constitute the structural integrity of the vehicle. This means that rust is not just an eyesore. The unibody car has more welded joints in critical structural areas where corrosion can do serious damage. It is an ever present danger to the unibody vehicle since rusting of structural panels and rails can affect the driveability of the car and the safety of its passengers.

WHAT IS CORROSION?

Corrosion—or rust, when it occurs on steel—is the product of a complex chemical reaction with serious, costly consequences (Figure 6-1). Chemical corrosion requires three elements (Figure 6-2):

- Exposed metal
- Oxygen
- Moisture (electrolyte)

FIGURE 6-1 Closeup of car's number one enemy—rust

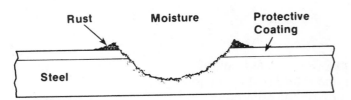

FIGURE 6-2 Breakdown in protective coating causes rapid rust formation.

In other words, the formula for rust in a car body is:

Iron + Oxygen + Electrolyte = Rust Iron Oxide

There are several kinds of rust (Figure 6-3). Three basic types of corrosion protection used on today's automobiles are:

- Galvanizing or zinc coating
- Paint
- Anticorrosion compounds

Galvanizing is a process of coating steel with zinc. It is one of the principal methods of corrosion protection applied during the manufacturing process. On galvanized steel, the zinc forms a natural barrier between the steel and the atmosphere. As the zinc corrodes, a layer of zinc oxide will form on the surface exposed to the atmosphere. Unlike iron oxide or rust, the zinc oxide adheres to the zinc coating tightly, forming a natural barrier between the zinc and the atmosphere. When the surface of the car's finish is damaged by a scratch or nick, the zinc coating undergoes corrosion, sacrificing itself to protect the iron under it. The resulting zinc oxide actually forms a protective coating and repairs the

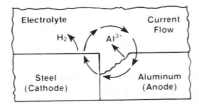

Galvanic or Bimetallic Corrosion

Galvanic corrosion occurs when two metals of dissimilar activity are placed in contact with one another in the presence of an electrolyte. The more active metal will anodize and corrode in preference to the less active metal which, as the cathode, is protected.

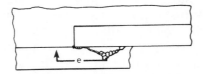

Crevice Corrosion at Lap Joint

Crevice corrosion also can occur between tightly sealed joints where the concealed metal surface is oxygen starved and electrolyte might seep between irregularities in the mating surfaces. This condition also occurs where moisture-bearing materials (such as felt) are in contact with the steel.

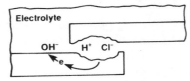

Crevice Corrosion at Lap Joint

Crevice corrosion showing acid formation and increased chloride ion concentration within the crevice.

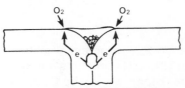

Crevice Corrosion at Joint

Crevice corrosion is caused by a gradient between the oxygen at the surface of the electrolyte and oxygen-starved electrolyte at the bottom of the crevice. Typical of weldments, sheet-metal joints, and rough surfaces where water might be trapped, the oxygen gradient also causes a rough microfinished surface to corrode faster than a smooth surface.

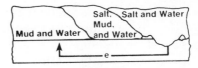

Poultice Corrosion

Electrolyte composition gradients are probably the most common cause of corrosion. Clumps of mud frequently collect under car fenders. The varying concentrations of salt and water encourage corrosion.

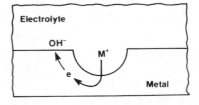

Pitting Corrosion

Similar to crevice corrosion, pitting corrosion occurs at localized areas where oxygen has been depleted, pH has become lowered and chloride has become enriched.

FIGURE 6-3 The many different kinds of rust *(Courtesy of American Iron and Steel Institute)*

FIGURE 6-4 The paint system used on the vehicle is a barrier against corrosion. *(Courtesy of Sherwin-Williams Co.)*

FIGURE 6-5 Anticorrosion material should be applied to an enclosed body section by a body technician.

exposed area of the steel. Thus, zinc performs a two fold protective process; first, it provides a natural barrier, and second, if it is exposed to the atmosphere, it is transformed into a protective zinc oxide coating over the exposed steel.

A paint system such as those described in later chapters of this book will provide a barrier between the atmosphere and the steel surface. When this barrier is in place (Figure 6-4), the moisture and impurities in the air cannot interact with the steel surface and the steel is protected from corrosion. If the paint surface or barrier is broken by a stone chip or scratch, the steel in this area is no longer isolated from the moisture and impurities in the air. Corrosion will then take place in this region. Corrosion will spread between the paint and steel surface. If the adhesion of the paint to the steel is poor, large sections of the paint can be separated from the steel. This will result in a large area of the steel being left unprotected, and severe rust in this region will quickly follow. If impurities are present between the paint and the steel, oxygen in the air can pass through the paint, reacting with the impurities and the steel to form rust. In this case, corrosion will take place on the steel surface and the protective paint barrier will be destroyed. Paint, by itself, is only effective as long as the paint film remains intact.

Anticorrosion compounds are additional coatings applied over the paint film. Protective coatings can be applied either by the manufacturer or as an aftermarket process. The two most popular types of anticorrosion coatings are:

- Petroleum-based compounds
- Wax-based compounds

Anticorrosion compounds are primarily used in enclosed body sections (Figure 6-5) and other rust prone areas.

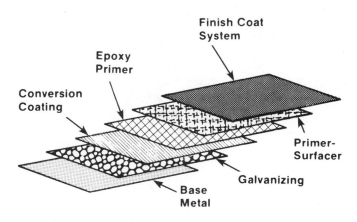

FIGURE 6-6 Typical buildup of corrosion prevention material used by car manufacturers.

The auto manufacturers are increasing their corrosion protection measures all the time. New processes and methods, including the use of coated steels, zinc rich primers, and more durable base coatings, have made it possible for modern cars to survive corrosive forces for longer periods than before. The following is a typical new car finishing sequence (Figure 6-6) used by major auto manufacturers:

1. Use coated or galvanized steel (Figure 6-7).
2. Chemically clean and rinse.
3. Apply conversion coating.
4. Apply epoxy primer.
5. Bake primer.
6. Apply primer-surfacer.
7. Apply color coats.
8. Bake color coats.
9. Apply anticorrosion materials.

Because of these better finishing procedures, corrosion protection warranties (Figure 6-8) of up to

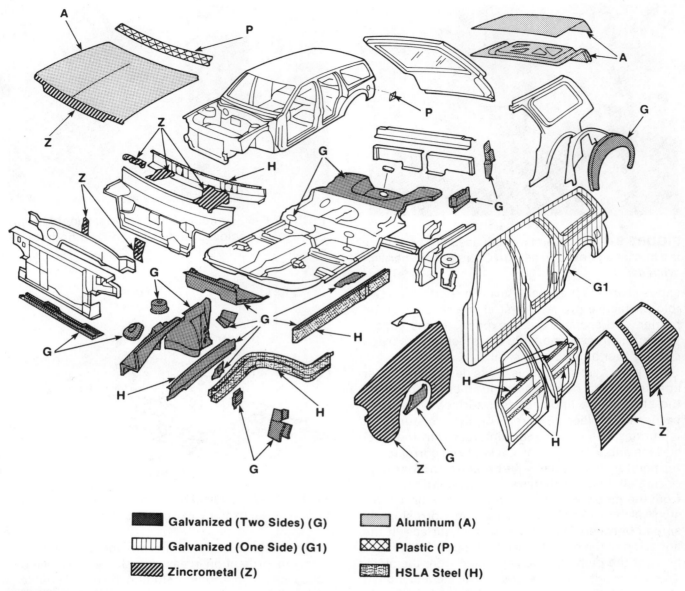

Galvanized (Two Sides) (G)   Aluminum (A)

Galvanized (One Side) (G1)   Plastic (P)

Zincrometal (Z)   HSLA Steel (H)

FIGURE 6-7 Exploded view of car body showing parts and types of coating

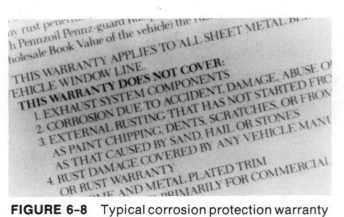

FIGURE 6-8 Typical corrosion protection warranty policy in use today

ten years are likely within the next few years. With these dramatic improvements in the performance of OEM products, the repair industry must rise to the challenge of producing corrosion resistance in repaired areas that matches or exceeds the durability of the original product. Repair work that does not stand up will draw attention to itself next to the outstanding durability of many original finishes. It can also draw liability challenges where issues of vehicle safety are involved. Remember, the paint shop technician is responsible for the quality and durability of the repairs completed. Remember that the customer is entitled to a car restored to the way it was before the damage occurred.

CAUSES FOR LOSS OF FACTORY PROTECTION

Even with all of the care taken to protect vehicles, breakdown still occurs. The breakdown of corrosion protection falls into three general categories:

- Paint film failure
- Collision damage
- Repair process

The paint film is the result of the entire process of coatings, primers, and color coats that the manufacturer applies. When the paint film fails, corrosion begins. Stone chips (Figure 6-9), moisture, and improper surface preparation can all lead to film failure.

During a collision, the protective coatings present on a car are damaged (Figure 6-10). This occurs not just in the areas of direct impact, but also in the indirect damage zones. Seams pull apart, caulking breaks loose, and paint chips and flakes. Locating and restoring the protection to all affected areas remains a key challenge for the paint technician.

Vehicle repair is possibly one of the major causes of protective coating damage. For example, repair procedures often require cutting body panels and seams either mechanically or with a plasma torch. Even minor straightening and stress relieving procedures can damage these protective coatings so corrosion can start. Normal welding temperatures cause zinc to vaporize and be lost from the weld area (Figure 6-11). Abrasive operations during repair and refinishing can also leave areas unprotected. After all welding and repair work has been completed, these damage points need careful attention to eliminate contaminants. Then steps must be taken to exclude the atmosphere from the metal by sealing all surfaces thoroughly.

FIGURE 6-10   During a collision, corrosion protection is usually damaged.

Other precautions that should be taken to protect the factory corrosion protection are:

- Remove only the minimum amount of paint film from affected areas such as welded points.
- Be extremely careful not to scratch any part except that to be repaired. If there is an accidental scratch, take necessary remedial measures.
- When clamping or holding the affected panels during body repair work (Figure 6-12), clamping tools can cause scratches on the panel. They must be treated to avoid rusting.
- While grinding (Figure 6-13), cutting, or welding panels, place protective covers over adjacent painted surfaces and surrounding

FIGURE 6-9   Stone chips can lead to rust spots.

FIGURE 6-11   Heat from welding and cutting operations destroys factory corrosion protection.

FIGURE 6-12 When clamping for body pulling, the body technician must be sure that all hold areas are corrosion treated after repairs are made.

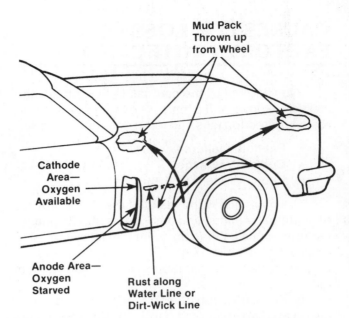

FIGURE 6-14 Inside-out corrosion caused by mud and debris packed against the underside of fenders is usually undetected until it eats through the metal.

FIGURE 6-13 Be sure all metal chips caused by grinding are cleaned up.

areas to protect them from the flame or metal chips.

- Cover any opening of the body sills and similar area with masking tape to prevent metal chips from entering during the grinding, cutting, or welding operation.
- Completely remove any metal chips from inside the body. Use a vacuum cleaner, not dry compressed air, to remove metal chips. If dry compressed air is used, metal chips can be blown out and accumulate in corner areas.

There are also some environmental and atmospheric conditions that help to influence the rate of corrosion. They are:

- **Moisture.** As the amount of sand, dirt, mud, and water on the underside of the body increases, so will the chances of corrosion accelerate (Figure 6-14). Floor sections that have snow and ice trapped under the floor matting will not dry. Likewise, if holes at the bottom of the doors and side sills (Figure 6-15) are not kept open, water will accumulate. Remember, water is one of the requirements for rust.
- **Relative Humidity.** Corrosion will be accelerated in areas of high relative humidity, especially those areas where the temperatures stay above freezing and where atmospheric pollution exists and road salt is used.
- **Temperature.** A temperature increase will accelerate the rate of corrosion to those parts that are not well ventilated.
- **Air Pollution.** Industrial pollution and acid rain, the presence of salt in the air in coastal areas, or the use of heavy road salt will accelerate the corrosion process. Road salt will also accelerate the disintegration of paint surfaces.

Another type of corrosion that must be considered when working on automobiles is known as galvanic corrosion. This occurs when two dissimilar metals are placed in contact with each other. The more chemically active of two metals will corrode, protecting the other metal in the process. As shown in Table 6-1, this is why zinc will sacrifice itself to

TINTING

BASE COLOR	ALUMINUM LETDOWN	MASS TONE	WHITE LETDOWN	BASE COLOR	ALUMINUM LETDOWN	MASS TONE	WHITE LETDOWN
1. Yellow Gold				15. Indo Orange			
2. Lt. Chrome Yellow	*Not to be used with Aluminum Letdown.*			16. Moly Orange (Red Shade)	*Not to be used with Aluminum Letdown.*		
3. Oxide Yellow				17. Red Oxide			
4. Indo Yellow				18. Transparent Red Oxide			
5. Transparent Yellow Oxide				19. Deep Violet			
6. Rich Brown				20. Quindo Violet			
7. Black				21. Magenta Maroon			
8. Strong Black				22. Phthalo Green (Yellow Shade)			
9. Organic Orange (Light)				23. Phthalo Green			
10. Oxide Red				24. Scarlet Red	*Not to be used with Aluminum Letdown.*		
11. Permanent Red				25. Perrindo Maroon			
12. Organic Scarlet				26. Phthalo Blue (Medium)			
13. Phthalo Blue (Green Shade)				27. Phthalo Green			
14. Permanent Blue				28. Phthalo Green (Yellow)			

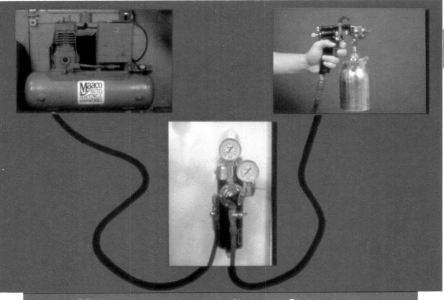

29. Important spray equipment: Compressor, Regulator and Gun

30. Easy way of determining the proper spray gun distance

31. Keep the gun parallel to the surface when spraying horizontally or downward

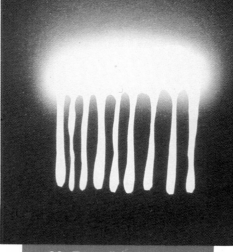

32. Split pattern

33. Even flood pattern

34. Heavy centered pattern

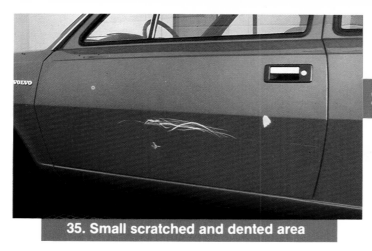

35. Small scratched and dented area

36. Sand and featheredge the damaged area

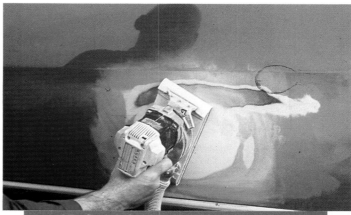

37. Sand the body filler with a flat sander or a sanding block.

38. After two or three coats of primer-surfacer have dried, wet-sand the surface

39. Applying the topcoat finish

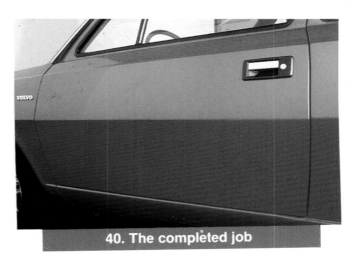

40. The completed job

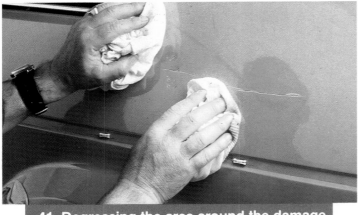

41. Degreasing the area around the damage

DENT AND DEEP SCRATCH PAINT REPAIRS

42. After sanding, fill with body filler. Avoid filling edges and scrape the outside edge away completely.

43. Dry sand the surface with a machine or by hand

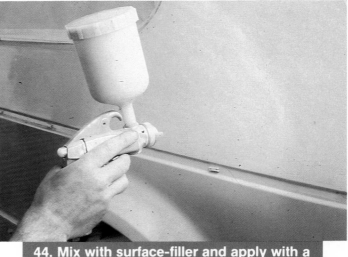

44. Mix with surface-filler and apply with a gravity feed spray gun

45. Remove the dirt with a tack rag. Keep the pressure light

46. Spraying the topcoat

47. The new panel installed

NEW PANEL PAINTING

48. Remove transport primer, if required by panel manufacturer, with paint stripper and clean with scraper and strong solvent

49. Sand surface with #120 or #150 grit, then remove the dust

50. After degreasing, apply 2 or 3 medium coats of primer-surfacer

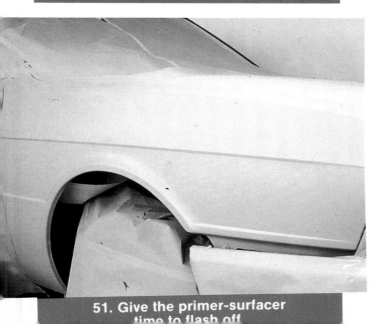

51. Give the primer-surfacer time to flash off

52. Applying the final topcoat

53. An undamaged car or a car that has been repaired

54. Apply primer-surfacer or sealer on any spots that need it, then degrease the surface

55. Abrade the surface with fine or extra fine sandpaper and remove the dust with a tack rag

A COMPLETE RE-SPRAY

56. Mix sealer as directed on the container, using a marked measuring stick

57. Applying the medium coat of sealer.

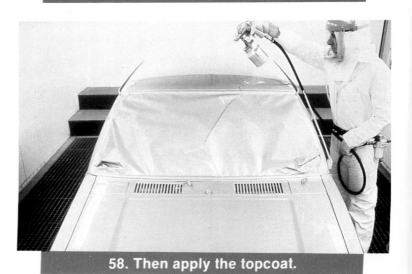
58. Then apply the topcoat.

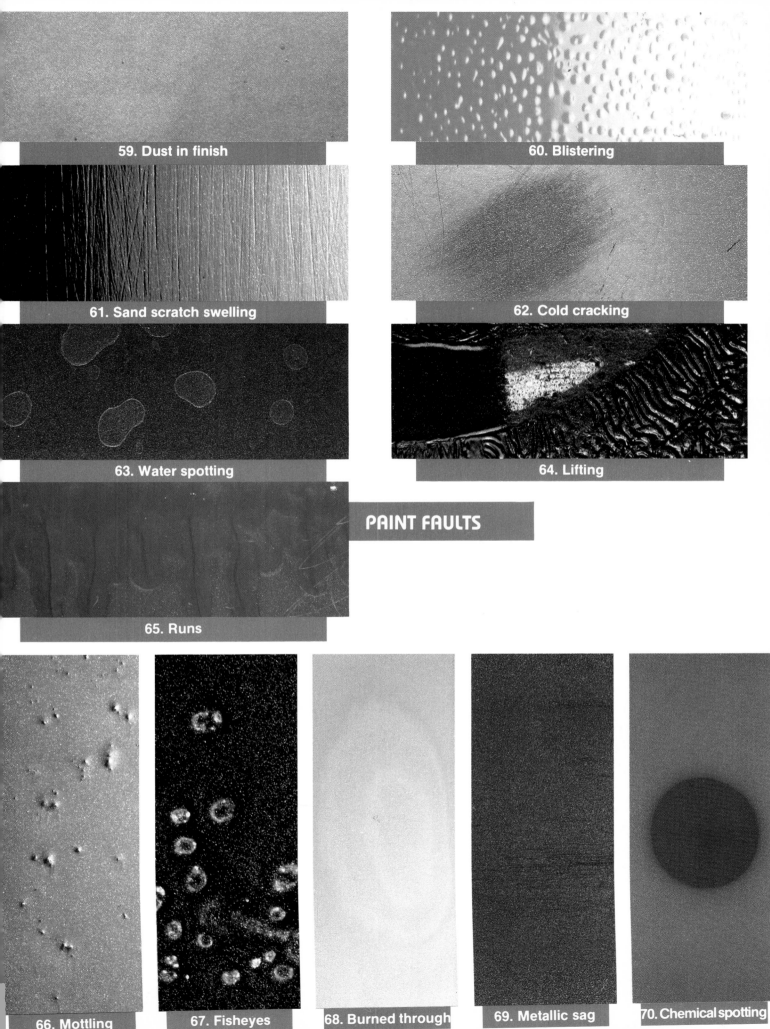

59. Dust in finish

60. Blistering

61. Sand scratch swelling

62. Cold cracking

63. Water spotting

64. Lifting

65. Runs

PAINT FAULTS

66. Mottling

67. Fisheyes

68. Burned through

69. Metallic sag

70. Chemical spotting

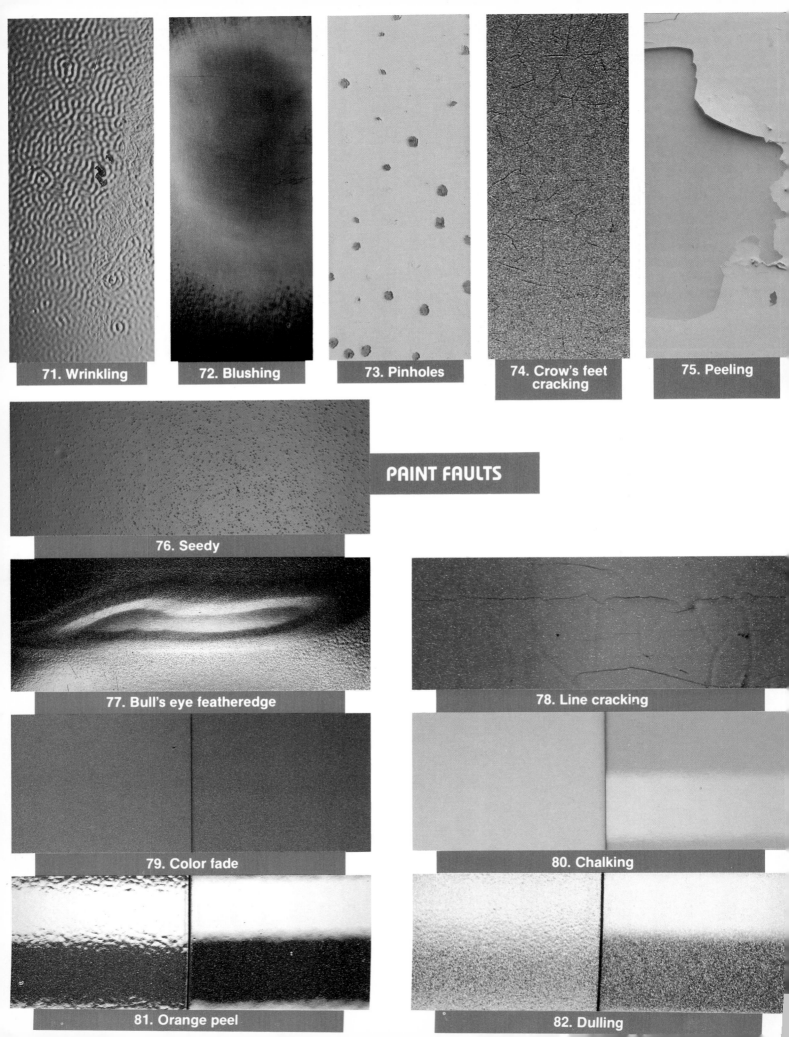

71. Wrinkling

72. Blushing

73. Pinholes

74. Crow's feet cracking

75. Peeling

PAINT FAULTS

76. Seedy

77. Bull's eye featheredge

78. Line cracking

79. Color fade

80. Chalking

81. Orange peel

82. Dulling

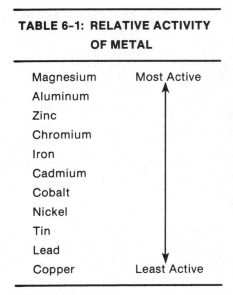

TABLE 6–1: RELATIVE ACTIVITY OF METAL

Magnesium	Most Active
Aluminum	
Zinc	
Chromium	
Iron	
Cadmium	
Cobalt	
Nickel	
Tin	
Lead	
Copper	Least Active

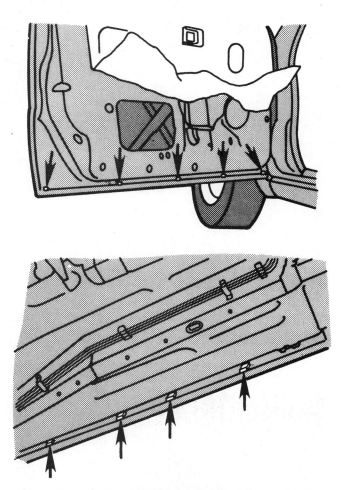

FIGURE 6–15 Keep drain holes open at the bottom of the doors, side sills, and so forth to avoid water accumulation. *(Courtesy of Nissan Motor Corp.)*

protect steel. In the case of other metals, as mentioned later in the chapter, galvanic corrosion can cause problems.

Regardless of the cause, if corrosion prevention is not practiced, the cost to the paint shop and insurer is comebacks or lost customers. Inadequate preparation that leaves dirt, grease, or acids on the metal will cause the loss of adhesion. Rust will start, a little at first, creating corrosive "hot spots" at the points of failure. Surface failure will progress quickly in unseen or enclosed areas, spreading under the surface coatings, eating deeper and deeper into the metal. Figure 6–16 illustrates some of the more common hot spots found on an automobile.

The main interests of the body shop in renewing corrosion protection generally are

- **Enclosed interior surfaces.** Includes body rails and rocker assemblies.
- **Exposed interior surfaces.** Including floor pan, apron, and hood sections.

- **Exposed joints.** Such as quarter-to-wheelhousing and quarter-to-trunk floor joints.
- **Exposed undercar exterior surfaces.** Such as fenders, quarter panels, and door skins.

The paint shop's main interest is the finishes of the vehicle's surface. But, like when performing minor repair techniques, the refinisher should know about the materials used.

ANTICORROSION MATERIALS

The paint shop's efforts in protecting car bodies from rusting should focus on creating a clean, chemically neutral surface on the sheet metal, then sealing the material under layers of paint. Under certain conditions, as mentioned earlier in the chapter, a wax- or petroleum-based anticorrosion compound is used to exclude air and moisture from the metal surface.

More and more new vehicles come off the assembly line today with anticorrosive materials that are available to the paint shop. Being able to replace or install these wax- or petroleum-based materials is very important to the knowledgeable refinisher.

Corrosion prevention has not always been a common paint shop operation. The original rustproofing was called undercoating, and it was an asphalt-based product that was sheer agony to apply, because it got not only on the underside of the car, but also on everything else within 20 feet of the application bay. But, worst of all, it did not work very well. In time, the solvents used would evaporate, the asphalt would harden and crack, and the moisture

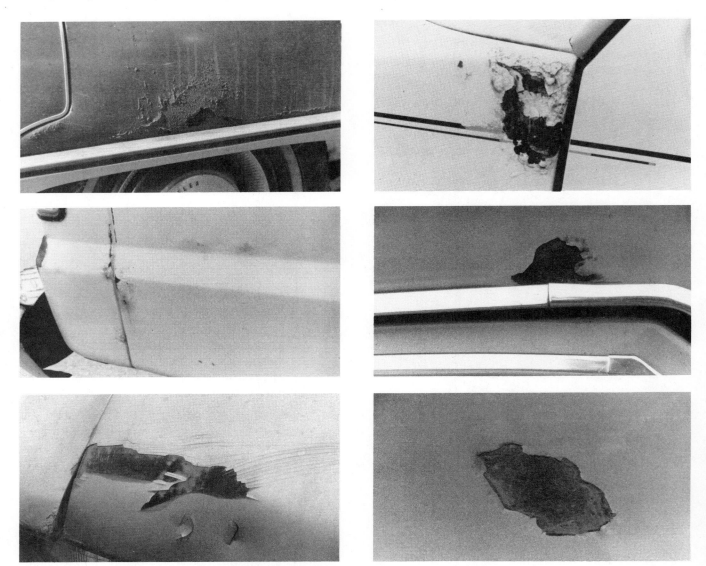

FIGURE 6-16 Common rust hot spots found on vehicles that would interest the painter

that causes oxidation would actually become trapped under the undercoating.

The asphaltic undercoats did have benefits in terms of sound deadening and preventing stone marks under fenders. And it is useful today on fiberglass panels for the same reasons. As a rustproofer, however, it probably was not the best.

When selecting a modern anticorrosive material, there are several things that should be considered:

- The material should be thin enough to flow or penetrate pinch weld cracks and to creep adequately to protect the exposed metal of such areas as the steel immediately adjacent to spot welds—a particularly tough rustproofing proposition.

- The material should have good adherence to both bare metal and painted surfaces. In addition to adhering to the surface, it should be highly resistant to water, cutting from stones thrown up from the road, ordinary solvent type materials used in the engine and elsewhere, and so forth. In other words, it should not only protect initially, it should also continue to protect. Material that does not retain some pliability and toughness will not do the job.
- It is important to choose a material without solvents that might have a lingering bad odor which could be present in a car when it is delivered.
- The product should be easy to clean up with ordinary and safe solvents.

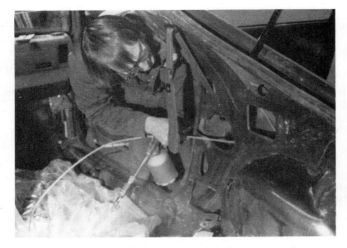

FIGURE 6-17 A body technician applying a typical anticorrosion compound

Anticorrosive materials or agents can be divided into three broad categories:

- **Anticorrosion compound (Figure 6-17).** As already mentioned, either wax- or petroleum-based compounds are resistant to chipping and abrasion; they can undercoat, sound deaden, and completely seal the surface of a car from the destructive causes of rust and corrosion. They should be applied to the undercarriage and inside body panels so that they can penetrate into joints and body crevices to form a pliable, protective film.
- **Body sealer or sealant (Figure 6-18).** These prevent the penetration of water or mud into panel joints and serve the important role of preventing rust from forming between adjoining surfaces.
- **Antirust agents (Figure 6-19).** Antirust agents are used where it is difficult to get anticorrosive material coverage. This includes such areas as the backsides of welded

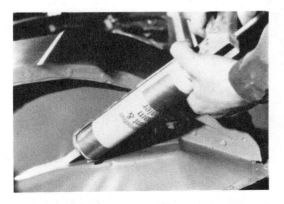

FIGURE 6-18 Applying a typical body sealer or sealant

FIGURE 6-19 A body technician applying a typical antirust agent

parts with boxed cross-sectional structures such as side members and body pillars that cannot be painted.

 **SHOP TALK** _____

Be sure to carefully read the manufacturer's instructions on the container (Figure 6-20) and follow them. Several of these anticorrosive materials can be used on the same part or section.

EXPOSED EXTERIOR SURFACES

Exterior surfaces are subjected to much greater exposure to chips and nicks than interior surfaces.

FIGURE 6-20 Always read carefully the manufacturer's instructions and literature before using the product.

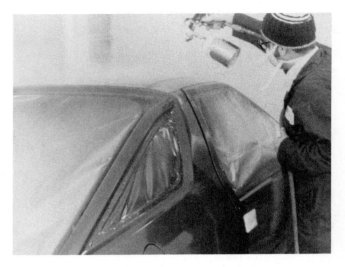

FIGURE 6-21   Applying the color coat

This is why the use of etching and conversion coating agents is of critical importance on exterior surfaces. Conversion coating provides the kind of superior paint film adhesion that retards creeping rust from working its way under the paint when chips and nicks do occur.

Exposed exterior surfaces are of two types:

• Cosmetic (Figure 6-21)
• Underbody (Figure 6-22)

When the completely repaired and corrosion-protected vehicle comes from the body shop, the anticorrosion procedures for exterior cosmetic surfaces are performed by the painter generally as follows:

1. Clean with a wax and grease remover.
2. Apply a metal conditioner.

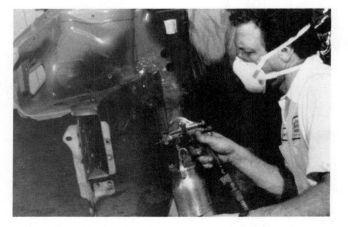

FIGURE 6-22   Spraying a primer onto underbody areas

3. Rinse with water.
4. Apply a conversion coating and allow to thoroughly air dry. Drying can be speeded with compressed air or a clean, white rag.
5. Rinse with water.
6. Apply a primer—two part epoxy primer recommended.
7. Apply a primer-surfacer.
8. Apply color coat system.

Who does the underbody corrosion proofing—the mechanic or the painter—depends on the shop. But, in any case, if a lift is available, it makes underbody corrosion protection work easier. However, it can be done on the floor as shown in Figure 6-22. When corrosion-proofing the underbody, start by spraying the fenders and wheel wells, paying particular attention to the fender beads. On some cars it will be necessary to remove the wheels in order to do an adequate spraying job. Fender skirts should be removed and done separately.

Spray the remaining underbody and splash pans adjacent to the front and rear bumpers. Spray the underside of the floor pan, welded joints, frame, tank straps, and seams. Remove any loose debris or sound deadener, particularly around joints, before spraying. Loose sound deadening materials or dirty surfaces at critical locations will only create pockets for rust to form and will prevent the rustproofing material from reaching the metal.

CAUTION: Never apply undercoating compounds to parts that reach high temperatures such as the exhaust pipe or muffler, and do not apply it to the suspension and drivetrain parts, brake drums, and other related moveable parts.

Anticorrosion procedures for exterior underbody surfaces are generally as follows:

1. Clean with a wax and grease remover.
2. Apply a metal conditioner.
3. Rinse with water.
4. Apply a conversion coating.
5. Rinse with water.
6. Apply a primer—self-etching primer recommended.
7. Apply anticorrosion compound and sound deadening materials to restore to factory specifications.
8. Most undercoat overspray can be removed with enamel reducer, stoddard solvent, or kerosene and washing.

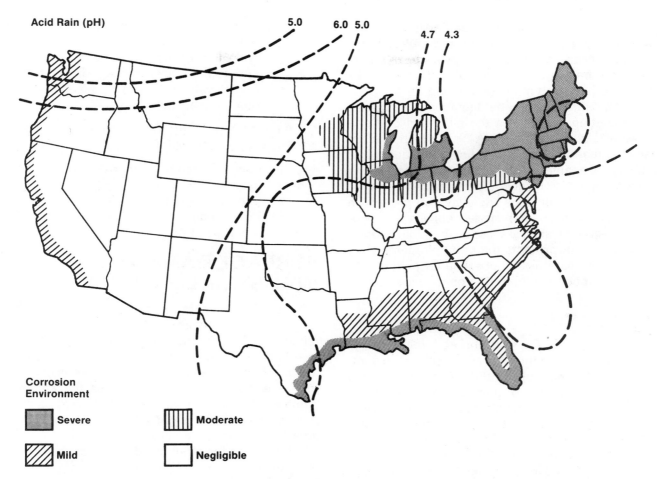

Acid Rain (pH)   5.0   6.0 5.0   4.7 4.3

Corrosion Environment

Severe   Moderate

Mild   Negligible

FIGURE 6-23 While corrosive environments are most severe in the northeast and along the southern seaboard, acid rain has become a factor in much of the country.

ACID RAIN DAMAGE

As mentioned earlier, air pollutants can damage an automotive finish. Since most of their damage is done to exterior, finished surfaces, they are a major concern of the refinisher.

Acid rain and other pollutants have generated a lot of controversy in recent years, and there has been some confusion as to their causes and effects. Sulfur dioxide or nitrogen oxides create acid rain when released into the atmosphere, and combine with water and the ozone to create either sulfuric or nitric acid. It is estimated that the United States alone pumps out 30 million tons of sulfur dioxide and 25 million tons of nitrogen oxides yearly. More than two-thirds of the sulfur is emitted from power plants burning coal, oil, or gas. Iron and copper smelters, automobile exhaust and natural sources like volcanoes, wetlands, and forest fires account for most of the remaining pollutants.

The standard for measuring acid rain is the pH scale. It runs from zero to 14, with 7 being neutral or

equal to distilled water. A pH reading of 4 is ten times more acidic than a solution of acid and water with a pH of 5, and 100 times more acidic than a pH of 6. Once released into the ozone, these acids are readily dissolved into cloud droplets which, if low enough in pH, can cause significant damage.

The level of acid rain varies greatly around the country (Figure 6-23). For example, South Carolina is reported to be one of the most acidic states in the nation. In Los Angeles, fog has been measured to have the acidic strength of lemon juice.

Rainfall in the northeastern states is extremely corrosive to car paints and finishes. For example, the average pH of rainfall in New Jersey is an acidic 4.3. General Motors now has clauses in some of its new car warranties that exempt them from liabilities involving paint damage in high pH areas.

Acid rain damage generally occurs to the paint pigments, with lead-based pigments the most susceptible. Typically, the damage looks like water droplets that have dried on the paint and caused discoloration. Sometimes the damage appears as a white ring with a clear, dull center. Severe cases show pitting. Discoloration varies depending on the color. For example, acid rain damage to a yellow finish might appear as a white or dark brown spot. Medium blue might have a whitening look. White might be discolored pink, and medium red, purple.

Metallic finishes can be damaged because the acidic solution reacts with the aluminim particles and etches away the finish. A fresh finish is more easily damaged than an aged finish. Lacquers and uncatalyzed enamel finishes are most susceptible to damage, followed closely by catalyzed enamels.

Clear-coated finishes add a layer of protection against acid rain, so later-model vehicles with two- and three-coat finishes are less susceptible to damage. A clearcoat protects the paint pigments from discoloration, but it is still possible for acid rain to create a peripheral etch, or ring on the clearcoat.

RESTORING

The procedure for restoring acid rain damage varies depending on the level and depth of the damage. The following steps outline repair procedures according to the level of damage as illustrated in Figure 6-24. When the problem has been corrected, stop at that stage. Remember that polishing or compounding removes part of the original finish, and thereby reduces its overall life.

If the surface damage is like that shown in Figure 6-24A, proceed as follows:

1. Wash with soap and water.
2. Clean with wax and grease remover.
3. Neutralize the area by washing with baking soda solution (1 tablespoon baking soda to 1 quart of water) and rinse thoroughly.

If the damage is embedded in the surface coat (Figure 6-24B), proceed as follows:

1. Follow cleaning and neutralizing steps already listed.
2. Hand polish problem area (inspect and continue if necessary).
3. Buff with polishing pad (inspect frequently and remove as little of the original finish as possible to cure the problem).

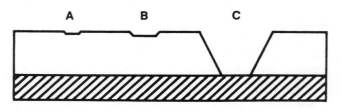

FIGURE 6-24 Levels of acid rain damage

4. Use rubbing compound (inspect and continue if necessary).
5. Wet sand with 1500 or 2000 grit sandpaper and compound. If damage is still visible, repeat with 1200 grit. Do not use grits coarser than 1000.

If the damage is through to the undercoat (Figure 6-24C), proceed as follows:

1. Follow cleaning and neutralizing steps listed in Figure 6-24A.
2. Sand with 400 to 600 grit sandpaper.
3. Reclean and reneutralize prior to priming and repainting.

SURFACE DAMAGE INDUSTRIAL FALLOUT

Generally speaking, damage from industrial fallout is caused when small, airborne particles of iron fall and stick to the vehicle's surface. The iron can eventually eat through the paint, causing the base metal to rust. Sometimes the damage is easier to feel than see. Sweeping a hand across the apparent damage will likely reveal a gritty or bumpy surface. Rust-colored spots might be visible, however, on light-colored vehicles.

The steps for repairing damage caused by industrial fallout are similar to those used when repairing acid rain damage, but with the following exception. After washing the car, treat the repair area with a "fallout remover," a chemical treatment product made especially for industrial fallout damage. Do not buff the damaged area before removing the fallout because buffing will drive the particles into the paint surface. If the particles break loose and become lodged in the buffing pad, deep gouges can occur.

EXTERIOR ACCESSORIES

To prevent corrosion, it is very important to install a barrier between dissimilar metal components such as aluminum bumpers and stainless and aluminum body trim. The plastic or rubber isolating pads accomplish this effectively. Mounting stainless and aluminum body trim must be done correctly to avoid galvanic corrosion. For example, when mounting trim requires drilling holes in a new or repaired panel, drill all holes (Figure 6-25) before applying the primer, coating the inside edges of all holes completely. When using a kit (Figure 6-26) for replacement trim, be sure to use all parts supplied with the kit. If parts are not purchased as a kit, duplicate the original assembly exactly. Clearly, there is a great

FIGURE 6-25 When drilling any hole in a body surface, be sure to take appropriate corrosion protection.

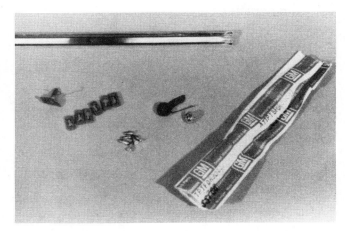

FIGURE 6-26 Typical exterior trim kit

FIGURE 6-27 Always follow manufacturer's instructions when using a kit.

variety of body trim and accessories requiring many different application techniques. In all cases, be sure to follow the manufacturer's recommendations to avoid future problems when making these repairs (Figure 6-27).

SHOP TALK

Where an accessory kit is not being used, duplicate the original installation.

REVIEW QUESTIONS

1. Corrosion prevention is the phase that is replacing _____ .
   a. rustproofing
   b. undercoating
   c. sound deadening
   d. all of the above
   e. both a and b

2. Corrosion will be accelerated in areas _____ .
   a. of high relative humidity
   b. where temperatures drop below freezing
   c. both a and b
   d. none of the above

3. The higher the pH number rises above 6.0, the _____ .
   a. greater chance of acid rain
   b. less chance of acid rain
   c. more acidic the substances
   d. both a and c

4. When two dissimilar metals are placed in contact with each other, the more chemically active will corrode, protecting the other metal in the process. This is called _____ .
   a. zinc coating
   b. galvanic corrosion
   c. all of the above
   d. none of the above

5. Which of the following prevents rust from forming between adjoining surfaces?
   a. anticorrosion compounds
   b. body sealant
   c. antirust agents
   d. none of the above

6. Painter A uses a conversion coating and then a metal conditioner. Painter B uses a metal conditioner and then a conversion coating. Who is right?
   a. Painter A
   b. Painter B
   c. Both A and B
   d. Neither A nor B

7. Painter A uses a conversion coating on inside closed sections. Painter B uses a primer. Who is right?

a. Painter A
b. Painter B
c. Both A and B
d. Neither A nor B

8. How often should cleaning solvent be sprayed through the spray wand?
   a. every half day
   b. once a day or as needed
   c. once a week or as needed
   d. once a month or as needed

9. The worst way to clean an enclosed interior weld area is to use a _____.
   a. plastic abrasive
   b. captive sandblaster
   c. regular sandblaster
   d. wire brush

10. These sealants are not paintable, and attract dust and dirt with time.
    a. silicone sealant
    b. tooling sealant
    c. thin-bodied sealants
    d. heavy-bodied sealants

11. Heavy-bodied sealers are used to fill seams from _____.

a. 1/16 to 1/8 inch wide
b. 1/8 to 1/4 inch wide
c. 1/4 to 1/2 inch wide
d. all of the above

12. Any seams that might be exposed to automotive fluid should have a _____.
    a. thin-bodied sealer
    b. heavy-bodied sealer
    c. brushable seam sealer
    d. solid seam sealer

13. Which of the following can be used for exposed interior surfaces?
    a. epoxy primers
    b. self-etching primers
    c. lacquer-based primers
    d. all of the above
    e. both a and b

14. Undercoating compounds should never be applied to _____.
    a. the exhaust pipe or muffler
    b. suspension parts
    c. drivetrain parts
    d. brake drums
    e. any of the above

CHAPTER SEVEN

AUTOMOTIVE REFINISHING MATERIALS

Objectives

After reading this chapter, you will be able to:

- explain the uses and properties of paints used in the trade for undercoats and topcoats.
- define the four components of automotive paints.
- define the characteristics of a good primer-surfacer.
- name five types of primer-surfacers.
- identify the types of body finishes and refinishing.
- explain the functions of the four types of undercoats.
- name the types of topcoats.
- discuss the advances made in refinishing by basecoat/clear coat finishes.
- explain the advantages of basecoat/clear coat finishes.
- describe the role of solvents and the variables that affect their spraying.
- determine the proper solvent to be used for a particular paint job.

Automobile finishes perform four very important functions:

- **Protection.** The automobile is constructed primarily of steel sheet metal. If this steel was left uncovered, the reaction of oxygen and moisture in the air would cause it to rust. Painting serves to prevent the occurrence of rust, therefore protecting the body.
- **Appearance improvement.** The shape of the body is made up of several types of surfaces and lines, such as elevated surfaces, flat planes, curved surfaces, straight and curved lines, and so forth. Therefore, another objective of painting is to improve the body appearance by giving it a three-dimensional color effect.
- **Quality upgrading.** When comparing two vehicles of identical shape and performance capabilities, the one with the most beautiful paint finish will have a higher market value. Hence another object of painting is to upgrade the value of the product.

- **Color designation.** Still another objective of painting the automobile is to make them easily distinguishable by application of certain colors or markings. Examples are police and fire department vehicles.

The typical automotive finishing system consists of several coats of two or more different materials:

- Undercoat or primer coat(s)
- Topcoat (color coat or basecoat/clear coat)

The undercoat provides a sound foundation for the topcoat and makes it adhere better. If applying topcoats to bare substrates (metal, fiberglass, or plastic), they might peel or look rough; that is why the undercoat is "sandwiched" between the substrate and the topcoat. The undercoat also protects against rusting and will fill scratches and other flaws in the metal or plastic.

The topcoat is the finish that is seen on the car. From an appearance standpoint, it is smooth, glossy, and eye catching. Functionally, it is tough and

FIGURE 7-1 The painter or refinishing technician is responsible for the final appearance of a vehicle. *(Courtesy of DeVilbiss Co.)*

FIGURE 7-2 Paint is composed of four ingredients: (A) pigment/metallic flake; (B) binder; (C) solvent; and—on occasion—(D) additives. *(Courtesy of Du Pont Co.)*

durable. The topcoat thickness on a new car when it comes from the factory is only about 2.5 mils.

A refinisher should know the uses and properties of all paints used in the trade—both undercoats and topcoats. That knowledge will help in choosing the best refinishing system for each job.

Refinishing paints are complex. Those applied to automobiles at the factory have been changing through the years. Many domestic manufacturers have begun to use high-solids finishes and clear coating. Most recently, mica is being used in certain topcoats to provide a pearlescent finish. In more fuel efficient cars, body parts that were once steel are now manufactured from one or more of the many choices of plastics available to car manufacturers. Each, though labeled plastic, exhibits its own characteristics and differences that determine its repairability and refinishing requirements.

In order to provide the perfect matches demanded by the customer on a refinishing job, the painter (Figure 7-1) must respond to these changes. Keeping up-to-date on the changes is crucial. The paint manufacturers providing finishes for use by the automotive refinisher have quickly responded to the car manufacturer's changes and are getting products to the painter that will enable the painter to effectively repair that new car. In addition to keeping informed and using the right products, the bottom line of a good paint job is the skill and care of the painter in the refinishing process. The techniques employed can vary color, cause loss of adhesion, cause sand scratch swelling, and create a multitude of other problems.

CONTENTS OF PAINT

Basically, automotive paints are composed of three and—with some topcoats—four components (Figure 7-2).

- Pigment/metallic or pearl flakes
- Binder
- Solvent
- Additives (with some finishes)

PIGMENT

Pigment is one of two nonvolatile film forming ingredients (that part which remains in the dried film) found in paint. It provides the color and durability of the finish. It also gives the paint the ability to hide what is underneath. In addition to providing durability and hiding, pigment can also improve the strength and adhesion, change gloss, and modify flow and application properties.

The size and shape of pigment particles are important, too. Pigment particle size affects hiding ability, while pigment shape affects strength. Pigment particles can be nearly spherical or rod- or plate-like. Rod-shaped particles, for example, reinforce paint film like iron bars in concrete.

BINDER

The other nonvolatile film forming paint ingredient, the binder, holds the pigment in liquid form, makes it durable, and gives it the ability to stick to the surface. The binder is the backbone of paint.

The binder is generally made of a natural resin (such as rosin), drying oils like linseed or cottonseed, or a man-made synthetic resin (such as methyl methacrylate, polyurethane, polystyrene, polyvinyl chloride, and so forth). The binder dictates the type

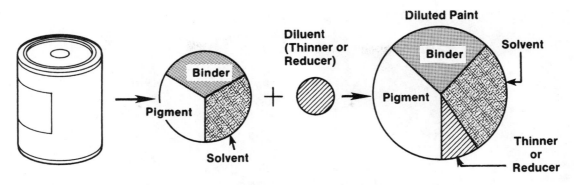

FIGURE 7-3   Ratio of pigment/binder/solvent that makes up paint.

of paint to be produced because it contains the drying mechanism.

Binder is usually modified with plasticizers and catalysts. They improve such properties as durability, adhesion, corrosion resistance, mar-resistance, and flexibility.

SOLVENT

The solvent (or **vehicle** as it is sometimes called) is the "volatile" ingredient of the paint. Most solvents are derived from crude oil. The main function of a volatile in paint is to make it possible to properly apply the material, and it must be of sufficient solvent power to dissolve the binder portion of the film. High-quality solvents improve the application and film properties of topcoats. They also enhance gloss and minimize paint texture, so less buffing is needed. They also help with more accurate color matches.

In addition to the solvent already in paint, so-called **diluent** solvents are used to give the paint a viscosity that makes it easier to apply. When used with lacquer, the diluent solvent is called a **thinner.** When used with enamel, it is called a **reducer.** This is an important distinction in the automobile refinishing business, and the respective products are so labeled. Remember that a lacquer is **thinned,** while an enamel is **reduced.** The ratio of pigment/binder/ solvent that makes up paint is given in Figure 7-3.

ADDITIVES

With the extensive changes made in paint technology during the last decade, additives have become a way of life for most refinishers. While comprising no more than 5 percent of the paint at most (and usually much less), additives perform a variety of vital functions. Some speed up drying and improve gloss; others slow drying; and still others lower gloss. And some perform a combination of functions—such as eliminate wrinkling, provide faster through cure (the final drying), prevent blushing (a milky, misty look), and improve chemical resistance.

Those additives that speed up cure and improve gloss are often referred to as **hardeners.** Those that slow drying are called **retarders.** And those that lower gloss are called **flatteners.**

Flexible paint additives are used in various color coat systems to afford the necessary elasticity of an otherwise rigid paint coating. When a flexible part is compressed or crinkled, the part will return to its normal shape. These additives allow the paint system to flex with the part.

TYPES OF BODY FINISHES

The exterior of an automobile is painted with a basic finish of either lacquer or enamel. Other terms such as nitrocellulose, acrylic, alkyd, or polyurethane sometimes can be used to describe an automobile paint. However, these products are still either lacquer or enamel (Figure 7–4). As the solvents evaporate, the binder and pigments left behind combine into a solid state. If the solvents are reintroduced into physically hardened paint products, they will soften and, if enough solvents are added, will eventually return to a liquid state.

Lacquers can be made hard and then soft again and, therefore, are reversible. As solvents evaporate, the painted film shrinks; as solvents are added, it expands. Lacquers are quick to surface dry but take a very long time to dry all the way through. Herein lie

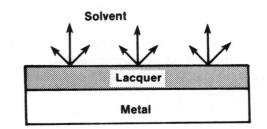

FIGURE 7-4   Lacquers and acrylic lacquers dry by evaporation.

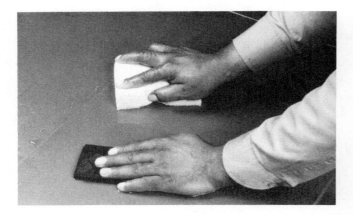

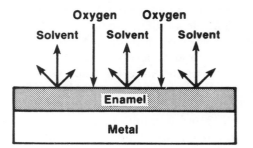

FIGURE 7-5 Lacquer topcoat being compounded by hand or machine to bring out the gloss. *(Courtesy of 3M).*

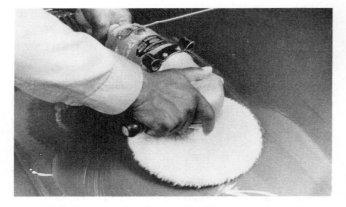

FIGURE 7-6 Enamels dry by evaporation and oxidation.

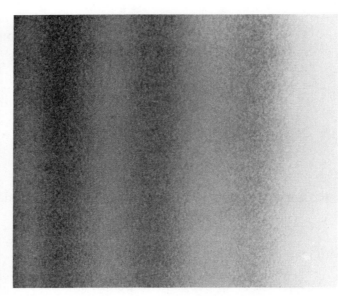

FIGURE 7-7 Orange peel is a fairly common problem. *(Courtesy of PPG Industries, Inc.)*

some of the problems refinishers encounter with lacquer-primers and putties when not properly used.

Lacquer topcoats usually must be compounded or rubbed with a compound or polish to bring out the gloss (Figure 7-5). Most acrylic lacquer basecoat/clear coat finishes can allow a lacquer basecoat to be clear coated with an enamel topcoat. This helps eliminate the need for compounding or polishing to bring out the gloss.

Enamels dry by evaporation of the solvents as the first stage and by oxidation of the binder as the second stage (Figure 7-6). The oxidation is a change in the binder as a result of combining with the oxygen in the air. Heat makes these actions more rapid. Thoroughly dry synthetic films are quite insoluble in ordinary solvents. The longer the drying period, the more insoluble and tougher they become. A thorough sanding when repainting is therefore necessary. Enamel finishes dry with a gloss and do not require rubbing or polishing because of a chemical change rather than simply solvent evaporation. Since enamels generally dry slower, there is more of a chance for dirt and dust to stick in the finish. Also, enamel finishes often dry with a texture called **orange peel** (Figure 7-7). While there is generally a slight amount of orange peel in an enamel film, too much will cause surface roughness or lower gloss.

The bulk of today's passenger cars is finished either in acrylic lacquer, Thermosetting Acrylic Enamel (TAE), or the new high-solids basecoat/clear coat enamel finishes. These finishes are baked in huge ovens to shorten the drying times and cure the paint. It is important to know what type of finishes the car manufacturers use because there are slightly different methods required for refinishing them.

There is a difference between the lacquer used by the car manufacturers and that used in the paint shops. Both are fast drying, but Original Equipment Manufacturers (OEMs) bake lacquers to produce reflow that assures leveling and a mirror-like gloss without need for compounding. Refinish lacquers—on the other hand—are made to air dry and often require compounding to achieve the proper gloss.

Since high-temperature ovens are generally not used in the shop, refinishers need faster drying thinners than the OEMs.

The thermosetting acrylic enamel finishes used by the car manufacturers must also be baked in ovens in order to dry and cure properly. Very few, if any, refinishing shops have these large bake ovens, but even if they did, the high temperatures might damage a car's upholstery, glass, or wiring. Therefore, refinishing shops require an easy-to-apply, yet durable enamel that will:

- Air dry without baking.
- Dry when baked at low temperatures. Again, air dry refinishing shop conditions require faster drying (and a wider range of) solvents than OEMs.

More information on the various lacquers and enamels used as topcoats in the automobile industry is given later in this chapter. As shown in Figure 7–8,

in addition to the topcoat, there are other materials that play an important role in the refinishing operation.

TYPES OF REFINISHING

With a wide number of refinishing paint materials available, the refinisher uses them to do only one of three types of jobs:

- Spot refinishing repairs (Figure 7–9)
- Panel refinishing repairs (Figure 7–10)
- Overall repainting of the entire vehicle (Figure 7–11)

SPOT REPAIR

This type of repair is often called "ding and dent" work. That is because the damaged area is

Functional Nomenclature	Resin/Pigment Ratio	Primary Objective	Use and Features
Primer		Adhesion and anticorrosion	Applied directly to panel surface
Primer-Surfacer		Adhesion, anticorrosion, and smoothness	Intermediate between primer and surfacer. Applied to metal surface or over primer.
Putty	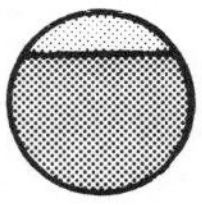	Filler	To smooth out rough spots
Sealer	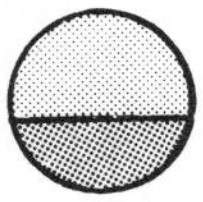	Prevent absorption of topcoat	Intermediate between surfacer and topcoat. Prevents absorption of topcoat and helps avoid troubles arising from old (previous) paint.
Topcoat		Upgrades external appearance	Gives color, gloss, and body to help upgrade merchandising value

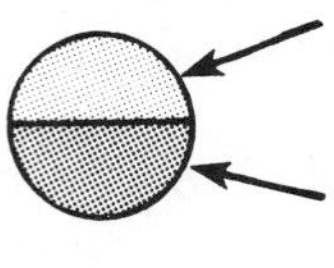

Resin Portion
Pigment Portion

(The more resin, the better gloss and less absorption)

(The more pigment, the better covering of rough spots and smoothness, but less gloss and more absorption.)

FIGURE 7-8 Functions of automobile paint materials. *(Courtesy of Toyota Motor Corp.)*

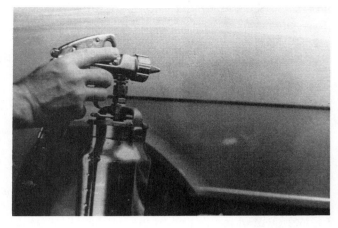

FIGURE 7-9 Spot refinishing repair generally involves minor body repair, featheredging, an application of primer-surfacer, and sanding. *(Courtesy of America Sikkens, Inc.)*

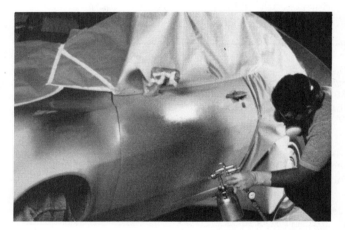

FIGURE 7-10 Panel or block refinishing repair, basically the same as spot repair, covers an entire panel or panels of the car (door, hood, and so forth).

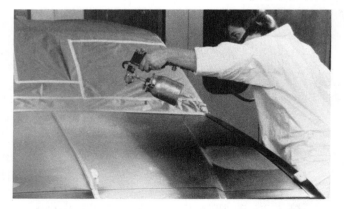

FIGURE 7-11 Overall repainting can be dictated by the extent of the repair, the condition of the finish, or by the owner's preference. *(Courtesy of Maaco Enterprises, Inc.)*

usually small—either a ding or a dent. Other possibilities might be scratches or a breakdown of the substrate due to rust or corrosion.

Spot repair generally involves:

- Minor body repair.
- Metal conditioning.
- Undercoat applications.
- Topcoat application that is blended into the old finish surrounding the repair.

PANEL REPAIR

Basically, panel repair work uses the same technique as spot repair except that the area covers an entire panel or panels of the car (door, hood, and so on) and the match is made at the panel joints. As in spot repair, any imperfections within the panel must be featheredged and the undercoats applied before the topcoats go on. Sometimes when the color match is especially difficult, it is recommended that the new color be blended into the adjoining panels.

Both spot and panel repair could be considered small area finishing. Oftentimes the refinisher must decide whether to do a spot or a panel repair. If the area to be repainted is large, panel repair can be easier.

OVERALL REPAINTING

Overall repainting is just what it says, the whole vehicle is painted. Some reasons for refinishing the entire car include:

- Size and/or number of spots to be repaired
- Dull, cracked, or worn finish
- Car owner wishes to change color

There are also specialty paint shops that do mostly overall painting as well as custom shops that develop glamour finishes for custom, antique, and classic cars.

UNDERCOAT PRODUCTS

Proper undercoating is part of the foundation for an attractive, durable topcoat. If the undercoat—or combination of undercoats—is not correct, the topcoat appearance will suffer and might even crack or peel.

Undercoats can be compared to a sandwich filler that holds two slices of bread together. The bottom slice of bread is called the substrate (or surface of the vehicle). That surface can be bare metal or plastic, or a painted or preprimed surface. The

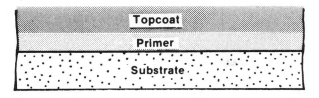

FIGURE 7–12 Primers are generally applied in a thin coat and do not require sanding. Primers are applied over bare substrates. *(Courtesy of Du Pont Co.)*

FIGURE 7–13 Primer-surfacers—unlike primers—must be sanded. They can be applied over bare metal or sanded old finishes. *(Courtesy of Du Pont Co.)*

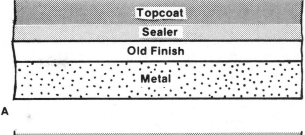

A

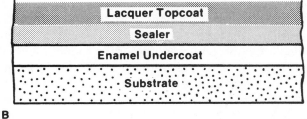

B

FIGURE 7–14 (A) Sealers improve topcoat adhesion. They can be applied over primers, primer-surfacers, or (in this case) old finish. (B) When a topcoat different from the old finish (in quality as well as color) is applied, a sealer should be used. *(Courtesy of Du Pont Co.)*

undercoat is the sandwich filler applied to the substrate. It makes the substrate smooth and provides a bond for the topcoat. The upper slice is the topcoat, the final color coat that the customer sees.

Undercoats contain pigment, binder, and solvent. There are four general or basic types of undercoats:

- Primer (Figure 7–12)
- Primer-surfacer (Figure 7–13)
- Primer-sealer
- Sealer (Figure 7–14)

Most surfaces must be undercoated (Table 7–1) before refinishing for several reasons: to fill scratches to provide a good base for applications, to promote adhesion of the topcoat to the substrate, and to assure corrosion resistance. A primer alone, however, will not fill sand scratches or other surface flaws. Primer-surfacers are used to provide both priming and filling in one step. Primer-sealers are applied to prevent solvents in the topcoat from being absorbed into the porous primer-surfacer. These three undercoats—primer, primer-surfacer, and primer-sealer—can be used together, singularly, or in various combinations, depending on the surface condition and size of the job (Table 7–2). Sealers are employed to improve adhesion between the old and new finishes. To provide good adhesion, a sealer should always be used over an old lacquer finish when the new finish is to be enamel. Under other conditions, a sealer can be desirable but not absolutely necessary.

TABLE 7–1: FUNCTIONS OF UNDERCOATS

Undercoat Function	Primer	Primer-Surfacer	Primer-Sealer	Sealer
Resists rust and corrosion	Yes	Yes	Yes	No
Makes topcoat adhere better	Yes	Yes	Yes	Yes
Fills scratches and nicks	No	Yes	No	No
Provides uniform hold out of the topcoat	No	No	Yes	Yes
Prevents show through of sand scratches	No	No	Yes	Yes

TABLE 7–2: SURFACES FOR UNDERCOATS

Undercoat Surface	Primer	Primer-Surfacer	Primer-Sealer	Sealer
Bare substrate (metal, fiberglass, or plastic)	Yes	Yes	Yes	No
Sanded old finish	No	Yes	Yes	Yes

With a great number of different kinds of under-coat products on the market, the refinisher is often faced with the problem of what one to use. No matter which type of undercoat product is used, the golden rule for selecting surface preparation and all other refinish products is the same: Never mix manufacturers' products.

Refinish products are formulated to work as systems. Manufacturers spend millions of dollars in research and development to design "systems" of products that work together to provide a specific result. Mixing one manufacturer's reducer with another manufacturer's primer-surfacer or topcoat is almost surely to create a lot of headaches. Putting one manufacturer's primer-sealer over another's primer-surfacer is just as risky. It is important to remember that manufacturers only test and guarantee their own systems.

When selecting an undercoat system, it is best to choose products that match the quality of the topcoat. Especially when refinishing a luxury car or applying a top quality basecoat/clear coat system, it can be worth the extra investment in a premium undercoat system to get the additional assurance against finish failure that these products provide.

Quite often, a premium undercoat system actually might be less costly than an economy grade product when labor and materials costs are considered. Premium primer-surfacers typically provide greater fill, so the surface can be prepared with fewer coats using less product.

PRIMERS

By definition, a primer (or prep coater as it is sometimes called) is generally the first coat in any finishing system (Figure 7–15). It is designed to prepare the bare substrate and to accept and hold the color topcoat. Primers should provide maximum adhesion to the surface and produce a corrosion-resistant foundation. Primers generally do not fill surface imperfections and therefore often do not require sanding.

Straight primers are predominantly used by original equipment manufacturers rather than paint shops. Primers are usually enamel type products because they provide better adhesion and corrosion resistance than lacquers. (Where the original surfaces are plastic or fiberglass, some lacquer-primers are used.)

There are several special primers available to the shop refinisher. For example, the two-part, self-etching **epoxy primers** are probably the most versatile and valuable primer products on the market today. An epoxy primer system consists of the primer

itself and an activator (or catalyst). When mixed together (known as **catalyzing**), it often requires an induction time; that is, the period of time that the components must be allowed to thoroughly mix with each other before spraying. It must be remembered that these two-part or two-component mixtures have a "pot" life, or a limited time before they become unusable.

Epoxy primers are a good choice where a great deal of fill is required. On sandblasted, coarse surfaces, for example, a high-build epoxy primer adheres to the bare substrate and provides the fill necessary for a smooth finish. Using a two-part epoxy primer is also the best way to restore corrosion prevention to a damaged vehicle. The epoxy primers are easy to apply (Figure 7–16) and offer the extra pro-

FIGURE 7-15 Application of a primer is generally the first step in refinishing. *(Courtesy of America Sikkens, Inc.)*

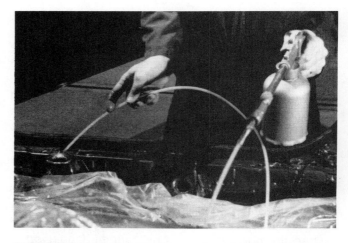

FIGURE 7-16 Application of a two-part epoxy primer to interior enclosed parts of a vehicle.

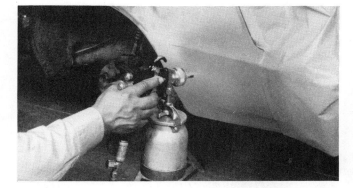

FIGURE 7-17 Application of a chip resistant primer provides resistance to chipping, salt spray, and the abrasive action of stones, sand, and other road particles. It dries fast and can be painted 30 minutes after applying. *(Courtesy of 3M)*

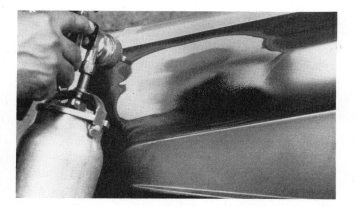

FIGURE 7-18 Application of a plastic primer over a flexible plastic part. Apply a wet coat on the part and then after 10 minutes, apply a second coat. *(Courtesy of 3M)*

tection that vehicles require because of the high degree of wear and tear to which they are exposed. Virtually any automotive or commercial vehicle topcoat can be used over an epoxy primer. Most epoxy primers are available in lead-free gray and lead- and chromate-free red iron oxide. They enable topcoat color to be sprayed only 1 hour after primer application, with no sanding or sealing.

Zinc chromate primer is a product that has been around for many years. It is a primer designed mainly for adhesion to aluminum. Today, however, epoxy primer will actually do a better job in this application.

Zinc chromate primer should always be used in applications where dissimilar metals will come in contact with each other, such as in a truck body where steel ribs might be used to support aluminum sides and top. One thin coat of zinc chromate will prevent an electrolysis reaction, which causes rapid corrosion. Most zinc chromate primers are reduced with enamel reducer and can be topcoated only with enamels.

Zinc weld-through primer is a zinc rich material that is frequently used to protect welded joints against corrosion. The zinc in the primer will provide galvanic protection in the weld zone.

When corrosion resistance is very important, **wash-primers** (also called **vinyl wash-primers**) are used under primer-surfacers or sealers. The reducer in a wash-primer contains phosphoric acid that "bites" into the surface to provide superior adhesion to steel, aluminum, rigid and flexible plastics, and certain kinds of zinc-coated metal. The bond is so strong, in fact, that when a primer has been applied to bare metal it is extremely difficult to remove without grinding it off.

To use the wash-primer it must be reduced with a special reducer-catalyst and must be used within a specific period of time. It offers high-corrosion resistance to alkalies, oils, grease, and even salt water. Another benefit of this type of resin primer is that it is more forgiving of metal cleaning problems.

Chip resistant primers are specially formulated for use on lower body sections that are prone to gravel and stone impact damage (Figure 7-17). They give improved resistance against corrosion and help to reduce drumming noise.

Adhesion to plastic panels that have come from the factory unprimed can be improved by the use of a special plastic primer. Flexible plastics in particular require **plastic primer** (Figure 7-18). Many rigid plastics also benefit from priming with a plastic primer. Plastic primers promote bonding, eliminating peeling and other adhesion problems.

🔫 SHOP TALK ⎯⎯⎯⎯⎯

Some metal replacement parts are supplied by the car manufacturers with a primed surface. The car manufacturer might recommend that this primer not be removed as it is an anticorrosive as well as for paint adhesion. It is necessary to apply a primer over the factory primers.

Another ready-to-spray primer product designed specifically for use with basecoat/clear coat OEM finishes is the so-called **adhesion promoter** or **mid coat primer.** This product is a water-clear primer with good durability and excellent adhesion to the very hard clear coats. It is recommended that it be applied beyond the repaired area on a spot repair before any other primer is used. Its purpose is to provide a surface to which a blend edge can adhere.

PRIMER-SURFACERS

Primer-surfacers are the most popular of all the undercoats in refinish applications. They are used to build up featheredged areas for rough surfaces and to provide a smooth base for lacquer and enamel topcoats (Figure 7-19). A good primer-surfacer should have all of the following six characteristics (Figure 7-20):

- **Adhesion.** A strong bond between the substrate and the topcoat to be applied.

FIGURE 7-21 Most primer-surfacers are easy to sand. *(Courtesy of Carborundum Abrasives Co.)*

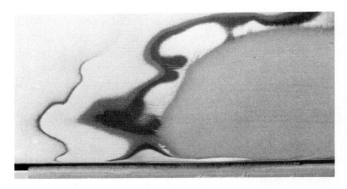

FIGURE 7-19 Primer-surfacers are very important where featheredging has been done. *(Courtesy of Carborundum Abrasives Co.)*

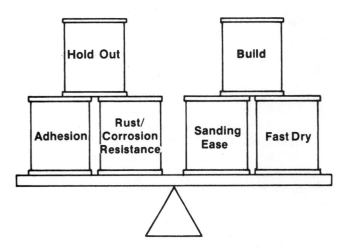

FIGURE 7-20 A "balance of properties" is vital in a primer-surfacer. The three properties on the right build the proper foundation for the topcoat; the three on the left make the job fast and easy. *(Courtesy of Du Pont Co.)*

- **Rust/corrosion resistance.** A durability characteristic that prevents loss of adhesion and, ultimately, disintegration of the metal.
- **Build.** A quality that provides the necessary fill for grinder marks and sand scratches in repair work.
- **Sanding ease.** A characteristic that allows the primer-surfacer to be sanded smooth and leveled quickly and easily (Figure 7-21).
- **Hold out.** A sealing quality that prevents the topcoat from sinking into the primer-surfacer, resulting in a dull look.
- **Drying speed.** A time-saving quality that permits the refinisher to go on to the next operation. (A good primer-surfacer should be ready to sand in 20 to 30 minutes.)

There are five types of primer-surfacers:

- Nitrocellulose lacquer
- Acrylic lacquer
- Alkyd or synthetic enamel
- Self-etching
- Acrylic urethane

Nitrocellulose primer-surfacer was, until the last few years, the most popular with the majority of painters—primarily because it dries fast and is easy to sand. While it has adequate adhesion in most cases, it does not have these two qualities that the other four primer-surfacers do: rust and corrosion resistance and a tough, flexible film. And it can be used on aluminum. The use of nitrocellulose lacquer primer-surfacers currently is recommended only for small area repairs.

Acrylic primer-surfacers have replaced nitro-cellulose-based primer-surfacers as the painter's number one choice because of their good fill and fast dry times. They can be directly recoated with a wider variety of topcoats than nitrocellulose primer-surfacers, making them suitable for more jobs. They offer greater durability, shrink less, and provide the same fill in fewer coats. Other desirable characteristics of an acrylic resin sealer are:

- **Sanding.** Easy sanding.
- **Drying.** It dries in 30 minutes or less when applied correctly.
- **Hold out.** The hold out is good and not porous.
- **Settling.** It does not settle too hard in the cup. It can be stirred back into solution quickly if it stands for a while.

Alkyd or synthetic enamel primer-surfacer is excellent in most respects. It requires a much longer drying time—2 to 3 hours. If it is to be wet sanded, overnight drying is recommended. Because of its tough, flexible film and high degree of corrosion resistance, it is recommended for surfacing large areas—either panel repair or complete repainting. It also can provide an overspray problem.

Though fairly new on the market, **self-etching primer-surfacers** are rapidly gaining in popularity because in one step they etch the bare metal and provide the fill needed for a smooth finish. Etching filler ensures outstanding paint adhesion and corrosion resistance and can reduce surface preparation time and materials costs by more than 25 percent.

The two-component **acrylic urethane primer-surfacers** were created for use with today's more sophisticated and expensive topcoats. Acrylic urethane primer-surfacers provide even higher film build than conventional acrylics, better color hold out, and virtually no film shrinkage, substantially reducing the risk of overnight dull-back. The trade-offs are longer dry times, cost, overspray damage, and the need to apply these products at controlled shop temperatures and in a very clean shop environment. An acrylic urethane primer-surfacer is a good choice for overall refinishing when a long-lasting, superior paint job is the goal.

Another excellent product is the new polyester primer-surfacer that primes, fills, and seals in one easy operation. It develops a tough, flexible polyester resin that offers its user high build-up capabilities. It quickly levels, fills, and reconditions sand scratches, pinholes, stone chips, grinder marks, crazed and lacquer-checked surfaces, and most mi-

nor surface imperfections. Polyester primer-surfacers can be sprayed—preferably with a gravity feed spray gun (Figure 7–22).

All primer-surfacers should be thinned as per label directions and applied in medium coats, allowing 15 to 20 minutes flash time between coats. Applying heavy coats or not allowing enough flash time will result in a thick coat of surfacer that can gum up the sandpaper, featheredge poorly, and cause loss of gloss or peeling of the topcoat. Excessive thickness of a primer-surfacer coat under a topcoat could lead to premature crazing and/or cracking conditions.

Recommended topcoats for both lacquer and acrylic primer-surfacers include lacquer and enamel. In some cases, urethanes can be applied over an acrylic primer-surfacer. Check manufacturers' recommendations regarding proper primer products for urethanes before making any suggestions because they can vary greatly from brand to brand.

PRIMER-SEALERS

A primer-sealer—like a primer—is used to prime bare metal to resist rust and corrosion and to provide topcoat adhesion. In addition, primer-sealers can be used to seal aged painted surfaces that have been sanded. In contrast to primer-surfacers, primer-sealers do not fill and do not have to be sanded.

A primer-sealer is generally an enamel-based product that must be reduced with an enamel reducer. The main reason for using this type of primer is to insure that the ready-to-paint surface is consistent

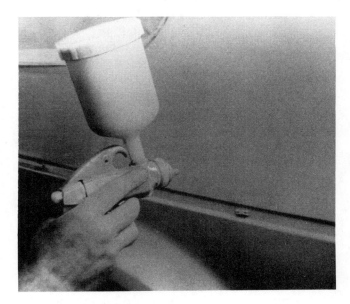

FIGURE 7–22 Spraying a polyester primer-surfacer with a gravity feed spray gun.

FIGURE 7-23 Spraying a sealer will provide better adhesion for the topcoat. *(Courtesy of Du Pont Co.)*

in color (to prevent primer spots from showing through the finish) and porosity (to prevent topcoat solvents from soaking into the primer spots, causing dull spots or featheredge ring).

SEALERS

Sealers differ from primer-sealers in that they cannot be used as a primer. Sealers are sprayed over a primer or primer-surfacer or a sanded old finish. They are used in automotive refinishing for four specific purposes:

- They offer better adhesion between the paint material to be applied and the repair surface (Figure 7-23). Sanding of the surface is usually required before application.
- They act as a barrier type material that prevents or retards the mass penetration of refinish solvents into the color and/or undercoat being repaired.
- They provide uniform hold out. If the old finish is good and hard and if a primer-surfacer with good hold out is used for spot repairing, a sealer is not mandatory. Obviously, if only one or neither of these conditions is present, a sealer is recommended (Figure 7-24). However, a sealer is always recommended to provide uniform color hold out and to prevent die-back.
- They prevent show-through or sand-through. If sand scratches (Figure 7-25) are present in the undercoat, particularly if noticeable to the eye, they will show through the topcoat. The safest procedure is to apply a coat of sealer, especially on large areas of sand

scratches. Small areas, such as sand scratches around a featheredge, can be removed by compounding.

Sealers also provide the following benefits:

- Improve adhesion of the repair color to very hard undercoats and enamel surfaces
- Improve gloss
- Prevent bleeding (when designed for this purpose)
- Usable on small, clean bare metal surfaces

FIGURE 7-24 This stepped up panel—from scratches in the old finish to sealer to new topcoat color—shows how scratches can be minimized or eliminated through the use of the proper sealers. *(Courtesy of PPG Industries, Inc.)*

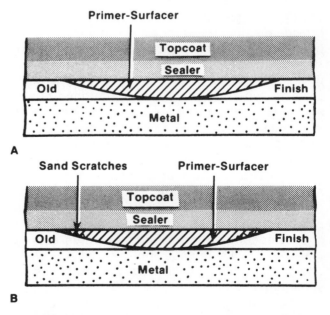

FIGURE 7-25 (A) If a primer-surfacer has been used, there might be a difference in the hold out between the two types of finishes. (B) If so, a sealer will solve the problem, use of a sealer might prevent show through of sand scratches. *(Courtesy of Du Pont Co.)*

There are situations in which some kind of sealer must be used, and there are conditions in which a sealer should be used to improve adhesions, the following application rules must be kept in mind:

- **Alkyd enamel over lacquer.** To insure adequate adhesion, a sealer must be used.
- **Enamel over enamel.** Adequate adhesion might be present between two enamels, but there is no guarantee, so a sealer should be used.
- **Lacquer over enamel.** Spot repairs generally are not a problem, but a sealer is recommended in panel repair or complete repainting (Figure 7-26).
- **Lacquer over lacquer.** Sealer not required to insure adequate adhesion but can be desired for hold out and hiding sand scratches.

Two basic types of sealer available to refinishers are:

- Those designed for an acrylic lacquer paint system. This sealer, when so stated on the label, is not to be topcoated with enamel finishes.
- Those designed for air dry enamel paint systems. This sealer, when so stated on the label, is not to be topcoated with lacquer or acrylic lacquer finishes.

More recently, however, universal sealers have been developed that can be used under the majority of topcoat systems available.

Like primers, there are several specialty sealers on the market, including **barrier coat sealers,** which are designed for extremely sensitive substrates. Old finishes that are on the verge of cracking or that have been exposed to too much sun can require the use of a barrier coat sealer. These sealers eliminate lift when an enamel topcoat is going to be sprayed over a previous enamel paint job that has been buffed through to an OEM lacquer.

Recoat sealer is a special purpose primer that is made only by a few paint companies to be used only with their acrylic enamel system when there is a need to repaint a panel that is in a sensitive stage. Recoat sealer is packaged ready to spray, requires no reduction, and has poor adhesion if it is used on a paint film that is not sensitive. The only way to find out whether or not recoat sealer is required is to test a small painted area by applying some enamel reducer. If the reducer has no effect or if it dissolves the finish, recoat sealer is not needed. If the finish is wrinkled or lifted by the reducer, recoat sealer must be applied before any repainting. If an isocyanate

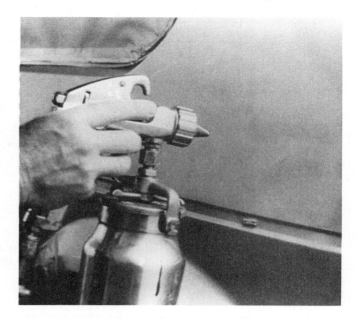

FIGURE 7-26 Sealer should be used when making panel refinishing repairs or when doing a complete refinishing job.

additive is used in the acrylic enamel, there is no sensitive time and recoat sealer is not necessary.

Bleeder sealer is a special sealer to be used over colors that contain a bleeding dye pigment. Some reds and maroons contain such a pigment; however, there are others that result in a yellowing rather than the familiar reddish tone. A spot check using a white color will generally establish whether a bleeding color is present or not.

Tie coat sealers provide extra adhesion when a lacquer topcoat is being sprayed over an OEM enamel. The transparent resin in the tie coat sealer provides the extra "bite" into the OEM enamel that refinish lacquer topcoats require.

PUTTIES AND BODY FILLERS

Putties and body fillers, while not precisely defined as undercoats, might be termed solid undercoats since they are frequently used in conjunction with one or more of the four liquid undercoats and perform many of the same functions. There are several types of putty that are called by different names depending on the manufacturer, but normally putty is classified as body filler, polyester putty, or lacquer putty (Figure 7-27).

Body filler is primarily used during body repair work to smooth out rough spots in the metal. Also called plastic filler, it features pliability and can be applied rather thickly (Figure 7-28). There is also a type that contains wax. When applied, the wax rises to the surface and cuts off air contact so as to pre-

	Body Filler	Polyester Putty	Lacquer Putty
Primary Use	Used to smooth out large depressions and fill in scratches.	Used to fill holes in body filler and sandpaper scratches in the metal.	Used to cover pinholes and small scratches after application of primer-surfacer, and to fill in small scratches in the old paint film.
Maximum Film Thickness per Application	Below 1/4" 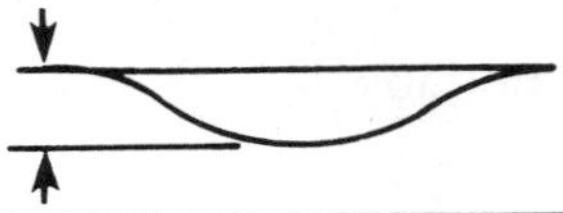	Below 1/8" 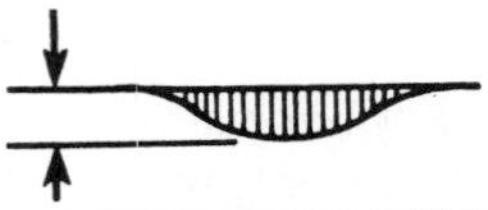	Below 1/16" 

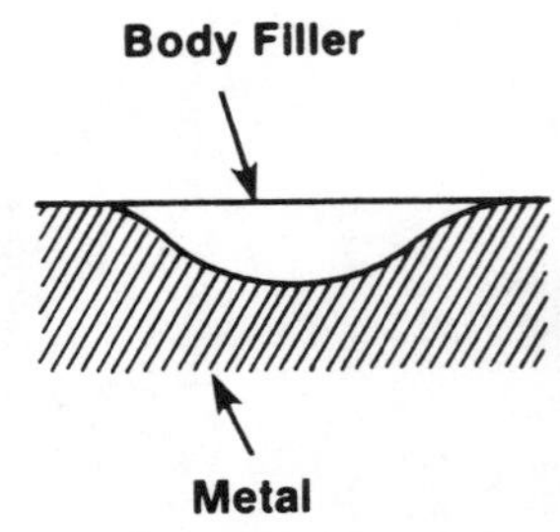

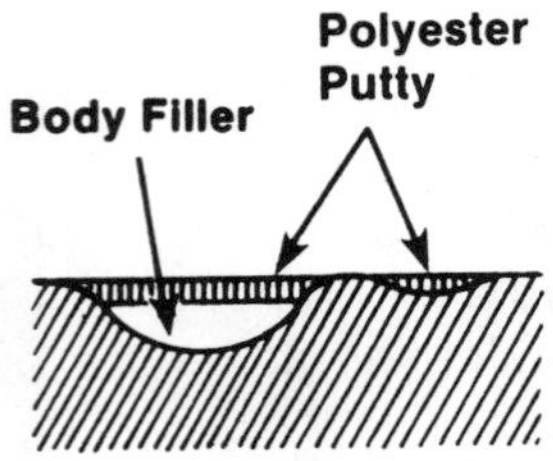

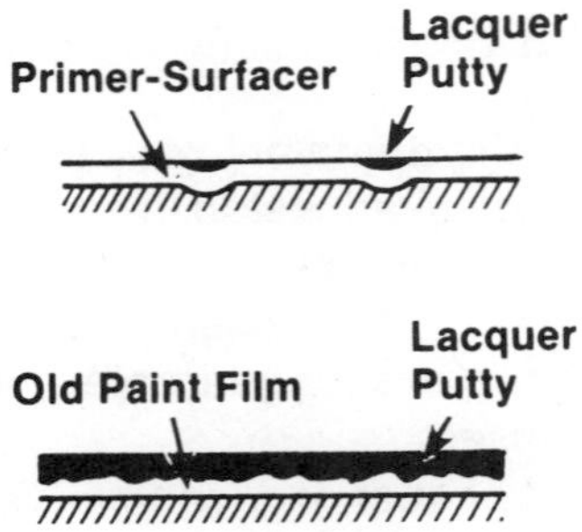

FIGURE 7-27   Use of three major types of putties and body fillers

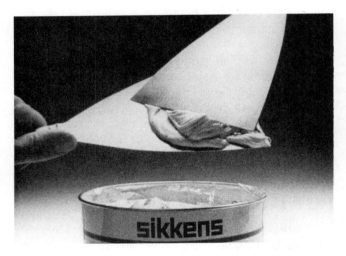

FIGURE 7-28   Body fillers are applied rather thick. *(Courtesy of America Sikkens, Inc.)*

FIGURE 7-29   Body fillers are frequently shaped with a surform tool. *(Courtesy of Carborundum Abrasives Co.)*

vent the adverse effects that oxygen has on the chemical reaction that occurs during hardening. Because it is easy for sandpaper scratches to occur during polishing, it is necessary to later remove the wax with a surform tool after the putty has partially dried (Figure 7-29). However, there is also a nonwax type that does not require scraping with a surform tool, but it is inferior to the wax type in respect to the maximum application thickness. In the past, wax

type body filler was used a great deal, but recently there is wider use of the nonwax type, similar to polyester putty. Because it is also possible to apply polyester putty rather thickly, little distinction is made between body filler and polyester putty.

Polyester putty is used to fill in small holes or slight scratches in the body filler. Its formal name is unsaturated polyester putty, but most refinishing personnel called it "poly putty." It is not as pliable as body filler and cannot be applied as thickly, but it has a fine texture, spreads easily (Figure 7–30), and does not require surform treatment. Like body filler, polyester putty is a two-component type requiring mixing of a main agent and a hardening agent. As there is no volatile component during application, the paint film maintains its body after hardening.

Lacquer type putty is a companion product to lacquer primer-surfacer and is used to fill scratches and flaws that the primer-surfacer cannot. Like primer-surfacers, a quality putty must offer a balance of properties, including fast drying, ease of sanding, good adhesion, and hold out. Putty is designed for the application to spot locations rather

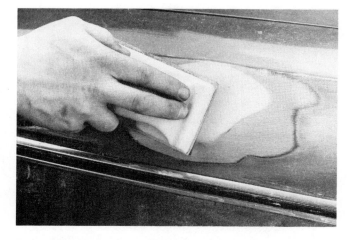

FIGURE 7–32 All putties usually require sanding.

than over a large area (Figure 7–31). Putty is not designed to straighten or finish straightening metal-work. On occasion multicoats of putty are used.

In composition, putty is made up of a very high solid material of the same nature as surfacer, but with a low thinner or solvent content. Therefore it is used to fill any small imperfections or flaws remaining in the substrate after primer-surfacer has been applied. Putty must be sanded (Figure 7–32).

CAUTION: After sanding the putty, it is important to recoat the putty with a **thin** coat of primer-surfacer before applying topcoats.

FIGURE 7–30 Polyester putties spread easily. *(Courtesy of America Sikkens, Inc.)*

Nitrocellulose-based spray putties are a special type of putty that gives the build of spray fillers coupled with fast drying. They can be applied by a siphon feed spray gun or pressure feed spray gun. The latter is preferable for speed and ease of application. These putties can be applied over large areas with less danger of imperfections than with putties applied with a squeegee or glazing knife. More details on the use and application of putties and body fillers can be found in Chapter 5.

In summary, the selection of one or more undercoats will be determined by the following characteristics of a job:

- **Type of surface.** Bare metal or previously finished.
- **Condition of that surface.** Repaired area or sanded aged finish.
- Whether **hold out** and **show-through** are problems.

Depending upon these circumstances the painter might use a:

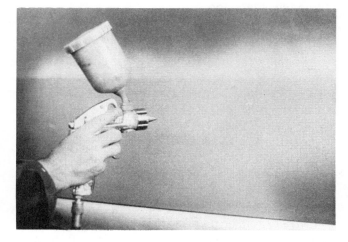

FIGURE 7–31 Gravity feed sprayer is used with some putties on small areas. *(Courtesy of America Sikkens, Inc.)*

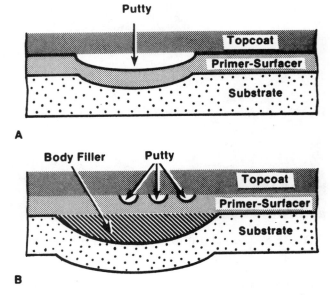

FIGURE 7-33 (A) Where scratches are too deep for primer-surfacers, use a putty after application of the primer-surfacer. (B) When scratches are too severe for putty, use a body filler on the surface and then the primer-surfacer. *(Courtesy of Du Pont Co.)*

- Primer by itself
- Primer-surfacer by itself
- Primer-sealer
- Primer-surfacer with a sealer
- Sealer over a sanded old finish

While a primer-surfacer will cover small imperfections, it will not handle deep scratches, gouges, or other similar defects. When these conditions exist, the painter has two other options:

- Where the scratches are a bit deeper, it is possible to apply putty over the primer-surfacer (Figure 7-33A).
- When the scratches are too severe for putty, the painter has to use body filler on the metal and then prime it (just as it is used in the metalworking area to repair larger dents) (Figure 7-33B).

No matter what type of refinish job confronts the painter, the purpose of the undercoat is always the same: to provide the best possible foundation for a beautiful, long-lasting finish. Making the right product choices is an important step in paving the way for a successful paint finish.

TOPCOATS

From the customer's standpoint, the topcoat (or color coat) is the most important in refinishing be-cause that is all he/she sees. The expert refinisher takes special pride in producing a beautiful finish on spot and panel repairs, or in an overall repaint job that matches both the color (or color effect) and the texture of the original finish. Therefore, it is of great importance to fully understand the topcoat materials and how they are applied. The latter is covered in detail in Chapter 11.

AUTOMOBILE COLORS

Like all colors, automotive refinishing colors are a result of the way they react to light. The color seen is the result of the kind and amount of light waves the surface reflects. When these light waves strike the retina, they are converted into electrical impulses that the brain sees as color. The same color will look very different under natural daylight, incandescent lamps, or fluorescent bulbs. That is why it is so important to check color match in daylight or a balanced artificial light. There are two basic automobile general finish types: solids and metallic colors.

SOLID COLORS

For many years all cars were solid colors, such as black, white, tan, blue, green, maroon, and so on. These colors are composed of a high volume of opaque type pigments. Opaque pigments block the rays of sun and absorb light in accordance with the type of color they are. That is, the darker the solid color is, the more light it absorbs and the less it reflects. Black will absorb more light and will reflect less; white absorbs less light but reflects a great deal more. When polished, solid colors reflect light in only one direction. Solid colors are still used by the refinisher, but to a lesser degree when compared with a few years ago.

METALLIC COLORS

Metallic (or polychrome) paint contains small flakes of metal suspended in liquid. The metal particles combine with the pigment to impart varying color effects. The effect depends on the position the flakes assume within the paint film (Figure 7-34). The position of the metal flakes and the thickness of the paint affect the overall color of the painted surface. The flakes reflect light, but some light is absorbed by the paint. The thicker the layer of paint, the greater the light absorption.

When metallic paint is sprayed on dry, the metallic flakes are trapped at various angles near the surface. Light reflection is not uniform, and because the light has less film to travel through, little of it is absorbed (Figure 7-35). The result of nonuniform light reflection and a minimum of light absorption is a painted surface with a metallic appearance and a light color.

When metallic paint is sprayed on wet, the metallic flakes have sufficient time to settle so they lie parallel to and deeper within the paint film. Light reflection is uniform and, because the light has to go farther into the paint film, light absorption is greater (Figure 7–36). The result is a painted surface that appears deeper and dark in color.

CAUTION: Metallic color paints must be stirred and mixed thoroughly before using. As shown in Figure 7–37, the pigment settles below the binder; the metal flakes settle below the pigment. If flakes stay at the bottom of the can, the paint will not match the same color on a vehicle being repaired or refinished.

BASIC TYPES OF TOPCOATS

Automotive topcoat finishes range from paints that have been available for 50 years to new multi-

FIGURE 7–34 In metallic finishes the light enters the finish and is reflected by metal flakes to produce metallic color effect. *(Courtesy of Du Pont Co.)*

FIGURE 7–35 Dry spray traps the metallic particles at various angles near the surface and causes a high-metallic color effect. *(Courtesy of Du Pont Co.)*

FIGURE 7–36 Wet spray allows time for metallic particles to settle in the paint film and causes a strong pigment color effect. *(Courtesy of Du Pont Co.)*

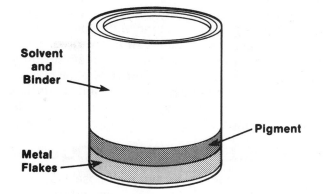

FIGURE 7–37 Metallic paint is composed of solvent, binder, pigment, and metal flakes. The pigment settles below the solvent and binder, while the flakes sink below the pigment.

FIGURE 7–38 The use of lampblack pigment and varnish was the standard car finish before 1924.

component systems that provide the ultimate in durability. No single finish is the best for all applications; it all depends on a careful matching of finish capabilities and characteristics with the requirements of the application.

Here is a brief review of the history and highlights of various materials used as topcoats. The application of those still being employed by the automotive trade is detailed in Chapter 11.

Starting with 1900 and into the early 1920s, the wooden bodies and spokes of cars built during this period were painted by hand. Using a mixture of lampblack pigment and varnishes, this material was brushed on by hand, coat after coat, until coverage and hiding was achieved (Figure 7–38). This pigment, having very few solids and being weak, could not give enough coverage with 1, 2, 3, 4, or 5 coats. This buildup of material, lacking any modern driers, would take from 40 to 50 days to dry.

When the bodies were finally dry enough to work on again, a pumice stone, water folded into the damp rag, along with plenty of elbow grease were applied and any flaws—such as remaining brush marks, dirt, or runs—were removed in this manner. No color selection had been developed at this time, nor did this material have any durability. It dulled and cracked within a year after all that hard work.

NITROCELLULOSE LACQUERS

The introduction of nitrocellulose lacquer in 1924 revolutionized automobile finishing. The use of this lacquer, applied with a spray gun, allowed the steel vehicle bodies to be completed in one day, in turn eliminating a major bottleneck in automobile production.

Nitrocellulose lacquer required several coats of color that did air dry very quickly but faded and chalked because of weak pigment. The color range was just beginning to show improvement, with something other than black, as the greens came into focus. Reds, blues, and yellows (Figure 7-39) were also developing, along with solvents and other technology. Nitrocellulose lacquers were used by the American automobile refinishing trade well into the 1950s.

ALKYD ENAMELS

Introduced in 1929, alkyd resin enamel has been satisfying refinisher needs in the overall repainting of passenger cars and commercial vehicles for more than half a century. This finish is basically the same today as it was when it was first introduced with a slight modification. The name "synthetic" was given to this enamel finish because the resin used in its formulation was modified by synthesizing the enamels with simple petroleum chemical compounds. Now, of course, all paint resins are synthesized, but the name synthetic enamel is still used to identify these alkyds.

Synthetic or alkyd enamels dry to a lustrous high gloss (Figure 7-40), requiring no compounding or buffing. It is the least expensive and the least durable of the commercial finishing systems and tends to dry slowly, generally overnight. It is prone to wrinkling in hot weather during the first 24 to 48 hours and cannot be two-toned or repaired for about 8 to 24 hours. Synthetic enamel also has poorer resistance to water, chemicals, and gasoline during the first few days after application.

Over the past few years, alkyd synthetic enamels have given away some of their popularity to newer finishes, namely acrylic and polyurethane enamels. However, many refinishers still select this enam-el because it provides an economical two-coat system with high initial gloss that hides surface imperfections better than newer enamels. This is especially true when a synthetic enamel is reduced with hardener. The synthetic is applied the same as without hardeners, but the drying time is shortened when the hardener has been added. The finish can be two-toned when it is dry enough to tape and generally can be recoated at any time without fear of lifting. The hardener also makes the synthetic enamel highly wrinkle-resistant, though it does not improve durability.

ACRYLIC LACQUERS

Introduced in 1956, acrylic lacquer quickly replaced nitrocellulose lacquer because it dried to a higher gloss and retained its appearance longer. It found immediate acceptance as a favored OEM and repair finish. It is used for spot and panel repair of both lacquer and enamel original finishes and in overall repainting. When used over enamel, a sealer is recommended.

FIGURE 7-39 The introduction of nitrocellulose lacquers brought color to the automotive industry.

FIGURE 7-40 With the introduction of alkyd resin enamels in 1929, cars took on a lustrous high gloss.

Properly applied, an acrylic lacquer system can give excellent results. It combines the features of durability, color and gloss retention, high gloss, and fast drying time. But, to achieve these features, both the undercoats and thinners must be those recommended for acrylic lacquer paints. The manufacturer's instructions should always be followed. If products from different manufacturers are mixed, failure of the paint film might occur by cracking or crazing.

Acrylic lacquers respond readily to hand or machine polishing, using rubbing or polishing compounds. Some degree of polishing is usually necessary, depending on the gloss level required.

ACRYLIC ENAMELS

Developed in the 1960s, acrylic enamels are more durable and faster drying than alkyd enamels and eliminate the compounding step associated with acrylic lacquer. Generally recommended for panel repairs and overall repainting, some acrylic enamels are used for spot repair of both lacquer and enamel original finishes. Acrylic enamel costs slightly more than synthetic enamels but is less expensive than other finishing systems available today.

Acrylic enamel combines the properties and advantages of the very durable color and gloss retentive acrylic lacquer with the excellent flow characteristics and gloss of the enamel systems. It is fast drying and is about 50 percent more durable than synthetic enamel. It is also easy to apply, produces a deep luster and high gloss, and has excellent color and gloss retention. Two-toning or recoating is possible within the first 6 hours of drying. During this period, the solvent evaporates from the film, leaving the finish nontacky and dry to the touch.

For the next 6 to 48 hours, however, most acrylic enamels enter the hard-curing period. Recoating must be done before this period since strong solvents of another coat could cause lifting because the original coat has become too cured to be dissolved and melt in with the new coat. If recoating is necessary during this time, most paint manufacturers recommend the use of a recoat sealer that serves as a barrier coat and permits recoating of acrylic enamel during the critical cure period when lifting might otherwise occur.

Some of the problems created when using acrylic enamels can be reduced or eliminated by the use of a hardener or urethane catalyst. The addition of a hardener or catalyst (often referred to as a second stage or second component) provides a greater initial gloss than synthetic enamel or acrylic enamel alone. It also improves the DOI (Distinctiveness Of Image, or measurement of the sharpness of images

FIGURE 7-41 Before applying any paint material, carefully read the manufacturer's instructions on the container.

reflected from the surface), chemical resistance, flexibility, and chip resistance of the finish while eliminating the self-lifting that might occur during the recoating within the 6-to-48-hour hard-curing period of the acrylic enamel without hardener. When adding a hardener or catalyst to acrylic enamel, a recoat or barrier coat sealer is not necessary to prevent lifting.

After reducing the acrylic enamel color and just prior to spraying, add the catalyst or hardener to the reduced material as per label directions (Figure 7-41). Once the catalyst is added and mixed, the topcoat should be sprayed immediately. The pot life, or working time, of these paints will generally be in the range of 4 to 8 hours. After this time all mixed paints should be discarded.

The advent of ultraviolet absorbers has greatly increased the durability and exterior weathering of the acrylic enamel. Acrylic enamel with hardeners and ultraviolet absorbers or stabilizers is sprayed in the same manner as acrylic enamel but provides 50 percent greater durability than acrylic enamels and 100 percent greater durability than the alkyd or synthetic enamels.

POLYURETHANE ENAMELS

Ordinary polyurethane enamels provide significantly greater durability than alkyd or synthetic enamels, acrylic enamels, and acrylic enamels with hardeners.

The polyurethane enamel—made with a polyester resin—dries by evaporation of the solvents and by chemical cross-linking between the two principal base components to cure the paint film. A high-gloss, extremely durable, chemical and solvent resistant finish results. Without an accelerator, dry time to tape is about 16 hours. With an accelerator, dry time to tape can be reduced to approximately 3 to 5 hours.

ACRYLIC URETHANE ENAMELS

A recent development in the urethane family is the acrylic urethane enamel. It is formulated with an acrylic resin that is much more durable than any other finish. Because of the characteristics of this resin, an acrylic urethane enamel offers higher gloss retention and, ultimately, a much longer life. Recent manufacturer tests have shown that this finish retains its gloss from 50 percent to 100 percent longer than ordinary polyurethane enamels.

The acrylic urethane enamel also dries tack-free and out of dust faster than polyurethane enamels. It is also more resistant to film degradation caused by the sun's ultraviolet (UV) rays. While degradation of the finish cannot be totally stopped, chemical composition of this material substantially retards damaging UV effects. When compared to metallic polyurethane colors, acrylic urethane enamel metallic colors have twice the durability. The urethane's durability also offers exceptional resistance to stone chipping and does not break down when exposed to weather, gasoline (Figure 7-42), chemicals, dirt, and road grime. It virtually eliminates sand scratch swelling.

To achieve proper results from this two component high-quality material, it is necessary to closely follow the manufacturer's instructions to the letter. The pot life of the activated material is 6 to 8 hours. To achieve the best results the material should be sprayed as soon as possible after components are mixed together. Some possible additives for acrylic urethane enamels include fish eye eliminators; accelerator (for temperatures below 70 degrees Fahrenheit) or retarder (for temperatures above 85 degrees Fahrenheit); and acrylic enamel reducers. If these additives and reducers are employed, they must be used in amounts specified by the manufacturer.

Typical application times are as follows:

- **Nonmetallic (nonpolychromatic).** Apply two to three medium wet coats and allow 20 to 30 minutes drying time between coats.
- **Metallic (polychromatic).** Apply three medium wet coats and allow 20 to 30 minutes drying time between coats. If necessary, apply a final mist coat to even out the metallic color (polychromatic).

Urethane clear coats can be applied over polyurethane enamel and properly prepared acrylic enamels 30 minutes after the color coat application. The result is an ultimate wet look that gives the basecoat additional depth, maximum color and gloss retention, plus extended durability.

WARNING: Polyurethane and acrylic urethane enamels as well as the two-component or catalyzed type finishes (acrylic and alkyd) use isocyanates as a hardener. Isocyanates, however, are highly reactive and can become health hazards if not handled carefully. Because isocyanates react with many common substances, they must be used, stored, and disposed of with care. All urethane paints and products contain isocyanates and, therefore, share the same potential health hazards regardless of brand.

Appropriate measures must be taken to prevent overexposure or sensitization whenever urethane or any other paints containing isocyanates are being sprayed. These paints should only be used in areas with adequate ventilation. For maximum protection when isocyanates are being sprayed, an air line respirator (Figure 7-43) should be worn until the work area has been exhausted of all vapors and spray mist.

Table 7-3 shows the relative durability of the various types of topcoat systems previously discussed and a comparison to Original Equipment (OE) high-baked thermosetting acrylic enamels.

FIGURE 7-42 Polyurethane finishes are not affected by gasoline spills.

FIGURE 7–43 When spraying isocyanate-based paints, wear a complete body cover and respirator. *(Courtesy of Sherwin-Williams Co.)*

TABLE 7-3: COMPARATIVE DURABILITY OF TOPCOATS

0	10	20	30	40	50	60	70	80	90	100

Acrylic Urethane Enamel

Two Component Acrylic Enamel

Polyurethane Enamel

Acrylic Enamel With Hardener

Acrylic Enamel

Synthetic (Alkyd) Enamel

Costs can be deceiving, particularly with the polyurethane and acrylic urethane colors, both of which are substantially more expensive in their unreduced prices per gallon. When costs are viewed in terms of life cycle—for example, the length of time the finish will continue to present an acceptable appearance before requiring refinishing—acrylic urethane enamels prove to be the most economical.

The type of paint used for the topcoat ultimately determines the attractiveness of the color, gloss, and finish. Table 7–4 is a general summary of the properties of paint used for repainting.

POLYOXITHANE ENAMELS

Recently introduced, these enamels are part of the first isocyanate-free basecoat/clear coat and single stage system. They were developed with health considerations in mind as well as providing the highest quality in OEM color and quality matching. Tests show that these provide excellent hiding, durability against industrial pollution and extreme weather conditions, and protection from fading caused by ultraviolet light. More information about polyoxithane enamels will be available in the near future, but for now these initial enamels promise to be the answer to one of the refinishing industries' major health problems.

BASECOAT/CLEAR COAT FINISHES

In the past few years, OEMs around the world have increasingly adopted basecoat/clear coat systems as the finish of choice for new cars rolling off assembly lines. The technology for basecoat/clear

coat finishes was developed in Europe. The durability and popularity of these finishes prompted Japanese and American automobile manufacturers to begin offering them, too. In fact, most automotive finishing experts agree that the basecoat/clear coat system will be used on the vast majority of refinished vehicles before the turn of the century. When the system was first used, it utilized either an acrylic lacquer clear or a polyurethane enamel clear over an acrylic lacquer basecoat. Early in 1985, the first acrylic enamel basecoat/clear coat refinish system to actually simulate the OEM basecoat/clear coat finish was introduced. Like OEM finishes, the new system loads more transparent pigments into the basecoat and locks the metallic flakes into a flat arrangement, enabling it to match the brightness, the color intensity, and the travel of an OEM basecoat/clear coat finish. This makes it easy to get the best color match available.

An added benefit of this new basecoat technology is a 30-minute recoat time with the clear coat. Conventional basecoats use a "chemical drying" to build solvent resistance. Chemical drying generally requires 4 to 6 hours to prevent the clear coat solvents from redissolving the basecoat and allowing the aluminum or mica flakes to streak and mottle. Another new basecoat technology builds the necessary solvent resistance without chemical drying in just 30 minutes at 75 degrees Fahrenheit and 1.5 mils dry film thickness. These qualities enable this new basecoat/clear coat system to be applied quickly and easily with superior results.

More recently, painters have been switching to the new acrylic urethane basecoat/clearcoat system. Many refinish paint manufacturers now offer

TABLE 7-4: SUMMARY OF TOPCOAT PAINT FEATURES

Nomenclature		One-Component Type			Two-Component Type	
		Alkyd Enamels	Acrylic Lacquer	Acrylic Enamel	Polyurethane	Acrylic Urethane Enamel
Spray characteristics		Excellent	Excellent	Good	Good	Good
Possible thickness per application		Fair	Fair	Good	Excellent	Excellent
Gloss	without polishing	Fair	Good	Good	Excellent	Excellent
	after polishing	Good	Good	Good	—	Good
Hardness		Good	Good	Good	Excellent	Excellent
Weather resistance (frosting, yellowing)		Fair	Fair	Good	Excellent	Excellent
Gasoline resistance		Fair	Fair	Fair	Excellent	Good
Adhesion		Good	Good	Fair	Excellent	Excellent
Pollutant resistance		Fair	Fair	Fair	Excellent	Excellent
Drying time	to touch	68°F 5–10 minutes	68°F 10 minutes	68°F 10 minutes	68°F 20–30 minutes	68°F 10–20 minutes
	for surface repair	68°F 6 hours 140°F 40 minutes	68°F 8 hours 158°F 30 minutes	68°F 8 hours 158°F 30 minutes	—	68°F 4 hours 158°F 15 minutes
	to let stand outside	68°F 24 hours 140°F 40 minutes	68°F 24 hours 158°F 40 minutes	68°F 24 hours 158°F 40 minutes	68°F 48 hours 158°F 1 hour	68°F 16 hours 158°F 30 minutes

this excellent two-stage system, and they have quickly achieved a strong following. The reason for its popularity stems from not only meeting the practical needs of the painter, but also because of its advanced technology. Acrylic urethanes are fast, offer the best color matches, and provide better coverage and hiding. Thus, they increase productivity and improve customer satisfaction.

In a few years, most cars probably will be finished in basecoat/clear coat colors. This trend is certain to have several effects on the paint shop. Surface preparation and a clean shop environment will be more important than ever, as the higher gloss and DOI of the clear coat make imperfections easier to see. A greater emphasis on cleanliness will result in more use of downdraft booths in progressive paint shops.

With good surface preparation and a clean shop, however, painters will find that the new acrylic enamel basecoat/clear coats are very easy to apply and result in better looking, more durable finishes.

For example, painters no longer have to balance flow for metal control in a metallic color, and streaking and mottling are eliminated. Spot repair is made easy because basecoat/clear coat finishes make it simple to blend in an edge. And the need for buffing is just about eliminated. But most important to paint shop refinishers is the outstanding color match that state-of-the-art basecoat/clear coat systems provide.

One challenge the paint shop refinisher faces is becoming well-educated about the many different systems available in order to select the best one. No customer likes a streaked finish or color drift. No paint shop can afford to lose potential income because shop time is tied up due to the difficult application procedures and long dry times. When choosing a refinishing system, the key factors involved are probably appearance and ease of application.

It is a good idea to look for a system that provides fast dry time and locks in the metallic flakes for consistent color match. Also, the amount of pigment in the basecoat should be considered. A good basecoat will contain enough pigment to achieve hiding in 1 to 1-1/2 mils (two coats basecoat). Some basecoats will require four to six coats of basecoat, which means more application time, more materials, and longer dry times due to higher film thickness. To assure long-term durability and customer satisfaction, the system should contain light stabilizers and ultraviolet light absorbers.

Identifying cars that are clear coated is easy. Looking at the vehicle identification code and the color chip book is a quick way to find out if the car has the basecoat/clear coat system. If the code has been removed or destroyed, sanding a small spot in a concealed area of the vehicle to be finished, using a fine sandpaper, can help determine the type of finish. If the dust is white, the car has a basecoat/clear coat finish. If the dust is the color of the car, it does not.

PEARL LUSTER FINISHES

Most recently, in their effort to attract buyers in a market where cars are starting to look alike, car manufacturers are offering highly iridescent colors applied in three layers. The first stage is a mica or "pearl" coat, and the final stage is the clear topcoat.

In 1960, a synthetic pearl luster pigment using a mica particle covered with thin layers of titanium dioxide was developed. The mica particles made very good carriers for the titanium dioxide because of their highly transparent qualities. The titanium dioxide layers provide the rainbow or pearl effect as light reflects and passes through the layers.

This transparent quality of the pearl luster pigments is what allows a much higher reflective brilliance that cannot be obtained with aluminum flakes. Aluminum flakes act as miniature mirrors that reflect light (Figure 7–44A). However, they will not let light pass through to the color. If too many aluminum flakes are added to a brilliant color, the color will be washed out.

Pearl luster pigments of titanium dioxide-covered mica flakes reflect light while also allowing some to pass through to other mica flakes and colored pigments below (Figure 7–44B). The brilliance and high iridescent effect of the finish are created this way. Because the pearl coat stage of this system is translucent and reflective, the amount of mica in this stage is critical for matching.

The repaint formulas available for the pearl colors on new cars usually have colored pigments and mica pigments combined. These formulas are applied like any other two-stage paint, except when they are to be sprayed over a repaired area that has been primed. Several additional coats with the prop-

er flash times between them will be necessary because of the transparent quality of the paint. Allow more spraying time when scheduling jobs with mica finishes.

Several things should be kept in mind when working with the pearl luster paints:

- Mica flakes are heavy. Keep the paint agitated to ensure even distribution.
- Spray test panels (with primer spot). Do not test on the customer's car.
- Continually blend.
- Do not rush. Allow enough flash time between coats.
- Spray in a well-lighted booth.
- Ultraviolet lights can help in checking the pearlescent effect.
- Direct sunlight is the best source of light for evaluating touch-ups.
- Check work from three angles in direct sunlight. Straight in, from a 45-degree angle to the surface with the light behind the observer, and from the opposite 45-degree angle with the light ahead of the observer.

Some experimenting with tinting of the base colors, tinting of the pearl coat with colored pigments or pearl pigments, or a combination of both, might be necessary to accomplish a good match.

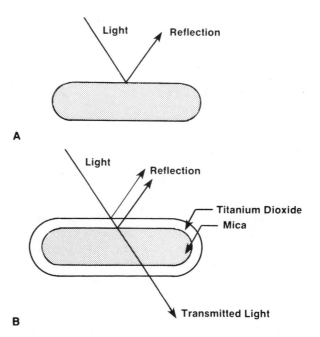

FIGURE 7–44 As opposed to (A) an aluminum flake, which only reflects light off its surface, (B) colored mica particles can be designed to reflect, absorb, and refract differing amounts of light striking them, thereby changing the color.

TRI-COAT FINISHES

Tri-coating, a three-stage basecoat/clear coat technique, which for 20 years has been used in glamour coating custom cars and for other special applications, has now found its way into the production line of several manufacturers deluxe models.

As the name implies, these tri-coat finishes consist of three distinct layers which produce a pearlescent appearance: a basecoat, a midcoat or interference coat, and a clear coat. Unlike other coating systems such as metallics and some micas, which change the value of a color (lightness/darkness) when viewed from different angles, the new three coats actually change the hue (color) as the angle of view changes (Figure 7-45). Thus a three-coat finish might look red viewed from straight on and blue when seen from the side. The effect is similar to that of a thin layer of oil floating on water.

In a three-coat finish the interference coat, or midcoat (or sandwich), is the layer contributing the most to the final appearance of the color. Particles making up the midcoat color can be designed to reflect, absorb, and refract differing amounts of the light striking them as in all pearl luster finishes. Changing the amount, or color, of the mica flake's coating drastically alters the color of the finish when viewed from straight on or from an angle. While most of the three-coat finishes currently used by automakers are pastels, darker shades are also feasible. Three-coat finishes have given automotive stylists an exciting new palette of variable colors. Anywhere from one to five coats of a pearl luster sandwich coat need to be applied to achieve the desired effect.

FORCE DRYING ENAMEL TOPCOATS

Force drying enamels by means of heat convection ovens or infrared lights will greatly reduce the drying period but care must be exercised to avoid wrinkling, blistering, pinholing, or discoloration. It is generally better to force dry at lower temperatures for longer periods rather than to run high temperatures for shorter periods. The following will serve as a guide for force drying times and temperatures for alkyd enamels: 125 degrees Fahrenheit for 90 minutes; 150 degrees Fahrenheit for 45 minutes; 180 degrees Fahrenheit for 30 minutes; and 200 degrees Fahrenheit for 15 to 20 minutes. Usually, acrylic enamel will dry in 15 to 20 minutes at 175 degrees Fahrenheit. While enamel can be force dried up to 200 degrees Fahrenheit, maximum care should be taken to allow sufficient flash-off time for solvents to escape before force drying or blistering is possible. Generally speaking, pastel colors are heat sensitive

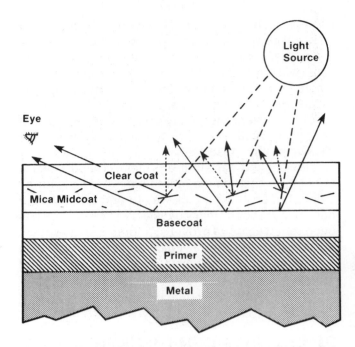

FIGURE 7-45 As this example shows, tri-coat finishes will alter the hue (color) of the finish as the angle of view changes.

and extreme caution must be used in force drying them to avoid discoloration.

It is especially necessary to avoid heavy coats of enamel in hot weather or when force drying. The temperature at which the enamel is sprayed, rather than the temperature at which it is dried, determines the reducer selected. Further information on the operation of force drying equipment is given in Chapter 2.

SOLVENTS (REDUCERS AND THINNERS)

As mentioned earlier in the chapter, when used with lacquer undercoats or topcoats, the blend of diluent solvents is called a **thinner**. When used with enamel undercoats or topcoats, the blend of diluent solvents is called a **reducer**. While the principles for making automotive paint solvents are similar, the ingredients that go into reducers are entirely different from the ones used in thinners. Therefore, the two materials never should be used interchangeably.

The basic function of diluent solvent such as a reducer and a thinner is to lower the viscosity of undercoats and topcoats that are too thick to spray as they come from the container. To accomplish this, a reducer or thinner must be properly balanced. That is, it must be made of the right ingredients to:

- Provide proper dilution of the material so that it will not only pass through the gun smoothly but also atomize easily as it leaves the gun.
- Keep the material in solution long enough for it to flow out and level a smooth, even surface and not allow the film to sag or run.
- Provide complete evaporation of the solvent so as to leave a tough, smooth, and durable film.
- Aid in blending lacquers and enamel spot repairs.

WARNING: Solvents are also used to clean painting equipment, and frequently the painter. However, before using the solvent to remove paint or undercoats from the skin, check to see if the manufacturer has any warnings against using it for this purpose. Some solvents used with newer finishes contain materials that can cause skin rashes and dermatitis. Always be sure to wash the area immediately after using solvent or paint, or undercoat is removed.

SELECTING THE PROPER SOLVENT

There are two vital variables that affect the spraying of materials: **temperature** and **humidity.** Unless a shop has year-round temperature control, these variables must be carefully observed and compensated for with use of the proper solvent. Of the two variables, temperature is the most critical.

Here is how temperature and humidity affect sprayed material:

- Hot, dry weather produces the **faster dry time.**
- Hot, humid, or warm, dry weather produces a **fast dry time,** but slower than hot, dry weather. (High humidity can cause problems.)
- Normal weather—70 degrees Fahrenheit with 45–55 relative humidity—produces a **normal dry time.**
- Cold, dry weather produces a **slower dry time** than normal.
- Cold, wet, or humid weather produces the **slowest dry time.**

Thus, to do quality refinishing, many auto paint shops use up to four different types of solvents for each paint system employed during the course of a year:

- **Slow drying solvent.** The flash time evaporation rate for slow lacquer thinners ranges from 3-1/2 to 5 minutes at about 75 degrees Fahrenheit when applied wet. For a slow drying enamel reducer, the flash time is slightly longer.
- **Medium drying solvent.** The average flash time evaporation rate for medium thinner is about 2 minutes when applied wet. Flash time for a medium reducer is slightly longer.
- **Fast drying solvent.** The flash time evaporation rate for fast thinners ranges from 15 to 20 seconds when applied wet at about 72 degrees Fahrenheit. The flash time for a fast reducer is slightly longer.
- **Retarder.** This is a very slow drying solvent. The flash time evaporation rate of retarder is about 30 minutes when applied wet at about 75 degrees Fahrenheit.

A good general rule to follow when selecting the proper solvent is: The **faster** the shop drying conditions, the slower drying the solvent should be.

In hot, dry weather, use a slow drying solvent. In cold, wet weather, use a fast drying solvent. If a solvent evaporates too rapidly, the following problems can be caused:

- **Orange peel.** As illustrated earlier in the chapter (Figure 7–7), the droplets formed in the spray pattern hit the surface and dry before they have time to flow out. This causes a roughness in the surface. In enamel topcoats this condition is referred to as orange peel. In lacquers this texture is often called dry spray. When this occurs with primer-surfacers, excessive sanding is required to make the surface smooth enough to apply the topcoats. With lacquer topcoats, excessive compounding and polishing is required to produce a smooth, high-luster film. While there can be a slight amount of orange peel in an enamel film, too much will cause roughness, low gloss, or both.
- **Blushing.** In hot, humid weather, some of the thinner evaporates as it leaves the gun and some as it hits the surface. This evaporation of the thinner creates a cooling condition that causes the moisture in the air to condense into droplets and mix with the spray stream. As the spray hits the surface and the film forms, the condensed moisture droplets are trapped. This gives the film a dull, hazy, or cloudy look (Figure 7–46A).
- **Overspray.** Similar to dry spray, overspray (Figure 7–46B) occurs where the spray pat-

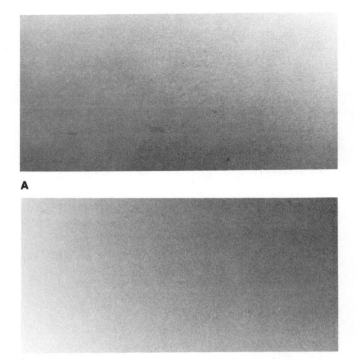

A

B

FIGURE 7–46 Improper selection of a solvent that drys too fast can cause problems like (A) blushing and (B) overspray.

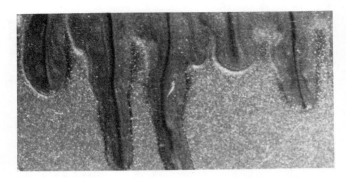

A

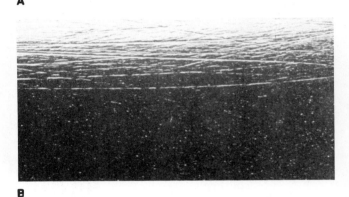

B

C

FIGURE 7–47 Too slow an evaporation rate can cause such problems as (A) sags and runs, (B) sand scratch swelling, and (C) mottling. *(Courtesy of PPG Industries, Inc.)*

tern overlaps an area already sprayed. (If a slow-dry thinner is used, the overspray will generally melt into the previously sprayed area.)

If on the other hand, a reducer or thinner evaporates too slowly, look for these problems (Figure 7–47):

- **Sags and runs.** A topcoat must lose part of its solvent before and part after it hits the surface. If the evaporation is too slow, the droplets will be too wet when they contact the surface and they will tend to flow. The weight of the film will cause it to slide or roll down the surface. Sags and runs are by far the most common problem where evaporation is too slow.
- **Sand scratch swelling.** A very slow drying thinner will tend to penetrate an old finish. This condition, which makes the sand scratches more pronounced, is called sand scratch swelling.
- **Mottling.** When metallic colors are sprayed too wet, the metallic flakes float and group together distorting the appearance of the finish.

While the use of an improper thinner or solvent might cause other problems, the six previously outlined cover the most common situations. Perhaps the best rule to follow in selecting reducers or thinners is to choose the slowest drying reducer or thinner that can be handled safely without sags, runs, or mottling (in metallic finishes). This will assure a smooth, glossy surface and generally the best color match. Lacquer topcoats often help to minimize buffing time. Such a selection will also improve the performance of most undercoats (for example,

FIGURE 7–48 Before thinning or reducing a paint material, check the label for proper percentage.

by reducing the sanding time for primer-surfacers and allowing sealers to flow better).

BASECOAT ADDITIVE

Instead of using a regular paint reducer, many paint manufacturers for their basecoat/clear coat system are recommending the use of a basecoat additive or stabilizer. This material not only acts as a reducer for base colors, but works as a "fixer" to lock the flake in place. Locking the flake into place makes it easier to achieve a more accurate color match to today's OEM colors. This additive also minimizes sand scratch swelling to give a smoother looking basecoat and ultimately a better looking topcoat.

When using most stabilizer additives, add the material in a 200 to 250 percent reduction. Be sure to use an additive that is correct for the shop's temperature. Check the additive label for this information and any other directions.

THINNING PRIMER-SURFACER

When thinning lacquer-based primer-surfacers, the object of the thinner selection is to be slow enough to provide a relatively smooth surface, which will require a minimum amount of sanding.

Faster drying thinners will cause the film to be rough, thus increasing sanding time.

The use of a slower drying topcoat thinner should also be avoided. The reason is that there is a tendency to spray heavy coats of primer-surfacer because of the high-solids content. When slow dry thinners are used, longer flash times and dry times are required. If the refinisher fails to allow sufficient flash and dry time, the primer-surfacer might shrink and crack at the featheredge.

When thinning or reducing, refer to the paint label for the proper solvent percentage (Figure 7–48) so there will be no danger of over or under reducing. Table 7–5 shows how to convert these percentages to the proper proportions of paint and solvent (Figure 7–49).

OTHER REFINISHING MATERIALS

There are several other products available to the refinisher that will help produce a better finishing job. The application of these products is covered in later chapters in this book.

Wax and Grease Removers. The adhesion of any paint film to any surface depends first on whether or not the surface is absolutely clean, not just physically clean, but chemically clean. The slightest film of oil, grease, wax, or moisture will prevent the paint from sticking to the surface.

Wax and grease removers (also called dewaxers) are solvent type materials that will dissolve part-

TABLE 7–5: REDUCTION RATIO GUIDE			
Reduction Percentage	Mixing Ratio	Paint Material	Solvent Material
12-1/2	8:1 =	8 parts	1 part
25	4:1 =	4 parts	1 part
33	3:1 =	3 parts	1 part
50	2:1 =	2 parts	1 part
75	4:3 =	4 parts	3 parts
87	1.5:1 =	1-1/2 parts	1 part
100	1:1 =	1 part	1 part
125	4:5 =	4 parts	5 parts
150	2:3 =	2 parts	3 parts
175	4:7 =	4 parts	7 parts
200	1:2 =	1 part	2 parts
225	4:9 =	4 parts	9 parts
250	4:10 =	4 parts	10 parts
275	4:11 =	4 parts	11 parts
300	1:3 =	1 part	3 parts

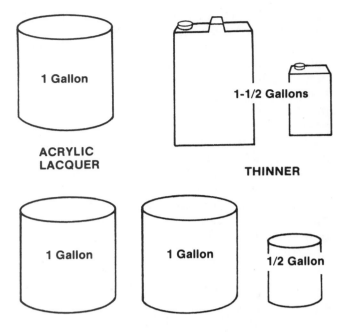

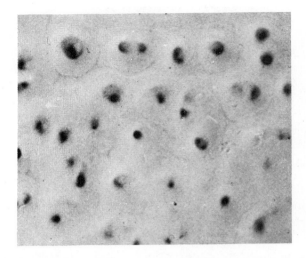

FIGURE 7-51 Fish eyes caused by painting over silicone. *(Courtesy of PPG Industries, Inc.)*

2-1/2 GALLONS READY TO SPRAY

FIGURE 7-49 Various materials work best as given percentages. For example, lacquer primer-surfacers and acrylic lacquer colors work best when thinned 150 percent. *(Courtesy of PPG Industries, Inc.)*

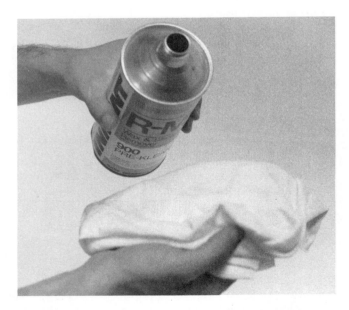

FIGURE 7-50 A dewaxing and degreasing is a very important operation in most refinishing operations. When applying be sure to follow manufacturer's recommendations.

ly oxidized waxes and greases that are embedded in the old finish (Figure 7-50). They should be strong enough to dissolve the several types of waxes used in automobile polishes but not so strong as to attack

the old finish. A final wipe off with a clean rag saturated in wax and grease remover before applying the paint is the best insurance against peeling and silicones. If the silicones are not removed before refinishing, fish eyes might form in the final finish (Figure 7-51). An additive or eliminator can also be put in to prevent fish eyes.

Metal Conditioners and Rust Inhibitors. Some auto paint jobs fail to hold up because the metal over which the finish was sprayed contains microscopic rust particles or pits of rust. Unless this rusting action is eliminated and further rusting prevented, the action will continue and the swelling effect of the rust will eventually pop off the paint.

As described in Chapter 1, metal conditioner and rust inhibitor is an acid that, when it comes into contact with rust, changes the iron oxide (rust) into another compound. This compound is fairly stable and if the surface containing it can be sealed over with paint after its use, there will be no further developof the oxidizing action.

The application of metal conditioner also creates negatively charged ions on the metal surface. The positively charged paint products are thus attracted to the metal, enhancing the paint-to-metal bond. This is the principle of "bonderizing" that is used in the car factories duplicated in a refinish shop through the use of metal conditioner. This material also etches metal to give the primer-surfacer a better and therefore better adhesion.

Rubbing Compounds. Rubbing compounds are composed of an emulsion of water and oils combined with abrasive compounds. Selection and grading of the abrasives determines the difference between good and bad compounds. Uniformity of size and hardness of the grits must be carefully con-

FIGURE 7-52 Use of a mechanical polishing compound. *(Courtesy of PPG Industries, Inc.)*

trolled. Sharp, hard abrasives or irregular size results in scratching the surface in place of doing a smooth cutting job.

Mechanical polishing compounds (Figure 7-52) are designed for use with a power polisher/ buffer. Those classified as rubbing compounds are into be used by hand. The very fine grit hand compound is called a polishing compound.

Glaze compounds are in fine finishing work. Similar to polishing compounds, they can be hand or machine finished. Complete details on using these materials can be found in Chapter 11.

Luggage Compartment or Trunk Finishes. Abrasion and moisture-resistant spatter finishare designed especially to duplicate the original car and truck finishes. Most spatter finishes are reduced with water and are easy to apply. White undercoats are recommended, but these spatter finishes will adhere to virtually any clean surface. These finishes are applicable to many other areas where an attractive finish is desired and where high scuff and wear resistance is needed.

Vinyl Spray Colors. Vinyls dry by evaporation of the volatiles. They dry rapidly to a permanent flexible film. The use of vinyl liquid over vinyl that is cleaned and pretreated with vinyl conditioner results in chemical bonding of the two films. Clear coats are essential to provide abrasion resistance and proper gloss level.

Some auto finishing shops apply vinyl spray paint on lower body panels. This abrasion-resistant coating protects these panels from being chipped by stones and other flying objects.

Flex (Elastomeric) Additives. Flex additives import flexibility to most topcoat qualities. They can be blended with acrylic lacquers, acrylic enamels, polyurethane acrylic enamels, and acrylic urethanes to produce flexibility for bumpers, fascia, and other flexible parts. The basic characteristics of the topcoat remain the same except for the flexibility.

There are several other additives available that help to improve the finish. For example, there are fish eye eliminators on the market. This material can be added to acrylic enamels, acrylic enamel basecoat/clear coat, synthetic enamels, and urethane enamels to keep fish eyes under control. However, they cannot be used with acrylic lacquer. All additives must be used as per manufacturer's instructions on the label.

Antichipping Paint. Most modern automobiles come with an antichipping paint applied to the rocker panels. Compared with other paints, antichipping paint has better coherence and pliability and helps prevent rust occurrence due to stone damage. When repainting, care is needed to apply antichipping paint at the designated areas so as not to lower the anticorrosion effectiveness.

Rocker Black Paint. This is either a semigloss or flat enamel coat that is applied to the rocker panel. After first masking off the surrounding area to protect it from paint overspray, the rocker panel is hand sprayed with a two-component urethane paint that has good adhesion qualities. If there are any other panels, such as the back panel, that require blacking, they should also be sprayed.

Paint Removers. There are many types of paint removers on the market. Two types of chemical paint removers are popular in refinishing shops. They are:

- Paint removers designed primarily to remove lacquer-type products
- Paint removers designed to remove all types of finishes (including enamel and urethane colors) down to the bare metal

Apply chemical strippers freely with a brush. When the old finish bubbles, flush off with a stream of water. Steel wool might be required to remove the finish in the case of acrylic lacquers. Other stubborn old finishes might have to be lifted from the surface with the aid of a putty knife. Further details on the use of paint removers in removing an old finish can be found in Chapter 9.

CAUTION: Never use a paint remover on plastic or fiberglass substrates.

Another chemical remover that is found in most paint shops is the decal remover. This material makes easy work of taking off decals.

Adhesives, Compounds, and Sealants. Perhaps more so than any other refinishing materials, adhesives are used where the action is—on those body parts subject to constantly changing conditions of temperature, moisture, friction, and pressure. Some of the more common adhesives in a refinishing shop include trim cement, glass sealer, weatherstrip adhesive, and caulking compounds and body seam sealer.

When using any of these paint products mentioned here—as well as when applying undercoats and solvents—be sure to carefully read the instructions detailing how to mix, how to apply, and how long to dry. These instructions on the container are important because they help to do the job right.

REVIEW QUESTIONS

1. Which is the volatile ingredient of the paint?
   a. pigment
   b. binder
   c. solvent
   d. none of the above

2. Which additives improve gloss?
   a. hardeners
   b. retarders
   c. flatteners
   d. none of the above

3. Which dries by evaporation of the solvents as the first stage and by oxidation of the binder as the second stage?
   a. lacquers
   b. enamels
   c. both a and b
   d. neither a nor b

4. When is a sealer absolutely necessary?
   a. when an old lacquer finish is to be covered with lacquer
   b. when an old lacquer finish is to be covered with enamel
   c. when an old enamel finish is to be covered with enamel
   d. when an old enamel finish is to be covered with lacquer

5. Which of the following is a characteristic of primers?
   a. They fill surface imperfections.
   b. They require sanding.
   c. They are usually enamel type products.
   d. All of the above
   e. None of the above

6. Which is the most popular primer-surfacer used today?
   a. nitrocellulose primer-surfacer
   b. acrylic primer-surfacer
   c. alkyd primer-surfacer
   d. self-etching primer-surfacer

7. The main reason for using a primer-sealer is to _____ .
   a. resist rust and corrosion
   b. provide topcoat adhesion
   c. insure a surface consistent in color and porosity
   d. none of the above

8. Which provides extra adhesion when a lacquer topcoat is being sprayed over an OEM enamel?
   a. barrier coat sealer
   b. recoat sealer
   c. bleeder sealer
   d. tie coat sealer

9. Painter A says that sand scratch swelling results when a thinner evaporates too quickly. Painter B says that this condition results when a thinner evaporates too slowly. Who is right?
   a. Painter A
   b. Painterer B
   c. Both A and B
   d. Neither A nor B

10. How many coats does it take for a good basecoat to achieve hiding?
    a. one
    b. two
    c. three
    d. four to six

11. Which of the following conditions results when the solvent evaporates too quickly?
    a. sand scratch swelling
    b. mottling
    c. sags and runs
    d. orange peel

12. Which solvent has an average flash time evaporation rate of 2 minutes when applied wet?
    a. slow-drying thinner
    b. slow-drying reducer
    c. medium-drying thinner
    d. medium-drying reducer

CHAPTER EIGHT

SANDING MATERIALS AND METHODS

Objectives

After reading this chapter, you will be able to:

- determine whether or not the existing finish is defect-free and adheres soundly to the vehicle.
- recognize surface defects that require additional surface preparation.
- select the correct abrasive and sanding techniques for specific sanding operations.

The life of a finish and the appearance of that finish will depend considerably upon the condition of the surface over which the paint is applied. In other words, proper surface preparation is the foundation of a good paint job. Without it, there will be a weak base for the topcoat that eventually can result in the failure of the finish.

The word "surface" as used in the automobile refinishing trade is the stage in the painting process just before the application of the final color coats. To get a smooth, level surface is therefore going to involve the steps necessary to get good adhesion and also the subsequent filling and sanding operations. Any painter knows that the color coat does little filling of rough areas and that the finished job is no smoother than the surface over which these materials are applied.

DETERMINATION OF SURFACE CONDITIONS

The very first job for the refinisher is to correctly identify the surface and overall condition of the existing paint system. Failure to identify defects at this stage can be very expensive to correct. It could even involve the complete removal of the repair and the original finish.

- Clean the areas to be inspected.
- Look carefully for any signs of surface or other forms of film breakdown—such as checking, cracking, and blistering (Figure 8-1). Horizontal surfaces usually show the greatest film deterioration; careful inspection of the hood and trunk areas will give a good indication of the overall condition of the paint system. Use light reflection to obtain the best view of the surface.
- Note particularly the gloss level. Low gloss will often indicate surface irregularities

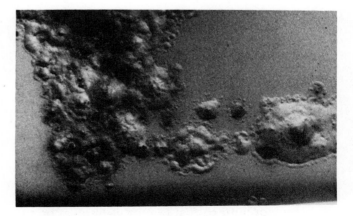

FIGURE 8-1 Carefully check the surface for signs of film breakdown such as blistering.

FIGURE 8-2 To check to see if rust has developed under a paint film, sand through a small spot and featheredge it.

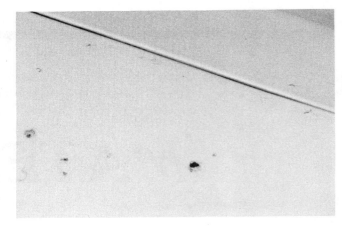

FIGURE 8-3 A chip or chips is a problem that can easily be solved by proper sanding.

caused by such defects as checking or microblistering, which will need more thorough investigation with a magnifying glass.

- Any signs of disfigurement or discoloration of the paint film due to attack by industrial fallout/acid rain must be completely removed.
- It must be determined that the old finish has good adhesion and that rust is not developing under the paint film. To test adhesion, sand through the finish (Figure 8-2), and featheredge a small spot. If the thin edge does not break or crumble, it is reasonable to assume that the old paint will stay on when the refinish color is applied over it. Developing rust can be detected by a roughness or pitting of the surface. The paint on those areas where either poor adhesion or rust is found must be removed to bare metal.

SANDING

Sanding is one of the most important steps of surface preparation. In fact, this operation is a standard part of most surface preparation procedures. Sanding prepares the surface for painting in several ways:

- Chipped paint (Figure 8-3) is sanded to taper the sharp edges that would show up as ridges under the new finish.
- Cracking or peeling paint (Figure 8-4) and minor surface rust (Figure 8-5) must be removed before applying a fresh topcoat. If not, these conditions will continue to deteriorate and will eventually ruin the new finish.

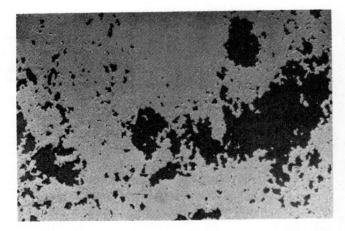

FIGURE 8-4 Cracking or peeling paint can be repaired by sanding. *(Courtesy of Maaco Enterprises, Inc.)*

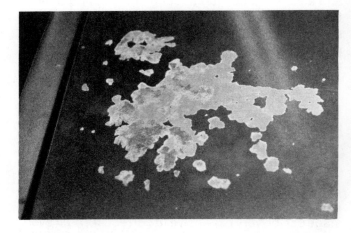

FIGURE 8-5 Rust must be removed by sanding before a new finish can be applied. *(Courtesy of Maaco Enterprises, Inc.)*

- Primed and puttied areas must be smoothed and leveled (Figure 8–6).
- The entire surface to be refinished must be scuff sanded to improve adhesion of the new paint (Figure 8–7). Scuff sanding removes any trace of contaminants on the existing finish. A clean, scuffed surface is very important for proper bonding of the new topcoat.

Because coated abrasives (sandpaper) perform the actual cutting and leveling in the sanding operation, selecting the correct abrasive is critical to the quality of the finished work.

COATED ABRASIVES (SANDPAPER)

When modern coated abrasives (sandpaper) are constructed, a flexible or semirigid backing attaches to the abrasive grains, which are bonded by an adhesive. Hence, the most efficient results on a particular application depend on the selection and manufacturing of suitable combinations of grains, adhesives, and backings available. The automotive refinishing professional must then select and correctly use the proper sandpaper product for optimum productivity, material cost efficiency, and the best finish.

ABRASIVE TYPES

The abrasive grains used to manufacture sandpaper products used in automotive refinishing are selected on the basis of their hardness, toughness, resistance to grinding heat, fracture characteristics,

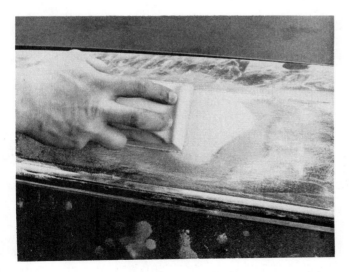

FIGURE 8–6 Primed and puttied areas must be smoothed and leveled by sanding.

FIGURE 8–7 Scuff sanding is used to improve the adhesion of the new paint. *(Courtesy of Maaco Enterprises, Inc.)*

and particle shape. The kind of grain a refinisher chooses depends on the purpose for which the coated abrasive is to be used.

As for abrasive types, most paint shops stock two: silicon carbide and aluminum oxide. Silicon carbide is a very sharp and fast-penetrating grain, customarily used (in paper sheet and disc form) for featheredging and dry sanding soft materials, such as old paint, fiberglass, and body putty. The major limitation of silicon carbide grain is that it tends to break down and dull rather readily when sanding hard surfaces.

Aluminum oxide is an extremely tough, wedge-shaped grain that better resists fracturing and dulling. Traditionally popular in coarse grits for grinding damaged metal, stripping old paint, and shaping plastic filler, numerous tests have demonstrated the superior performance of aluminum oxide sanding sheets and discs over silicon carbide on today's modern paint systems. Aluminum oxide is also preferred for use with today's paint finishes, which are predominantly basecoat/clear coat, have harder surfaces, and are applied in thinner layers than traditional lacquers and enamels. The blocky shape of the aluminum oxide abrasive when compared to silicon carbide makes it not as likely to create deep scratches right through to the base material and so reduces the risk of overcutting. The greater durability of aluminum oxide versus silicon carbide enables the abrasive sheet or disc to better resist edge wear and dulling for longer effective life on these harder finishes.

A third type of abrasive, zirconia alumina, has been developed through advanced technology and continues to gain widespread preference in paint shops. Zirconia alumina grain has a unique, self-sharpening characteristic that provides continuous new cutting points during the sanding operation for reduced labor and increased efficiency and longer effective life compared to traditional abrasives. Also, the fact that zirconia alumina products run cooler is particularly important when removing OEM clear coat finishes because of the extra heat generated when sanding these harder paint surfaces. A hot-running disc or sheet will load faster as the material being sanded softens and "balls up" in the abrasive. The self-sharpening action reduces the amount of

sanding pressure required—and often refinishing professionals find that they can save money by using one grit finer and get a better finish. The net result is that zirconia alumina abrasive products are being recognized as the more cost-effective alternative to traditional aluminum oxide and silicon carbide for a growing number of auto body repair and refinish operations.

GRIT NUMBERING SYSTEM

The rough side of the sandpaper is called the grit side. Grit sizes vary from coarse to micro fine grades and are ordered by number (Table 8–1). The

TABLE 8-1: TYPES OF GRIT AND NUMBERING SYSTEM

Grit	Aluminum Oxide	Silicon Carbide	Zirconia Alumina	Primary Use for Auto Body Repair
Micro fine	—	2000 1500 1250	—	Used for basecoat/clear coat paint system
Ultra fine	—	800	—	Used for color-coat sanding.
Very fine	—	600	600	Used for color-coat sanding. Also for sanding the paint before polishing.
	400 320 280 240	400 320 280 240	400 — 280 240	Used for sanding primer-surfacer and old paint prior to painting.
	220	220	—	Used for sanding of topcoat.
Fine	180 150	180 150	180 150	Used for final sanding of bare metal and smoothing old paint.
Medium	120 100 80	120 100 80	— 100 80	Used for smoothing old paint and plastic filler.
Coarse	60 50 40 36	60 50 40 36	60 — 40 —	Used for rough sanding plastics filler
Very coarse	24 16	24 16	24 —	Used on sander or grinder to remove paint.

FIGURE 8-8   As the grit number increases, so does the smoothness. *(Courtesy of Maaco Enterprises, Inc.)*

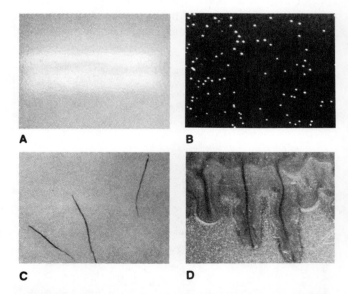

FIGURE 8-9   The micro fine grids are frequently used to remove such problems as: (A) orange peel; (B) dust nibs; (C) small surface scratches; and (D) paint sags.

FIGURE 8-10 Various sizes and shapes of abrasive papers and discs.

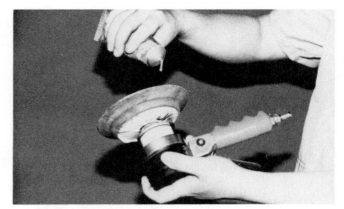

FIGURE 8-12 Applying a self-adhesive disc. *(Courtesy of Maaco Enterprises, Inc.)*

A

B

FIGURE 8-11 (A) Spread the adhesive on the pad, then (B) press the sandpaper disc in place. *(Courtesy of Carborundum Abrasives Co.)*

lower the number, the coarser the grit (Figure 8-8). For example, a #24 grit is used to remove old paint film; while a #320, #360, or #400 grit is used to sand the gloss of an old finish to be repainted. Very fine and ultra fine abrasive papers are used primarily for color coat sanding. The so-called compounding papers, the #1250, #1500, and #2000 grits, are used to solve problems on basecoat/clear coat paint surfaces such as those shown in Figure 8-9.

All domestic manufacturers conform to the same grading system for uniform consistency of standards. Differences in performance when using the same mineral, grit, bond, and backing from different manufacturers can be attributed to differences in manufacturing processes or quality, and/or operator methods.

As shown in Figure 8-10, the abrasive papers are available in various sizes and shapes. The most common forms found in paint shops are sheet stock and discs. The sheet stock—usually 9 by 11 inches—can then be cut into smaller pieces. Sheets are also available in jitterbug and board or body file sizes.

The most common abrasive sanding disc sizes for disc and dual action sanders are 5, 6, and 8 inches. Sandpaper disc grit sizes generally range from #50 to #400 grit. To apply nonstick sandpaper to the backing pad of a disc, orbital, or dual action sander, squeeze a few drops of adhesive on the backing pad. Spread the adhesive evenly with the pad (Figure 8-11A). Then center the disc on the pad and press it into place (Figure 8-11B). When using a self-adhesive sandpaper disc (Figure 8-12), be sure to center the paper on the pad before pressing it into place. Immediately after finishing the sanding operation, remove the used sandpaper from the backing pad. If it is not removed right away, the adhesive will harden and cause the disc to stick fast to the backing pad. Should this occur, use solvent on a rag to dis-

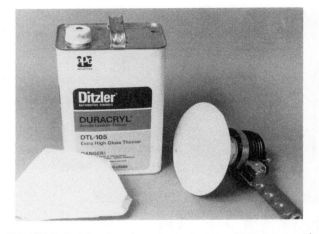

FIGURE 8-13 A solvent can be used to remove the sandpaper from the pad.

A

B

FIGURE 8-14 (A) Dual action sander and (B) air grinder can be used to grind rust and paint.

solve the adhesive and then remove the paper (Figure 8-13).

Grinding abrasive discs are used for rough jobs, such as grinding off rust and paint. They are available in numbers of #16 to #50 grits and in diameters of 3 to 9 inches. A dual action sander can be used to remove light rust, but heavy surface rust must be removed with a grinder (Figure 8-14). The grinder disc is first assembled to the backing plate (Figure 8-15) and then the disc/plate assembly is attached to the grinder (Figure 8-16). Some sandpaper discs are available with a center hole and are fastened to the sander in the same manner as the grinding abrasive disc. This manner of fastening is necessary in some wet sanding operations.

Although grinding discs are thicker and stronger than sandpaper discs, they are rather thin and easily bent. For this reason, the backing plate is necessary to provide stiffness for the revolving disc. Two types of back-up pads or plates are shown in Figure 8-17.

COATED ABRASIVE SURFACES

Coated abrasives are generally manufactured in two types of surface distributions (Figure 8-18):

- Closed coat abrasive paper
- Open coat abrasive paper

A closed coat product is one in which the surface grains completely cover the sanding side of the backing. An open coat product is one in which the abrasive grains are spaced to cover between 50 and 70 percent of the backing surface.

As for uses, open coat products are the popular choice on softer materials such as old paint, body filler, and putty, plastic, and aluminum—where premature loading of the abrasive would otherwise be a problem. Closed coat products generally provide a finer finish and are most commonly used in wet sanding applications.

In addition to open coat construction, many abrasive sheets and discs are surface coated in manufacturing with a zinc stearate solution to further prevent the premature loading of the sandpaper and to extend its useful life. This is particularly true of fine grit papers commonly used for scuff sanding old paint and primer-surfacer and finishing body filler. During those applications, the materials tend to soften because heat is generated while sanding and loading the abrasive. Remember also that with talc-coated products, the coating breaks away from the abrasive during use, taking with it sanding residue, and thereby freeing the abrasive to cut longer.

A

B

FIGURE 8-15 (A) Grinder disc and backing plate; (B) assembling the disc and plate. *(Courtesy of Maaco Enterprises, Inc.)*

FIGURE 8-16 Attaching abrasive disc/plate assembly to air grinder. *(Courtesy of Maaco Enterprises, Inc.)*

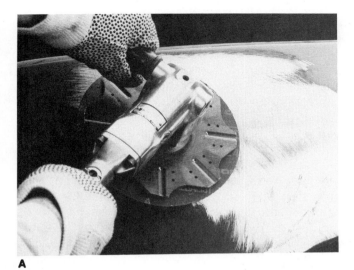

A

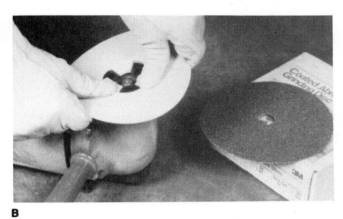

B

FIGURE 8-17 (A) Hard rubber backing plate and (B) a 3-inch fiber back-up plate

FIGURE 8-18 (Top) Closed coat abrasive paper; (bottom) open coat abrasive paper surfaces. *(Courtesy of Norton Co.)*

Talc remains an excellent load-resistant feature. However, with the evolution of paints, in particular today's popular basecoat/clear coat paint systems, certain elements of surface preparation become more critical, necessitating a possible alternative to the standard zinc stearate-coated sanding product.

One critical element is a contamination-free surface. Although talc can extend abrasive life, it also contributes another contaminant to the auto body surface. A clean surface under the basecoat is extremely critical for the success of the basecoat/ clear coat paint job—more so than with standard enamels and lacquer. In the past, dust "nibs" or contamination under the first color coat could be sanded down, spot recoated, and blended in without detracting from the appearance of the final finish. With basecoat/clear coat, however, spot sanding of the basecoat is to be avoided without necessitating a complete redo, as any defects or mismatches are magnified by the clear coat. With metalite flake and pearl color coats, subsurface dirt is a disaster. A key, then, is to minimize the contaminants on the auto body surface whenever possible. To this end, new sanding products have been introduced for auto body and paint professionals that employ high-tech, antistatic bonding agents to retard loading without zinc stearate.

In addition, new advanced abrasives such as zirconia alumina, anchored by resin type adhesives, are becoming more and more popular in the automotive refinishing trade because they cut faster and cooler. In other words, they will cut through paints, primers, and plastic fillers before they can soften and load the abrasive. And from a safety standpoint, sanding with products that do not have a zinc stearate coating creates less nuisance dust in the air as well as on the auto body surface.

WEIGHT OF PAPER

The proper selection of backings likewise depends on the application involved. Paper-backed abrasive products used in automotive refinishing are designated under uniform standards by all manufacturers as A-, C-, D-, or E-weight. A-weight paper is the lightest, most conformable paper backing available. It is popular for wet color sanding and dry finish sanding. The C- and D-weight paper products are progressively heavier, tougher, and less flexible. They are suitable for coarser sanding applications. E-weight paper is being more widely used by refinishing personnel for paint stripping and shaping of filled areas, as it is more durable than the traditional D-weight paper backings once popular for these applications. D- and E-weight papers are sometimes referred to as "production" papers because their construction produces a fast cutting, long lasting abrasive surface.

Cloth backings employed in products used by the auto body trade are likewise designated by a letter code. J-weight is a light, flexible cloth, popular for general clean-up, and deburring in sheet or handy roll form. X- and Y-weight cloths are heavier,

more rigid backings often used in small disc form for tight-quarter coarse sanding.

Fiber backings are most common in grinding discs. This very tough, semirigid backing is best suited for heavy operator pressure applications, such as weld grinding and rust removal. The most suitable fiber backing for automotive application is 30 mil vulcanized fiber because of its extra durability and greater resistance to breakdown and edge chipping.

Safety Pointers with Abrasives

The following points must be kept in mind when working with abrasives:

- Grinding discs should never be run if the edges are nicked, torn, or show excessive wear. Whenever in doubt do not use the product. Recommended fiber disc grinding speeds are 5 inch, 7650 rpm; 7 inch, 5500 rpm; 9-1/8 inch, 4200 rpm.
- Fiber grinding discs should be seated flat against a back-up pad and never overhang a pad by more than 1/4 inch.
- When paper discs are used on a slow speed polisher, the recommended speed is 3000 rpm or less.
- Curled discs generally indicate improper storage and should not be used until the shape is corrected. Storage of discs at 65 to 75 degrees Fahrenheit will prevent excessive curling of abrasive products prior to usage.
- Insure proper ventilation at all times when grinding or sanding and particularly avoid breathing dusts/fumes that are generated by "grinding aid" disc products. Refer to precautions on box labels, discs, or charts for detailed instructions.

METHODS OF SANDING

Refinishing sanding can be done:

- By hand or
- By power equipment

Most heavy sanding—such as the old finish—is done by power sanders. But some conditions—particularly the delicate operations—dictate hand sanding.

HAND SANDING

Hand sanding is a simple back and forth scrubbing action with the sandpaper flat against the sur-

FIGURE 8-19   Fold sandpaper in thirds. *(Courtesy of Maaco Enterprises, Inc.)*

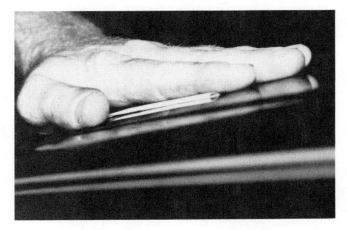

FIGURE 8-20   Method of holding the paper

FIGURE 8-21   Result of finger sanding. *(Courtesy of Maaco Enterprises, Inc.)*

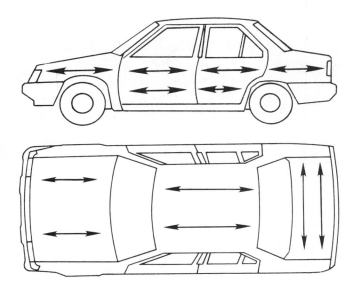

FIGURE 8-22   Sand with body lines.

face. It can be achieved by following a general procedure such as this:

1. Cut the sheet of sandpaper in half crosswise and then fold in thirds (Figure 8-19).
2. Place the paper in the palm of the hand and hold it flat against the surface. Apply even, moderate pressure along the length of the sandpaper using the palm and extended fingers (Figure 8-20). Sand back and forth with long, straight strokes. If the palm of the hand is not flat on the surface, the fingers will be doing the sanding. This will result in uneven pressure being applied in the spaces between the fingers (Figure 8-21). Finger sanding should be avoided.
3. Do not sand in a circular motion. This will create sand scratches that might be visible under the paint finish. To achieve the best results, always sand in the same direction as the body lines on the vehicle (Figure 8-22).
4. Be sure to thoroughly sand areas where a heavy wax buildup can be a problem, such as around trim, moldings, door handles (Figure 8-23), radio antennae, and behind the bumpers. Paint will not adhere properly to a waxy surface.
5. Use a sanding block or pad for best results. To sand convex or concave panels (Figure 8-24), employ a flexible sponge rubber backing pad. Use a sanding block (Figure 8-25) to sand level surfaces.
6. Carefully sand areas where coarser grit paper has been used. Hard-to-reach areas are easier to sand with a small abrasive pad similar to the one shown in Figure 8-26.
7. When hand sanding primer or putty, make certain to sand the area until it feels smooth and level. Rub a hand or a clean cloth (Figure 8-27) over the surface to check for rough spots.

   —**Dry.** This is basically the back-and-forth procedure just described. But one of the

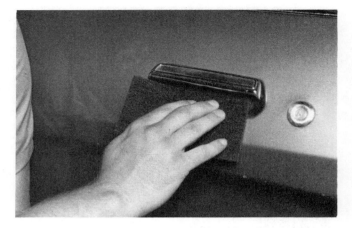

FIGURE 8-23 Sand around trim, handles, molding, and other similar items.

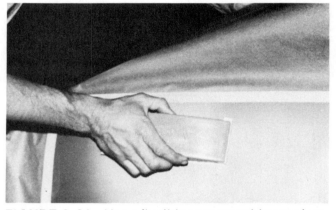

FIGURE 8-24 Use a flexible sponge rubber pad on convex and concave panels. *(Courtesy of Maaco Enterprises, Inc.)*

FIGURE 8-25 Use a sanding block on flat surfaces. *(Courtesy of Maaco Enterprises, Inc.)*

FIGURE 8-26 Use an abrasive pad in tight spots.

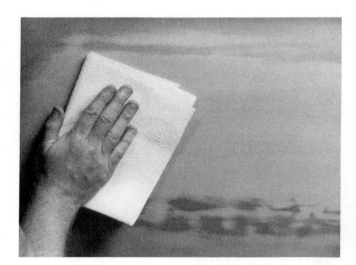

FIGURE 8-27 Feel for rough spots.

problems with it is that the paper tends to clog with paint or metal dust. Tapping the paper from time to time will remove some of the dust. Another suggestion is to use talc-coated or dry-lubricated sandpaper, which tends to prevent clogging. Special-treated open coat paper resists loading for long life. The majority of acrylic primer-surfacers should be sanded dry.

—**Wet.** Wet sanding also solves the problem of paper clogging. It is basically the same action as dry sanding except that water, a sponge, and a squeegee are used in addition to the sanding block. Sandpapers are available in dry, wet, or wet-or-dry abrasive types.

FIGURE 8-28 When wet sanding, water can be applied by a sponge. *(Courtesy of Carborundum Abrasives Co.)*

TABLE 8-2: COMPARISON OF WET AND DRY SANDING

Item	Wet Sanding	Dry Sanding
Work speed	Slower	Faster
Amount of sand-paper required	Less	More
Condition of finish	Very good	Final finish difficult
Workability	Normal	Good
Dust	Little	Much
Facilities required	Water drain necessary	Dust collector and exhaust necessary
Drying time	Necessary	Not necessary

When wet sanding, dip the paper in the water or wet the surface with the sponge (Figure 8-28). Use plenty of water, employing short strokes and light pressure. Never allow the surface to dry during the wet sanding operation. Also do not allow paint residue to build up on the abrasive paper. It is possible to tell how well the paper is cutting by the amount of drag felt as it moves across the surface. When the paper begins to slide over the surface too quickly, it is no longer cutting. The grit has become filled with paint particles or sludge. Rinse the paper in water to remove the paint and sponge the surface to remove the remaining particles. Then the sandpaper will cut

the surface again. Check the work periodically by sponging the surface off and wiping it dry with a squeegee. This will remove all excess water, so that it is easier to evaluate the surface condition. It is usually wise to complete one panel or body section at a time, then remove the sanding residues with the sponge and dry off with the squeegee before sanding the next panel.

Once the wet sanding operation is completed, be sure that all surfaces are dry. Blow out the seams and molding with compressed air at a lower pressure and tack-rag the entire surface.

A comparison of the advantages and disadvantages of wet and dry sanding is given in Table 8-2.

POWER SANDING

As described in Chapter 2, there are four types of power sanders used by the refinisher (Figure 8-29):

- Disc sander or grinder
- Orbital or jitterbug pad sander
- Dual action (DA) sander
- Straight line or board sander

All four types of sanders are powered by air or electricity.

In general, the type of power sander dictates sanding procedures (Table 8-3). Disc sanders or grinders, for example, have high-speed discs that turn from 2000 to 6000 rpm. They use circular discs from 5 to 9 inches in diameter and are used for such operations as grinding off an old finish. Heavier grinders (Figure 8-30) generally take a 9-inch diameter disc and—because of the obvious safety hazard involved—many have both a rear and side handle for better control.

When using a disc grinder, care must be taken to tilt it slightly so that only about 1 inch of the leading edge of the sanding disc contacts the surface (Figure 8-31). Never use the disc flat on the surface because it will twist the grinder and can even cause it to fly out of one's grip. Also when held flat, it makes circular sand scratches, which are difficult to get rid of. Never use a disc grinder at a sharp angle with just the edge of the disc in contact, because this will cause it to gouge or dig deeply into the surface. When a disc grinder is properly held, the sanding marks are nearly straight.

Orbital sanders have an eccentric (off center) action that produces either a partly circular scrubbing action (orbital pad or dual action types) or a straight back-and-forth reciprocating action (flat orbital or straight line type). Unlike the disc sander

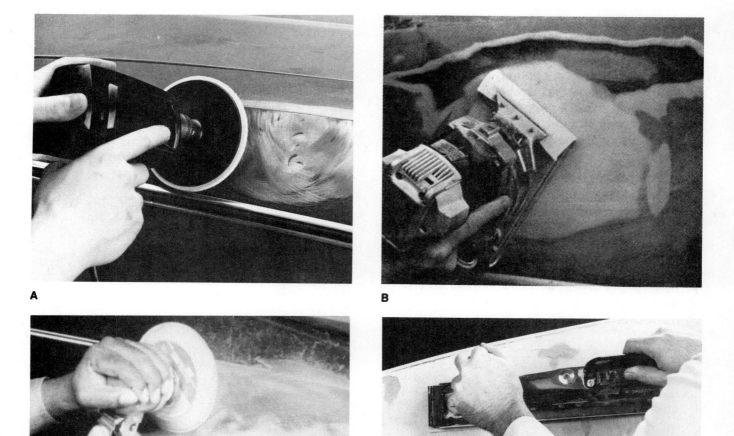

FIGURE 8-29 The types of sanders in operation: (A) disc sander; (B) jitterbug pad sander; (C) dual action sander; and (D) straight line sander.

		Normal Use							
Sander Type	Normal Area of Operation	Sanding old finishes	Paint stripping	Feather-edging	Rough sanding of solder	Rough sanding of metal putty	Rough sanding of poly putty	Sanding of metal putty	Sanding of poly putty
Disc Sander	Suitable for narrow areas	A	A	C	B	A	C	C	C
Dual Action Sander		A	C	A	C	A	A	A	A
Orbital Sander		B	C	B	C	A	A	A	A
Straight Line Sander	Suitable for wide open spaces	C	C	C	C	A	A	A	B
Long Orbital Sander		C	C	C	C	A	A	A	B

TABLE 8-3: USE OF SANDERS

NOTE: It is important that the correct type of sander and abrasive paper be used for each type of job. Also, always wear a mask or use some sort of dust arrester when using the sander.
A Preferred
B Acceptable
C Least preferred

FIGURE 8-30 Heavy-duty sander/grinder in operation

FIGURE 8-31 When using a disc, be sure only the leading edge does the cutting.

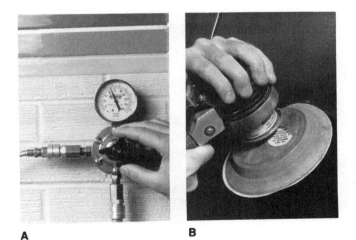

A   **B**

FIGURE 8-32 (A) Setting the correct air pressure; (B) handling a sander correctly. *(Courtesy of Maaco Enterprises, Inc.)*

FIGURE 8-33 Avoid ornamental and chrome items.

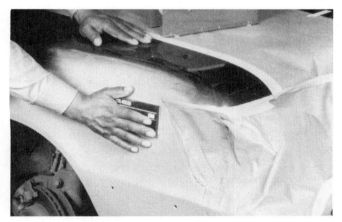

FIGURE 8-34 Masking can cut down the chance of surface scratch damage.

just discussed, orbital sanders should be pressed flat so they will not leave surface scratches. Orbital and board sanding can be done either dry or wet.

To operate an air sander, set the air pressure at 65 to 70 pounds. Then if right-handed, hold the handle of the sander in the right hand, while using the left hand to apply light pressure and guide the tool (Figure 8-32).

To protect the chrome from damage, do not machine sand closer than 1/2 inch from the trim and moldings (Figure 8-33). Mask nearby trim, decals, glass, handles, and emblems (Figure 8-34) to prevent metal spraks from pitting these surfaces. In fact, it is a good idea to double-tape (Figure 8-35) all moldings and trim on the panel before sanding.

When using any mechanical sander—and particularly a disc grinder—keep it moving so that no deep scratches, gouges, or burn-throughs develop. And do not, except when sanding bare metal, power

FIGURE 8-35 To prevent spark damage, double-tape all trim in the area. *(Courtesy of Maaco Enterprises, Inc.)*

sand styling lines as this will quickly distort the styling edge.

WARNING: Always wear a dust mask (Figure 8-36A) when sanding, and wear both a dust mask and face shield (Figure 8-36B) when grinding.

When power sanding, replace the sandpaper when paint begins to cake or "ball" up (Figure 8-37). This paint buildup can scratch the surface and reduce the sanding action of the disc. Slowing down the speed of the sander will also help prevent paint buildup on the sanding disc and prolong sandpaper life. Generally, six to eight sanding discs or pads will be required to featheredge the chips and scratches on the average automobile.

TYPES OF SANDING

There are several types of sanding that a refinisher must master. Some can be completed with power sanders alone, others with a combination of power and hand, and still others by hand alone.

Most occur during the surface preparation stage, but one—scuffing—is performed after undercoating.

BARE METAL SANDING

If the metal work has been done properly, little sanding of bare metal should be required. But once in a while the metal arrives very rough from coarse sanding in the metal shop. In such cases, it might be necessary to sand it with #50 grit to level out the burrs, nibs, and deep scratches. Remember, the smoother the bare metal, the easier the refinish

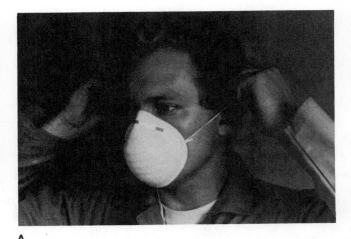

A

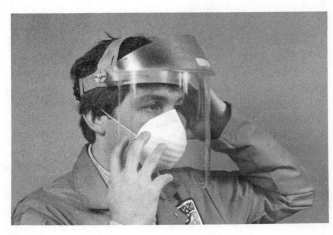

B

FIGURE 8-36 (A) When just sanding, wear a dust respirator, but when sanding and grinding, wear both a dust respirator and face mask. *(Courtesy of Maaco Enterprises, Inc.)*

work. For more details on bare metal sanding, check **grinding** later in this chapter.

THOROUGH SANDING

Use this procedure for two specific conditions:

- Where the old finish is rough or in poor shape
- To level and smooth primed areas

Since the primer-surfacer is primarily intended to fill low spots and scratches, sanding must be done in a manner that will leave material in the low spots and cut away the high. Block sanding is highly recommended for this purpose. A guide coat is very helpful and assists in pointing out the depressions. Spray a very light coat of a different color material over the primer-surfacer. Quickly sand through the high spots, and the low spots immediately become evident. The sanding itself can be done mechanically or by hand with a sanding block. For the average hand wet sanding job, use #360 or #400 grit when applying an acrylic lacquer or enamel topcoat and #320 when the topcoat is an alkyd enamel. Dry sanding runs 100 grit coarser because sanding the dust partially fills in the grit.

LIGHT SANDING

This procedure should be done on all areas where the old finish is in good condition. The purpose is to partially reduce the gloss and to improve adhesion. Use an orbital or dual-action sander, or do it by hand (Figure 8-38), but **never** use a disc grinder or sander.

If the new topcoat will be lacquer or enamel, use a #360 or #400 sandpaper. If it will be alkyd enamel, use a #320 sandpaper. For basecoat/clear coat finishes, proper surface preparation is critical. It is important to sand all surfaces to be refinished with #400 grit or finer paper. Sanding can be wet or dry.

COLOR SANDING

To achieve the smoothest finish and best results in acrylic work, wet sand (Figure 8-39) the next-to-the-last coat of color with #600 or #800 grit paper.

FEATHEREDGING

If a new coat of paint was applied right over the broken areas of the old finish, the broken film would be very noticeable through the topcoat (Figure 8-40). So the broken areas must be featheredged. That is, the sharp edge of the broken film must be tapered down by sanding (Figure 8-41). Then the bare metal areas are filled with a primer-surfacer and the entire area is sanded smooth and level.

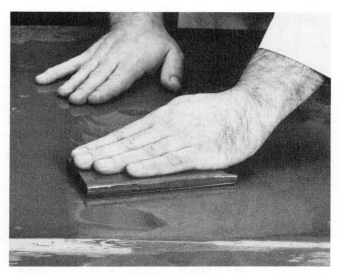

FIGURE 8-39 Use plenty of water when color sanding.

FIGURE 8-37 Paint caked on sandpaper. *(Courtesy of Maaco Enterprises, Inc.)*

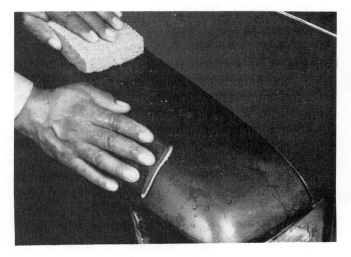

FIGURE 8-38 Light sand when the old finish is in good condition.

FIGURE 8-40 Squeegee helps show the featheredge areas.

Featheredging by hand is usually a two-step procedure:

1. First, cut down the edges of the broken areas with a coarse #100 paper and follow with #220 sandpaper.
2. Then, complete the taper of the featheredge with a sanding block and either a #360 or #400 grit sandpaper and water to produce a finely tapered edge and eliminate coarse sandpaper scratches.

If the old finish is lacquer, an alternate Step 1 can be used. Cut down the edges chemically by using lacquer removing solvent. Roll a cloth into a ball or thick pad and soak with lacquer removing solvent. Then rub back and forth in a circular motion until a tapered edge is obtained. Finish the edge by light sanding with #360 or #400 sandpaper and water.

When featheredging with a power sander, an orbital or dual action type equipped with a flexible

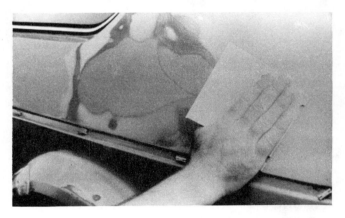

FIGURE 8-41 Featheredging tapers successive coats of paint and primer away from the metal to create a smooth surface.

FIGURE 8-42 Correct angle for featheredging. *(Courtesy of Maaco Enterprises, Inc.)*

FIGURE 8-43 Crosscutting with a sander

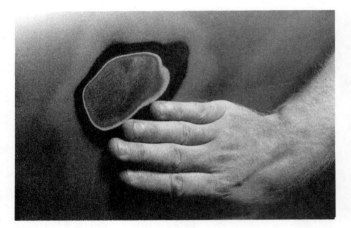

FIGURE 8-44 Feel for rough spots.

backing pad is recommended. Use a #80 grit for the rough cut followed by a #280 or #360 sandpaper for the fine work. When featheredging a chip, start by positioning the sanding disc at a 5 to 10 degree angle from the work surface (Figure 8-42). Using the outer edge, approximately 1 inch of the sanding disc, cut away the rough paint edges. Do not hold the sander at an angle greater than 10 degrees from the surface. Doing so will cut a deep gouge in the paint.

After initially leveling the rough paint edges in this manner, flatten the sander on the panel and finish tapering the paint layers by moving the sander back and forth in a crosscutting pattern (Figure 8-43). Start over the chipped area and work in an outward direction. Stop frequently and run a hand over the sanded area to feel for rough edges (Figure 8-44). The total outside edge should be cut new and all original chipped edges should be removed to avoid any lifting during refinishing. When the surface feels smooth, and rings of old paint and primer color are visible, the featheredging is complete.

FIGURE 8-45   Featheredging brittle paint. *(Courtesy of Maaco Enterprises, Inc.)*

FIGURE 8-46   Feathering an edge

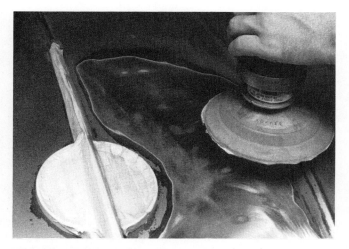

FIGURE 8-47   Removing brittle paint

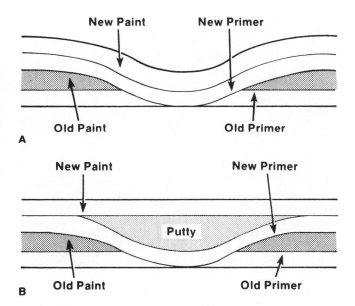

FIGURE 8-48   Causes of "bull's eye" and how to correct it

Certain localized peeling paint problems can be corrected using the featheredging technique (Figure 8-45). Slowing down the sander's speed helps produce a smooth edge on brittle paint. However, if the paint is extremely brittle, it will continue to chip away as sanding progresses. When this happens, move the sander several inches beyond the edge of the peeling paint and feather an edge in the undamaged finish (Figure 8-46). Once the layers of paint film have been successfully tapered, remove the damaged paint between the feathered edge and the original bare metal area using a buffing action (Figure 8-47).

If the successive layers of paint are not properly tapered, a depression called a "bull's eye" will show up under the new paint finish (Figure 8-48A). This condition can usually be corrected by extending each paint and primer ring farther from the bare metal. Do this until the depression can no longer be felt when a hand is run over the featheredged area. Occasionally, when featheredging areas with several layers of paint, primer and putty might be necessary to fill the bull's eye to the level of the existing film buildup (Figure 8-48B).

GRINDING

Start grinding with a #24 grit disc (Figure 8-49) followed by a #50 grit disc to remove the #24 sand scratches. If possible, do not operate a grinder at full speed. The high speed could cause the metal to heat up and warp or cause the disc to break.

FIGURE 8–49 When grinding, first use a #24 grit disc on a disc sander/grinder. *(Courtesy of Du Pont Co.)*

FIGURE 8–50 Any sanding operation, unless extreme care is taken and #800 grit or finer grit is used, is going to produce some scratches.

Safety Pointers when Grinding

In addition to the safety procedures given in Chapter 2, the following pointers must be remembered:

WARNING: Be sure to wear eye protection.

- When disc grinding, hold the grinder firmly at a low 5 degrees Fahrenheit angle to the work surface.
- Grinding should direct dust away from the face and toward the floor.

- Be conscious of the grinder or polisher cord at all times to prevent entanglement.
- Do not grind or sand too close to trim, bumpers, or any projection that might snag or catch the grinding disc's edge.
- Never start or stop a disc grinder in contact with the work surface.
- Never "free run" a grinding disc or set a grinder down until it stops completely.
- Make certain the back-up pads are designed for the work, free of cuts or nicks at the edge or at the center hole. Make certain pads are seated on the shaft properly. Check for proper balance. Retainer nuts should not show excessive thread wear, must have at least three-thread contact, and should not cause damage to the grinding discs.
- Back-up pads for use with the "self-adhesive" type discs must be dry, clean, and dust free. Avoid using pads with frayed, torn, dirty, or paper contaminated surface. If necessary wipe pad face with clean dry cloth. Do not immerse pad or clean pad face with solvent.

SCUFFING

Once all surface reconditioning is completed, the final sanding operation is to scuff the surface to remove nibs and dust specks on nonsanding primers, sealers, or where dirt shows up. It should be done with a very fine grit sandpaper such as #400.

Place the paper in the palm of the hand and hold it flat against the surface. Apply even, moderate pressure along the length of the sandpaper using the palm and extended fingers. Sand back and forth with long, straight strokes. Remember that scuffing the surface is only to improve adhesion of the new paint. Care should be taken not to cut into the film. When sanding large panels, one stroke back and forth in an overlapping pattern will be sufficient. More sanding than this is not only a waste of energy, but could possibly risk creating scratches that could show up under the new finish. Do not oversand.

SAND SCRATCH SWELLING

The first requirement for a good paint job is a smooth surface. The refinishing technician can make it doubly hard for the painter if the metal is not properly finished. The best practice is to use a #24 disc for restoring the contours and finishing off the metal with #50 and then #80 paper. Even this method will not eliminate some sources of sand scratches (Figure 8–50) because there are often little burrs or fins on the crests of the scratches, and these cause uneven shrinkage in the surfacer coat (Figure 8-51A). To eliminate them, sand with #220 paper to round off the tops of these crests (Figure 8-51B). Do not worry about getting the metal too smooth. Sanded metal that looks and feels smooth will still have plenty of "tooth" for the surfacer (Figure 8-52).

Modern primer-surfacers will do a lot of filling in one coat. It is not hard to understand, however, that the thicker the coat, the slower the drying, so spray two or three coats with 5 to 15 minutes between them, and thus save time over spraying a real heavy coat and having to wait a long time for it to dry through. It is difficult to tell when a thick coat is really dry because the surface will appear to be dry while there is still a lot of thinner trapped below the surface and shrinkage is still going on. Where the imperfections or scratches in the metal are unusually deep, the use of a lacquer glazing putty will save time in getting a smooth surface.

After the primer-surfacer has dried thoroughly, the next thing to consider is the sanding operation. The use of coarse sandpaper such as #220 or #240 will produce scratches in the primer-surfacer that will be hard to fill by the final finish coats. With the present day surfacers, sanding is so easy it is not necessary to use paper coarser than #320 or #360. In order to get the smoothest finish, the use of #400 paper as a final sanding is recommended.

When a lacquer or acrylic lacquer finish coat is used, the thinner penetrates and swells the undercoat and where the undercoat is the heaviest, as in the deep scratches, the swelling will be the greatest. If the color is compounded and polished before all of

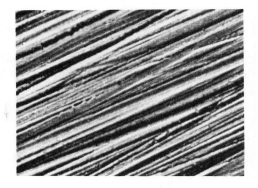

FIGURE 8-52   Sand scratches in primer-surfacers enlarged 40 times. *(Courtesy of PPG Industries, Inc.)*

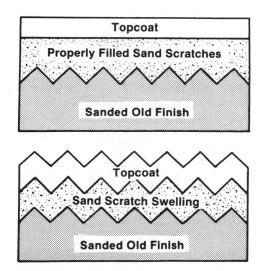

FIGURE 8-53   The best way to prevent sand scratches from showing is to use the proper grit sandpaper and proper sanding technique. In hand sanding always sand in a straight line, never circular. *(Courtesy of Du Pont Co.)*

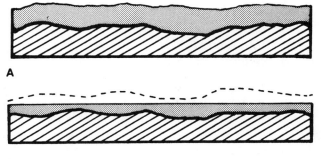

A

B

FIGURE 8-51   Enlarged cross-section of rough metal. (A) Some metal coated with primer-surfacer. Surface of undercoat follows approximate contours of original metal when thoroughly dry. (B) Sanding levels off high spots, producing a flat, smooth surface. If not dry when sanded, further shrinking over deep fills produces uneven surface and shows abrasive marks.

the thinner has evaporated from the primer-surfacer, there will be further shrinkage at the point of deepest fill. Therefore, it is important to give finish coats plenty of dry time before sanding and polishing.

The danger of sand scratch swelling is greatest on the featheredge. The spraying of a light fog coat for the first color coat keeps the solvent content on the low side when it first comes in contact with the old featheredge finish.

It can be seen from Figure 8-53 that the shrinkage and swelling of lacquer undercoats is an important point to consider in the elimination of sand scratches. If the undercoat is not allowed to dry down to its final position before sanding or applying finish coats, scratches are likely to result.

REVIEW QUESTIONS

1. Which of the following is least likely to show film deterioration?
   a. hood
   b. trunk
   c. doors
   d. roof

2. Which of the following must be sanded?
   a. chipped paint
   b. peeling paint
   c. puttied areas
   d. the entire surface to be refinished
   e. all of the above

3. Silicon carbide is _____.
   a. a very sharp grain
   b. customarily used for featheredging and dry sanding soft materials
   c. an abrasive type that tends to break down and dull when sanding hard surfaces
   d. all of the above
   e. both b and c

4. Which type of abrasive has a self-sharpening characteristic that provides continuous new cutting points during the sanding operation?
   a. silicon carbide
   b. aluminum oxide
   c. zirconia alumina
   d. none of the above

5. Painter A says the lower the grit grade number the finer the grit. Painter B says the lower the number the coarser the grit. Who is right?
   a. Painter A
   b. Painter B
   c. Both A and B
   d. Neither A nor B

6. Painter A uses a dual action sander to remove heavy surface rust. Painter B uses an air grinder to remove light rust. Who is right?
   a. Painter A
   b. Painter B
   c. Both A and B
   d. Neither A nor B

7. Closed coat abrasive paper is used _____.
   a. on aluminum
   b. on old paint
   c. on body filler
   d. in wet sanding applications

8. Which backing is becoming more widely used for paint stripping and shaping of filled areas?
   a. A weight
   b. E weight
   c. C weight
   d. D weight

9. Painter A hand sands in the same direction as the body lines on the vehicle. Painter B sands in a circular motion. Who is right?
   a. Painter A
   b. Painter B
   c. Both A and B
   d. Neither A nor B

10. Which type of sander should not be held flat against the surface?
    a. disc
    b. orbital
    c. dual action
    d. board

11. Thorough sanding is best done with a _____.
    a. disc sander
    b. straight line sander
    c. jitterbug pad sander
    d. sanding block

12. Painter A does light sanding using a dual-action sander. Painter B does light sanding by hand. Who is right?
    a. Painter A
    b. Painter B
    c. Both A and B
    d. Neither A nor B

13. Painter A starts the disc grinder in contact with the work surface. Painter B does not. Who is right?
    a. Painter A
    b. Painter B
    c. Both A and B
    d. Neither A nor B

14. Painter A is careful not to sand the bare metal too smooth so that it will have plenty of "tooth" for the surfacer. Painter B is not. Who is right?
    a. Painter A
    b. Painter B
    c. Both A and B
    d. Neither A nor B

15. Which of the following characteristics belong to wet sanding?
    a. slower work speed
    b. less sandpaper required
    c. condition of the finish is very good
    d. all of the above

CHAPTER NINE

SURFACE REFINISHING PREPARATION

Objectives

After reading this chapter, you will be able to:

- prepare existing paint films and bare metal substrates for refinishing.
- describe the three methods of removing a deteriorated paint film.
- explain how conversion coating enhances primer adhesion to bare metal.
- determine when to apply a primer, a primer-sealer, a primer-surfacer, or glazing putty.
- mask a car, panel, or spot repair for refinishing.

It is unwise to apply any kind of finish to a surface that has not been prepared properly. Quality suffers, customer dissatisfaction is inevitable, and finally, costs increase because the job usually has to be done over. A good beginning pays off in a savings of materials and time and in a higher quality refinishing job.

There are two types of automotive refinishing surfaces:

- Previously painted
- Bare metal or substrate

Even if the original paint finish is in good condition, it should be lightly sanded or scuff sanded after washing to remove dead film and to smooth out imperfections. If the surface is in poor condition, all the paint should be removed down to the bare metal. In this way, a good foundation is achieved.

PAINTED SURFACE IN GOOD CONDITION

It is simple to repaint over an existing paint film in good condition, whatever the type of finish, providing it is stable and does not react to the solvent of the refinish paint. The procedure for surface preparation in good condition is as follows:

CLEANING THE VEHICLE

The vehicle should be washed to remove any mud, dirt, or other water-soluble contaminants before being brought into the shop (Figure 9-1). Hose down the car, sponge with detergent and water, then

FIGURE 9-1 Wash the car very carefully. *(Courtesy of Maaco Enterprises, Inc.)*

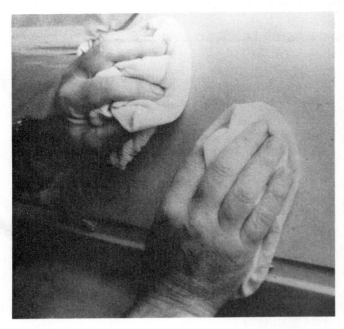

FIGURE 9-2 Applying wax and grease remover

rinse thoroughly. Wash the top, front and deck, then the sides—and allow to dry.

CLEAN WITH WAX AND GREASE REMOVER

Be sure there is no wax, grease, or other contaminants imbedded in the old finish. Gasoline is a dangerous, poor wax solvent and can itself deposit contaminating substances on the surface. It is ill advised to use synthetic reducers for cleaning up a surface, particularly acrylic lacquer, because they absorb reducer into the paint film and blistering or lifting can result.

Before the job is sanded, use a specially blended wax and grease remover or solvent to thoroughly clean the surface and repeat the operation after sanding. Be sure to thoroughly clean areas where a heavy wax buildup can be a problem, such as around trim, moldings, door handles, radio antennae, and behind the bumpers. Paint will not adhere properly to a waxy surface.

To apply the wax and grease remover (or silicone and wax remover as it is sometimes called) fold a clean, dry cloth, soak it with solvent (Figure 9-2), and apply it to the old painted surface. While the surface is still wet, fold a second clean cloth and wipe dry. Work small areas that are 2 or 3 feet square, wetting the surface liberally. Never attempt to clean too large an area; the solvent will dry before the surface can be wiped. Maximum effectiveness will be achieved by wiping up the wax and grease remover while it is still wet. Always use new wiping

cloths because laundering might not remove all oil or silicone residue.

To remove any last trace of moisture and dirt from seals and moldings, blow out with compressed air at low pressure. Wax and silicone can penetrate beneath the surface. This contamination is not easily detectable. It is wise to assume that it is present, so always include some wax and grease cleaner or detergent in the sanding water.

Special attention should be paid to tar, gasoline, battery acid, antifreeze, and brake fluid stains. These can also penetrate well beneath the surface of old paint films and their residues must be removed during the sanding operation.

REPAIR FLAWS IN PAINTED SURFACES

First, sand or grind off the rust and old paint in the damaged areas (Figure 9-3). If the grinding operation goes down to bare metal, it will be necessary to perform the appropriate metal conditioning later. These steps are described later in this chapter.

Be sure that all the dings, dents, and built-up areas have been made as described in Chapter 5. Many dings and dents are too deep to be filled by a primer-surfacer and/or putty. In such cases use a lightweight body filler. But when using a body filler, there are some precautions that should be kept in mind:

- **Do not** use body filler directly over a metal conditioner.
- **Do not** use too much hardener because it will cause pinholes.
- **Do not** return any unused mixture to the can.

The following is a review of the procedure for using body filler as given in Chapter 5 concerning

FIGURE 9-3 Grinding a rustout. *(Courtesy of Maaco Enterprises, Inc.)*

minor surface repairs. For small dents, squeeze a 1-1/2-inch ribbon of hardener on a mass of body filler about the size of a golfball. Mix well with a putty knife or paint paddle (Figure 9-4). Mix only as much as can be handled properly because the mixture will harden. Apply immediately with a spreader or squeegee (Figure 9-5). Work to the contour of the surface. Then let it harden for 8 to 10 minutes. Use a grater to shape the repair, bridging the dent to prevent gouging. Sand as needed.

If using a power sander—such as an orbital or dual action sander—use a #80 sandpaper for the rough cut followed by a #180 or #220 grit for the fine work. Next, feather the broken paint edges. This must be done so that a continuous smooth surface can be developed when filled with a primer-surfacer. Featheredging can be done by hand with a sanding block or with an orbital sander.

Taper the broken edges first. If hand sanding, use a #220 grit sandpaper for the rough work. Then complete the job with a #240 or #320 paper and water to produce a fine tapered edge and eliminate sandpaper scratches.

To remove decals from a painted surface, a razor blade slipped under the edge of a decal will start a small area that can be pulled up and the whole decal peeled off. If the decal will not peel off, disc grinding is usually employed or, if a heat gun is available, heat the decal and surrounding surface to soften the adhesive and peel off. There are also decal removers on the market, however, they must be used with care since they may damage the surface on which the decal is applied.

PAINT WORK IN POOR CONDITION

Most forms of paint failure are progressive. These conditions cannot be stopped by any form of repairing; in fact, repairing will usually accelerate the deterioration of the original finish. If the old finish is badly weathered or scarred, it is **not** suitable for recoating. When this situation occurs, the old finish should be completely removed. There are three common ways of stripping paint from metal surfaces:

- Sanding or grinding
- Sandblasting
- Chemical stripping

With any of these methods, remove all chrome trim strips, lamp surrounds, badges, and so forth that are adjacent to the area to be painted, or in

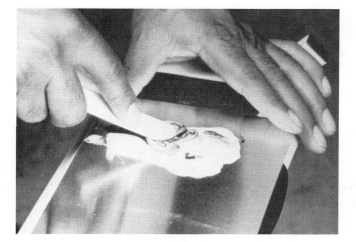

FIGURE 9-4   Mixing a body filler

FIGURE 9-5   Applying a body filler

direct contact with it. A chemical paint remover can be trapped and retained by these parts, or they can be accidentally damaged by the sander/grinder or sandblaster. In any case, corrosion is often found beneath exterior trim parts, and this can only be dealt with if they are removed.

SANDING OR GRINDING

Machine sanding/grinding is suitable for removing old finish from small flat areas and gently curved areas. Start with a #24 grit open-coated disc, and by holding the face of the disc at a slight angle to the surface, work forward and backward evenly over the area to get off the bulk of the old finish down to the metal. Follow this with a #50 or #80 close-coated disc, go over the entire area and slightly out on the surrounding surface to clean up the work, and eliminate the troughs or steps caused by the coarse disc. When using the grinder, care must be taken to prevent gouging or scarring the metal.

After all of the paint is removed with the grinder and the coarse grit disc, resand the area with the orbital or dual action sander and #100 grit paper to remove the metal scratches. Then finish sand the panel using #180 grit sandpaper. In this way most of the scratches created by the stripping operation will be eliminated. Remember that any metal that has been scratched with very coarse abrasive paper will require filling to the depth of the scratch plus the height of the burr.

SANDBLASTING

Sandblasting can be done on nearly all types of body construction—even aluminum sheet, with caution—and it leaves a clean, dry surface in an ideal condition for refinishing. It is a very fast method and has the further advantage of revealing rusted areas and places where hidden rusting can result in scaling after the job has been refinished. In addition, sandblasting makes hard-to-reach areas accessible to the technician. Also this method saves time when compared with sanding/grinding and chemical stripping.

A sandblaster concentrates the pressure and flow of air and sand. Usually found in shops in a smaller version (40 to 300 pound models), the technician using it can vary the blast volume, focusing the pattern on the spot at hand, rather than blasting in a wide pattern.

Blasters in the shop are one of two kinds: pressure or siphon. Pressure blasters are pressurized containers filled with abrasive material (such as silica sand). The sand travels down one hose, the high-velocity air comes down another hose. Both meet at another hose and travel out toward the surface together at tremendous speed and force.

In a siphon blaster, compressed air draws the abrasive from the reservoir as suction is applied. The abrasive accelerates and is shot out of the nozzle at the intended surface. Small bottle blasters are available for spot type jobs (Figure 9–6).

The basic procedure in operating sandblasters is as follows:

1. Mark off the areas that will not be affected by the spot repair. For instance, when spot repairing a rocker panel, mask the wheel caps and the top of the car (as described later in this chapter).

2. Put on the necessary safety gear. It is a good idea to wear gloves, eye protection, a helmet, and a respirator (Figure 9–7). A respirator should be worn because sand can build up in the lungs over an extended period of time causing silicosis.

3. Before blasting, check the manufacturer's instructions for proper blasting pressures, sand load procedures, and setup arrangements (Figure 9–8). When ready to blast, apply the abrasive material directly on the area to be blasted. Eventually, the area will turn a gray or white color. Blasting has textured the surface by opening the pores of the metal in these colored areas. This etched texture makes an excellent surface for primer adhesion. When the area shows no signs of brown rust, remove the pressure. Be on guard against heat warpage.

Pressure should be applied by holding the hose 8 to 12 inches back from the area being repaired. It should hit the surface at a 20 to 30 degree angle. That way, the cutting edges of the blasting are away from the operator.

FIGURE 9–6 Typical bottle type blaster. *(Courtesy of A.L.C. Co.)*

FIGURE 9–7 Typical safety gear worn by a sand blaster.

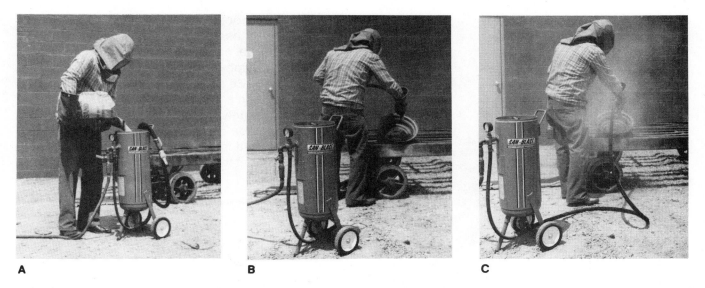

FIGURE 9-8 Conventional type sand blaster operations: (A) fill the reservoir with adhesive material; (B) aim the gun nozzle; (C) trigger the gun to release the abrasive. *(Courtesy of Truman's Inc.)*

CAUTION: Care should be taken where sheet metal is light gauge. High air pressure and/or coarse blasting media can warp the metal.

---

4. Watch the surface carefully. The blasting might reveal a hole, in which case blast as much of the hole out as possible. Blasting is designed to reveal weak spots like these. Before priming the rusted out area, weld a patch on it.

5. After the paint has been removed, use an air blow gun to remove the sand from other parts of the vehicle, particularly the glass. If it is not removed, the sand or abrasive will eventually get stuck in windshield wiper blades or window slots and scratch the windows.

6. It is advisable to prime coat the metal as soon as possible after any stripping process, but a sandblast job actually requires that the job be primed almost immediately because the metal is really in a raw state after this treatment and will start rusting if allowed to stand overnight.

Until recently, all sandblasting work was done outdoors. As mentioned in Chapter 2, some of the newer blaster models provide "dust-free, captive" sandblasting (Figure 9-9). They contain a built-in vacuum and filtration system that cleans up and recycles the abrasive, while it blasts away paint, rust, and other debris.

To operate this newer type of blaster, hold the designed nozzle directly against the surface being treated (Figure 9-10). As the abrasive strikes the surface, it is sucked back by the vacuum, along with rust and debris. A rubber nozzle and stiff brush seal in the abrasive and debris to keep them from escaping. The rust and debris fall into an easy-to-empty pail, while the blasting abrasive is recycled and sent back into action.

FIGURE 9-9 Typical "dust-free, captive" sand blaster. *(Courtesy of Clements National Co.)*

FIGURE 9-10 Blasting with "captive" sand blaster. *(Courtesy of Clements National Co.)*

CHEMICAL STRIPPING

A chemical paint remover is recommended for stripping large areas of paint. It is very effective in those places that a power sander cannot reach and there is no danger of the metal warping.

Before applying paint remover, mask off the area to insure that the remover does not get on any area that is not to be stripped. Use two or three thicknesses of masking tape to give adequate protection. Cover any crevices to prevent the paint remover from seeping to the undersurface of a panel. Slightly scoring the surface of the paint to be stripped will help the paint remover to penetrate more quickly.

Paint remover should be applied following the manufacturer's instructions. Pay attention to warnings regarding ventilation, smoking, and the use of protective clothing such as PVC or rubber gloves, long sleeve shirts, and safety glasses or goggles. If remover comes in contact with the skin or eyes, it will cause irritation and burning.

To apply, brush on a heavy coat of paint remover in one direction only to the entire area being treated (Figure 9-11). Use a soft bristle brush, but do not brush the material out. Allow the paint remover to stand until the finish is softened. Although paint remover is quickly effective on most vehicle topcoats, some modern car undercoats can prove stubborn. (For example, acrylic lacquer becomes sticky, making it more difficult to remove.) Because the active strength of the paint remover must be held at a safe level to prevent the risk of serious skin and eye injury to the operator, more than one application might be needed.

Caution should be taken when removing the loosened paint coatings. Some paint removers are designed to be neutralized by water. Others are more easily removed with a squeegee or scraper (Figure 9-12). Be sure to rinse off any residue that remains using cleaning solvent and steel wool, followed immediately by wiping with a clean rag. This rinsing operation is essential. Many paint removers contain wax, which, if left on the surface, will prevent the refinish paint from adhering, drying, and hardening properly.

CAUTION: Do not use paint remover on fiberglass or other plastic substrates.

Rusting occurs very rapidly on metal that has been chemically stripped. In fact, any bare metal substrate should be treated immediately. But before selecting the type of metal treatment or conditioning system, first consider the types of rust. The least amount of rust might be considered **microscopic rust** (Figure 9-13) that is not really visible to the eye but can be a hazard to the performance of a refinish job. The second type of rust might be called **flash rust** that usually develops when there is moisture or humidity present. The other types of rust are the types that are very visible and might even be large and scabby.

The decision about which metal conditioning system to use depends on the type of rust and the type of substrate.

BARE METAL SUBSTRATE

Proper bare metal treatment is a critical step in every successful automotive painting operation. Yet

FIGURE 9-11 Applying chemical paint remover with a brush. *(Courtesy of America Sikkens, Inc.)*

FIGURE 9-12 Removing paint with a scraper. *(Courtesy of America Sikkens, Inc.)*

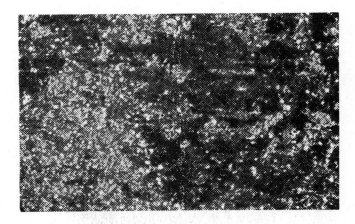

FIGURE 9-13 Rust-pitted sheet steel that has been sanded clean to the naked eye and put under a microscope (enlarged 125 diameters) still shows traces of rust in the pits. *(Courtesy of PPG Industries, Inc.)*

it is often ignored or carried out in a haphazard manner. This can only result in poor adhesion, corrosion, and—as a result—customer complaints. Though not noticeable when the original finish has been stripped down to bare metal, it is the single most important factor in original equipment finish life. Recognizing its importance, auto manufacturers devote more attention to this step than they do to priming and topcoating, using a seven-stage zinc phosphate metal treatment process to ensure adhesion of primers to the substrate.

Though the techniques and equipment used on the OEM level are not adaptable to paint shops, some metal treatment products on the market today can enable the refinisher to simulate original equipment metal treatment.

Why is bare metal treatment so important? Water vapor penetrates all paint films. The fresher the paint and the more humid the weather, the further the vapor penetrates, sometimes reaching the bare metal. Once water droplets form under the paint film, pressure starts to build, causing bubbling, blistering, and loss of adhesion. Rust can also begin to form, further pushing the paint film away from the metal.

The only way to prevent this potentially serious problem is to create such a strong bond between the primer-surfacer and the metal that water vapor cannot penetrate down to the substrate. If the water vapor is not allowed to condense under the paint film, it will return to the surface of the finish and eventually evaporate.

This bond between a negatively charged metal car surface and a positively charged primer can be created electrochemically. All that is needed is the application of an acidic metal treatment system that contains both positive and negative parts. The negative parts are attracted to the metal, while the positive parts are attracted to the primer, forming a superior bond that does not allow water droplets to collect. This type of system is called a conversion coating. The conventional system generally works the best and consists of the following three-step process called metal treating:

- **Cleaning to remove contaminants.** Use a wax and grease remover and apply it to the surface. While the surface is still wet, fold a second clean cloth and wipe dry. Work small areas, 2 to 3 square feet, wetting the surface liberally (Figure 9–14).
- **Cleaning with metal conditioner.** Mix the appropriate cleaner with water in a plastic bucket according to label instruction. Apply with a cloth, sponge, or spray bottle. If rust is present, work the surface with a stiff brush or abrasive plastic pad (Figure 9–15). Then while the surface is still wet, wipe it dry with a clean cloth.
- **Applying conversion coatings.** Pour the appropriate conversion coating into a plastic bucket (Figure 9–16). Using an abrasive pad, brush, or spray bottle, apply the coating to the metal surface. Then leave the conditioner on the surface 2 to 5 mintues. Apply only to an area that can be coated and rinsed before the solution dries. If the surface dries before the rinsing, reapply. Flush the coating from the surface with cold water. Wipe dry with a

FIGURE 9-14   Applying a wax and grease remover. *(Courtesy of Du Pont Co.)*

FIGURE 9-15   Applying metal conditioner. *(Courtesy of Du Pont Co.)*

clean cloth and allow to air dry completely. The desired primer or primer-surfacer can then be applied.

Another type of metal treatment system also can be applied to enhance adhesion and assure corrosion resistance. A washer-primer is a sprayable surface treatment that eliminates the need for a conver-

FIGURE 9-16   Mixing a conversion coating

sion coating. The vinyl resin in the washer-primer provides corrosion resistance and the reducer contains phosphoric acid for strong bonding.

A washer-primer with phosphoric acid reducer not only cleans, it also etches the metal and assists the adhesion of the subsequent paint film. It helps prevent the occurrence of rust and also eases sanding marks. The washer-primer is applied by the following procedure:

1. Carefully read the manufacturer's directions and special instructions, which should be closely followed.
2. Pour the washer-primer into a container and add a special washer-primer thinner to achieve a sprayable viscosity. Do not use a metal container because the washer-primer reacts with metal. If applying a two-component washer-primer, the solution must be used within 8 hours after mixing the main and subagents.
3. Pour the mix solution or thinned solution into the spray bottle container and spray the metal immediately. Do not allow any washer-primer to get on any part of the vehicle that is not to be repainted. The gun air pressure and discharge pressure should be kept low and the gun held close to the surface. The area should be masked off to prevent other areas from coming into contact with the washer-primer.
4. Apply a **thin** coat. Too thick an application will result in paint peeling and blistering.
5. The washer-primer should not be allowed to dry on the metal. Should this happen a second application of the material will soften and dissolve the dried residues. After the washer-primer has been applied,

wash well with plenty of clean water and dry thoroughly.

6. Wash out the spray gun immediately after spraying washer-primer. Washer-primer left in the spray gun or container will cause a chemical film to form on the metal, making the spray gun useless. Because of this, some manufacturers recommend that washer-primer be used with an acid-resistant brush or sponge.

WARNING: While phosphoric acid metal materials are not considered dangerous chemicals, they do have a drying action on the skin. Although this is comparatively harmless, it might cause chapping and render the skin susceptible to irritants. Rubber or PVC gloves should be worn, and rubber or PVC boots and aprons are recommended to protect the clothing.

Typically, metal conditioning and priming/surfacing are considered separate surface preparation steps. Some new products, however, actually make it possible to combine these steps. "Etching primer-fillers" etch the bare metal to improve paint adhesion and corrosion resistance, while providing the priming and filling properties usually offered by primer-surfacers. Etching primer-fillers work best on lightly sanded surfaces where a slight-to-moderate amount of filling is required. They must be applied as directed by the manufacturer.

SPECIFIC METAL TREATMENTS

The preparation of the various metals used in automotive construction require slightly different techniques. The more common bare metal procedures are for:

Steel-Body Metal (Including Blue Annealed) Preparation

1. Sand metal thoroughly. Remove all visible scale or rust.
2. Clean the surface with wax and grease remover and wipe dry.
3. Use any of the three bare metal treatments—conversion coating, washer-primer, or etching primer-filler—as previously described.
4. Apply an undercoater (primer or primer-surfacer). If the etching primer-filler is

used, this step might not be necessary.

5. Once the undercoat refinish system is dry and sanded, wipe with a tack rag. The surface is ready for the color coat.

Galvanneal, Plymetal, Galvanized, or Other Zinc-coated Metal

1. Follow Steps 1 and 2 of steel-body preparation.
2. Use either a conversion coating or special zinc metal conditioner. Apply the latter according to manufacturer's directions. Never use a washer-primer since it will attack galvanized and other zinc surfaces and must not be allowed to come into contact with them.
3. Apply one wet double coat of epoxy primer. If filling is required, allow the epoxy primer to dry a minimum of 1 hour and then apply a primer-surfacer.
4. Sand the primer-surfacer after a 30-minute dry period. Once the undercoat system is completed (as mentioned later in this chapter), the surface is ready for the topcoat.

New Anodized Aluminum or Untreated Aluminum and Oxidized Aluminum Preparation

1. Follow Steps 1, 2, and 3 of steel-body preparation.
2. Apply one wet double coat of epoxy primer or zinc chromate. If filling is required, allow the material a minimum of 1 hour to dry and then apply a primer-surfacer.
3. Sand the primer-surfacer after a 30-minute dry period. Once the undercoat system is completed, the surface is ready for the color coat.

CHROMIUM PLATING PREPARATION

Chromium presents a very difficult problem and at best the adhesion of a finish to this metal is not lasting. When painting is desired, prepare the surface by cleaning and sanding and proceed with the following system described for stainless steel preparation:

1. Clean the metal thoroughly with a wax and grease remover.
2. Sand metal thoroughly, using #320 wet or dry sandpaper.
3. Reclean with wax and grease remover.

4. Apply any of the metal treatments described earlier in this chapter.
5. Spray two coats of primer-surfacer. Allow 2 to 3 hours drying time before dry sanding.
6. Blow out cracks, then use a tack rag on the entire surface. The final coat can now be applied.

Regardless of the cleaning procedure, once the metal is clean and prepared, it must not be contaminated by fingerprints, so clean cotton industrial gloves should be worn when handling. Sometimes painters rub their hands over an area to determine the effect of the sanding without realizing that they are transferring oil from their hands to the surface. Oil comes from the skin and from shop tools, and even if the hands are freshly washed, a fine oily film will be left on the surface because there are not many people who have oil-free skin. Wiping off the surface with a good wax and grease remover, just before applying the finishing coat, is excellent insurance against peeling and/or blistering.

PREPARING METAL REPLACEMENT PARTS

Many car manufacturers and component suppliers protect panels in a primer. The function of this primer coat is to protect the metal against corrosion. It does not necessarily provide a firm basis for a paint system. Although most primers in use do have this dual function, the supplier should always be consulted. Certain major motor manufacturers supply components in electrocoat primers that are an essential part of their warranty repair systems and should not be removed. They should be suitably prepared for the painting process.

It must be remembered that some replacement parts are provided from the manufacturer with only a coating. This coating is **not** intended to serve as the primer. A primer must be applied to these replacement parts or the color coat will not stick properly. The usual procedure is to clean with wax and grease remover, then examine the part for imperfections such as drips or scratches. If drips or scratches are present, sand these imperfections until smooth but do not try to remove the coating completely. Scuff sand the entire panel, then apply primer before painting. If in doubt about the quality of the coating, check with the manufacturer of the part for the recommended finishing procedures.

Any bare metal replacement panels protected with grease should also be cleaned with a wax and grease solvent. They should be washed with liberal amounts of solvent, changing any rags frequently,

then treated with a bare metal conditioner, flushed down with water, and dried off.

UNDERCOAT REFINISHING SYSTEM

The decision to apply a primer, a primer-sealer, or a primer-surfacer by itself or combined with putty and/or a sealer depends on three factors. These are:

- The condition of the substrate—smooth or rough, bare or painted
- The type of finish on the substrate—if painted
- The type of finish to be used for the topcoat

Full details on the use of undercoats are given in Chapter 7. These products are applied primarily to protect the bare metal against corrosion and to improve adhesion of the topcoats of paint (Figure 9-17). Due to their excellent filling and leveling qualities, they also fill minor sand scratches and level rough edges or depressions that remain after machine sanding. Before applying any undercoater, be sure to treat all bare metal with metal conditioner. Reduce the undercoater chosen according to the manufacturer's instructions. Be careful to select the

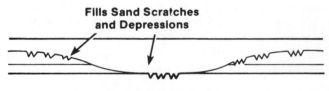

Fills Sand Scratches and Depressions

Protects Bare Metal

FIGURE 9-17 How undercoaters or primer-surfacers protect bare metal

FIGURE 9-18 Applying the undercoater—in this case a primer-surfacer

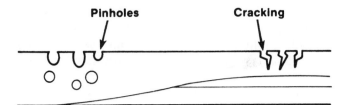

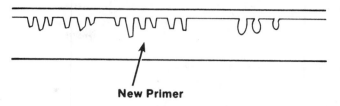

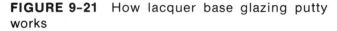

FIGURE 9-19 The problems of excessive primer-surfacer

FIGURE 9-21 How lacquer base glazing putty works

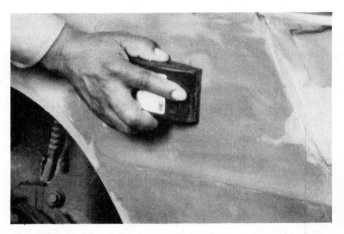

FIGURE 9-20 Block sanding the undercoater or primer-surfacer

FIGURE 9-22 Applying putty to the squeegee

FIGURE 9-23 Applying putty to the surface

proper solvent for the weather conditions and mix the material thoroughly.

Apply the first coat of undercoater primer-surfacer (Figure 9-18). Allow this coat to flash dry, following the recommendations on the label for flash time. Then apply two or three more medium wet coats for additional film buildup, with flash time between each application. When making a spot repair, extend the undercoater (primer-surfacer) several inches around the first coat.

Allow the undercoater to dry thoroughly. Do not apply extra heavy coats to speed up the operation. Film applied in this manner will require more time to dry and can lead to cracking, crazing, pinholes, and poor holdout (Figure 9-19).

After the undercoat is dry, block sand the area until it is smooth (Figure 9-20). For best results, use #320 grit sandpaper. If very fine scratches still appear, another coat of primer-surfacer might be all that is required to fill them.

PUTTY APPLICATIONS

Some sand scratches might require additional filling with a thin lacquer type glazing putty. This putty is generally used to fill small scratches and pinholes (Figure 9-21), but use it sparingly. To apply the putty, squeeze a small amount from the tube onto the edge of a squeegee (Figure 9-22). Quickly press the putty onto the repair and level it off with a flat scraping motion. Use moderate pressure to assure that the putty fills the depression completely (Figure 9-23). Make additional passes quickly, if necessary.

Allow the putty to air dry until it is hard. Test with a fingernail for hardness before sanding. If it is sanded too soon, the putty will continue to shrink, leaving part of the scratch unfilled (Figure 9-24). Once it hardens, the putty should be dry sanded with #220 grit paper or wet sanded (Figure 9-25). Wet

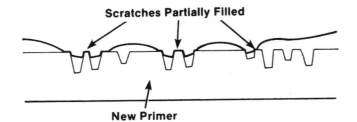

FIGURE 9-24   How putty shrinks

FIGURE 9-25   Sanding the putty

FIGURE 9-26   Re-priming the puttied area

sanding is carried out in the same manner as dry sanding; however, it requires special paper and plenty of water. After sanding the puttied area, clean the surface and then reprime (Figure 9-26). If the putty has been wet sanded, make sure to dry the surface thoroughly before applying primer-surfacer.

Lacquer-based glazing putties are being partially replaced by polyester putties, or finishing fillers as they are also called, and by polyester primer/fillers. Both products must be mixed with hardener before starting application and can be applied to filler, metal, or old paint finishes. The use of these high-viscosity, finely textured "fillers" eliminates the traditional primer/putty/primer process. Because they

chemically harden, they cure quickly and can be primed and refinished without the worry of sand scratch swelling commonly associated with lacquer-based glazing putties. For complete details on working with all types of putties, see Chapter 5.

COMPOUNDING

Compounding is sometimes done as a final smoothing step to remove light scratches, small dirt particles, and minor grinding or sanding marks before applying a final topcoat. Compounding can be done either by hand or machine. Rubbing compounds are available in various cutting strengths for both hand and machine as a final smoothing operation. A hand-rubbing compound is usually coarser than a machine-rubbing compound. It is used on small spot repairs, but it can be used on an entire car. It is applied with a damp rag to one small area at a time in a straight back-and-forth motion, not in circles. It is then buffed by machine or by hand.

Machine-rubbing compound is made for use with a portable polisher or buffer (see Chapter 2). It is finer than hand-rubbing compound because the machine provides more power. This compound should be thinned with water before it is applied to the surface.

Details on both hand and machine compounds can be found in Chapter 11.

MASKING

Masking is a very important step in the painting preparation process. Masking keeps paint mist from contacting areas other than those that are to be repainted (Figure 9-27). This has become even more important since the popular use of acrylic urethane and two component type paints. Once these types of paints dry, the paint mist cannot be removed with a thinner or other solvent. These paints will have to be removed with a compound or other time-consuming means.

MASKING MATERIALS

The basic materials for any masking job is masking paper and tape. Automotive paper comes in various widths—from 3 to 36 inches. Automotive masking paper is heat resistant so that it can be used safely in baking ovens. It also has good wet strength, freedom from loose fibers, and resistance to solvent penetration. **Never** use newspaper for masking a vehicle since it does not meet any of these requirements. Newspaper also has the added disadvantage of containing printing inks that are soluble in some

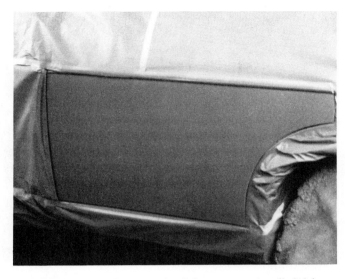

FIGURE 9-27 Car masked for a panel refinishing job. *(Courtesy of Du Pont Co.)*

FIGURE 9-29 Typical masking paper and tape dispensing equipment

FIGURE 9-30 Typical plastic tire covers in use. *(Courtesy of DeVilbiss Co.).*

paint solvents. These can be transferred to the underlying finish causing staining.

Automotive masking tape comes in various widths from 1/4 to 2 inches. The most frequently used tapes are shown in Figure 9-28. Larger width tapes are used only occasionally since they are expensive and difficult to handle. Automotive masking tape should not be confused with tapes bought in hardware or paint stores for home use. The latter will not hold up to the demanding requirements of automotive refinishing. It is interesting to note that the average size vehicle takes 2 to 2-1/2 rolls of tape to be completely masked.

The use of masking paper and tape dispensing equipment (Figure 9-29) makes it easy to pull and tear the exact amount of paper needed. Some masking machines permit tape to adhere to one or both edges of the paper as it is rolled out.

There are several types of masking covers available. One type of cover is the plastic tire cover that

eliminates the need for masking off the tire (Figure 9-30). Others include a body cover (Figure 9-31) and a frame cover. Light covers in a variety of sizes and shapes (Figure 9-32) are available to mask light assemblies including headlights and tail lights (Figure 9-33). These various covers can be used as the situation demands.

HOW TO MASK

Before any masking materials are applied, the vehicle must be completely cleaned (Figure 9-34) and all dust blown from the vehicle. The masking tape will not stick to surfaces that are not clean or dry. It is most important that the tape be pressed down firmly and adhered to the surface. Otherwise, paint solvents will creep under the tape. In the case of a two-color job, where the color break is not hidden by a capping strip or molding, it is **vital** that the masking tape edge is firmly pressed down.

FIGURE 9-28 Most common sizes of tape used in the paint shop. All widths are in 60-yard rolls.

FIGURE 9–31 Typical plastic car cover. Note the door panel is the area to be painted. *(Courtesy of Fibre Glass Evercoat Co., Inc.)*

FIGURE 9–32 Typical light covers save time masking head and tail lights. *(Courtesy of Marson Corp.)*

FIGURE 9–33 How the headlight covers are used. *(Courtesy of Lenco, Inc.)*

FIGURE 9–34 Clean the car thoroughly before masking

🔫 **SHOP TALK** _____

It is wise to completely detail (that is, check to see that all prior steps have been performed) the car before the masking job is started and, of course, after the paint job is completed. Reason: Improper masking can also cause a dirty paint job if done over a dirty car.

If the paint shop is cold and damp with little air movement, the masking tape probably will not stick to glass or chromium parts because of an almost invisible film of condensation that has formed on these parts. It must be wiped off before the tape will adhere properly.

Masking tape generally will not stick on the black rubber weatherstripping used around the doorjambs and deck lid opening. To mask rubber weatherstripping, apply clear lacquer thinner with a rag, allow it to completely dry, and then apply the tape. When masking doorjambs, be sure to cover both the door lock assembly and the striker bolt.

Although masking tape has an elastic property, it should be stretched only on curved surfaces. This is especially true when masking newly applied finishes that are still soft beneath the surface. It is also wise to avoid stretching the tape because this can increase the degree of tape marking on the finish.

When applying masking tape, most experienced maskers find it is easier to hold and peel the tape in one hand while they use the other hand to guide and secure it (Figure 9–35). This gives tight edges for good adherence and also allows the masker to change directions and go around corners with tape.

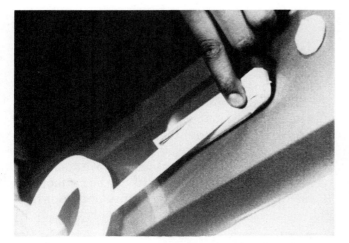

FIGURE 9–35 Proper way to handle masking tape

FIGURE 9–37 Masking an antenna and windshield

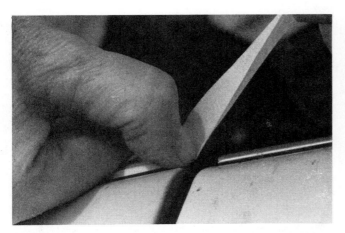

FIGURE 9–36 Easy method of cutting masking tape

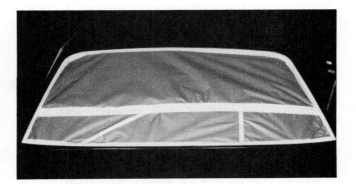

FIGURE 9–38 Masking the rear window

To cut the masking tape easily, quickly tear upward against the thumbnail as shown in Figure 9–36. This procedure will permit a clean cut of the tape without any stretching.

Be careful that the tape does not overlap any of the areas to be painted. Loop or overlap the inner tape edge to make, and follow, curves. The tape will stretch to conform to curves. Difficult areas such as a wheel can be masked using this process, but more often wheel covers are used to save time.

Here are some general recommendations on masking paper and tape size for the various areas of a car to be masked:

- Mask antennas by making a sleeve with pre-taped 3-inch masking paper and secure at the base with masking tape. On windshields, use two widths of either 15- or 18-inch masking paper. The top layer must overlap the bottom to prevent overspray (Figure 9–37).

- Rear windows are masked similarly to windshields with the use of two widths of 15- and 18-inch masking paper (Figure 9–38).
- Apply 12- or 15-inch masking paper to windows for fast, economical protection. On door handles, apply 3/4-inch tape in a lengthwise continuous strip to insure faster removal. Chrome drip rails and moldings also require 3/4-inch or wider widths of masking tape. Outside mirrors can be masked with 2-inch tape or 6-inch masking paper (Figure 9–39).
- The wide variety of shapes and widths of grilles and bumpers might require various widths of masking paper; 6, 9, 12, and 15 inches are the most popular widths to use (Figure 9–40).
- Mask protective side molding and wheel well molding with two strips of 3/4-inch or greater widths, 1-1/2, 2, or 3 inch as required. For protecting the tire and wheel, wrap two adjoining pieces of 18-inch masking paper around the tire (Figure 9–41).

FIGURE 9-39 Masking the side window, door handles, and side mirror

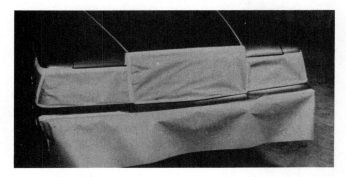

FIGURE 9-40 Masking the grille and the bumper

FIGURE 9-41 Masking side moldings and wheel well moldings

- Tail lights are masked with 6- or 9-inch masking paper. Mask letters and emblems with 1/8-inch or 1/4-inch tapes (Figure 9-42). A pocket knife is a handy tool to work the tape into place on such small items. If these items are too difficult to mask, they can often be removed during the masking operation and replaced after refinishing.
- Use two or three pieces of 36-inch masking paper to protect the inside of the trunk area.

Use clear lacquer to promote tape adhesion when masking weatherstrip (Figure 9-43).

- Mask around doorjambs with 6-inch pre-taped masking paper (Figure 9-44).

When masking large areas, such as bumpers, it is easier to manage the paper if it is tacked in the middle of the bumper with tape first. Then each side can be masked without the paper dragging on the floor and getting in the way.

Before masking glass areas, remove such items as wiper blades. The wiper shafts can be protected in the same manner as radio antennas and door han-

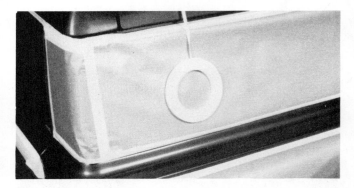

FIGURE 9-42 Masking tail lights

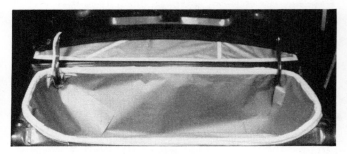

FIGURE 9-43 Masking a trunk

FIGURE 9-44 Masking the doorjambs

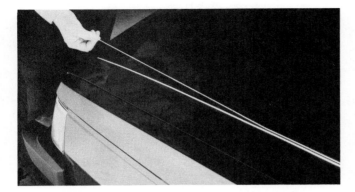

FIGURE 9–45 Fine line tape, as described in Chapter 12, can also be used to paint stripes; special tapes are available to create custom designs. *(Courtesy of Spartan Plastics Inc.)*

FIGURE 9–46 Using a special masking tape for making stripe painting easier. *(Courtesy of 3M)*

dles. Glass areas themselves can be masked by first applying tape along the very top and edges of window moldings. Then, use two pieces of masking paper to cover the glass area. The tape on the edge of the paper should overlap the tape placed on the molding. The top piece of paper should overlap the bottom layer of paper. If necessary, fold and tape any pleats in the paper so that there is no dust seep-

age. To mask lights that cannot be completely covered by tape or light covers, masking paper can be cut, folded, and worked around before being held down with tape.

One-sixteenth and 3/32-inch fine line tape can be used to protect existing stripes from overspray or damage of adjacent panels (Figure 9–45). Use fine line tape for precise color separation in two tone painting and for painting vivid, clean stripes. Its added flexibility and conformability makes painting of curved lines easier, with less reworking (Figure 9–46).

When spraying horizontal surfaces (hood, trunk, and so on), two layers of paper should be used to prevent bleed-through of finish-dulling solvents. Another method to prevent bleed-through is to reverse tape the paper. The paper is taped on the inside and allowed to bellow slightly, which keeps the paper lifted slightly from the surface.

A reverse masking method is often used during spot repainting to restrict the shading area and to make it less noticeable. At times a **line of definition** such as a door edge or a body seam next to a refinished panel will accentuate a slight difference in an otherwise acceptable color match. This is particularly true with metallics. This situation can be avoided by sanding the adjacent panel (crossing the line) when preparing the panel to be refinished. Then reverse mask the adjacent panel and refinish the repaired panel. Now remove the masking paper. If there is a slight difference, just paint across the line and blend in smoothly as with any spot repair. In Figure 9–47, reverse masking method A is used for flat surfaces and method B for curved surfaces.

Inspect the masking very carefully for any over-masked or undermasked areas that will make extra work after the vehicle is painted. Overmasked areas mean that the painter must touch up the part of the car that should have been painted. On the other hand, undermasked areas must be cleaned with solvent to remove overspray that detracts from the overall appearance of an otherwise good job.

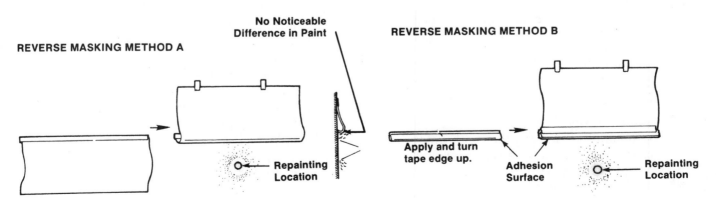

FIGURE 9–47 How to make a reverse mask. *(Courtesy of Toyota Motor Corp.)*

REVIEW QUESTIONS

1. If the original paint surface is in good condition, Painter A simply washes the car. In the same instance, Painter B washes and scuff sands the vehicle. Who is right?
   a. Painter A
   b. Painter B
   c. Both A and B
   d. Neither A nor B

2. When filling a dent, Refinsher A first applies a metal conditioner and then the body filler. Painter B applies the body filler alone. Who is right?
   a. Painter A
   b. Painter B
   c. Both A and B
   d. Neither A nor B

3. Which of the following methods is used to strip paint from the metal surfaces of a vehicle?
   a. sanding
   b. sandblasting
   c. chemical stripping
   d. all of the above

4. Painter A sandblasts at a 20- to 30-degree angle. Painter B sandblasts holding the hose 8 to 12 inches back from the area being repaired. Who is right?
   a. Painter A
   b. Painter B
   c. Both A and B
   d. Neither A nor B

5. Painter A brushes paint remover on the surface with a back and forth motion along the body lines. Painter B brushes it on in one direction only. Who is right?
   a. Painter A
   b. Painter B
   c. Both A and B
   d. Neither A nor B

6. Which method of paint removal is the quickest?
   a. sanding
   b. grinding
   c. sandblasting
   d. chemical stripping

7. Paint removers are _____.
   a. neutralized and removed with water
   b. removed with a squeegee or scraper
   c. not to be used on fiberglass
   d. all of the above

8. Painter A applies a metal conditioner before applying a conversion coating. Refinisher B does not. Who is right?
   a. Painter A
   b. Painter B
   c. Both A and B
   d. Neither A nor B

9. A washer-primer with phosphoric acid _____.
   a. cleans
   b. etches the metal
   c. assists in adhesion
   d. all of the above

10. After the putty hardens, Painter A dry sands it. Painter B wet sands. Who is right?
    a. Painter A
    b. Painter B
    c. Both A and B
    d. Neither A nor B

11. Lacquer-based glazing putties are being partially replaced by _____.
    a. polyester putties
    b. finishing fillers
    c. polyester primer/fillers
    d. all of the above
    e. none of the above

12. Painter A applies compound in a back-and-forth motion. Painter B uses a circular motion. Who is right?
    a. Painter A
    b. Painter B
    c. Both A and B
    d. Neither A nor B

13. Newspaper _____.
    a. has freedom from loose fibers
    b. has resistance to solvent penetration
    c. contains inks that are soluble in some paint solvents
    d. all of the above
    e. none of the above

14. Two layers of paper should be used to prevent bleed-through, when _____.
    a. spraying more than one coat
    b. using a urethane topcoat
    c. spraying horizontal surfaces
    d. using an acrylic topcoat

15. Painter A stretches the masking tape to gain adhesion. Painter B never stretches the tape. Who is right?
    a. Painter A
    b. Painter B
    c. Both A and B
    d. Neither A nor B

CHAPTER TEN

CHOOSING AND MATCHING PAINT

Objectives

After reading this chapter, you will be able to:

- determine the type of paint on a car and whether or not the car has been repainted.
- match color and texture by tinting.

From the customer's standpoint, the topcoat or color coat is the most important operation in body repair because that is all the customer sees. The expert refinisher takes special pride in producing a beautiful finish on spot, panel repairs, or overalls that matches both the color (or color effect) and the texture of the original finish. Sometimes this color effect can be a basecoat/clear coat finish that more and more customers are viewing as a premium-looking finish. It is the painter's job to satisfy the customer with the paint application. So it is of great importance to fully understand all the working application instructions for applying topcoats. The best place for this is the paint label (Figure 10-1).

Since the customer sees only the topcoat and judges the quality of the refinisher's work on its appearance and its appearance alone, there is little appreciation for all the work done underneath the topcoat. As already pointed out in previous chapters, the cleaning, filling, and sanding of the substrate must be done very painstakingly. A perfectly smooth surface must be readied before the topcoat is applied. Otherwise, any imperfection—even the smallest—will show in the topcoat.

TYPE OF PAINT AND REPAINTING PROCESS

The conditions determining the type of topcoat paint to be used are: the extent of the area to be covered, the extent of deterioration of the previous paint film, and whether or not the vehicle had been previously repainted. The type of paint used and the process in which it is applied in accordance with these conditions are very important factors governing work efficiency and speed.

DETERMINING IF THE AUTOMOBILE HAS BEEN REPAINTED

There are two ways to determine if the automobile has been repainted in the past. They are:

- **Sanding method.** Sand an edge on the area to be repainted until the bare metal appears.

FIGURE 10-1 Carefully read the manufacturer's instructions that appear on the paint container.

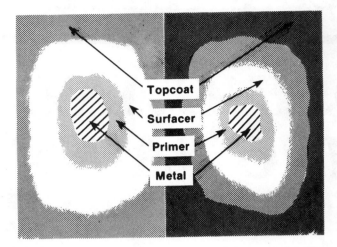

FIGURE 10-2 Sanding method of determining the type of old finish

FIGURE 10-3 Visual inspection method of determining the type of old finish

The make-up of the paint coating will determine whether or not it was repainted previously (Figure 10-2).

• **Paint film thickness measurement method.** A paint film thickness that is greater than the standard for a new vehicle is an indication of previous repainting. The standard paint film thicknesses of new vehicles are:

Domestic vehicles	3 to 5 mils
European cars	5 to 8 mils
Japanese vehicles	3 to 5 mils

Normally, an electromagnetic thickness gauge or a mechanical thickness gauge mentioned in Chapter 3 is used to measure the paint film thickness.

DETERMINING THE TYPE OF PREVIOUS PAINT COATING

If the vehicle has never been repainted (the finish is the original one), the problem of determining the type is fairly easy. Shop manuals or the so-called "world color" book will identify the topcoat type.

If it is confirmed that the vehicle had been repainted in the past, it is now necessary to determine what type of paint was used. The methods for doing this include:

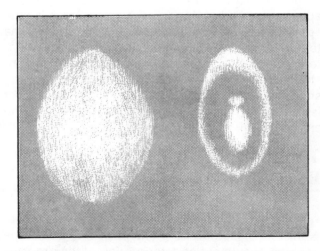

FIGURE 10-4 Solvent application method of determining the type of old finish

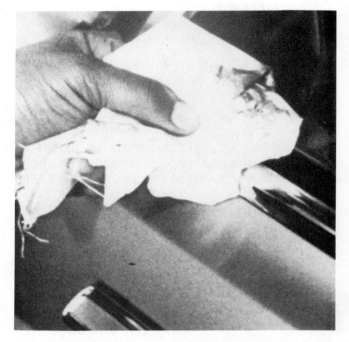

FIGURE 10-5 Heat application method of determining the type of old finish

TABLE 10-1: HARDNESS ACCORDING TO PENCIL BRAND (REFERENCE ONLY)

Test Sample Number	Brand Name				
	A	B	C	D	E
1	5B	6B	5B	4B	3B
2	3B	4B	5B	4B	3B
3	2B	2B	2B	2B	HB
4	HB	F	HB	HB	HB
5	HB	F	HB	HB	H
6	F	H	H	H	2H
7	F	F	F	H	2H
8	H	H	H	H	2H
9	2H	2H	2H	4H	3H
10	3H	3H	3H	4H	4H

1. **Visual inspection method.** If the skin texture near a character line is rough or if what is known as a "polished texture" appears when rubbed (Figure 10–3), it indicates that a polish type paint was used for repainting. If a gloss peculiar to acrylic urethane appears, it can be determined that it was repainted with an acrylic urethane type paint.

2. **Solvent application method.** With this method, the paint film is rubbed with a white shop cloth soaked in lacquer thinner to determine the extent to which it will dissolve the previous film. If the paint film dissolves and leaves a mark on the rag (Figure 10–4), the previous paint is an air-dry type. If it does not dissolve, it is either an oven dried or a two-component reaction type paint. An acrylic urethane lacquer paint film will not dissolve as easily as an air-dried paint, but sometimes the thinner will penetrate sufficiently to blur the paint gloss.

3. **Heat application method.** First, the area is wet sanded with #800 to #1000 grit abrasive paper to dull the paint film. Next, the area is heated with an infrared lamp. If a gloss returns to the dulled appearance, the paint is acrylic lacquer (Figure 10–5).

4. **Hardness method.** This method is based on the fact that different kinds of paint do not dry to the same hardness. Generally, two-component reaction and bake-dried type paints dry to a harder film than air-

TABLE 10-2: CLASSIFICATION STANDARD FOR PREVIOUS PAINT COATINGS

Previous Paint Coating	Classification Method			
	Visual Inspection	Solvent Method	Heat Application Method	Hardness Method (pencil hardness)
Alkyd enamel	Caulking surface	Does not dissolve	Some softening	F to H
Acrylic lacquer	—	Dissolve	Softens	B to H
Acrylic enamel	—	—	Some softening	F to H
Polyurethane	Polished skin	—	—	—
Acrylic urethane lacquer	Polished skin	Difficult to dissolve	Some softening	—
Acrylic urethane enamel	Gloss with some orange peel	—	—	—

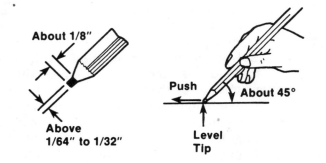

FIGURE 10-6 Hardness method of determining the type of old finish

dried paint. The most common method of determining the paint film hardness is with a pencil. The lead of the pencil tip should be shaped as shown in Figure 10-6, held at a 45 degree angle to the surface and pushed forward. If the lead pierces the paint, the hardness is considered to be one number below that of which the lead pierced. As indicated in Table 10-1, the pencil lead hardness varies depending on the manufacturer so the same brand of pencil should be used for all tests.

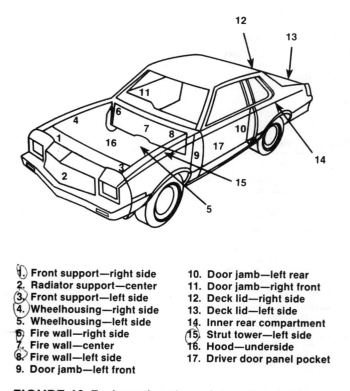

1. Front support—right side
2. Radiator support—center
3. Front support—left side
4. Wheelhousing—right side
5. Wheelhousing—left side
6. Fire wall—right side
7. Fire wall—center
8. Fire wall—left side
9. Door jamb—left front
10. Door jamb—left rear
11. Door jamb—right front
12. Deck lid—right side
13. Deck lid—left side
14. Inner rear compartment
15. Strut tower—left side
16. Hood—underside
17. Driver door panel pocket

FIGURE 10-7 Locating the paint code number on various car makes. *(Courtesy of Du Pont Co.)*

Table 10-2 classifies standard paints for determining previous painted coating. Table 10-3 lists the types of previously applied paints and those topcoats that can be applied over them.

COLOR AND TEXTURE MATCHING

Color matching is probably the single most recurring problem in the automotive refinishing industry. Most of the color matching problems are experienced when attempting to match metallic colors. Although some problems are encountered with solid colors, they cause the fewest problems for the average painter.

The first step in the color matching procedure is to learn the original color from the manufacturer's paint code in the vehicle identification number. Use the paint code in the vehicle identification number. Use Figure 10-7 and Table 10-4 to find the position of the paint code number on almost all vehicles, except General Motors. Location of paint code numbers for General Motors is shown in Figures 10-8 and 10-9.

Most auto refinishing shops have a color book (Figure 10-10). This book contains color chips and color information for almost all makes and models worldwide (Figure 10-11). First locate the car manufacturer's code number. This permits the refinisher to identify the color chip next to it. As a double check, it is wise to compare the color chip with the

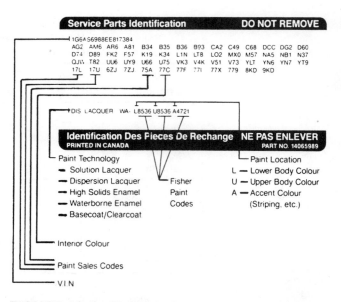

FIGURE 10-8 Typical General Motors' service parts identification label. *(Courtesy of Du Pont Co.)*

TABLE 10-3:   APPLICATION CHART—PREVIOUSLY APPLIED PAINT AND REPAINTING PAINT

Topcoat	Previously Applied Paint					
	Alkyd Enamel	Acrylic Lacquer	Acrylic Enamel	Polyurethane Enamel	Acrylic Urethane Lacquer	Acrylic Urethane Enamel
Alkyd enamel	A	B	A	A	B	A
Acrylic lacquer	A	B	B	A	A	A
Acrylic lacquer enamel	A	B	A	A	A	A
Polyurethane enamel	B	B	B	A	A	A
Acrylic urethane lacquer	B	B	B	A	A	A
Acrylic urethane enamel	A	A	A	A	A	A

A   Good to repaint with
B   Good if primer-surfacer or sealer specified by paint manufacturer is used

TABLE 10-4:   PAINT CODE LOCATION (See Figure 10-7)

Model	Position	Model	Position
Acura	9	Jaguar	1, 9
Alfa Romeo	4, 13	Lancia	4, 8, 13
AMC	9,10	LUV 1972–80	7
Arrow	3	1981–82	2
Audi	12, 13	Masarati	2, 4
Austin Rover	17	Mazda	1, 2, 3, 4, 6, 8
BMW	4,5	Mercedes	2, 7, 9
Challenger 1978–82	3	Mitsubishi Starion	7
1983	16	Montero/Pickup	3
Champ	5	Cordia/Tredia	4
Chrysler	3, 5, 16	Others	1, 2, 3
Chrysler Imports	1, 2, 4	Nissan	1, 3, 4, 6, 8, 15,*
Citroe‰n	4, 6, 7, 8	Opel—GM	1, 2, 3, 4, 5, 8
Colt 1974–82	5	Peugeot	2, 3, 4, 5, 8
1983–84	3	Porsche	9
Colt Vista	16	Renault	1, 3, 4, 5, 8
Conquest	7	Rover	1, 3, 4, 5
Courier	3, 4, 10	SAAB	5, 6, 8
Daihatsu	1, 6, 7	Sapporo 1978–82	3
Datsun	2	1983	16
Dodge D50	3	Sterling	9
Ferrari	12	Subaru	2
Fiat	4, 8, 13	Suzuki	7, 11
Ford	10	Toyota Passenger	7, 8, 14
Ford Europe	2, 6, 8	Truck	4
GM Imports	2, 12, 13, 14	Triumph	5, 6, 9
Honda	8, 10	Volkswagen	2, 11
Hyundai	6,7	Volvo	6, 7, 8
Isuzu	2, 10	Yugo	12

*Under right front passenger seat

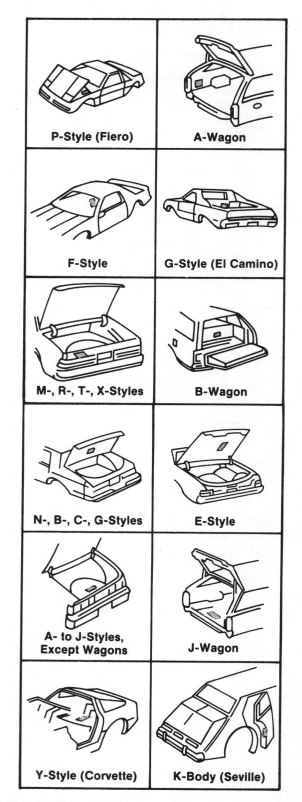

FIGURE 10-9 Beginning with 1985 production, General Motors has added identification colors used on various parts of the car. These labels or tags define the type of paint used. *(Courtesy of Du Pont Co.)*

FIGURE 10-10 Refer to the shop's color book containing color chips that identify make and model year. *(Courtesy of Du Pont Co.)*

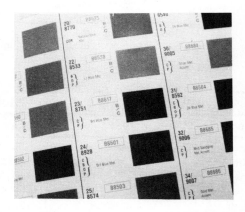

FIGURE 10-11 Locate the manufacturer's paint code number in the book. Identifying color chip is located next to it. *(Courtesy of Du Pont Co.)*

car color, for there is always the chance that the car has been repainted with a different color.

If the color match is correct, order the topcoat from a local supplier by color stock number. Refinish suppliers supply topcoat colors in two ways:

- If it is a recent model or a popular color, chances are they will have it ready-mixed in pint, quart, and occasionally gallon cans. These ready-mixed colors are called **factory packaged** (Figure 10-12).
- If it is an older color, they might have to mix it in pint, quart, or gallon quantities. Paint manufacturers work extensively to develop OEM matches with mixing color formulas for all top qualities. Custom-mixed colors are those colors that are mixed to order at the paint supply distributor. Custom-mixed color can always be identified easily because

the contents of the container must be written on the label by the paint distributor that mixed the paint (Figure 10–13).

In recent years, most of the major automobile paint manufacturers have made available to refinisher shops a color mixing system. Under such an "intermix" system, it is possible to mix thousands of colors at a savings of up to 35 percent of the cost of factory-packaged colors.

With this service, inventory can be reduced, keeping only the fast-moving current colors on hand. Yet, the service takes up little space. It is fast and easy to mix a color that matches car maker's standards.

- Formulas are scientifically developed by the laboratory from base tints, which are rigidly controlled by plant chemists to assure batch-to-batch uniformity.
- Formulas come completely indexed on microfiche ready to use with directions for mixing exact quantities.
- Measurements by weight, not volume, insure completely accurate measurements.
- Pour-spout allows precise control of material flow.

It must be remembered that the color code might not be exactly the right color because all automotive finishes gradually change color when exposed to light. Some colors fade lighter, others go darker. Yellow, for instance, fades fairly rapidly. If the yellow fades from a cream, the color will usually

FIGURE 10-13 Custom-mixed colors are mixed and packaged at a local paint dealer or distributor for use on a specific job.

go lighter and whiter. If the yellow fades from a green composed of blue and yellow, the color will go bluer and usually darker.

Every color weathers a little differently than any other color depending on its pigment composition. Each color weathers a little differently on each car depending on its care and the part of the country in which it is driven. In general, cars that are in a garage a good share of the time change less. Those that are rubbed and polished a lot, change more. Those parked under trees, change depending on the type of tree spray or drippings. Those in the South change more rapidly due to increased ultraviolet radiation from the sun. Those in industrial areas or in areas of the country where there are natural chemicals in the air, such as alkali flats, change depending on the chemical to which they are exposed. If a refinish material made with the same pigmentation of the original equipment material is used, the weathering will be the same (unless the type of care or exposure has changed) and in a few months, the refinished area will change to the same weathered color as the original finish. Weathering is the fastest in the first few months, and then the change slows down. For that reason, a fresh touch up spot will catch up in time.

In order to give the customer the best match at the time the vehicle is delivered, most shops tint colors to match the weathered color on the car. This matching process is made much simpler through the use of test cards. First the original finish must be compounded to bring it up to its original shine.

FIGURE 10-12 Factory-packaged colors are mixed and packaged at the paint factory. (Courtesy of FAC-PAC).

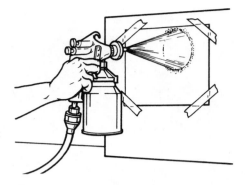

FIGURE 10-14 To match the color exactly, make a test card by spray painting a piece of cardboard.

Then, a thin piece of cardboard (not corrugated) can be taped to newspaper or another protective backing and propped up so that it hangs vertically (Figure 10-14). The cardboard is spray painted and held against the car to see if it matches. A number of adjustments can be made to make slight changes in the paint's color. Several test cards might be needed in order to achieve a good match. Although the ability to match is mostly a matter of experience, there are some things that can be pointed out that will be helpful.

TINTING COLORS FOR A PERFECT MATCH

There are three basic reasons for tinting colors:

- To adjust color variations in shades for cars of the same color as they come from the manufacturer.
- To adjust color because of aged or weathered finish. (Color might change due to exposure to the weather, other elements, or age.)
- To tint or make a color for which there is no formula. They are cars painted with bench colors (a color that was never formulated or a color that has no color codes available).

To do color matching, the refinisher must be able to recognize colors as they actually are. It is important not only to see the color that is to be worked on, but also the overtones within that color, including the shades of darkness or lightness and the richness or fullness of the color (Table 10-5).

Tinting should only be used as a last resort. If the color of the refinish paint varies from the car finish, check the following possible reasons for the mismatch before deciding to tint the paint:

- The original may have faded. Check the paint on unexposed areas such as door jambs or

under the trunk or hood lid to determine if the finish has faded. If this is the case, you can restore the paint's luster by compounding the old finish well beyond the repair area.
- Was the wrong color used? Check the auto manufacturer's code and the paint company's stock number of the color being used to make sure that it is the right color. It may be necessary to know the VIN number as well as the paint code in order to check the manufacturer's code.
- The pigment and/or flakes might not have been mixed thoroughly. Leaving pigment, flake or pearl in the bottom of the can could cause a mismatch, so be sure to agitate thoroughly.
- Has the amount of thinner or reducer been measured carefully? Overthinning will lighten or desaturate a color. Remember that it is easy to add more thinner, but it cannot be taken out.
- Be sure to clean and compound the old finish to remove all chalking and oxidation before making a color comparison.
- The type of light in the shop could alter the appearance of the finish. Colors vary depending on the light they are viewed under. When the color match between two paints changes under different lighting conditions, it is referred to as **metamerism.** This is the reason why it is possible for a refinish paint to match the car color under shop lighting conditions, and then show up as a less than perfect match when the car is viewed in natural daylight. The color match seen under shop lighting conditions can vary depending on the type of lights used. For example, incandescent lights tend to give paint a red cast; fluorescent lights could give paint a yellow or blue cast, depending on the type of fluorescent in the light; both cool white light and soft white lights can also alter the ap-

TABLE 10-5: HOW COLORS ARE DESCRIBED	
Lighter—Darker (called depth)	1. Direct look (panel to panel) 2. Side angle look (panel to panel)
Cast differences	1. Redder 2. Bluer 3. Greener 4. Yellower
Cleanliness	1. Grayer (dirtier or more muddy) 2. Brighter (cleaner appearance)

pearance of paint color, the cast they throw on the finish will vary with the color of the paint.

- When using a test panel, allow the paint enough time to dry. Be sure to allow proper flash and dry times for each coat, because paint usually gets darker as it dries. If using a lacquer clear coat, remember that compounding the clear will make the paint appear darker. If testing for a base/clear finish, color judgment cannot be made until the clear is applied to the basecoat. Further information on making a test panel is given later in this chapter.

- Vary the spraying technique. The three shades shown in Figure 10-15 were sprayed out of the same gun cup of material. The section on the left was sprayed dry with the gun quite far away. The section in the middle was sprayed with the gun at the normal distance from the panel. The section on the right was sprayed wet with the gun held close. Here is a list of shading adjustments:

Darker
1. Open fluid valve more.
2. Reduce size of fan pattern.
3. Decrease gun distance.
4. Slow down stroke.
5. Allow less flash time.

Lighter
1. Close fluid valve slightly.
2. Increase size of fan pattern.
3. Increase gun distance.
4. Speed up stroke.
5. Increase flash time.

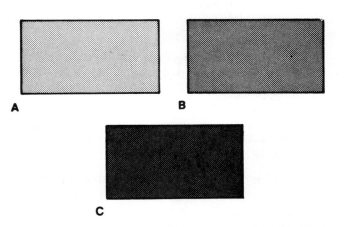

FIGURE 10-15 Matching colors with a spray gun: (A) lighter than normal—dry spray; (B) standard color—normal spray; and (C) darker than standard—wet spray.

Oddly enough, a mismatch in a panel repair will usually show up more than a mismatch in a spot repair—even though the spot repair is smaller. That is because a panel—such as a car door—has a distinct edge. And the repair, obviously, cuts off at that edge. Any mismatch—as in the case of front and rear doors—will be right next to the adjoining panel and will show a sharp contrast.

A spot repair, on the other hand, is performed by blending the repair into the surrounding area. In spot repairing, the first coat is applied to the immediate area being repaired. Subsequent coats extend beyond this area gradually. Finally, a blend coat extends beyond the color coats. Thus, if there is a slight mismatch, the blend coat and the last color coat will allow enough show through of the old finish to make the color difference a gradual one.

ANALYZING COLOR

Through various application techniques, lightness/darkness, cast, and brightness can be adjusted so that the painter can achieve a good match. To determine what must be done, the color must first be analyzed to determine whether the color is too light or too dark, looking at the finish from an angle and head-on. Then the refinisher must check the cast to see if the color sprayed is redder, bluer, greener, or yellower than the original finish. Before adjusting begins, the color must be checked to see if the finish just sprayed is brighter or grayer than the original. The sprayed portion must always be allowed to dry before any adjustments are made.

Adjustments for lightness or darkness rely primarily on shop conditions, spraying techniques, and solvent usage (Table 10-6). Other variables include the amount of paint applied, the air pressure at the spray gun, and the amount of color added to the mix.

Once the lightness or darkness has been adjusted, tinting might be required to get the right cast. Each color can only vary in cast in two directions.

- Colors that are either greener or redder in cast include:

Blues	Purples
Yellows	Beiges
Golds	Browns

- Colors yellower or bluer in cast are:

Greens	Blacks
Maroons	Grays or Silvers
Whites	

- Colors yellower or redder in cast are:

Bronzes	Reds
Oranges	

- Colors bluer or greener in cast include:

Aqua	Turquoise

TABLE 10-6: ADJUSTING LIGHTNESS/DARKNESS

Variable	To Make Colors	
	Lighter	Darker
Shop Condition 1. Temperature 2. Humidity 3. Ventilation	1. Increase 2. Decrease 3. Increase	1. Decrease 2. Increase 3. Decrease
Spraying Techniques 1. Gun distance 2. Gun speed 3. Flash time between coats 4. Mist coat	1. Increase distance 2. Increase speed 3. Allow more flash time 4. Will not lighten color	1. Decrease distance 2. Decrease speed 3. Allow less flash time 4. Wetter mist coat
Solvent Usage 1. Type solvent 2. Reduction of color 3. Use of retarder	1. Use faster evaporator solvent 2. Increase amount of solvent 3. Do not use retarder	1. Use slower evaporator solvent 2. Decrease amount of solvent 3. Add retarder to solvent

TABLE 10-7: METHOD OF CHANGING CASTS

Color	Add		Cast
Blue	Green	to kill	Red
Blue	Red	to kill	Green
Green	Yellow	to kill	Blue
Green	Blue	to kill	Yellow
Red	Yellow	to kill	Blue
Red	Blue	to kill	Yellow
Gold	Yellow	to kill	Red
Gold	Red	to kill	Yellow
Maroon	Yellow	to kill	Blue
Maroon	Blue	to kill	Yellow
Bronze	Yellow	to kill	Red
Bronze	Red	to kill	Yellow
Orange	Yellow	to kill	Red
Orange	Red	to kill	Yellow
Yellow	Green	to kill	Red
Yellow	Red	to kill	Green
White	White	to kill	Blue
White	White	to kill	Yellow
Beige	Green	to kill	Red
Beige	Red	to kill	Green
Purple	Blue	to kill	Red
Purple	Red	to kill	Blue
Aqua	Blue	to kill	Green
Aqua	Green	to kill	Blue

Charts and manuals available from manufacturers can help the painter decide on what tint color to use for the appropriate system. Once the color necessary to correctly adjust the cast is determined (Table 10-7), the amount must then be calculated, utilizing the least amount necessary to effectively change the color. The color must be thoroughly mixed; the gun triggered to clear the chamber; and then a small panel can be sprayed, allowed to dry, and checked against the original color.

After the color is correct in lightness/darkness and cast, the color might be made grayer or dirtier. Attempting to make a color brighter at this point will throw off the previous two corrections. To gray the finish, a wet coat must be sprayed followed by a coat sprayed at half trigger at a slightly greater distance and a small amount of white mixed with a very small amount of black.

There are three angles the refinisher should use to look at a vehicle's finish when determining whether a color adjustment is necessary:

- **Head-On.** Viewing the repaired area from an angle that is perpendicular to the vehicle.
- **Near-Spec.** Viewing the repaired area from an angle just past the reflection of the light source.
- **Side-Tone.** Viewing the repaired area at an angle of less than 45 degrees.

The color of the repaired area should be the same as the rest of the vehicle. If there is any difference, the color shold be corrected until it is the same when viewed from all three angles.

HINTS ON COLOR TINTING

Here are some additional tips that might prove helpful when tinting a color:

- Check the color in daylight as well as artificial light. It might not look the same in both lights. When a refinish color matches in one light but not another, it often indicates that the same pigments were not used in the refinish material as in the original finish. The original equipment supplier is usually very careful to use the same pigments in the refinish material that are used in the original finish. To control the uniformity of colors, every batch is checked for exact color match in three different lights—yellow, blue, and daylight.
- Determine what the color problem is and select the proper tinting colors. Do not use mixed colors from the bench for this because they probably have overcasts of the wrong shades. Adjust the color to make the hue redder, greener, bluer, or yellower.
- To understand what the overcasts are to a tinting color, put a few drops on a quart lid with a few drops of white, then intermix these two and make a finger smear on the lid. This will allow the refinisher to determine what the overcast of that tinting color is (Figure 10-16).
- Do all tinting systematically.
  —Use a measuring device such as those described in Chapter 2.
  —Keep a list of tinting colors used.
  —Keep a record of the amount used.
- A formula of the color is a help in tinting because it shows the original base colors and indicates which color has faded out and has to be toned down in the refinish material.
- Be sure to mix all tinting colors thoroughly before using; also thoroughly mix the tinting color every time any color is added.

- Add tinting colors in small amounts because it is very easy to overtint. Keep in mind that more color can be added but it cannot be taken out.
- Do not tint the whole can of paint at one time. Make progressive tryouts with small samples until a color match is achieved.
- Be conservative when tinting near the limits of the color range. Correct the most noticeable color differences first.
- Use caution when adding white to metallics or pearls and always use low-strength whites.
- Stay with the same pearls and metallic flakes used in the formula.
- Do not use reduced material when using the drawdown bar.
- An agitator cup is preferred when spraying metallics or pearls.
- Allow the color to dry before attempting to adjust it. To shorten dry time, use heat lamps, heat guns, or other drying methods. Be sure the method chosen has been approved for use in the paint/body shop.
- To check the true color, spray out a small panel and allow it to dry. Compare it to the panel to be matched. When it is possible, an old panel from the car to be matched is good to use because it can be masked in the center for an excellent comparison.
- Keep the tint on the light side until the final match is determined. Do not make a final judgment of the color match while the color is wet or still damp because it will change until it is completely dry.
- Once the color is tinted "close enough," complete the repair. Many times that last "just a little bit closer" is the thing that ruins a successful tinting.

Tinting can be divided into two categories: major color tinting and minor color tinting. Major color tinting consists of making up a color for which there is no color mixing formula available. Find a color chip as close as possible to the desired color and look at that formula. Break the formula down into percentages. For example, gold metallic is 45 percent coarse metallic, 20 percent sparkle metallic, 15 percent gold toner, 10 percent yellow gold, 3 percent soft white, 2 percent soft black. Using these percentages, make only half of a can; stir and tint to match the desired color.

Minor color tinting is used to adjust a color in a given repair situation to achieve an acceptable color match. To achieve this, each major paint supplier has a basic color tinting kit, a set of instructions, and

FIGURE 10-16 One method of determining the overcast of the tinting color

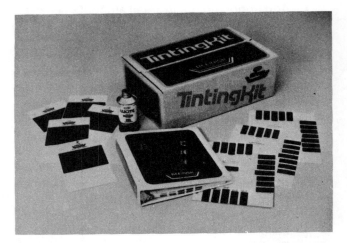

FIGURE 10-17 Typical tinting guide and kit that is designed for the refinisher to provide a color matching tool that will help to visualize color changes and develop the experience and skill to accomplish successful color tinting. *(Courtesy of Du Pont Co.)*

a tinting guide that is available to the paint shop and painter (Figure 10-17). Any painter, once familiar with the tinting information and kits that are available, should be able to do minor color tinting to achieve top quality color matches. For more information on the tinting colors and/or for a copy of a company's tinting guide with color chips, contact the shop's local paint jobber or a paint manufacturer's sales and service representative.

MATCHING METALLIC FINISHES

In most cases, solid color finishes—when properly prepared, thinned, and sprayed—will provide a good color match. The matching of metallic (polychrome) finishes, however, is probably the most skillful operation the refinisher has to perform. There are more cars on the road with metallic rather than solid-colored finishes; that means there are more metallic repairs to be made.

The reason much difficulty is experienced in matching metallic color is that metallic colors are made with a pigment and aluminum flake in the binder that allows light to penetrate beyond the surface of the paint film. When viewing a metallic color at right angles or perpendicular to the surface, this is the face of the color (Figure 10-18A). When viewing it at a 45 degree angle or less, it is the pitch or side tone of a color (Figure 10-18B).

As the position of metallic and/or pigment particles changes in a color film, the color shade of the metallic finish changes accordingly. Each metallic particle is like a tiny mirror. That is what changes the appearance of metallic colors when viewed from different angles. Metallic color also appears to be different when viewed under different kinds of light, such as daylight, shade, sun, or artificial light.

In standard color shades, the aluminum and pigment particles are spread uniformly throughout the paint film. Also notice that the metallic particles point in all directions, not just one predominate direction. This random mixing of the tiny mirrors in the paint film causes the light to reflect in all directions. The uniform distribution of pigment particles is what creates the standard color shade (Figure 10-19). To achieve this standard color proceed as follows:

- Use the label directions for the reduction of the color.
- Use slow evaporating solvents in temperatures of 65 to 85 degrees.
- Use 35 to 40 psi at the gun for lacquer and 50 to 55 psi at the gun for enamels.
- Apply in medium wet color coats with correct flash off time between coats.
- Remember to always be sure the paint material is stirred properly or put on the paint shaker.

Light Color Shades (Lighter Than Standard)

Light color shades are caused when the aluminum particles lie nearly horizontally at the top of the

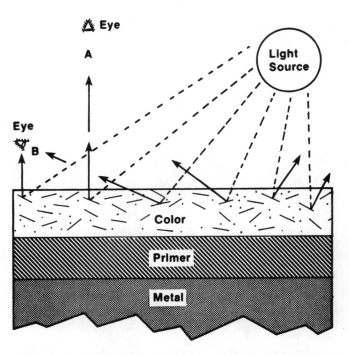

FIGURE 10-18 Metallic color construction showing face and side tone appearance of color. *(Courtesy of General Motors Corp.)*

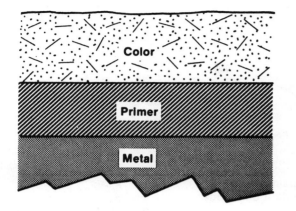

FIGURE 10-19 Standard shade of metallic color. *(Courtesy of General Motors Corp.)*

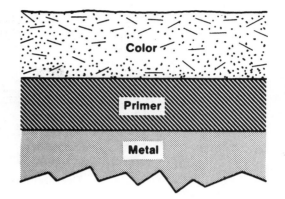

FIGURE 10-20 Light shade of metallic color. *(Courtesy of General Motors Corp.)*

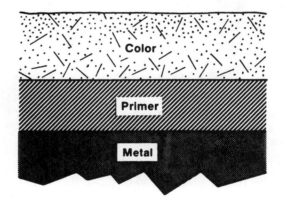

FIGURE 10-21 Dark shade of metallic color. *(Courtesy of General Motors Corp.)*

paint film and hide most of the pigment particles underneath them (Figure 10-20). The flat or horizontal positioning of the tiny metallic mirrors reflects a higher than normal amount of light. This causes lighter than standard color shades of the metallic finish. A match to these shades can be achieved by one or a combination of the following procedures:

1. Use more solvent than is called for on the label directions.
2. Use medium or fast thinner to reduce acrylic lacquer. Use only fast drying solvents in reducing acrylic enamel.
3. Use a higher than recommended air pressure at the gun.
4. Apply light to medium coats with complete flash off between coats.
5. Hold the spray gun farther from the surface during spraying.
6. Increase speed of spraying applications.

Dark Color Shades (Colors Darker Than Standard)

Dark color shades have a dense flotation of pigment particles near the surface of the paint film. The aluminum flakes are positioned nearly perpendicularly to the surface (Figure 10-21). This effect is achieved on the vertical sides of a car the same as on the horizontal panels and is not simply the settling of the metallic flakes.

Dark shades are produced by very slow solvents and extra wet coats. Darker shades of colors are achieved by one or a combination of the following:

- Reduce color with 10 to 25 percent less solvent than the label indicates.
- Use 9 parts slowest solvent to 1 part retarder for color reduction in temperatures of 65 to 85 degrees. Usually a 100 percent reduction

works well for dark shades of lacquer metallic colors, 25 percent for acrylic enamels.
- Use lower than normal air pressure for application; 35 to 40 psi is normal for lacquer, 55 to 60 psi for acrylic enamels.

Flip-Flop of Color

Flip-flop is a condition that occurs in metallics involving the positioning of the aluminum particles and the manner in which light is reflected to the observer (Figure 10-22). The cause of this effect results from the percentage of aluminum particles oriented in a specific direction and their depth in the paint film. The direction and intensity of the light being reflected back through the paint film is the flip-flop phenomenon that is observed.

The first approach to correct the problem is to adjust your spraying technique to compensate for this effect. Spraying the fender a little wetter will slightly darken the appearance when looking directly into the panel. When viewed from an angle, the resulting appearance is lighter. This occurs because

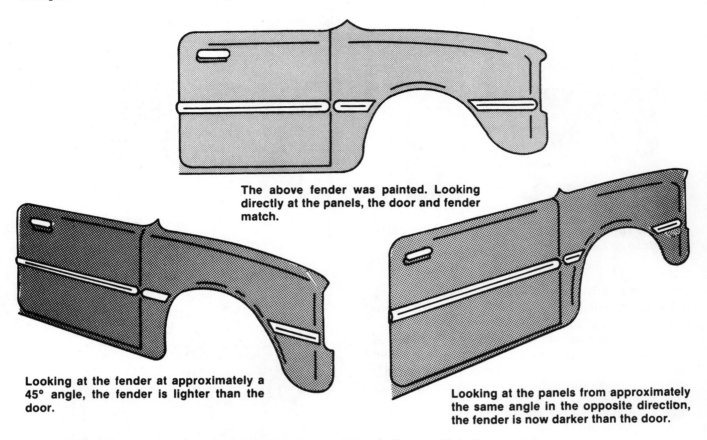

The above fender was painted. Looking directly at the panels, the door and fender match.

Looking at the fender at approximately a 45° angle, the fender is lighter than the door.

Looking at the panels from approximately the same angle in the opposite direction, the fender is now darker than the door.

FIGURE 10-22 The cause of flip-flop. *(Courtesy of Martin-Senour Paint)*

the aluminum particles are positioned flatter and deeper in the paint film.

Spraying the panel slightly dryer reverses the effect, giving a light appearance when looking directly at the panel. This is because the aluminum particles are closer to the surface. The result is a darker appearance viewed at the angle, as light becomes trapped. Both of these techniques are a compromise and should be used to correct minor conditions of flip-flop because the match in one direction can be changed too severely to be acceptable.

If spray techniques cannot correct this condition, the addition of a small amount of white will eliminate the sharp contrast from light to dark when the surface is viewed at various angles. The white acts to dull the transparency, giving a more uniform, subdued reflection through the paint film. Care should be taken when adding white since the change occurs quickly. Once too much white is added, recovering the color match becomes virtually impossible.

When confronted with an extremely difficult flip-flop condition, the best method involves adding white, plus blending the color into the adjacent panels. When blending, extend the color in stages. In acrylic lacquer, for example, use a recommended

blending clear material, and thin the appropriate color when spraying farther into the adjacent panel. The blending agent protects the metallic edges, eliminating the halo or bright edge where the blend ends.

A good painter must know how to handle metallic colors. They are very sensitive to the solvents with which they are reduced and the air pressure with which they are applied. Metallic colors are also affected by a number of variables. A **variable** is part of the spray painting conditions: such as temperature, humidity, and ventilation, or a part of the spray painting process such as amount of reduction, evaporation, speed of solvents, air pressure, and type of equipment. If a painter is to get good color matches, it is important to understand how certain paint variables affect the shades of metallic colors.

Variables are divided into two categories: positive and negative. Positive variables are those things that a painter does to duplicate the original finish, which in turn results in a good color match. They are:

- Slowness of solvent evaporation. This allows the painter to reproduce the factory finish.
- Wetness of color application.

- Proper spraying technique and the correct air pressure.

Negative variables are those that cause the shades of colors to be off standard. Most common are:

- Improper reduction.
- Improper agitation.
- Improper application; primarily too high or too low air pressure.

In summary, the shades of metallic colors are controlled by:

- Choice of solvents.
- Color reduction.
- Air pressure.
- Wetness of application.
- Spraying techniques.

TEST PANELS

While a test panel sprayout is **recommended** in many refinish applications, with pearl luster and three-coat finishes, it is **vital.** Test panels for three coats are needed to determine the correct amount of midcoat color that must be applied to achieve an exact color match. The midcoat color is the most critical portion of the three-coat repair. Because gun pressure, reduction, and spray technique can affect the amount of color being applied to a given job, the extra time spent spraying one or more test panels will be repaid many times over with a finished job that satisfies the customer and does not come back later.

Here is how to make a test panel for a tri-coat finish.

1. Prepare a test panel with the same color undercoat being used on the job. If a sealer is going to be used, apply the sealer to the test panel also. Generally, a light color undercoat (or sealer) is preferred for three-coat repairs.

2. Apply the basecoat color to hiding, using the same pressure and spray pattern that you will on the job. Duplicating the actual spray techniques when preparing the test panel is an important point. Make sure not to vary the procedures because the work is a small panel and not a full repair.

3. After the panel has dried, divide it into four equal sections (Figure 10–23). Next, mask off the lower three quarters of the panel, exposing the top quarter.

4. Apply one coat of mica midcoat color over the top quarter of the panel.

5. After the first mica coat has flashed, remove the masking paper and move it down to the middle of the panel, exposing the top half.

6. Apply another coat of mica midcoat color over the exposed top half of the panel.

7. After this second coat has flashed, remove the masking paper and move it down to expose three quarters of the panel.

8. Apply another coat of mica midcoat color over the exposed three quarters of the panel.

9. After flashing, remove the masking paper entirely.

10. Apply a fourth coat of mica midcoat color, as always, spraying the coating in the same way as would be done on the repair.

11. After the entire panel has dried, mask off the panel **lengthwise** this time.

12. Apply the manufacturer's recommended number of coats of clear to the exposed side.

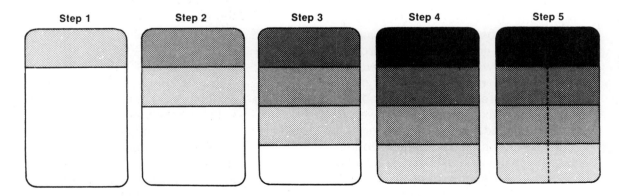

FIGURE 10–23 This example shows the step-by-step creation of a three-coat test panel. A test panel is always recommended when spraying paint. However, when spraying three-stage paint, it is necessary in order to achieve a proper color match.

Once the test panel is completed, lay it on the vehicle to determine the number of mica midcoat coatings needed to achieve a precise color match. Be sure to view the match from different angles and under sunlight if at all possible. And be sure that the panel on the vehicle is thoroughly cleaned before making the comparison.

If the refinisher prefers, instead of using one panel divided into small sections, separate panels can be prepared to provide a larger work area. If separate panels are used, start by spraying all four panels with the midcoat color. Remove one of the panels and then spray the remaining three with a second coat. Spray a third coat on the last two panels and a fourth coat on the last panel only. Then, the panels should be masked vertically and receive the recommended coats of clear.

If, after completing the test panel procedure, a proper color match is still not achieved, recheck the coating with the manufacturer's product number. Be sure that the correct basecoat color is used for this match. Slight variations in the basecoat color can produce an unmatchable final finish. Also, be sure that the paint manufacturer's label directions for each product are followed.

Do not mix brands of products. From primer to final clear coat, stay with one manufacturer's system. The use of a single system also includes solvents and reducers. Paint company laboratories match colors with a balance of solvents or reducers recommended for their products. Using another manufacturer's thinner might save a few dollars, but will often result in hours of color matching problems. Keep in mind that individual coatings manufacturers might have slightly different approaches and these should be followed carefully.

Once the test panel work is completed, the job is ready for repair. The following are some points to keep in mind when making a spot repair:

1. Prepare the surface as desired for any spot repair. That is, begin, as in spot repair jobs, by washing the entire repair and surrounding areas with water and a mild detergent soap. Rinse thoroughly and let dry. Then clean the entire panel and surrounding areas with a wax and grease remover. Repair all damaged and bare metal areas. Use a light-colored primer-surfacer or primer-sealer if possible. Sand the repaired area if necessary. Wet sand with #400 grit (or finer) sandpaper or dry sand with #320 grit (or finer) sandpaper. Next, compound the undamaged area of the panel. Use a fine rubber compound. Sand the repaired area

if necessary. Wet sand with #400 grit (or finer) sandpaper or dry sand with #320 grit (or finer) sandpaper. Compound the undamaged area of the panel. Use a fine rubbing compound. Scuff and sand the compounded area with #1200 grit (or finer) sandpaper. Clean the entire panel with a prepaint cleaner to remove the sanding and compound residue. Use an air gun to remove all dirt from the cracks and surfaces of the panel. Complete the preparation job by tacking the entire panel with a clean tack cloth.

2. Properly reduce the basecoat color by strictly adhering to the paint manufacturer's ratios.

3. Apply the basecoat color over the repair area only, using the blend technique. Apply single coats until proper hiding is achieved using 30 to 40 pounds of air pressure at the gun (or the paint manufacturer's recommended pressure). Normally two to three coats with 5 minutes of flash time between coats will suffice.

4. Allow 15 minutes of flash time between the basecoat color and mica midcoat color. (It is not necessary to "melt in" the dry overspray from the basecoat color because the mica midcoat will be applied directly over it.)

5. Tack the entire panel with a clean tack cloth.

6. Properly reduce the mica midcoat color by strictly adhering to the paint manufacturer's ratios. Use the same reduction ratio used when preparing your test panel.

7. Apply the mica midcoat color over the basecoat color and beyond, again using the blend technique. Apply single coats until a color match is achieved based on the test panel. Use 30 to 40 pounds of air pressure at the gun (or the paint manufacturer's recommended pressure) and allow 5 minutes of flash time between coats.

8. Allow 15 minutes of flash time between the mica midcoat color and the clear coat. As with the basecoat, there is no need to "melt in" the mica midcoat color dry overspray because the clear coat will be applied directly over it.

9. As with the basecoat and the mica midcoat, carefully follow the manufacturer's recommended mixing procedures. This is especially important with the ratio of clear coat to hardener.

10. Again, tack the entire panel with a clean basecoat/clear coat tack cloth.
11. Apply medium wet coats of clear coat over the entire panel. Unlike application pressures for basecoat and midcoat, the clear coat should be applied using 50 to 55 pounds of air pressure at the gun (or manufacturer recommendation). Allow 5 to 10 minutes of flash time between coats. The number of coats of clear will vary, depending upon the type of clear coat material being used and the depth of the original finish. If the clear coat must be blended, use the recommended thinner to melt in the dry overspray.

If the repair includes a flexible surface, products and approaches vary. Some coating products require additives in the clear coat, others call for flex agents to be used in the basecoat, midcoat, and clear coat. Still others do not require an additive or flex agent in any of the three coats. It may be necessary to spray a separate test panel with the flexible material if additives are used in any of the three layers of the three-coat procedure because there could be slight color variations imparted by the additives. Pay careful attention to the manufacturer's requirements when three-coating flexible surfaces.

Drawdown Bar.   The drawdown bar is a precision tool with a machined blade to give an even paint film distribution. To use it, a black and white test panel is taped to a perfectly flat surface, such as an aluminum clipboard. Paint is distributed onto the test panel and the drawdown bar is drawn through the paint, spreading it into a uniform paint thickness. After the first drawdown flashes, the process is repeated until the black and white on the test panel is no longer visible through the paint film. Then the test panel is compared to the car.

When working on base/clear, make the drawdown over a strip of clear film (place over a check hiding panel so the painter knows coating is achieving the desire hiding effect). Turn the clear film over and the painter will have a base/clear appearance.

If additional tinting is needed, another drawdown should be made on another test panel. This allows the refinisher to see the direction in which the tint is moving by comparing the panels to each other. When the desired color is achieved, the material can be sprayed and further adjusted through gun techniques and refinishing skills. The drawdown bar eliminates unnecessary waste of time, material, and labor to adjust color. It is a unique way to tint and is an important tool to any shop when applying pearl lusters and three-coat finishes.

REVIEW QUESTIONS

1. If the surface softens when a small spot of the finish is rubbed with a cloth saturated with thinner, what type of finish is it?
   a. enamel
   b. lacquer
   c. polyurethane
   d. acrylic urethane enamel

2. What cans have a paint film thickness of 5 to 8 mils?
   a. domestic vehicles
   b. European cars
   c. Japanese vehicles
   d. both a and c
   e. none of the above

3. Which of the following is a method used to determine if an automobile has been repainted?
   a. visual inspection method
   b. solvent application method
   c. sanding method
   d. all of the above
   e. both a and b

4. Which of the following is a method for determining what type of paint was used?
   a. heat application method
   b. hardness method
   c. sanding method
   d. all of the above
   e. both a and b

5. In which method is the surface wet-sanded to dull the paint film?
   a. paint film thickness measurement method
   b. sanding method
   c. visual inspection method
   d. heat application method

6. Colors exposed to light tend to go
   _____ .
   a. darker
   b. lighter
   c. both a and b
   d. neither a and b

7. Painter A says that polyurethane enamel can be applied over acrylic enamel without first applying a sealer. Painter B says a sealer must be used. Who is right?
   a. Painter A
   b. Painter B
   c. Both A and B
   d. Neither A nor B

8. Which spray technique is used to make a color lighter?
   a. open fluid valve more
   b. reduce size of fan pattern
   c. allow less flash time
   d. speed up stroke
   e. none of the above

9. Painter A adds yellow to maroon in order to kill blue. Painter B adds red to maroon in order to kill blue. Who is right?
   a. Painter A
   b. Painter B
   c. Both A and B
   d. Neither A nor B

10. Painter A adds green to beige in order to kill red. Painter B adds yellow to beige in order to kill red. Who is right?
    a. Painter A
    b. Painter B
    c. Both A and B
    d. Neither A nor B

11. Which of the following variables tends to make colors lighter?
    a. temperature decrease
    b. humidity increase
    c. slower evaporator solvent
    d. increased amount of solvent

12. Which of the following variables tends to make colors darker?
    a. increased ventilation
    b. retarder added to solvent
    c. temperature increase
    d. more flash time allowed

13. Darker color shades are achieved by
    _____ .
    a. reducing the color with 10 to 25 percent less solvent than the label indicates
    b. using lower than normal air pressure for application
    c. increasing speed of spray applications
    d. all of the above
    e. both a and b

14. When confronted with an extremely difficult flip-flop condition, _____ .
    a. adjust spraying technique
    b. spray the panel slightly dryer
    c. spray the panel slightly dryer and add a small amount of white
    d. add white and blend the color into the adjacent panels

15. Which of the following is a positive variable in spray painting conditions?
    a. slowness of solvent evaporation
    b. improper reduction
    c. improper agitation
    d. none of the above

CHAPTER ELEVEN

APPLICATION OF COLOR COATS

Objectives

After reading this chapter, you will be able to:

- identify the steps in applying various types of color coats.
- apply basecoat/clear coat systems.
- recognize and correct defects occurring in a paint finish.

A complete description of various topcoat materials is given in Chapter 7. In this chapter, a general application procedure is given. But, before getting into these application techniques, it would be best to **review** the basic preparation procedure necessary to achieve a fine final finish. They are:

1. Thoroughly wash the car with soap and water (Figure 11-1).
2. Chemically clean the car with a wax and grease remover to remove wax buildup, tar, and other nonwater soluble grime.
3. Sand the repair area by hand with a block (#400 grit) or machine (#320 grit).
4. Reclean the area with the wax and grease remover (Figure 11-2).
5. If bare metal is showing, pretreat the area to eliminate any hidden corrosion.

6. Then spot-prime these areas with an epoxy chromate primer.
7. Apply primer-surfacer as needed to fill low areas and eliminate sand scratches (Figure 11-3).
8. Sand primer-surfacer level to the surrounding area and blow off to clear dust. Use #400 grit for hand sanding and #320 grit if machine sanding (Figure 11-4).

After properly masking the vehicle and preparing the surface for repainting as just described, once again blow off any remaining dust with an air gun. Give a final touch-up cleaning with the wax and grease remover and rub the surface with a tack cloth (in this order). From this point on be careful not to touch the surface being refinished.

FIGURE 11-1 Wash the vehicle with soap and water.

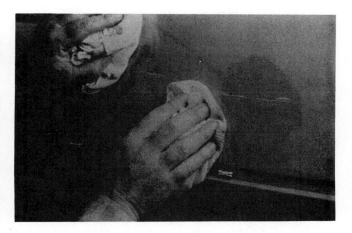

FIGURE 11-2 Clean the area with wax and grease remover.

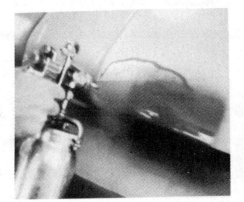

FIGURE 11-3 Apply primer-surfacer to eliminate scratches.

FIGURE 11-4 Wet sanding before applying the topcoat

SPRAYING PROCEDURE

Before the topcoat material can be applied by spraying, it must be:

- Properly stirred or mixed.
- Thinned or reduced with proper solvent to the desired viscosity.

STIRRING PAINT

The failure to properly stir all the settled pigment into the liquid is a principal cause of paint problems. Stirring or mixing can be done by hand or by machine.

The part of paint that settles is the pigment, which gives the paint its color, opacity, and specific performance properties. These pigments vary greatly as to weight. Some of the commonly used pigments are seven to eight times as heavy as the liquid part of the paint. Because of their weight, the heavy pigments slowly settle and it is impossible to keep them in suspension. Some of the pigments are light and fluffy and have very little tendency to settle. The commonly used pigments that settle quite rapidly are the whites, chrome yellows, chrome oranges, chrome greens, and red and yellow iron oxides.

The consistency or viscosity of the liquid part of the paint has much to do with the rate of settling. The heavier the consistency, the slower the settling. Heavy pigments will settle out of a straight thinner in a few minutes, whereas in a paint vehicle it would take weeks or months. Careful judgment in thinning only sufficient material to do the job and discarding the small amount that is not used is the mark of an experienced painter.

If a color, which contains one or more of the heavy pigments (Table 11-1), is thinned or reduced to spraying consistency and allowed to stand 10 to 15 minutes without being stirred, it will have settled enough in that time to be off color when sprayed.

After a can of paint has been thoroughly agitated, empty out the contents of the can into another container or the gun cap, wash the can clean with a little solvent, and add this to the paint.

If a paint has settled out very hard, the liquid part should be poured off and the residue well broken up. The liquid part should then be slowly poured back with vigorous stirring.

Do not use sharp sticks or screwdrivers for stirring. At least a 1-inch wide flat bottomed, clean stirring paddle or steel spatula should be used.

When using an intermix system, agitate all base mixing colors for a minimum of 15 minutes. Before

TABLE 11-1:	WEIGHTS OF VARIOUS PIGMENTS
Name of Pigment	**Weight of Solid Gallon Pounds**
Toluidine Red	12.0
Indo Maroon	13.1
Carbon Black	14.4
Aluminum Powder	21.0
Titanium Dioxide White	35.0
Red Oxide of Iron	42.7
Chrome Yellow	50.0
Zinc Dust	60.7

putting the can on the scale, put in just enough universal retarder to cover the bottom. This will prevent small color additions from drying out and not mixing in with the rest of the colors.

VISCOSITY

Topcoat paint materials are usually shipped at as high a viscosity as practical to help in slowing down the rate of settling. In order to apply these paint materials, they must be reduced with thinner or reducer to a viscosity that can be properly atomized by the spray gun.

Compared with a two-component reaction, the air-dry type of topcoat has a higher resin viscosity so vaporization is not as rapid. Because the initial drying time is faster, more solvent is required to improve the finish and it is also necessary to increase the spraying air pressure. However, increasing the air pressure will cause the solvent to evaporate faster, resulting in an even faster initial drying time and a defective finish. For preventive measures, it is necessary to consider decreasing the distance between the gun and painting surface, increasing the discharge volume, increasing the number of coats, speeding up the painting operation, and so on.

Two-component reaction type paint can be used with less solvent than air-dry type paint. However, because the acrylic urethane lacquer dries faster than acrylic urethane, more thinner is needed to compensate.

To prevent unevenness, metallic colors with a lower viscosity than solid colors are used. The distance between the gun and the painted surface is greater and there is also more pattern overlap. Application is similar to that for a dry coat.

Clear coat is applied in a method similar to a solid color but care must be taken to avoid a heavy coat. This can cause residual unevenness or other defects.

The method of checking the viscosity of paint is described in Chapter 3. The recommended viscosities for spot repairs, body repairs, and overall paint, as well as spray gun pressure, are given later in this chapter. All spray gun air pressure recommendations in this reading are at the gun.

REPAINTING SPRAY METHODS

As mentioned in Chapter 7, repainting spray methods are classified according to the condition of the previous (original) paint coat, the size of the area

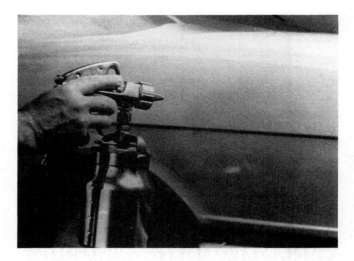

FIGURE 11-5   As described in Chapter 7, spot repair repainting involves small spots.

to be repainted, and the location. These methods are:

- Spot repair spraying
- Panel repair spraying
- Overall spraying

SPOT AND PANEL SPRAYING

Spot repainting repairs (Figure 11-5) are recommended where a complete panel repair is unjustified, being either uneconomical (size of repair or amount of masking involved) or impractical (difficulty of rendering the repair invisible, particularly in the case of metallic finishes). Shading is necessary so that slight differences in color or texture are not conspicuous.

Panel repainting is done to repair complete panels separated by a definite boundary, such as a door or a fender. Normally, it is not necessary to shade or graduate the paint unless the paint is difficult to match or if it is a metallic color. However, shading is done for such areas as between the quarter panel and roof panel, but this is still referred to as a panel repair.

Spot Repainting with Solid Colors

Definite rules cannot be laid down as to the range or degree of graduation for the shade area. The spot repair method should be used for light damage at the fender edge. In this case, there are two methods of graduation: at the boundary line between the fender and hood (Figure 11-6A) and at the press line. If graduation can be done within the

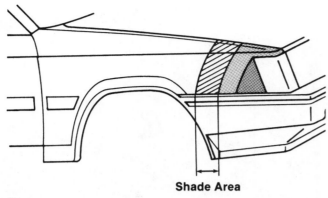

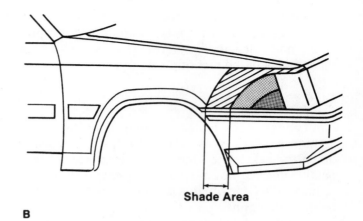

A — Shade Area

B — Shade Area

FIGURE 11-6 Range of spot repainting

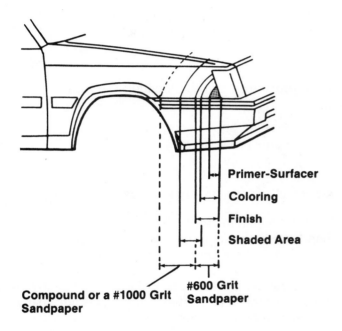

Primer-Surfacer
Coloring
Finish
Shaded Area

Compound or a #1000 Grit Sandpaper

#600 Grit Sandpaper

FIGURE 11-7 Preparing an area for spot repainting

range shown in Figure 11–6B, it will not be necessary to paint the upper portion of the fender where shading shows most conspicuously, thereby avoiding problems with color and texture differences.

Shown in Figure 11–7, when spot repainting with a solid color lacquer, the shaded area should be treated with compound or sanded using a #1000 grit sandpaper before repainting.

Apply the topcoat with a circular motion, working the spray gun from the center outward (Figure 11–8). This allows each coat to slightly overlap the previous one. An alternative method is to apply the finish in short strokes from the center outward. Again extend each coat so that it slightly overlaps the previous one. But in either method, the spray pattern should be narrowed and the fluid delivery reduced by adjusting the spray controls. To minimize overspray, the air pressure should be reduced, depending on the material to be sprayed. The spray pattern should never be reduced to a completely round jet; otherwise, both the paint control and overlapping of passes become difficult.

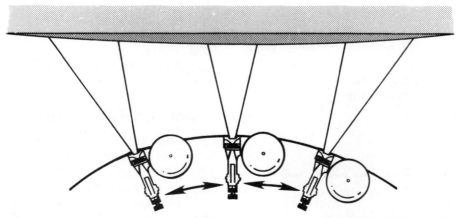

FIGURE 11-8 When spraying a shade area, it might be necessary to break "the arcing pattern" rule, but the arcing should be kept to a minimum.

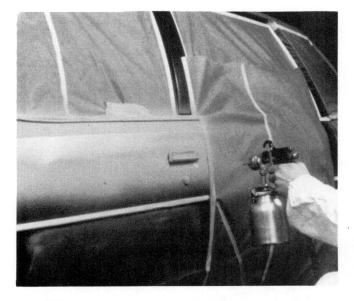

FIGURE 11-9 As the name implies, panel repairs are the usual concern in repainting a panel or panels.

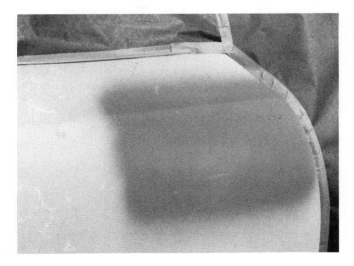

FIGURE 11-10 Once the area has been primed and the surface masked, the topcoat(s) can be applied.

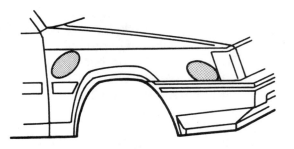

FIGURE 11-11 Panel repainting in two areas

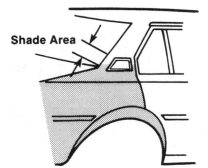

FIGURE 11-12 Repainting of quarter panel

Panel Repairs with Solid Colors

For complete panel or block repair (Figure 11-9), it is wise to properly mask off the area not to be painted (Figure 11-10).

If a panel has damage at two different locations, as shown in Figure 11-11, repairs should be done in a panel style. As shown, shading can be done at the molding area or extended below the molding.

For the quarter panel, it is generally necessary to graduate the shade area into the quarter pillar. If the vehicle has a ventilation louver on the quarter pillar, as shown in Figure 11-12, shading at that area will be less noticeable.

Spot Repainting of Metallic Colors

If spot repainting with a metallic color at locations shown in Figure 11-13, skill is required in matching the color tone and bringing out the metallic image through proper distribution of the paint. The shaded area will be less noticeable if it is angled off from the press line as shown in Figure 11-14.

Panel Repairs with Metallic Colors

Unevenness tends to be very noticeable with clear and bright metallic colors. Therefore, if it is impossible to match the paint exactly with the previous coat, extend the shade area over a wide range, as shown in Figure 11-15, to make it less distinguishable.

If one panel has damage at both ends or if the whole panel is to be repainted, shading of metallic paint must extend onto the adjacent panels. As shown in Figure 11-16, the clear coat extends beyond the fender onto one of the adjacent door panels and to the second press line of the hood.

OVERALL SPRAYING

When overall spraying, the painter can keep a wet edge while maintaining minimum overspray on

219

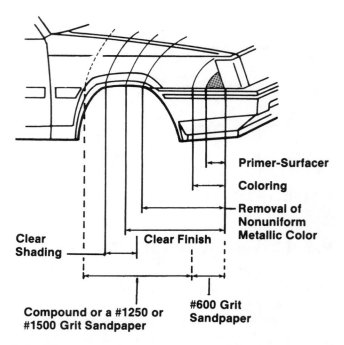

FIGURE 11-13 Spot repainting with metallic colors

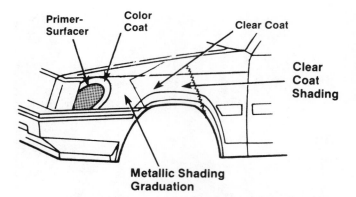

FIGURE 11-14 One method of making a shaded area less noticeable

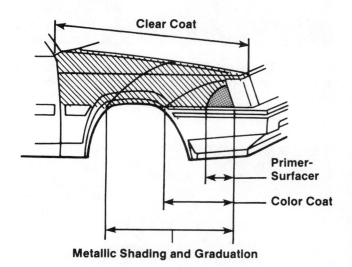

FIGURE 11-15 Panel repainting of metallic colors

the horizontal surfaces. This prevents spray dust from settling onto areas that have already dried, which would cause a gritty surface. Avoid sags in the overlap line by changing the point of overlapping as shown in Figure 11-17.

Although there is not a single most perfect procedure for repainting a car overall, most refinishers will agree that the diagrams in Figure 11-18 illustrate the best patterns. With a conventional booth, by starting with the top of the car and proceeding to the trunk deck lid, side, and so on, the painter can best keep a "wet edge" while maintaining minimum overspray on the horizontal surfaces (Figure 11-18). This prevents spray dust from settling onto areas that have already dried, causing a gritty or contaminated surface. If possible, it is better for two painters to work in a state-of-the-art downdraft booth. The spray pattern is different than that of the conventional booth because of the direction of the airflow (top to bottom). Following the pattern shown in Figure 11-19 allows the three main horizontal surfaces to remain as wet as possible while maintaining minimum overspray. These procedures also allow the painter(s) to continue to apply additional coats as needed without a significant loss of time due to flash off between coats.

 SHOP TALK _____

Before doing any spray procedure, pour the paint through a strainer when filling the spray gun to filter out any foreign particles.

APPLYING ALKYD ENAMELS
(PANEL REPAIR AND OVERALL REPAINT ONLY)

The following is a **general** procedure for the application of alkyd enamels. For specific details on a specific brand of alkyd enamel, follow the manufacturer's directions on the container. The spraying air pressure given in the following procedures are taken at the gun.

1. **Additives.** If the protection of an additive such as fish eye eliminator is desired, add 1 pint to a gallon of unreduced topcoat.
2. **Reducer.** Use a proper reducer for the shop temperature. Usual mixing ratio: 1 part reducer to 4 parts topcoat.
3. **Viscosity.** Allow 20 to 23 seconds in a #2 Zahn cup.
4. **Air pressure.** Use 50 to 60 pounds.
5. **Application.** For solid colors, spray a medium first coat and allow it to become

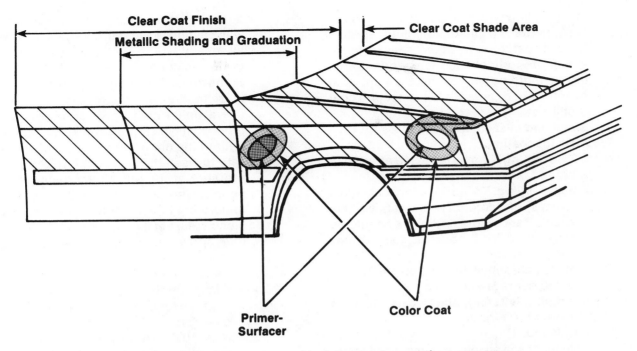

FIGURE 11-16 Panel repairs of metallic colors with damage at more than one area

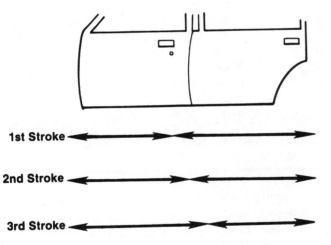

1st Stroke

2nd Stroke

3rd Stroke

FIGURE 11-17 Changing overlapping point

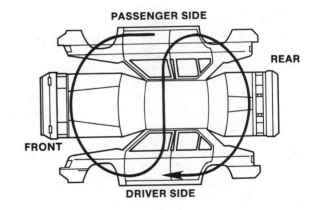

FIGURE 11-19 Painting procedure in a downdraft booth

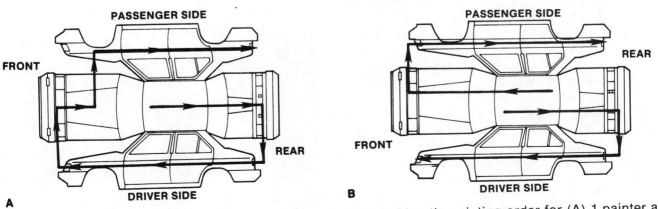

A

B

FIGURE 11-18 Overall painting procedures in a conventional booth; painting order for (A) 1 painter and (B) 2 painters

tacky. Follow with a full second coat within 1-1/2 hours. For metallic colors, spray a full wet coat. After it becomes tacky, apply a medium-to-light second coat. If streaking or mottling shows, dust a light coat over the entire area while the second coat is still wet.

6. **Blend and mist coats.** Not necessary.
7. **After topcoating.**
   - **Two-toning.** Can be recoated after 6 to 8 hours.
   - **Force drying.** To 1 gallon topcoat, add 4 ounces of force dry and antiwrinkle agent. Dark colors and black should be force-dried for 2 hours at 150 degrees Fahrenheit or 1-1/2 hours at 165 degrees Fahrenheit; light colors for 2 hours at 150 degrees Fahrenheit.
   - **Striping, lettering, and decals.** Allow to dry at least 6 hours.
   - **Cleanup.** Clean all equipment with reducer or solvent immediately after using.
   - **Waxing.** After 60 days, if desired.

APPLYING ACRYLIC LACQUERS (SPOT AND PANEL REPAIR AND OVERALL REPAINT)

As with alkyd enamels, always follow the specific brand recommendations. These are general application suggestions.

1. **Additives.** Use a fish eye eliminator to reduce the effect of silicone contamination only when necessary. However, acrylic chromate is frequently used on spot and panel repairs where bare metal is to be used under other lacquer primer-surfacers (Figure 11–20).
2. **Thinners.** In spot repair, panel repair, and overall repaint, use the proper solvent for the temperature conditions. The ratio is usually about 1 to 1-1/2 parts thinner to 1 part topcoat.
3. **Viscosity.** Allow 18 to 22 seconds for spot repair, panel repair, and overall repaint in a #2 Zahn cup.
4. **Air pressure.** Use 20 to 30 pounds for spot and panel repair; 40 to 50 pounds for overall repaint.
5. **Application.** For spot and panel repair, spray three full wet coats—each a little wider than the previous one. Let each coat flash 4 to 5 minutes. After the third coat, let the job set up for 10 to 15 minutes, then

apply two more wet coats, extending each well beyond the first three coats. For overall repaint, spray five or six wet coats, allowing each coat to flash.

6. **Blend coats.** To melt in the overspray, minimize buffing, and improve depth of color, use a uniforming finish after letting the topcoat flash. Empty the paint cup and pour in the uniform finish (it is not necessary to wash the cup out first). Set the air pressure at the gun to approximately 20 pounds and spray two medium coats of uniforming finish around the edges of the blend area. Let it melt in for a few minutes, then spray two wet coats over the entire area.
7. **After topcoating.**
   - **Compounding.** Allow at least a 4-hour dry time for panels and overnight dry for overall repainting at a temperature of at least 70 degrees Fahrenheit. Force drying at 165 degrees Fahrenheit for 15 minutes for spot and panel repairs or 1 hour for overall repainting will provide satisfactory dry. Compound with either hand rubbing compound or machine polishing compound.
   - **Waxing.** Can be done, if desired, 60 days after painting.

APPLYING ACRYLIC ENAMEL (SPOT AND PANEL REPAIR AND OVERALL REPAINT)

While these are general application procedures for acrylic enamel, always follow any specific direction given by the manufacturer of the material.

1. **Additive.** If the performance of a hardener is desired, use 1 pint to 1 gallon of topcoat.

FIGURE 11–20 Acrylic chromate primer can be used to quickly protect the metal for small "burn through" of bare metal. *(Courtesy of Du Pont Co.)*

2. **Retarder.** In hot weather only, 1 part reducer to 2 parts topcoat.
3. **Viscosity.** Allow 18 to 20 seconds for spot and panel repair or overall repainting in a #2 Zahn cup.
4. **Air pressure.** Use 30 to 40 pounds for spot and panel repair; 55 to 65 pounds for overall repaint.
5. **Application.** For spot and panel repair, spray medium coats until full hiding is obtained, extending each new coat beyond the previous one to achieve a tapered edge. For overall repaint, spray three wet coats, flashing as necessary.
6. **Blending and mist coats.** Mist coats can be applied by raising the gun distance to about 18 inches during the last coat to position the metallic flake in metallic colors.
7. **After topcoating.**
   - **Two-toning.** Use a hardener in the first coats. Can be recoated after 4 hours under normal drying conditions. Remove masking tape immediately after final coat is applied to prevent tape marking. Avoid masking paper contact with fresh enamel.
   - **Force drying.** Can be force dried at 160 degrees Fahrenheit for 15 minutes.
   - **Striping, lettering, and decals.** Allow to dry at least 4 hours before proceeding.
   - **Cleanup.** Clean all equipment with a reducer or an approved solvent immediately after spraying.
   - **Waxing.** After 60 days, if desired.

APPLYING POLYURETHANE ENAMELS (PANEL REPAIR AND OVERALL REPAINT ONLY)

1. **Activator.** Follow manufacturer's instructions as to the amount of the activator (catalyst).
2. **Reducer.** Use the reducer as per shop temperature, mixed with equal parts of activator and reducer.
3. **Viscosity.** Allow 18 to 22 seconds in a #2 Zahn cup. Check every 4 hours.
4. **Air pressure.** Use 50 pounds for solid colors; 65 pounds for metallics.
5. **Application.** For solid colors, spray a medium first coat. Allow to tack up and follow with a full second coat. For metallic colors, apply a light medium coat as a tack coat. Allow to set up for 20 minutes, then apply a

second light medium coat. Reduce remaining material 15 percent with appropriate reducer and apply a third light medium coat. Metallics can be clear coated with a clear coat following label directions.
6. **Blend and mist coats.** Not necessary.
7. **After topcoating.**
   - **Two-toning.** At 77 degrees Fahrenheit and 50 percent humidity, two-toning can be done in 6 to 10 hours. If hardener is used, two-toning can be done in 2 to 4 hours. (Pot life is 8 hours minimum at 70 to 75 degrees Fahrenheit.) For films cured over 72 hours, scuff sand before recoating, striping, lettering, or applying decals.
   - **Force drying.** Can be force dried for 30 minutes at 165 degrees Fahrenheit.
   - **Striping, lettering, and decals.** Recoating can be done at any stage of dry. Two-toning, striping, lettering, or decals can be applied when tape free. For films cured 72 hours, scuff sand before recoating, striping, lettering, or applying decals. Do not scuff sand metallics when clear finish coating.
   - **Cleanup.** Clean all equipment with lacquer thinner or reducers. **Do not** leave mixed material in equipment.

APPLYING ACRYLIC URETHANE ENAMELS (PANEL REPAIR AND OVERALL REPAINT ONLY)

General application data is as follows:

1. **Activator.** Mix equal parts of activator (catalyst) and topcoat color.
2. **Reducer.** Solid colors are normally thinned in ratio of 4 parts catalyzed color to 1 part proper reducer. Most metallic colors are thinned in a ratio of 2 parts catalyzed color to 1 part reducer.
3. **Viscosity.** Allow 20 to 22 seconds in a #2 Zahn cup.
4. **Air pressure.** Use 50 pounds for solid colors; 65 pounds for metallics.
5. **Application.** For solid colors, spray two or three wet double coats with a short flash time between double coats. For metallic colors, apply a light medium coat as a tack coat. Allow to set up for 20 minutes, then apply a second light medium coat. Reduce remaining material 15 percent with appropriate reducer and apply a third light me-

dium coat. Metallics can be coated with a clear coat following label directions.
6. **Blend and mist coats.** Not necessary.
7. **After topcoating.**
   - **Two-toning.** At 77 degrees Fahrenheit and 50 percent humidity, two-toning can be done in 6 to 10 hours. If hardener is used, two-toning can be done in 2 to 4 hours. (Pot life is 8 hours minimum at 70 to 75 degrees Fahrenheit.) For films cured over 72 hours, scuff sand before recoating, striping, lettering, or applying decals.
   - **Force drying.** Can be force dried for 30 minutes at 165 degrees Fahrenheit.
   - **Striping, lettering, and decals.** Recoating can be done at any stage of dry. Two-toning, striping, lettering, or decals can be applied when tape free. For films cured 72 hours, scuff sand before recoating, striping, lettering, or applying decals. Do not scuff sand metallics when clear finish coating.
   - **Cleanup.** Clean all equipment with lacquer thinner or reducers. **Do not** leave mixed material in equipment.

APPLYING POLYOXITHANE ENAMEL (SPOT AND PANEL AND OVERALL REPAINT)

The general application procedure is as follows:

1. **Additives.** Use fish eye eliminator to avoid the effect of silicone contamination only when necessary.
2. **Initiator/Reducers.** Mix 1 part initiator with 8 parts single stage enamel. Then add 2 parts (depending on temperature) fast reducer (60 to 75 degrees Fahrenheit) or mid-temperature reducer (70 to 85 degrees Fahrenheit) or slow reducer (85 to 90 degrees Fahrenheit) in hot and/or humid weather.
3. **Viscosity.** Allow #17 to #19 in Zahn cup.
4. **Air pressure.** Use 25 to 35 pounds for spot repair; 45 to 55 pounds for panel and overall repair.
5. **Application.** For spot repair, apply two to three coats until desired match is achieved. For panel and overall repair, apply three coats plus a final cross/mist coat if necessary to even out metallic flake. Allow 2 to 5 minutes flash between each coat. Dust-free in 15 minutes. Air dry overnight.

6. **Blending.** If blending is required, use a uniforming finish. Apply two to three coats using 15 to 20 pounds pressure at the gun.
7. **After topcoating.**
   - **Force drying.** Allow 15 minutes flash after final coat, then force dry for 60 minutes at 140 degrees Fahrenheit.
   - **Cleanup.** Immediately use acrylic lacquer thinner to clean equipment.

APPLYING BASECOAT/ CLEAR COAT

Basecoat/clear coat systems are very difficult to match and repair. They pose a major challenge to refinishers and paint manufacturers alike. To help match and repair basecoat/clear coat systems, paint manufacturers offer special clear coats for use over color base coats. These systems are designed to simplify this process of repairing basecoat/clear coat finishes. Since more and more domestic cars as well as European and Japanese cars have basecoat/clear coat finishes on them, it is even more important that professional painters familiarize themselves with an effective basecoat/clear coat system(s). The application procedure for the basecoat of either acrylic enamel, acrylic lacquer, or acrylic urethane have already been discussed.

When estimating a basecoat/clear coat repair, carefully examine the finish on the area adjacent to the damage. If it is chalked, dulled, or otherwise impaired, matching the old finish might prove impossible. Ideally, such jobs should be shot as overalls. This approach will eliminate many problems in repairing basecoat/clear coat finishes or any finish that is severely weathered.

There are several important points to remember when mixing basecoat color.

- Always read label directions first.
- Use only the manufacturer's recommended hardeners and reducers (or basecoat stabilizers if recommended).
- Use the proper reducer for shop conditions and size of job.
- Use only the proper mixing ratios.

The choice of a reducer is an important one. The refinisher must be careful to choose the product to complement the basecoat (and later the clear coat) in relation to the shop's temperature and humidity. Most major paint manufacturers offer a choice of reducers to offset these atmospheric conditions which may cause color shifting. Problems such as soak-in (too slow a reducer) or dry overspray (too fast a reducer) can also occur if the incorrect reducer is used.

In the case of some new systems, a basecoat stabilizer or additive replaces the standard reducer. The stabilizer contains a basecoat resin designed to give it a faster recoat time and allow better metallic control. This is especially important if any blending is desired because it prevents wash-out or a "halo-like" effect at the edge of the repair.

BASECOAT/CLEAR COAT SPOT AND PANEL REPAIRS

Once the repair area has been properly compounded with a rubbing compound to rough up the surface, reclean the area again with a wax and grease remover and tack off the entire area. Then proceed as follows:

1. Apply one coat of a bonding or blending clear (per manufacturer's directions) 6 to 12 inches beyond the repair area (the area where the color basecoat and clear coat will be applied).
2. Next, thin the basecoat in the ratio of 150 percent, that is 1 part color to 1-1/2 parts of the solvent most suited to the temperature needs.
3. Apply two medium coats of basecoat or until hiding is achieved allowing 10 to 15 minutes flash time between each coat. Viscosity should be 18 to 22 seconds in a #2 Zahn cup and applied at an air pressure of 25 to 40 pounds.

CAUTION: Do not extend color coat beyond the sanded area of the spot repair.

---

4. Allow 30 to 60 minutes dry time of the final color coat before beginning to clear coat.
5. If it has been predetermined by use of a color test panel that a color blend will be necessary to obtain an acceptable match, now is the time to execute that procedure. This is done by mixing equal parts of the already reduced basecoat with high-performance clear that has been thinned 200 percent with the appropriate thinner. Apply this mixture to the outer edge of the painted area, spraying toward the new paint. Repeat this procedure until the mismatch disappears adding reduced clear to the existing mixture each time.
6. Apply 3 to 4 full wet coats of clear that has been thinned 200 percent with the thinner

best suited for the shop conditions or two full wet coats of a polyurethane basecoat clear that has been properly catalyzed and reduced. In either case keep the clear coat within the area where the bonding clear has been applied. Viscosity should be 18 to 22 seconds in a #2 Zahn cup and applied at an air pressure of 50 pounds.

7. Allow 24 hours air dry or force dry 30 minutes at 180 degrees Fahrenheit. Compound lightly with a power-buffing compound if an acrylic urethane clear is used.

OVERALL PANEL REPAIRS

After sanding the entire vehicle by hand with a block (#400 grit) or machine (#320 grit), clean the entire surface with a wax and grease remover.

SHOP TALK ——————

Before chemically cleaning, be sure to make any metal or body filler repairs. If a polyester body filler is used, it generally is recommended that all bare metal first be primed with an epoxy chromate primer followed by body filler. (This will assure a corrosion resistant surface for better adhesion of the body filler.)

Now proceed with the overall panel repairs as follows:

1. Apply one full coat of sealer to the entire surface. Some paint manufacturers recommend a coat application of an "adhesion promoter" over the entire area to be refinished rather than a sealer. The absence of pigment in the clear coat makes the surface less porous, more glass-like, and hard to adhere to. It is, therefore, a good suggestion to apply adhesion promoter on "blending clear" after priming and before applying the basecoats in order to ensure adequate adhesion to the OEM finish.
2. Apply two medium coats of basecoat color or until hiding is achieved. It should be thinned at the rate of 150 percent (1-1/2 parts thinner to 1 part color). Allow a 10- to 15-minute flash between coats. After the final color coat, allow to dry 30 to 60 minutes before applying clear coat. The viscosity of the basecoat should be 18 to 22 seconds in #2 Zahn cup, while the air pressure should be at 45 to 55 pounds.
3. Apply 3 to 4 full wet coats of an acrylic urethane clear or two full wet coats of a

polyurethane clear. Follow directions on the respective labels for proper catalyzation and/or reduction. Viscosity should be 18 to 22 seconds in a #2 Zahn cup. The air pressure should be about 50 to 55 pounds.

4. Allow 24 hours dry time or force dry 30 minutes at 180 degrees Fahrenheit. Compound lightly with a polishing compound or a power-buffing compound if high-performance clear is used.

In a few years, as mentioned in Chapter 7, all new cars probably will be finished in basecoat/clear coat colors. This trend is certain to change some of the body/paint shops. For example, one change is the preparation before applying a basecoat/clear coat finish. The surface should be prepared in the same way as it would be for a normal acrylic enamel job, using at least #320 grit or finer no-fill type sandpaper, or #400 grit or finer wet or dry paper.

When spraying, two medium coats of basecoat should be applied for a maximum film build of approximately 2 mils. The basecoat does not need to be glossy and only enough should be applied to achieve hiding. Then two or three medium wet coats of clear should be applied with at least 15 minutes flash time between coats. Recommended film thickness for the clear is 1.5 to 2 mils, for a total film build of approximately 4 to 4.5 mils.

For best results, sanding of the basecoat should be avoided. If sanding is required because of dirt or imperfections after the first coat of clear, it can be done safely but carefully after approximately 3 hours at 70 degrees Fahrenheit, 50 percent relative humidity, and where adequate air movement is assured. With heat, the affected area can be sanded 1 hour after the basecoat is applied. A wet sand using at least a #1200 grit paper will minimize sand scratches. The sanded area must then be rebasecoated or streaking and mottling will result. Buffing of an acrylic enamel basecoat/clear coat finish is needed only if sanding was done.

CLEARS

Although clears are primarily used in two- and three-coat applications, there are two other areas of refinishing in which clears—or uniform finishes—are used. They are:

- Custom work
- Acrylic enamel or lacquer spot repair

CUSTOM WORK

Clears are used by custom paint shops in overall repairing to provide:

1. An overall basic uniform coat
2. Protective coats over graphics, murals, lace work, stripping, and other customizing techniques (see Chapter 12).

LACQUER AND ACRYLIC ENAMEL SPOT REPAIR

Generally referred to as "blending clears"—or uniforming finishes—these prethinned clears are used to melt in overspray and provide a light protective coating to prevent:

- Buffing through the repair
- Weathering of the blended edge

UNIFORMING FINISH MIST COATING LACQUER

A uniforming finish is used as a blend coat for the lacquer spot repair of both lacquer and enamel finished vehicles.

It not only smoothes and blends the repair, but it also improves the depth and gloss of the color. Its application often eliminates compounding, so that only a quick polish is required.

BASIC TECHNIQUES WITH CLEAR TOPCOATS

There are several things that a refinisher can do to help clear wear better:

- Do not load clears. Because these finishes are clear, refinishers have a tendency to use too much clear to increase the desired glamour effect. As a result, they "bury" the topcoat.
- Do not spray clears too thick. Contrary to some opinions, clears do not perform better when they are underreduced. Thin or reduce clears according to the label instructions.
- Do not use economy thinners or reducers when spraying clears. Fast thinners/reducers weaken the performance of clears by trapping solvents and hurting flow and leveling. Use a quality thinner/reducer according to label instructions and let each coat flash thoroughly before applying the next coat.

As already mentioned, there are three types of clear topcoats:

- Urethane enamel clear
- Acrylic urethane clear
- Blending clear

The general application data on these materials is as follows.

Urethane Enamel Clear

1. **Activator.** Activator (catalyst) must be to clear at a ratio of 1 part of catalyst to 4 parts added of clear.
2. **Reducers.** This mixture can be further reduced with up to 10 percent for better flow and leveling. Use a retarder if required.
3. **Viscosity.** Allow 18 to 22 seconds in a #2 Zahn cup.
4. **Air pressure.** Use 50 to 55 pounds.
5. **Application.** For spot and panel repair or overall refinishing, spray two medium wet coats over entire area to be refinished. Allow first coat to completely flash before applying second coat. Allow to cure overnight. Clean equipment with lacquer thinner immediately after use.

Acrylic Urethane Clear

1. **Activator.** Add activator or catalyst as per the directions on the label.
2. **Reducers.** If necessary, reduce with up to 10 percent proper reducers. Stir thoroughly and strain.
3. **Viscosity.** Allow 18 to 20 seconds in a #2 Zahn cup.
4. **Air pressure.** Use 50 pounds pressure at the gun and apply two medium coats.
5. **Application.** Allow basecoat color to flash 1 hour before applying clear. Apply two medium coats of clear. Allow 15 minutes flash time between coats. Heavy coats of clear should be avoided.
6. Clean all equipment immediately after use with lacquer thinner. A 24-hour cure is recommended for customer delivery.

Blending Clear (Panel Repair and Overall Repaint Only)

1. **Activator/Additives.** Must be activated with an activator or catalyst. Ratio: 1 part activator to 3 parts topcoat. Mix thoroughly and if faster tape-free time is desired, add recommended accelerator, using the ratio: 4 ounces of accelerator to 1 gallon of topcoat.
2. **Reducer/retarders.** If desired, material can be further reduced with a reducer or retarder that is recommended by the maker. Mix no more material than will be used in an 8-hour period. Pot life of mixture is 8 hours at 70 degrees Fahrenheit.
3. **Viscosity.** Allow 18 to 22 seconds in a #2 Zahn cup.

4. **Air pressure.** Use 50 pounds.
5. **Application.** Spray one medium coat of blending clear over freshly painted color, allow to tack, and follow with only one full second coat. Except for metallics, blending clear can be applied wet-on-wet or after overnight dry. Clean equipment promptly with proper solvent.
6. **Blend and mist coats.** Not necessary.

SPATTER FINISHES

The interior of luggage compartments—the side walls and floor—is often painted with a special latex finish and a lacquer color. The material is water-reducible and can be applied in one heavy or two medium coats. The spatter finish material should be agitated to a minimum. Hand paddle mixing is usually sufficient; do not shake on a paint shaker. When ordering spatter paint from a paint jobber, be sure to mention the make of the vehicle and the model year of the car.

The application procedure is as follows:

1. After all metal repair work and priming have been completed, clean the luggage compartment surfaces with a solvent.
2. Mask off the compartment area, as required.
3. Read the label directions carefully and follow them to the letter. As a rule, open the spray fan nozzle to give only 3/4 of the full pattern. The fluid feed should be wide open. Also, use the lowest air pressure that causes the desired spray pattern:
   - For smaller spatters, increase the air pressure.
   - For larger spatters, reduce the air pressure.
4. Apply the coating. If two coats are needed, allow several minutes of flash time. Allow the surface to dry completely before putting the vehicle back into service.

FINAL TOUCH-UP

Once the topcoat has been applied, the final touch-up or detail procedure can begin. This includes:

- Removal of masking tape and paper
- Polishing the surface
- Repairing small surface defects

FIGURE 11-21 When removing the masking material, be sure not to touch the paint.

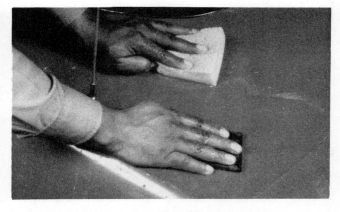

FIGURE 11-22 Use micro fine #1200 grit abrasive paper for leveling newly painted lacquer surface and to produce that "show car" finish. Use micro fine #1500 grit abrasive paper to remove dust nibs in enamel surfaces.

REMOVAL OF MASKING MATERIALS

After the topcoat has dried, the masking paper and tape must be removed. If the finish has been force dried, the masking should be removed while the paint finish is still warm. If the finish is allowed to cool, the tape is more difficult to remove and leaves adhesive particles on the paint finish.

The tape should be removed slowly so that it comes off evenly (Figure 11-21). Pull the tape away from the paint edge—never across it. Take care not to touch any painted areas because the paint might not be completely dry. Fingerprints or tape marks could result if the surface is touched. Also, be careful of loosely fitting clothing or belt buckles that could accidentally rub against the paint.

Never allow a lacquer type paint to dry thoroughly before removing the tape as the paint film might peel off along with the tape. It is best to remove the tape immediately after repainting, but when doing so, be careful not to touch the freshly painted surface.

POLISHING

Lacquer paint generally needs a light compounding or polishing to give it the desired gloss and to remove any unevenness (Figure 11-22). If any slight defects in new enamel finished surfaces should occur, they should not be compounded until the paint has had a chance to "set up." This could involve a period of several days.

Rubbing Compound and How It Works

Rubbing compounds (Table 11-2) are much like paste and liquid cleaners used before a car is waxed.

TABLE 11-2: POLISHING AND RUBBING COMPOUNDS

Grade	Liquid	Paste	Use and Application
Coarse	Machine	Machine	Used for compounding before final topcoating (see Chapter 9)
Medium	Machine or hand	Paste (add water for machine use)	Used for quick-leveling orange peel. Can be used to repair other minor paint defects.
Fine	Machine or hand	Hand (add water for machine use)	Used to level orange peel. Can also be used to clean, polish, and restore older finishes leaving no wheel marks or swirls.
Very fine	Machine or hand	—	Used to remove swirl marks on topcoat. Spread material evenly with buffing wheel pad before starting compounding.

Whether these rubbing compounds come in paste or liquid form, they contain an abrasive such as pumice that levels the top of the finish, making it smooth and lustrous. Rubbing compounds are available in various cutting strengths for both hand and machine compounding. (Hand compounds are oil based to provide lubrication; machine compounds are water based to disperse the abrasive while using a buffing wheel.)

Generally, compounds with coarse particles are called **rubbing compounds,** while those with fine particles of pumice are called **polishing compounds.**

A rubbing compound works two ways:

- When originally used, the pumice particles cut and smooth the compound.
- This action breaks down the pumice into small particles so it then works as a polish.

Uses of rubbing compounds are:

- To eliminate fine sand scratches around a repair area as described in Chapter 9
- To correct "orange peel" or a gritty surface
- To smooth and bring out the gloss of applied lacquer topcoats (Figure 11–23)

Small areas or blended areas are best done by hand. On large areas, however, machine compounding is recommended. Care must be taken not to cut through styling edges. To avoid cutting through styling edges, apply a strip of masking tape along the edge. After compounding is completed, remove the tape and compound the edge by hand—just enough to produce a smooth finish. Keep in mind that styling edges usually retain less paint than flat surfaces and should get only minimum compounding.

Compounding/Polishing Techniques

The technique for compounding/polishing is the same as sanding by:

- Hand
- Machine

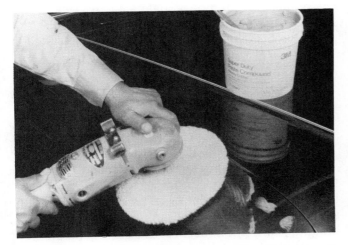

FIGURE 11–23 Rubbing compounds bring out gloss.

FIGURE 11–24 Always hand polish or compound in a straight direction. *(Courtesy of 3M).*

Hand Compounding. Fold a soft, lint-free, flannel cloth into a thick pad or roll into a ball and apply a small amount of compound to it (Figure 11–24). Rub area to be compounded in straight back and forth strokes using medium-to-hard pressure until desired smoothness is achieved.

When polishing over a blended or shaded area, it is a must to keep the following in mind:

- Rub in the direction shown in Figure 11–25. If rubbed in the opposite direction, there is danger of the shade texture appearing.
- Use either a very fine or extra-fine grain rubbing compound.
- Be careful because if the shade texture appears, it cannot be corrected.

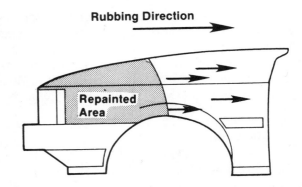

FIGURE 11–25 Polishing direction over shaded area

Hand compounding takes a lot of elbow grease and is time consuming. To keep the final compounding of lacquer topcoats to a minimum, it is important to apply the finish as wet as possible (without sags or runs) by using the right quality lacquer thinner.

Machine Compounding. Compounding/polishing machines are described in Chapter 2. Apply machine compound over a small area using a medium-to-coarse bristled paint brush or a squeeze bottle. Then compound using a buffing pad on the machine. Do not try to compound too large an area at one time because the rubbing compound has a tendency to dry out. Do not apply too much pressure and keep the machine moving to prevent cutting through the topcoat to the undercoat. Figure 11-26 shows how to install buffing and polishing pads.

A

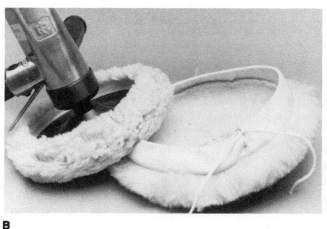

B

 **SHOP TALK** ⎯⎯⎯⎯⎯

During polishing, the abrasive material in the rubbing compound gradually crumbles into smaller pieces. The polishing effect is better in the early stages and gradually decreases with the gloss producing effect gradually becoming better. This is why a small amount of compound should be used over small areas without replenishing the compound for each area.

The primary advantages of machine compounding—in addition to saving time—are the achievement of the proper cutting action and the nonclogging of the compounding pad. When the compounding is completed, replace the buffing pad with a polishing pad or lamb's wool bonnet and polish. Remember to keep the machine moving.

MINOR SURFACE REPAIRS

A spray gun should not be used for small repairs of the topcoat. While minor surface defects such as dust nibs, orange peel, paint runs, and so on sometimes can be repaired by a knife and a whetstone, the best way to remove these defects is by following a four-step procedure (Table 11-3), which involves:

- Wet sanding
- Compounding
- Machine glazing
- Hand glazing

Several key factors stand out when working with new paints and attempting to repair any defects. First, it is most important that the paint specialist

FIGURE 11-26 (A) The buffing pad is usually fastened by a washer nut. (B) Most refinishers install the polishing pad over the buffing pad for extra softness. The pad is tied in place.

identify into which category (paint type and age) his/her work falls. There are basically four major categories of automotive paints in use—each of which requires specifically designed products for precision finishing. The four paint categories are:

1. Cured enamels/urethanes (air dried more than 48 hours or baked)
2. Fresh enamels/urethanes (air dried 24 to 48 hours)
3. Acrylic lacquers
4. All factory-applied (OEM) paints

Once the paint category in question is identified, the next step is to gauge the severity of the finishing problem. Paint systems generally involve several steps for handling any finishing problems ranging from minor dust nibs and surface scratches to major problems such as pits caused by acid rain, heavy orange peel, and paint runs or sags. In every case, the paint specialist will want to attack the prob-

TABLE 11-3: REPAIR PROCEDURE FOR NEWER PAINTS

Paint Type	Paint Condition	Procedure			
		Wet Sanding	Compounding	Machine Glazing	Hand Glazing
Refinish Paints: Cured enamels/urethanes* (air-dried more than 48 hours or baked)	1. Minor dust nibs of mismatched orange peel (light sanding) 2. Heavy orange peel, dust nibs, paint runs or sags	1. Fine 1500 2. Fine 1200	2. Microfinishing compound	1. Finishing material 2. Finishing material	1. Hand glaze 2. Hand glaze
Refinish Paints: Fresh enamels/urethanes* (air-dried 24 to 48 hours)	1. Minor dust nibs or mismatched orange peel (light sanding) 2. Heavy orange peel, dust nibs, paint runs or sags	1. Fine 1500 2. Fine 1200	1. Microfinishing compound 2. Microfinishing compound	1. Microfinishing glaze 2. Microfinishing glaze	1. Hand glaze 2. Hand glaze
Refinish Paints: Acrylic lacquer	1. Low gloss or overspray 2. Low gloss, minor orange peel, or overspray 3. Low gloss, moderate orange peel, or dust nibs 4. Low gloss, heavy orange peel, paint runs or sags	3. Fine 1200 4. Fine 1000	2. Paste or rubbing compound (heavy cut) 3. Microfinishing compound (medium cut) 4. Paste or rubbing compound (heavy cut)	1. Machine glaze 2. Machine glaze 3. Machine glaze 4. Machine glaze	1. Hand glaze 2. Hand glaze 3. Hand glaze 4. Hand glaze
All factory applied (OEM)	1. New car prep or fine wheel marks 2. Coarse swirl marks, chemical spotting, or light oxidation 3. Overspray or medium oxidation 4. Heavy oxidation or minor acid rain pitting 5. Dust nibs, minor scratches, or major acid rain pitting 6. Orange peel, paint runs or sags	5. Fine 1500 6. Fine 1200 or 1500	3. Microfinishing compound (medium cut) 4. Rubbing compound (heavy cut) 6. Microfinishing compound (medium cut)	2. Finishing material 3. Finishing material 4. Finishing material 5. Finishing material 6. Finishing material	1. Hand glaze liquid polish 2. Hand glaze 3. Hand glaze 4. Hand glaze 5. Hand glaze 6. Hand glaze

*Enamels/urethanes—as referred to in this chart— are catalyzed paint systems including acrylic enamel, urethane, acrylic urethanes, acrylic urethane enamels, polyurethane enamels, and polyurethane acrylic enamels), and nonisocyanate-activated paint systems used in color or clear coats.

lem with the least number of steps necessary, to save both time and materials. For example, if dealing with an acrylic lacquer painted surface with a minor orange peel problem, it might not be necessary to use sandpaper to handle the problem. It might be more appropriate to tackle the job at the beginning with a rubbing compound or perhaps with an even less-aggressive machine glazing product.

The four basic steps involved in a systemic approach to the finishing process can be summarized as follows, beginning with the most aggressive (for example, the most severe of finishing tactics) step:

1. **Wet Sanding.** Use very fine (#1000, 1500, 2000) grade sanding papers. Wet sanding is particularly appropriate for dealing initially with heavy or mismatched orange peel, paint runs and sags, dust nibs, minor scratches, and major acid rain pitting on all paint surfaces. Basically, wet sanding is used to remove a defect from the painted surface.

2. **Compounding.** As the second step in the process, compounding is necessary to remove sanding marks and scratches left on the surface from Step 1. At times, the painter might be able to start the finishing process at Step 2. This would be the case when dealing with a low gloss, minor orange peel or overspray problem on an acrylic lacquer surface, or with heavy-to-medium oxidation and minor acid rain pitting problems on OEM-painted surfaces. Again, in the system approach to paint finishing, the paint expert must determine at the beginning of the job both the type of defect involved and the severity of the problem, then base his/her decision to start the appropriate finishing step on this information.

3. **Machine Glazing.** Step 3 is essential to eliminate (remove) the compounding swirl marks produced by Step 2. The machine glazing step is critical to the overall success of the finishing process. It is always important to devote enough time to this step to complete it properly. Failure to properly complete this vital step can result in a "die-back" problem, in which the defective work reveals itself to the customer's eye weeks or months later, requiring costly rework, as well as damaging a body/paint shop's reputation for quality results.

   The choice of both the machine glazing product and the polishing pad is critical (Figure 11-27). Depending on the type

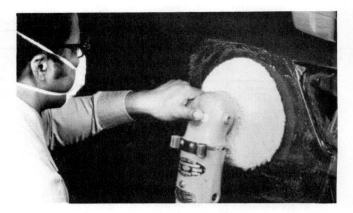

FIGURE 11-27 For a buffing job, use a polishing pad at low speed (1500 to 2500 rpm) to fill swirl marks from compounding and to produce a high-gloss finish. *(Courtesy of 3M)*

of automotive paint being finished, it is essential to choose the recommended machine glazing product for that particular type of paint.

It is also essential to use very high-quality polishing pads—pads designed specifically for machine glazing. Use of compounding pads or coarsely fibered polishing pads for the machine glazing step can result in surface marks that cannot be removed by the final hand glazing step. This is especially true on paints such as the fresh-air dried enamels and urethanes, which are extremely soft and easy to scratch. Machine glazing produces a near showroom-quality finish that will require only minimal polishing in the final step. Machine and hand glazing might be the only steps required to handle certain minor defects, such as low gloss with acrylic lacquers or coarse swirl marks, chemical spotting, and light oxidation problems on factory-painted surfaces.

4. **Hand Glazing.** Hand glazing is the final step in achieving a consistent high-quality finish. Hand glazing results in an exceptionally high gloss, defect-free finish. When dealing with very minor, superficial finishing problems such as those encountered in new car prep work, hand glazing might be the only required step. However, most refinish needs will require more than one step.

Repair with a Whetstone and Knife

As stated earlier, protruding defects in the topcoat such as sags or seeds (dirt spots) should be first corrected with a whetstone or a knife and then polished with a rubbing compound. Use of either a whetstone or a knife depends on the shape of the defect as shown in Figure 11-28.

If the protrusion is not so apparent, use a #1500 to #2000 FBB whetstone as follows:

1. First, prepare the whetstone by sanding a smooth edge with a #1200 grit abrasive paper to make it flat. Next, round the corners.
2. Place the sanded edge of the whetstone over the protrusion and move it in a left-right direction (Figure 11-29). If necessary, use a little oil to help make the movement smoother.
3. After the protrusion has almost disappeared, blow off the whetstone particles and finish the job with a very fine or extra-fine rubbing compound.

If the protrusion is rather noticeable, repair with a knife or single-edged razor blade:

1. Being careful not to take off more than necessary, cut off the protrusion with a knife or razor blade (Figure 11-30). The tip of the knife should be pointed slightly upward.
2. Take off the remaining protrusion with a whetstone or a #1500 to #2000 grit abrasive paper.
3. Blow off any particles and finish with an extra-fine grain rubbing compound.

Repairs with a Brush

A fine brush can be used to repair slight peeling or scratches by filling them in with touch-up paint. Here is the basic procedure:

1. First, degrease the defective area with silicone solvent or comparable material.
2. Lightly dip the tapered tip of a small brush handle into the touch-up paint and quickly allow the paint to drip onto the defective area (Figure 11-31).
3. Dip the brush into lacquer thinner and apply it around the boundary of the touch-up paint. This will cause the touch-up paint to smooth out and make it less noticeable.
4. Allow to set until completely dry.

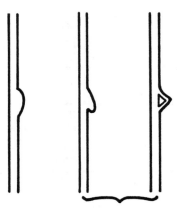

Use whetstone.   Use knife.

FIGURE 11-28 Type of defect and proper repair tool

FIGURE 11-29 How to polish defects with a whetstone

FIGURE 11-30 Making surface repair with a knife or razor blade

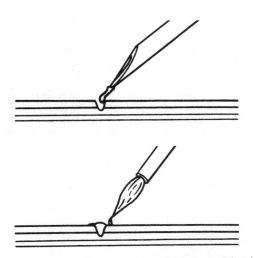

FIGURE 11-31 Making surface repairs with a brush

TABLE 11–4: SUMMARY OF REFINISHING OPERATIONS

Process	Total Repainting, Panel Repainting				Spot Repairing	Remarks
	Replacement Panel	Previous Coat Satisfactory	Previous Coat Unsatisfactory	Previous Coat Peeling		
Paint stripping and base sanding				A		
Featheredging		A	A		A	
Cleaning with solvent		A	A	A	A	
Surface treatment				A		
Application of metal putty and sanding		B	B	B	B	Depending on roughness, only poly putty might be necessary
Cleaning with solvent		B	B	B	B	
Application of poly putty and sanding		B	B	B	B	
Sanding of manufacturer primer	A					
Masking prior to application of primer-surfacer	A	A	A	A	A	
Cleaning with solvent	A	A	A	A	A	
Spraying of sealer			B			If previous coat deterioration is evident, apply anti-shrinking and antiabsorption sealer.
Spraying of primer-surfacer	A	A	A	A	A	
Touch-up putty and sanding		B	B	B	B	Cover areas not covered by primer-surfacer, pinholes in poly putty and sandpaper marks.
Base sanding	A	A	A	B	B	
Masking	A	A	A	A	A	
Cleaning with solvent	A	A	A	A	A	
Spraying of primer-surfacer		B	B	B	B	Apply thin coat of surfacer after touch-up putty application.
Topcoat	A	A	A	A	A	
Polishing	B	B	B	B	B	Not necessary if nonpolishing type paint used

A Applicable
B Applicable under certain conditions

PAINTING PROBLEMS

Most refinishing problems can usually be repaired, but the work requires time and time is money. Therefore, it is wise to prevent common paint problems before they occur. There is a variety of causes for defects occurring in a paint finish, and they usually originate in the preparation of the base metal, painting procedure, environment, paint ingredients, and external influences. If defects are noted, the remedy should be in accordance with the instructions given earlier in this chapter.

If defects are noted while painting, either stop work and take the proper steps immediately or wait until the painting is finished to take the proper remedy. One of the best ways to reduce the likelihood of defects occurring is to closely follow the proper fundamental painting procedures outlined in this book.

ACID AND ALKALI SPOTTING

Condition

Spotty discoloration that appears on the surface. (Various pigments react differently when in contact with acids or alkalies.)

Causes

Chemical change of pigments resulting from atmospheric contamination, in the presence of moisture (acid rain), due to industrial activity.

Prevention

1. Keep finish away from contaminated atmosphere.
2. Immediately following contamination, the surface should be vigorously flushed with cool water and detergent.

Solution

1. Wash with detergent water and follow with a vinegar bath.
2. Sand and refinish.
3. If contamination has reached the metal or subcoating, the spot must be sanded down to the metal before refinishing.

BLEEDING

Condition

Original finish discoloring—or color seeping through—the new topcoat color.

Causes

Contamination—usually in the form of soluble dyes or pigments on the older finish before it was repainted. (This is especially true with older shades of red.)

Prevention

Thoroughly clean areas to be painted before sanding, especially when applying lighter colors over darker colors. (Avoid using lighter colors over older shades of red without sealing first.)

Solution

Apply two medium coats of bleeder. Seal in accordance with label instructions. Then reapply color coat.

BLISTERING

Condition

Bubbles or pimples appearing in the topcoat film, often months after applications.

Causes

1. Improper surface cleaning or preparation. Tiny specks of dirt left on the surface can act as a sponge and hold moisture. When the finish is exposed to the sun (or abrupt changes in atmospheric pressure), moisture expands and builds up pressure. If the pressure is great enough, blisters form.
2. Wrong thinner or reducer. Use of a fast-dry thinner or reducer, especially when the material is sprayed too dry or at an excessive pressure. Air or moisture can be trapped in the film.
3. Excessive film thickness. Insufficient drying time between coats or too heavy application of the undercoats can trap solvents that escape later and blister the color coat.
4. Contamination of compressed air lines. Oil, water, or dirt in lines.

Prevention

1. Thoroughly clean areas to be painted before sanding. Be sure surface is completely dry before applying either undercoats or topcoats. Do not touch a cleaned area because the oils in the hands will contaminate the surface.

2. Select the thinner or reducer most suitable for existing shop conditions.
3. Allow proper drying time for undercoats and topcoats. Be sure to let each coat flash before applying the next.
4. Drain and clean air pressure regulator daily to remove trapped moisture and dirt. Air compressor tank should also be drained daily.

Solution

If damage is extensive and severe, paint must be removed down to undercoat or metal, depending on depth of blisters. Then refinish. In less severe cases, blisters can be sanded out, resurfaced, and retopcoated.

BLUSHING

Condition

A milky white haze that appears on lacquer films.

Causes

1. In hot humid weather, moisture droplets become trapped in the wet paint film. Air currents from the spray gun and the evaporation of the thinner tend to make the surface being sprayed lower in temperature than the surrounding atmosphere. This causes moisture in the air to condense on the wet paint film.
2. Excessive air pressure.
3. Too fast a thinner.

Prevention

1. In hot humid weather try to schedule painting early in the morning when temperature and humidity conditions are more suitable.
2. Use proper gun adjustments and techniques.
3. Select the thinner that is suitable for existing shop conditions.

Solution

Add retarder to the thinned color and apply additional coats.

CHALKING

Condition

Formation on the finish caused by pigment powder no longer held by the binder, which makes the finish look dull.

Causes (Other Than Normal Exposure)

1. Wrong thinner or reducer, which can harm topcoat durability.
2. Materials not uniformly mixed.
3. Starved paint film.
4. Excessive mist coats when finishing a metallic color application.

Prevention

1. Select the thinner or reducer that is best suited for existing shop conditions.
2. Stir all pigmented undercoats and topcoats thoroughly.
3. Meet or slightly exceed minimum film thicknesses.
4. Apply metallic color as evenly as possible so that misting is not required. When mist coats are necessary to even out flake, avoid using straight reducer.

Solution

Remove surface in affected area by sanding, then clean and refinish.

CHIPPING

Condition

Small chips of a finish losing adhesion to the substrate, usually caused by impact of stones or hard objects. While refinishers have no control over local road conditions—and thus cannot prevent such occurrences—they can take steps to minimize the effects if they know beforehand that these conditions will exist. (For details on the causes, prevention, and solution for **Chipping,** see **Peeling.**)

CRACKING (LINE CHECKING, MICROCHECKING)

Condition

A series of deep cracks resembling mud cracks in a dry pond. Often in the form of three-legged stars and in no definite pattern, they are usually through the color coat and sometimes the undercoat as well.

Causes

1. Excessive film thickness. Excessively thick topcoats magnify normal stresses and strains that can result in cracking even under normal conditions.
2. Materials not uniformly mixed.

3. Insufficient flash time.
4. Incorrect use of additive.

Prevention

1. Do not pile on topcoats. Allow sufficient flash and dry time between coats. Do not dry by gun fanning.
2. Stir all pigmented undercoats and top-coats thoroughly. Strain and—where necessary—add fish eye eliminator to top-coats.
3. Same as Step 1.
4. Read and carefully follow label instructions. Additives not specifically designed for a color coat can weaken the final paint film and make it more sensitive to cracking.

Solution

The affected areas must be sanded to a smooth finish or, in extreme cases, removed down to the bare metal and refinished.

LINE CHECKING

Condition

Similar to cracking, except that the lines or cracks are more parallel and range from very short up to about 18 inches.

Causes

1. Excessive film thickness.
2. Improper surface preparation. Oftentimes the application of a new finish over an old film that had cracked and was not completely removed.

Prevention

1. Do not pile on topcoats. Allow sufficient flash and dry time. Do not dry by gun fanning.
2. Thoroughly clean areas to be painted before sanding. Be sure the surface is completely dry before applying any undercoats or topcoats.

Solution

Remove color coat down to primer and apply new color coat.

MICROCHECKING

Condition

Appears as severe dulling of the film, but when examined with a magnifying glass, it contains

many small cracks that do not touch. Micro-checking is the beginning of film breakdown and might be an indication that film failures such as cracking or crazing will develop.

Solution

Sand off the color coat to remove the cracks, then recoat as required.

CRAZING

Condition

Fine splits or small cracks—often called "crow's feet"—that completely checker an area in an irregular manner.

Causes

Shop too cold. Surface tension of original material is under stress and literally shatters under the softening action of the solvents being applied.

Prevention

Select the thinner or reducer that is suitable for existing shop conditions. Schedule painting to avoid temperature and humidity extremes in shop or between temperature of shop and the job. Bring vehicle to room temperature before refinishing.

Solution

1. Continue to apply wet coats of topcoat to melt the crazing and flow pattern together (using the wettest possible thinner shop conditions will allow).
2. Use a fast-flashing thinner, which will allow a bridging of subsequent topcoats over the crazing area. (This is one case where bridging is a cure and not a cause for trouble.)

DIRT IN FINISH

Condition

Foreign particles dried in the paint film.

Causes

1. Improper cleaning, blowing off, and tack ragging of the surface to be painted.
2. Defective air regulator cleaning filter.
3. Dirty working area.
4. Defective or dirty air inlet filters.
5. Dirty spray gun.

Prevention

1. Blow out all cracks and body joints.
2. Solvent clean and tack-rag surface thoroughly.
3. Be sure equipment is clean.
4. Work in clean spray area.
5. Replace inlet air filters if dirty or defective.
6. Strain out foreign matter from paint.
7. Keep all containers closed when not in use to prevent contamination.

Solution

1. Rub out finish with rubbing compounds (not for enamels).
2. If dirt is deep in finish, sand and compound to restore gloss. Metallic finishes might show mottling with this treatment and will then require additional color coats.

DULLED FINISH

Condition

Gloss retards as film dries.

Causes

1. Compounding before thinner evaporates.
2. Using poorly balanced thinner or reducer.
3. Poorly cleaned surface.
4. Topcoats put on wet subcoats.
5. Washing with caustic cleaners.
6. Inferior polishes.

Prevention

1. Clean surface thoroughly.
2. Use recommended materials.
3. Allow all coatings sufficient drying time.

Solution

Allow finish to dry hard and rub with a mild rubbing compound.

FEATHEREDGE SPLITTING

Condition

Appears as stretch marks (or cracking) along the featheredge. Occurs during or shortly after the topcoat is applied over lacquer primer-surfacer.

Causes

1. "Piling on" the undercoat in heavy and wet coats. Solvent is trapped in undercoat layers that have not had sufficient time to set up.
2. Material not uniformly mixed. Because of the high pigment content of primer-surfacers, it is possible for settling to occur after it has been thinned. Delayed use of this material without restirring results in applying a film with loosely held pigment containing voids and crevices throughout, causing the film to act like a sponge.
3. Wrong thinner.
4. Improper surface cleaning or preparation. When not properly cleaned, primer-surfacer coats can draw away from the edge because of poor wetting and adhesion.
5. Improper drying. Fanning with a spray gun after the primer-surfacer is applied will result in drying the surface before solvent or air from the lower layers is released.
6. Excessive use (and film build) of putty.

Prevention

1. Apply properly reduced primer-surfacer in thin to medium coats with enough time between coats to allow solvents and air to escape.
2. Stir all pigmented undercoats and topcoats thoroughly. Select thinner that is suitable for existing shop conditions.
3. Select only thinners that are recommended for existing shop conditions.
4. Thoroughly clean areas to be painted before sanding.
5. Apply primer-surfacer in thin to medium coats with enough time between coats to allow solvents and air to escape.
6. Lacquer putty should be limited to filling minor imperfections. Putty applied too heavily (or too thick) will eventually shrink causing featheredge splitting.

Solution

Remove finish from the affected areas and refinish.

FISH EYES

Condition

Small, crater-like openings in the finish after it has been applied.

Causes

1. Improper surface cleaning or preparation. Many waxes and polishes contain silicone,

the most common cause of fish eyes. Silicones adhere firmly to the paint film and require extra effort for their removal. Even small quantities in sanding dust, rags, or from cars being polished nearby can cause this failure.
2. Effects of the old finish or previous repair. Old finish or previous repair can contain excessive amounts of silicone from additives used during their application. Usually solvent wiping will not remove embedded silicone.
3. Contamination of air lines.

Prevention

1. Precautions should be taken to remove all traces of silicone by thoroughly cleaning with wax and grease solvent. The use of fish eye eliminator is in no way a replacement for good surface preparation.
2. Add fish eye eliminator.
3. Drain and clean air pressure regulator daily to remove trapped moisture and dirt. Air compressor tank should also be drained daily.

Solution

After affected coat has set up, apply another double coat of color containing the recommended amount of fish eye eliminator. In severe cases, affected areas should be sanded down and refinished.

LIFTING

Condition

Surface distortion or shriveling, while the topcoat is being applied or while drying.

Causes

1. Use of incompatible materials. Solvents in new topcoat attack old surface, which results in a distorted or wrinkled effect.
2. Insufficient flash time. Lifting will occur when the paint film is an alkyd enamel and is only partially cured. The solvents from the coat being applied cause localized swelling or partial dissolving that later distorts final surface.
3. Improper dry. When synthetic enamel type undercoats are not thoroughly dry, topcoating with lacquer can result in lifting.
4. Effect of old finish or previous repair. Lacquer applied over a fresh air-dry enamel finish will cause lifting.

5. Improper surface cleaning or preparation. Use of an enamel-type primer or sealer over an original lacquer finish, which is to be topcoated with a lacquer, will result in lifting due to a sandwich effect.
6. Wrong thinner or reducer. The use of lacquer thinners in enamel increases the amount of substrate swelling and distortion, which can lead to lifting, particularly when two-toning or recoating.

Prevention

1. Avoid incompatible materials, such as a thinner with enamel products, or incompatible sealers and primers.
2. Do not pile on topcoats. Allow sufficient flash and dry time. Final topcoat should be applied when the previous coat is still soluble or after it has completely dried and is impervious to topcoat solvents.
3. Same as Steps 1 and 2.
4. Same as Step 1.
5. Same as Step 1.
6. Select the thinner or reducer that is correct for the finish applied and suitable for existing shop conditions.

Solution

Remove finish from affected areas and refinish.

MOTTLING

Condition

Occurs only in metallics when the flakes float together to form spotty or striped appearance.

Causes

1. Wrong thinner or reducer.
2. Materials not uniformly mixed.
3. Spraying too wet.
4. Holding spray gun too close to work.
5. Uneven spray pattern.
6. Low shop temperature.

Prevention

1. Select the thinner or reducer that is suitable for existing shop conditions and mix properly. In cold, damp weather use a faster dry solvent.
2. Stir all pigmented topcoats—especially metallics—thoroughly.
3. Use proper gun adjustments, techniques, and air pressure.

4. Same as Step 3.
5. Keep your spray gun clean (especially the needle fluid tip and air cap) and in good working condition.
6. Same as Step 1.

Solution

Allow color coat to set up and apply a drier double coat or two single coats, depending upon which topcoat is to be applied.

ORANGE PEEL

Condition

Uneven surface formation—much like that of the skin of an orange—that results from poor fusion of atomized paint droplets. Paint droplets dry out before they can flow out and level smoothly together.

Causes

1. Improper gun adjustment and techniques. Too little air pressure, wide fan patterns, or spraying at excessive gun distances cause droplets to become too dry during their travel time to the work surface and they remain as formed by gun nozzle.
2. Extreme shop temperature. When air temperature is too high, droplets lose more solvent and dry out before they can flow and level properly.
3. Improper dry. Gun fanning before paint droplets have a chance to flow together will cause orange peel.
4. Improper flash or recoat time between coats. If first coats of enamel are allowed to become too dry, solvent in the paint droplets of following coats will be absorbed into the first coat before proper flow is achieved.
5. Wrong thinner or reducer. Underdiluted paint or paint thinned with fast evaporating thinners or reducers causes the atomized droplets to become too dry before reaching the surface.
6. Too little thinner or reducer.
7. Materials not uniformly mixed. Many finishes are formulated with components that aid fusion. If these are not properly mixed, orange peel will result.

Prevention

1. Use proper gun adjustments, techniques, and air pressure.

2. Schedule painting to avoid temperature and humidity extremes. Select the thinner or reducer that is suitable for existing conditions. The use of a slower evaporating thinner or reducer will overcome this.
3. Allow sufficient flash and dry time. Do not dry by fanning.
4. Allow proper drying time for undercoats and topcoats (not too long or not too short).
5. Select the thinner or reducer that is most suitable for existing shop conditions to provide good flow and leveling of the topcoat.
6. Reduce to recommended viscosity with proper thinner/reducer.
7. Stir all pigmented undercoats and topcoats thoroughly.

Solution

Compounding might help—a mild polishing compound for enamel, rubbing compound for lacquer. In extreme cases, sand down to smooth surface and refinish, using a slower evaporating thinner or reducer at the correct air pressure.

PEELING

Condition

Loss of adhesion between paint and substrate (topcoat to primer and/or old finish, or primer to metal).

Causes

1. Improper cleaning or preparation. Failure to remove sanding dust and other surface contaminants will keep the finish coat from coming into proper contact with the substrate.
2. Improper metal treatment.
3. Materials not uniformly mixed.
4. Failure to use proper sealer.

Prevention

1. Thoroughly clean areas to be painted. It is always good shop practice to wash the sanding dust off the area to be refinished with clean-up solvent.
2. Use correct metal conditioner and conversion coating.
3. Stir all pigmented undercoats and topcoats thoroughly.
4. In general, sealers are recommended to improve adhesion of topcoats. In certain

cases (for example, alkyd enamels over lacquer finishes) sealers are required to prevent peeling.

Solution

Remove finish from an area slightly larger than the affected area and refinish.

PINHOLING

Condition

Tiny holes or groups of holes in the finish, or in putty or body filler, usually are the result of trapped solvents, air, or moisture.

Causes

1. Improper surface cleaning or preparation. Moisture left on primer-surfacers will pass through the wet topcoat to cause pinholing.
2. Contamination of air lines. Moisture or oil in air lines will enter paint while being applied and cause pinholes when released during the drying stage.
3. Wrong gun adjustment or technique. If adjustments or techniques result in application that is too wet, or if the gun is held too close to the surface, pinholes will occur when the air or excessive solvent is released during dry.
4. Wrong thinner or reducer. The use of a solvent that is too fast for shop temperature tends to make the refinisher spray too close to the surface in order to get adequate flow. When the solvent is too slow, it is trapped by subsequent topcoats.
5. Improper dry. Fanning a newly applied finish can drive air into the surface or cause a dry skin—both of which result in pinholing when solvents retained in lower layers come to the surface.

Prevention

1. Thoroughly clean all areas to be painted. Be sure surface is completely dry before applying undercoats or topcoats.
2. Drain and clean air pressure regulator daily to remove trapped moisture and dirt. Air compressor tank should also be drained daily.
3. Use proper gun adjustments, techniques, and air pressure.
4. Select the thinner or reducer that is suitable for existing shop conditions.

5. Allow sufficient flash and dry time. Do not dry by fanning.

Solution

Sand affected area down to smooth finish and refinish.

PLASTIC FILLER BLEED-THROUGH

Condition

Discoloration (normally yellowing) of the topcoat color.

Causes

1. Too much hardener.
2. Applying topcoat before plastic filler is cured.

Prevention

1. Use correct amount of hardener.
2. Allow adequate cure time before refinishing.

Solution

1. Remove patch.
2. Cure topcoat, sand, and refinish.

PLASTIC FILLER NOT DRYING

Conditions

Plastic filler remains soft after applying.

Causes

1. Insufficient amount of hardener.
2. Hardener exposed to sunlight.

Prevention

1. Add recommended amount of hardener.
2. Be sure hardener is fresh and avoid exposure to sunlight.

Solution

Scrape off plastic filler and reapply.

RUNS OR SAGS

Condition

Heavy application of sprayed material that fails to adhere uniformly to the surface.

Causes

1. Too much thinner or reducer.
2. Wrong thinner or reducer.
3. Excessive film thickness without allowing proper dry time.
4. Low air pressure (causing lack of atomization), holding gun too close, or making too slow a gun pass.
5. Shop or surface too cold.

Prevention

1. Read and carefully follow the instructions on the label.
2. Select proper thinner/reducer.
3. Do not pile on finishes. Allow sufficient flash and dry time in between coats.
4. Use proper gun adjustment, techniques, and air pressure.
5. Allow vehicle surface to warm up to at least room temperature before attempting to refinish. Try to maintain an appropriate shop temperature for paint areas.

Solution

Wash off the affected area and let dry until affected area can be sanded to a smooth surface and refinish.

RUST UNDER FINISH

Condition

The surface will show raised surface spots or peeling or blistering.

Causes

1. Improper metal preparation.
2. Broken paint film allows moisture to creep under surrounding finish.
3. Water in air lines.

Prevention

1. Locate source of moisture and seal off.
2. When replacing ornaments or molding, be careful not to break paint film and allow dissimilar metals to come in contact. This contact can produce electrolysis that might cause a tearing away or loss of good bond with the film.

Solution

1. Seal off entrance of moisture from inner part of panels.

2. Sand down to bare metal, prepare metal, and treat with phosphate before refinishing.

SAND SCRATCH SWELLING

Condition

Enlarged sand scratches caused by swelling action of topcoat solvents.

Causes

1. Improper surface cleaning or preparation. Use of too coarse sandpaper or omitting a sealer in panel repairs greatly exaggerates swelling caused by thinner penetration.
2. Improper thinner or reducer, especially a slow-dry thinner or reducer when sealer has been omitted.
3. Underreduced or wrong thinner (too fast) used in primer-surfacer causes "bridging" of scratches.

Prevention

1. Use appropriate grits of sanding materials for the topcoats being used.
2. Seal to eliminate sand scratch swelling. Select thinner or reducer suitable for existing shop conditions.
3. Use proper thinner and reducer for primer-surfacer.

Solution

Sand affected area down to smooth surface and apply appropriate sealer before refinishing.

SOLVENT POPPING

Condition

Blisters on the paint surface caused by trapped solvents in the topcoats or primer-surfacer—a situation that is further aggravated by force drying or uneven heating.

Causes

1. Improper surface cleaning or preparation.
2. Wrong thinner or reducer. Use of fast-dry thinner or reducer, especially when the material is sprayed too dry or at excessive pressure, can cause solvent popping by trapping air in the film.
3. Excessive film thickness. Insufficient drying time between coats and too heavy ap-

plication of the undercoats can trap solvents causing popping of the color coat as they later escape.

Prevention

1. Thoroughly clean areas to be painted.
2. Select the thinner or reducer suitable for existing shop conditions.
3. Do not pile on undercoats or topcoats. Allow sufficient flash and dry time. Allow proper drying time for undercoats and topcoats. Allow each coat of primer-surfacer to flash naturally—do not fan.

Solution

If damage is extensive and severe, paint must be removed down to undercoat or metal, depending on depth of blisters; then, refinish. In less severe cases, sand out, resurface, and retopcoat.

STONE BRUISES

Condition

Small chips of paint missing from an otherwise firm finish.

Causes

1. Flying stones from other vehicles.
2. Impact of other car doors in a parking lot.

Solution

1. Thoroughly sand remaining paint film back several inches from damage point.
2. Properly treat metal and refinish.

UNDERCOAT SHOW THROUGH

Condition

Variation in surface color.

Causes

1. Insufficient color coats.
2. Repeated compounding.

Prevention

1. Apply good coverage of color.
2. Avoid excessively compounding or polishing the surface.

Solution

Sand and refinish.

WATER SPOTTING

Condition

General dulling of gloss in spots or masses of spots.

Causes

1. Water evaporating on finish before it is thoroughly dry.
2. Washing finish in bright sunlight.

Prevention

1. Do not apply water to fresh paint job and try to keep newly finished car out of rain. Allow sufficient dry time before delivering car to customer.
2. Wash car in shade and wipe dry.

Solution

Use rubbing or polishing compound. In severe cases, sand affected areas and refinish.

WET SPOTS

Condition

Discoloration and/or slow drying of some areas.

Causes

1. Improper cleaning and preparation.
2. Improper drying of excessive undercoat film build.
3. Sanding with contaminated solvent.

Prevention

1. Thoroughly clean all areas to be painted.
2. Allow proper drying time for undercoats.
3. Wet sand with clean water.

Solution

Wash or sand all affected areas thoroughly and then refinish.

WRINKLING

Condition

Surface distortions (or shriveling) that occur while enamel topcoat is being applied (or later during the drying stage).

Causes

1. Improper dry. When a freshly applied topcoat is baked or force dried too soon, softening of the undercoats can occur. This increases topcoat solvent penetration and swelling. In addition, baking or force drying causes surface layers to dry too soon. The combination of these forces causes wrinkling.
2. "Piling on" heavy or wet coats. When enamel coats are too thick, the lower wet coats are not able to release their solvents and set up at the same rate as the surface layer, which results in wrinkling.
3. Improper reducer or incompatible materials. A fast-dry reducer or the use of a lacquer thinner in enamel can cause wrinkling.
4. Improper or rapid change in shop temperature. Drafts of warm air cause enamel surfaces to set up and shrink before sublayers have released their solvents, which results in localized skinning in uneven patterns.

Prevention

1. Allow proper drying time for undercoats and topcoats. When force drying alkyd enamel, baking additive is required to retard surface setup until lower layers harden. Lesser amounts can be used in hot weather. Read and carefully follow label instructions.
2. Do not pile on topcoats. Allow sufficient flash and dry time.
3. Select proper reducer and avoid using incompatible materials such as a reducer with lacquer products or thinner with enamel products.
4. Schedule painting to avoid temperature extremes or rapid changes.

Solution

Remove wrinkled enamel and refinish.

REVIEW QUESTIONS

1. How long should a basecoat of an intermix system be agitated?
   a. 5 minutes minimum
   b. 10 minutes minimum
   c. 15 minutes minimum
   d. 20 minutes minimum

2. When applying alkyd enamel, what should the viscosity be?
   a. 20 to 23 seconds in a #2 Zahn cup
   b. 18 to 22 seconds in a #2 Zahn cup
   c. 18 to 20 seconds in a #2 Zahn cup
   d. none of the above

3. When applying an acrylic lacquer for a spot repair, what should the air pressure be?
   a. 15 to 25 pounds
   b. 20 to 30 pounds
   c. 25 to 35 pounds
   d. 30 to 40 pounds

4. Painter A sprays a solid color polyurethane enamel with a medium first coat, allows it to tack up, and follows with a full second coat. Painter B sprays two or three wet double coats of the same paint with a short flash time between double coats. Who is right?
   a. Painter A
   b. Painter B
   c. Both A and B
   d. Neither A nor B

5. How much flash time should be allowed between medium wet coats of clear?
   a. 5 minutes minimum
   b. 10 minutes minimum
   c. 15 minutes minimum
   d. 20 minutes minimum

6. Clears are used in _____.
   a. basecoat/clear coat applications
   b. custom work
   c. acrylic enamel spot repair
   d. all of the above
   e. both a and b

7. Painter A applies a splatter finish in one heavy coat. Painter B applies it in two medium coats. Who is right?
   a. Painter A
   b. Painter B
   c. Both A and B
   d. Neither A nor B

8. Painter A force dries the topcoat and then removes the masking while the paint is still warm. Painter B waits till it cools. Who is right?
   a. Painter A
   b. Painter B
   c. Both A and B
   d. Neither A nor B

9. Which type of compound is used just before applying the final topcoating?
    a. very fine
    b. fine
    c. medium
    d. coarse

10. Which of the following should be used to repair dust specks in the topcoat?
    a. spray gun
    b. polish
    c. whetstone (knife)
    d. brush

11. How long should a new topcoat finish be cured before an automotive finish wax is applied?
    a. 24 hours
    b. one week
    c. 20 to 60 days
    d. 69 to 90 days

12. Bubbles appear in the topcoat film months after application. What could be the cause?
    a. acid rain
    b. excessive air pressure in the application
    c. excessive film thickness
    d. all of the above

13. Which of the following conditions can be caused by excessive amounts of silicone in the old finish?
    a. orange peel
    b. fish eyes
    c. pinholing
    d. sand scratch swelling
    e. all of the above

14. Which of the following steps can be taken to prevent wet spots?
    a. thoroughly clean all areas to be painted
    b. allow proper drying time for undercoats
    c. wet-sand with clean water
    d. all of the above

15. Which of the following problems can be solved by removing the affected area by sanding and recoating?
    a. microchecking
    b. chalking
    c. lifting
    d. all of the above
    e. both a and b

16. Painter A says that the topcoat must be properly stirred before it can be applied. Painter B says that the topcoat must be thinned with the proper solvent before it can be applied. Who is correct?
    a. Painter A
    b. Painter B
    c. Both A and B
    d. Neither A nor B

17. Which component of the topcoat settles in the can?
    a. pigment
    b. binder
    c. solvent
    d. none of the above

18. When spot repainting with solid colors, Painter A applied the topcoat with a circular motion, working the spray gun from the center outward. Painter B applies the finish in short strokes from the center outward and extends each coat so that it slightly overlaps the previous one. Who is correct?
    a. Painter A
    b. Painter B
    c. Both A and B
    d. Neither A nor B

19. When applying polyurethane enamel, what should the viscosity be?
    a. 18 to 20 seconds in a #2 Zahn cup
    b. 18 to 22 seconds in a #2 Zahn cup
    c. 20 to 22 seconds in a #2 Zahn cup
    d. 22 to 24 seconds in a #2 Zahn cup

20. When applying acrylic urethane enamel, what should the viscosity be?
    a. 18 to 20 seconds in a #2 Zahn cup
    b. 18 to 22 seconds in a #2 Zahn cup
    c. 20 to 22 seconds in a #2 Zahn cup
    d. 22 to 24 seconds in a #2 Zahn cup

21. When doing an overall panel repair, Painter A sands the entire vehicle by hand before chemically cleaning the entire surface. Painter B chemically cleans the surface before making any body filler repairs. Who is correct?
    a. Painter A
    b. Painter B
    c. Both A and B
    d. Neither A nor B

22. For which of the following are clears used?
    a. two- and three-coat operations
    b. custom work
    c. acrylic enamel or lacquer spot repair
    d. all of the above

23. Which of the following grades of rubbing compounds is used to level orange peel?
    a. coarse
    b. medium
    c. fine
    d. very fine

24. Which of the following is not involved in minor surface repairs?
    a. wet sanding
    b. compounding
    c. machine compounding
    d. none of the above

25. Which of the following does not cause blistering?
    a. improper surface cleaning
    b. temperature too high
    c. excessive film thickness
    d. none of the above

CHAPTER TWELVE

PAINTING PLASTIC PARTS AND ADDING FINISHING TOUCHES

Objectives

After reading this chapter, you will be able to:

- prepare plastic parts for refinishing.
- describe the paint finishing systems applicable to plastic parts.
- recognize custom painting and refinishing techniques.
- apply decals, pinstriping, and woodgrain transfers.
- explain the importance of final touchup and cleaning to the satisfaction of the customer.

In recent years, more and more plastic has been used in various parts of car bodies, particularly in the front end: in bumper and fender extensions, in soft front fascia, fender aprons, grille opening panels, stone shields, instrument panels, trim panels, and elsewhere (Figure 12–1). Because these parts are much lighter in weight than sheet metal, they have become an important part of every American manufacturer's fuel saving, weight reduction program. And because of the high strength-to-weight ratio of plastic, the weight decrease does not mean a decrease in strength. Every indication is that plastic body parts are here to stay, and new applications for plastic will probably be found in the future. Therefore, automotive painters can expect to be painting a greater number of plastic parts.

TYPES OF PLASTICS

There are two types of plastics used today in automotive production:

- **Thermoplastics.** These plastics are capable of being repeatedly softened and hardened by heating or cooling. They soften or melt when heat is applied and, therefore, are weldable.

- **Thermosetting plastics.** These plastics are materials that undergo a chemical change by the action of heating, a catalyst, or ultraviolet light leading to an infusible state. Catalyst/resin mix to form a new product. Thermosets are not weldable.

PLASTIC IDENTIFICATION

Before deciding upon the proper repair technique to use, it is first necessary to identify the type of plastic from which the component is made. This is very important, because a repair job that is based on incorrect identification of the plastic can quickly delaminate, crack, or discolor. There are several ways to identify an unknown plastic. For instance, various types of plastic can be identified according to national identification symbols, which can often be found on the parts to be repaired. When parts are not identified by these symbols, refer to the manufacturer's technical literature for plastic identification. Domestic manufacturers are using identification symbols more and more; unfortunately, there are many who do not. Another problem with this system is that it is usually necessary to remove the part to read the letters.

One of the best ways to identify an unknown plastic is to become familiar with the different types

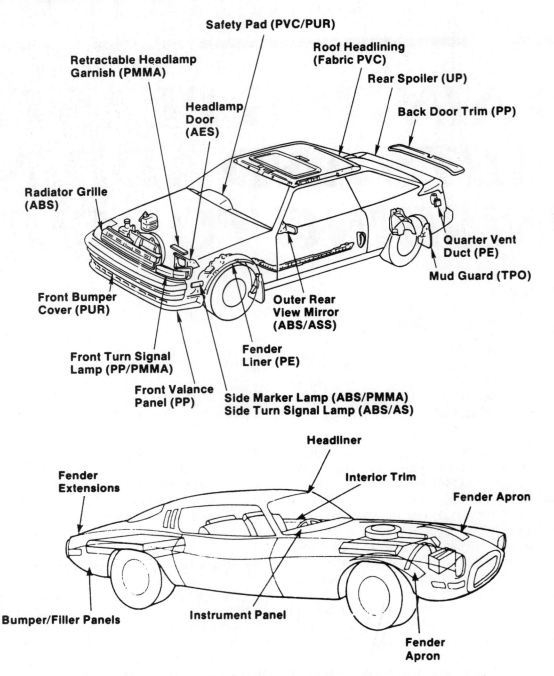

FIGURE 12-1 The use of plastics in automobiles has grown greatly in the last decade.

of plastics and where they are commonly used. Table 12-1 gives the identification symbol, chemical and common names, and applications of the more common automotive plastics. Plastic applications information can often be found in shop manuals or in special manufacturer's guides.

Another technique for identifying various types of plastic is the so-called **burn test** or **smoke test.** Different plastics have different burn characteristics and some produce unique odors.

To do a burn test, scrape off a small sliver of the unknown material, hold it with pliers or on the end of

a piece of wire, and carefully try to ignite it with a match or propane torch (Figure 12-2). The results of such burn tests are given in Table 12-2.

PLASTIC PARTS PREPARATION

Plastic parts are usually considered either hard (rigid) or flexible (semirigid). Some flexible plastic auto body replacement parts come from the factory

TABLE 12-1:   STANDARD SYMBOL, CHEMICAL NAME, TRADE NAME, AND DESIGN APPLICATIONS OF MOST COMMONLY USED PLASTICS

Symbol	Chemical Name	Common Name	Design Applications	Thermosetting or Thermoplastic
ABS	Acrylonitrile-butadiene-styrene	ABS, Cycolac, Abson, Kralastic, Lustran, Absafil, Dylel	Body panels, dash panels, grilles, headlamp doors	Thermoplastic
ABS/MAT	Hard ABS reinforced with fiberglass	—	Body panels	Thermosetting
ABS/PVC	ABS/Polyvinyl chloride	ABS Vinyl	—	Thermoplastic
EP	Epoxy	Epon, EPO, Epotuf, Araldite	Fiberglass body panels	Thermosetting
EPDM	Ethylene-propylene-diene-monomer	EPDM, Nordel	Bumper impact strips, body panels	Thermosetting
PA	Polyamide	Nylon, Capron, Zytel, Rilsan, Minlon, Vydyne	Exterior finish trim panels	Thermosetting
PC	Polycarbonate	Lexan, Merlon	Grilles, instrument panels, lenses	Thermoplastic
PRO	Polyphenylene oxide	Noryl, Olefo	Chromed plastic parts, grilles, headlamp doors, bezels, ornaments	Thermosetting
PE	Polyethylene	Dylan, Fortiflex, Marlex, Alathon, Hi-fax, Hosalen, Paxon	Inner fender panels, interior trim panels, valances, spoilers	Thermoplastic
PP	Polypropylene	Profax, Olefo, Marlex, Olemer, Aydel, Dypro	Interior moldings, interior trim panels, inner fenders, radiator shrouds, dash panels, bumper covers	Thermoplastic
PS	Polystyrene	Lustrex, Dylene, Styron, Fostacryl, Duraton	—	Thermoplastic
PUR	Polyurethane	Castethane, Bayflex	Bumper covers, front and rear body panels, filler panels	Thermosetting
TPUR	Polyurethane	Pellethane, Estane, Roylar, Texin	Bumper covers, gravel deflectors, filler panels, soft bezels	Thermoplastic
PVC	Polyvinyl chloride	Geon, Vinylete, Pliovic	Interior trim, soft filler panels	Thermoplastic
RIM	"Reaction injection molded" polyurethane	—	Bumper covers	Thermosetting
R RIM	Reinforced RIM-polyurethane	—	Exterior body panels	Thermosetting

TABLE 12-1: STANDARD SYMBOL, CHEMICAL NAME, TRADE NAME, AND DESIGN APPLICATIONS OF MOST COMMONLY USED PLASTICS (CONTINUED)

SAN	Styrene-acrylonitrite	Lustran, Tyril, Fostacryl	Interior trim panels	Thermosetting
TPR	Thermoplastic rubber	—	Valance panels	Thermosetting
UP	Polyester	SMC, Premi-glas, Selection Vibrin-mat	Fiberglass body panels	Thermosetting

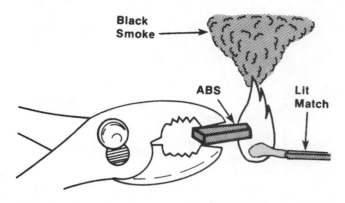

FIGURE 12-2 Conducting a burn test on ABS plastic

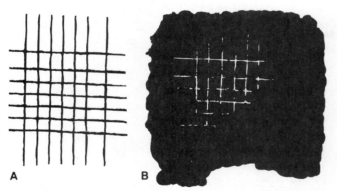

FIGURE 12-3 These test panels show the improved adhesion to TPO made possible by the use of a plastic primer. Panel A was primed; Panel B was not. *(Courtesy of Sherwin-Williams Co.)*

TABLE 12-2: BURN CHARACTERISTICS OF COMMON PLASTICS

Plastic	Burn Characteristic
Polypropylene (PP)	Burns with no visible smoke and continues to burn once the flame source is removed. Produces a smell like burned wax. Bottom of flame is blue and top is yellow.
Polyethylene (PE)	Also smells like burned wax, makes no smoke, and continues to burn once the flame source is removed. Bottom of flame is blue and top is yellow.
ABS	Burns with a thick, black, sooty smoke and continues to burn when the flame source is removed. Produces a sweet odor when burned. Flame is yellowish orange.
PVC	Only chars and does not support a flame when you try to burn it. Gives off gray smoke and an acid-like smell. End of flame is yellowish green.
Thermoplastic Polyurethane (TPUR) and Thermosetting Polyurethane (PUR)	Burns with a yellow-orange sputtering flame and gives off black smoke. The thermoset version of polyurethane, however, will not support a flame.

already primed, while others are delivered unprimed. If the parts are factory-primed, no additional priming is necessary. If they are not, both rigid and semirigid plastics might benefit from the use of a special plastic primer, primer-sealer, or vinyl washer-primer to improve paint adhesion. TPO, in particular (Figure 12–3), has an extremely slick, waxy surface that makes it difficult for the topcoat to form a strong bond to the substrate unless a primer is used. Adhesion to ABS used in exterior applications also is greatly enhanced by priming.

PREPARATION OF FLEXIBLE PLASTIC

Prepare the surface of semirigid unpainted material as follows:

1. Clean the entire part with a wax, grease, and silicone removing solvent applied with a water dampened cloth. Wipe dry.

 **SHOP TALK** ⸻

Unpainted rigid plastic parts should also be solvent cleaned to remove mold release agents (typically silicones) before a primer or topcoat is applied.

2. Featheredge the scuff or filler repair with #320 sandpaper, blow off dust and tack wipe.
3. Mix and apply four medium dry coats of a flexible primer-surfacer (Figure 12–4). Be sure to follow the manufacturer's instructions for the specific mix ratios and additives.

 SHOP TALK ⸻

Use a fast evaporating thinner as recommended to reduce the primer-surfacer and do not apply excessively wet coats. Bare flexible plastic surface and/or flexible filler materials have a tendency to swell from thinner absorption, causing visible or "highlighted" repair.

4. Allow to dry at least 1 hour and block sand with #400 sandpaper. Sand the entire part with #400 sandpaper to remove all gloss in preparation for color application.

When undercoaters are modified with a flex additive, the possibility of mixture "pot life" exists; therefore, spray equipment should be emptied and flushed immediately after use. Flex additives are needed for semirigid plastics because they expand, contract, and bend more easily than other substrates. The flex agent will keep the paint film flexible so it can accommodate the movement of the substrate without cracking.

PREPARATION OF POLYPROPYLENE PLASTIC PARTS

The system for painting polypropylene parts involves the use of a special primer. Since polypropylene plastic is hard, it can be color coated after priming with conventional interior acrylic lacquer. To prepare the surface, proceed as follows:

 1. Wash the part with a wax and silicone remover solvent. Follow the label directions.

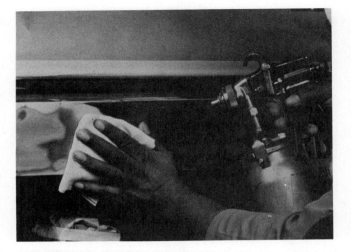

FIGURE 12–4   Applying a flexible primer-surfacer

2. Apply a thin, wet coat of polypropylene primer according to label directions. Wetness of primer is determined by observing gloss reflection of spray application in adequate lighting. Be sure primer application includes all edges. Allow primer to flash dry 1 minute minimum and 10 minutes maximum.
3. During the above flash time period (1 to 10 minutes), apply conventional interior acrylic lacquer color as required and allow to dry before installing part. Application of color during above flash time range promotes best adhesion of color coats.

PREPARATION OF RIGID PARTS

Exterior hard (rigid) parts should be treated as fiberglass when in doubt as to their makeup. In fact, fiberglass should be treated much the same—in preparation for a final coat—as body steel. It must be remembered that fiberglass parts do not require chemical conditioners. Replacement or new panels can contain contaminants on the surface due to the mold release agent used in the molds. Several common release agents are composed of silicone oils. These contaminants must be removed.

 1. Newly molded parts should be washed with denatured alcohol used liberally on a clean cloth.
2. Thoroughly clean the surface with a wax and grease remover.
3. Sand the exposed fiberglass with #220 or #280 grit paper by hand or #80 to #120 grit with sander.

FIGURE 12-5 Applying body filler to a plastic part

CAUTION: Do not sand down through the gel coat to the glass fibers that are used to reinforce the plastic. There is generally sufficient gel coating to allow thorough sanding for refinishing.

---

4. Reclean surface and wipe dry with clean rags.

Alternate Step: If there are joints to be filled or the sanding operation exposes air pockets or glass strands, glaze a coat of body filler over the entire surface (Figure 12-5). Allow to cure, sand, and reclean. Apply a single coat of sealer or a double coat of epoxy chromate primer.

5. Apply a primer-surfacer as directed on the label. Allow to dry and sand smooth with fine sandpaper to minimize sand scratches. Blow off with air and tack-rag the surface. If necessary apply another coat of sealer.

Alternate Step: A synthetic primer-surfacer is also recommended if topcoats are to be enamel or acrylic enamel.

6. The surface is now ready for the color coats.

When refinishing previously painted fiberglass parts, care should be taken not to sand through the gel coat, and a sealer should be used. Fiberglass parts are extremely porous. The gel coat keeps topcoat solvents from being absorbed into the substrate.

TOPCOATS FOR PLASTIC AUTOMOTIVE PARTS

After automotive plastic part(s) have been repaired or installed and the surfaces have been pre-

pared, the final color can be applied. Automotive plastics can generally be topcoated using most acrylic lacquers, acrylic enamels (catalyzed or uncatalyzed), and acrylic enamel basecoat/clear coat systems. Follow the manufacturer's recommendations to determine if a particular paint system can be used on a specific type of plastic, or if a special plastic primer or flexibilizing agent is required. Table 12-3 lists the more popular automotive plastics and suggested finishing systems.

Most rigid (hard) plastics generally require no primers. The paint will adhere properly to the plastic. Semirigid (flexible) plastics might require the addition of a "flex agent" to the paint system. The additive is needed because semirigid plastics expand, contract, and bend more easily than other substrates. The flex agent will keep the paint film flexible so it can accommodate the movement of the substrate without cracking.

Some refinish product manufacturers require that different flexible additives be used in the various paint systems. Others offer a universal flexible additive that can be used in a variety of paint systems. These products eliminate the need to stock several flexible additives and help keep costs down. As always, it is best not to mix manufacturers' products. The flexible additive, the topcoat, the undercoat products, and the reducer or thinner used all should be provided by the same manufacturer. Mixing labels or using different manufacturers' products on the same job can result in poor performance.

SHOP TALK

Plastic parts are normally painted before they are installed. However, if painting is done on the car, it is important that the surfaces are properly masked off.

PAINTING RIGID INTERIOR PLASTIC PARTS

Rigid or hard ABS plastic parts generally require no primer or primer-sealer. Interior colors are color keyed to trim combination numbers located on the body number plate (see Chapter 7). Conventional interior acrylic lacquer colors are designed for use only on hard trim parts, such as:

- Steel and fiberglass parts (primer or sealer required on new service parts)
- Hard ABS plastic (no primer necessary)
- Hard polypropylene plastic (special primer required)

Each major paint supplier provides an interior color chart that identifies the stock number, color

TABLE 12-3:   FINISHING SYSTEMS FOR POPULAR PLASTICS

KEY		Standard Lacquer System	Flexible Lacquer/ Enamel System	Polypropylene System	Vinyl System	Urethane System
I Interior E Exterior P Primer NP No primer SP Special primer/adhesion promoter NA None approved * Flexible primer and/or additive recommended						
ABS	Acrylonitrile-Butadiene-Styrene	I/NP E/NP				
ABS/PVC	ABS/Vinyl (Soft)		I/NP E/NP		I/NP	
EP I, EP II, or TPO	Ethylene Propylene			E/SP*		
PA	Nylon	E/P				
PC	Lexan	I/NP				
PE	Polyethylene	NA	NA	NA	NA	NA
PP	Polypropylene			I/SP		
PPO	Noryl	I/NP				
PS	Polystyrene	NA	NA	NA	NA	NA
PUR, RIM, or RRIM	Thermoset Polyurethane		E*			E
PVC	Polyvinyl Chloride (Vinyl)		E/NP I/NP		E/NP	E I/NP
SAN	Styrene Acrylonitrile	I/NP				
SMC	Sheet Molded Compound (Polyester)	E/P				
UP	Polyester (Fiberglass)	E/P				
TPUR	Thermoplastic Polyurethane		E*			E
TPR	Thermoplastic Rubber		E*			E

name, gloss factor, and trim combination number for each conventional interior color. When painting rigid interior surfaces, proceed as follows:

1. Wash the part with a cleaning liquid or solvent.
2. Apply conventional interior acrylic lacquer color according to trim combination (see paint supplier color chart for trim and color code). Apply only enough color for proper hiding to avoid washout of grain effect.
3. Allow to dry, following label directions, and then install part.

PAINTING RIGID EXTERIOR PLASTIC PARTS

Painting of rigid exterior plastic parts is basically the same for rigid interior plastic parts. While most rigid exterior plastics do not require a primer, some paint manufacturers recommend giving ABS exterior parts a primer coat before the color coat. When applying a coat to rigid (hard) plastic parts, proceed as follows:

1. Wash the part thoroughly with a cleaning solvent.
2. Color coat the part using the appropriate color of acrylic lacquer, acrylic enamel, urethane, or basecoat/clear coat systems (Figure 12-6).
3. Allow the color coat to dry, and reinstall the part.

In finishing fiberglass after the primer-sealer has been applied, the color or topcoat is applied following the basic procedures as for body steel.

When refinishing a previously painted sheet molded compound (SMC) with either a blend or full

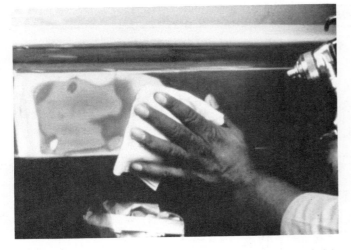

FIGURE 12-6 Apply the desired finish to a rigid exterior plastic part. *(Courtesy of 3M).*

panel paint procedure, it is necessary to apply a coat of an adhesion promoter. This must be applied 6 to 8 inches beyond the blend area, when performing a spot repair, or in the event of refinishing a full panel, the entire part must be coated. A flash time of at least 30 minutes is required before applying the base color. This will ensure adequate adhesion of the topcoat.

A spot repair can be accomplished in the following manner. The area that will receive the basecoat color should be sanded with #400 grit wet or dry paper. The blend area that will be clear coated should be sanded with #600 grit or finer wet or dry paper (Figure 12-7). It is important that the adhesion promoter extend beyond the blend area. The application of paint to new parts does not require an adhesion promoter prior to applying the topcoat.

FIGURE 12-7 Sanding plastic surface with a #600 grit or finer. *(Courtesy of 3M)*

When refinishing rigid plastic parts, a slow-drying lacquer solvent is recommended for reducing the basecoat color. Specific reduction ratios supplied by the paint manufacturer should be followed. Only enough film thickness to achieve full hiding is necessary, usually two or three medium wet coats are sufficient. The basecoat should be allowed to dry at least 20 minutes before the clear coat is applied. The clear coat can be either lacquer or enamel. The label directions for the product selected should be followed accordingly.

INTERIOR/EXTERIOR FLEXIBLE PLASTIC PARTS

As previously mentioned, most flexible or semi-rigid plastics require an additive to the paint to allow the paint to flex without cracking. There are several flexible or elastomeric topcoat systems available for the painter's selection; in most cases, it is a matter of personal preference. Basecoat/clear coat material can be either enamel or lacquer based. Some manufacturers do not recommend the use of flex additives in their base color material when using a clear topcoat, but do recommend its use for their lacquer and enamel clear coats.

To apply a flexible (elastomeric) finish, proceed as follows:

1. Thoroughly sand the entire part with #400 grit abrasive paper (Figure 12-8). Clean the surface with a cleaning solvent.
2. Follow manufacturer's label instructions, mix the base color, the flexible additive, and recommended solvent (Figure 12-9). A typical mixing procedure for either an acrylic lacquer or acrylic enamel, for example, to produce 3-1/2 pints yield, mix 1 pint of lacquer (or enamel), 1 pint of flexible additive, and 1-1/2 pints of thinner. For a 1-3/4 pints yield, cut these measures in half. Mix the lacquer (or enamel) color and the flexible additive thoroughly before adding the amount of solvent best suited for the shop temperature. Remember to mix only the amount of elastomeric material that is going to be used since the reduced material cannot be stored.
3. Using 30 to 35 pounds of air pressure at the gun, apply a sufficient number of wet double coats to achieve complete hiding and color match (Figure 12-10). Wet double coats are applied as follows: Spray first pass left to right. Spray second pass right to left, directly over first pass. Drop nozzle so that 50 percent of the pattern overlaps

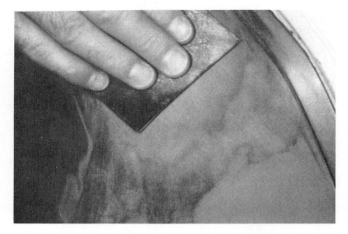

FIGURE 12-8   Thoroughly sand the entire part with a #400 grit abrasive paper.

FIGURE 12-9   Mix basecoat according to manufacturer's instructions.

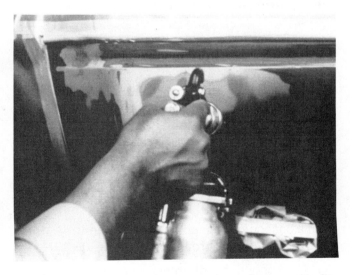

FIGURE 12-10   Apply enough color coats to achieve the proper color match.

the bottom half of the initial double coat. Continue the pattern until complete. Be sure to allow flash time between coats.

4. As the paint film builds, it will be necessary to allow more flash off time between coats to avoid trapping the thinner. If thinner is trapped, pinholes and bubbles might result.

5. Allow the base color coat to dry 30 to 60 minutes before applying the clear coat. Do not sand the basecoat before applying the clear coat. When not applying a topcoat, air dry for approximately 4 hours before installing or putting the part into service. If sanding of the base coat is necessary to remove imperfections, such as dirt or sags, sand with #400 grit or finer sandpaper, reclean the area(s). Apply one additional coat of base material and let dry.

Apply the clear coat, if desired, in the following manner:

1. Mix and reduce clear coat (lacquer or enamel) material per label instructions. Use flex additive if recommended by paint source.

2. Strain the mixture and apply 2 to 3 coats with 35 to 40 pounds air pressure at the gun (Figure 12–11).

3. Allow each coat to flash completely before applying the next coat. Allow at least 4 hours air dry time or force dry for 30 minutes with a heat lamp at 180 degrees Fahrenheit before putting into service.

SHOP TALK

Compounding is not necessary when a flexible additive is used in the topcoat paint material. The mixture will dry with acceptable gloss. Compounding dulls the gloss of elastomeric finishes, causing a flat appearance. The finish cannot be brought back to the same gloss level without applying more paint.

Flexible replacement panels are factory primed with an elastomeric enamel-based primer. The only preparation required prior to topcoating is solvent cleaning, sanding with #400 grit paper, and a second cleaning with solvent after sanding operations are completed. In the event the OEM primer has been scratched leaving the plastic substrate exposed, or the part has been repaired with a flexible filler material, it is necessary to cover the exposed area with a

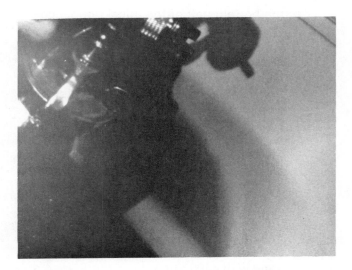

FIGURE 12-11 Applying a clear coat to a flexible plastic part

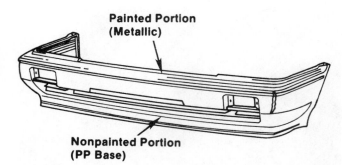

FIGURE 12-12 Typical colored bumper

flexible primer-surfacer prior to topcoating. If the exposed surface is not primed, the area will be highlighted after the topcoats are applied. A fast evaporating solvent should be used to reduce the primer-surfacer to prevent swelling of the base material by absorption.

 SHOP TALK

Spot repairs on OEM finished flexible panels and parts are not recommended because of the failure of elastomeric color to flow or "wet out" properly at the blend area.

Keep elastomeric paint material off regular vehicle finishes. If applied to them, there could be a problem color matching gloss differences, and if retopcoated with lacquer, the finish could lift or wrinkle, requiring the removal of the affected area. Conversely, keep conventional acrylic lacquers and enamels off all flexible exterior parts. If these finishes are applied to flexible parts, the finish will crack as the parts are flexed and will spoil the appearance of the car. Repair of cracked paint of flexible parts is very difficult because it requires the removal of the entire cracked finish.

PAINTING INTERIOR/ EXTERIOR POLYPROPYLENE PLASTIC PARTS

The system for painting interior polypropylene parts involves the use of a special primer. Since polypropylene (PP) plastic is hard, it can be color

coated after the primer with conventional interior acrylic lacquer.

The most common exterior use of polypropylene plastic parts is for bumpers. PP bumpers come in two types:

- One with a tinted base material (black, gray, and dark gray)
- One that is partially painted, called a colored bumper (Figure 12-12)

The quality of paint used for PP bumpers is different from that for metal surfaces and, in particular, adhesive and softening agents are required. Therefore, a special PP primer must be used for the undercoat and a flexing agent added to the topcoat paint. If not, it will result in peeling.

If a PP bumper has major structural damage, it must be replaced. Replacement bumpers of this type are usually primed and come ready to be painted. If they are not primed, they must be given a special PP primer over the entire bumper. Before starting the painting, be sure to wash with a solvent cleaner. When applying only a regular color coat proceed as follows:

1. Apply properly thinned, proportioned, and mixed special polycarbonate primer and flexible additive as directed by the manufacturer. Allow 1 to 2 hours drying time before application of color coats.
2. Apply proportioned and mixed acrylic enamel (appropriate color) and hardener additive. Flexible additive is **not** used in the topcoat.
3. Allow 8 hours-to-overnight drying time to assure paint hardness.

If a basecoat/clear coat is appropriate, read the container labels and proceed as follows:

1. Apply properly thinned and agitated special PP primer. Allow 1/2 to 1 hour drying time before application of acrylic lacquer.

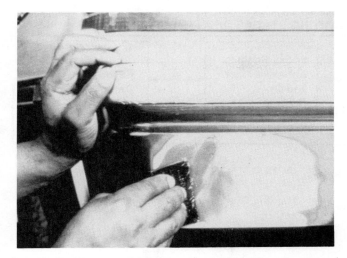

FIGURE 12-13   Applying a thin coat of body filler

Remember a flexible additive is **not** used with basecoat/clear coat finishes.

2. Apply properly thinned, proportioned, and mixed acrylic lacquer (appropriate color) and allow 15 to 30 minutes drying time before applying clear coat.
3. Apply properly thinned, proportional, and mixed acrylic enamel clear coat and urethane enamel clear hardener. Allow 8 hours-to-overnight drying time to assure finish coat hardness.

CAUTION: PP bumpers are made of thermoplastic resin, and force drying at more than 212 degrees Fahrenheit could result in deformation.

Minor surface scratches can usually be repaired by following the procedures for finishing painting replacement PP bumpers with the following changes.

1. If scratches do not penetrate the substrate, follow the entire procedure but do not apply primer.
2. If scratches penetrate the substrate, use a lightweight body filler (Figure 12-13) and primer the repair area only.

A summary of repainting procedures of a PP bumper can be found in Figure 12-14 and Table 12-4.

Repainting of Urethane Bumpers

Urethane bumpers include the colored type that have been painted and the tinted black bumpers. Although both are made of urethane, the black type has been made with an additive that helps prevent deterioration due to sunlight and rain. If painted, a black bumper would change color due to the additive. Light colors such as white would cause a noticeable change. Therefore, black bumpers cannot be painted.

Described here is the procedure for painting a colored urethane bumper:

1. Mask off the area to be repainted and clean with a silicone solvent. Keep in mind that insufficient cleaning will result in peeling or blistering.
2. Apply a coat of primer-surfacer over the entire surface (Figure 12-15). Repair any scratches with a brush.
3. It is extremely difficult to match the paint for spot repainting, so the entire bumper should be repainted. Prepare the entire surface by wet sanding with a #600 grit abrasive paper.
4. Clean the topcoat surface again.
5. Apply the topcoat over the entire bumper. Use a two part acrylic urethane paint with a softening agent added (Figure 12-16). For a metallic color, allow a flash time of ap-

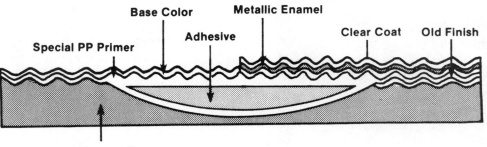

FIGURE 12-14   Repainting damaged PP bumper. *(Courtesy of Toyota Motor Corp.)*

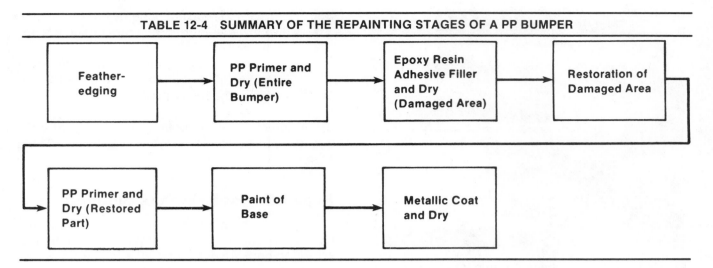

TABLE 12-4   SUMMARY OF THE REPAINTING STAGES OF A PP BUMPER

Feather-edging → PP Primer and Dry (Entire Bumper) → Epoxy Resin Adhesive Filler and Dry (Damaged Area) → Restoration of Damaged Area → PP Primer and Dry (Restored Part) → Paint of Base → Metallic Coat and Dry

FIGURE 12-15   Applying a coat of special primer to the surface that is to be finished. *(Courtesy of Urethane Supply Co.)*

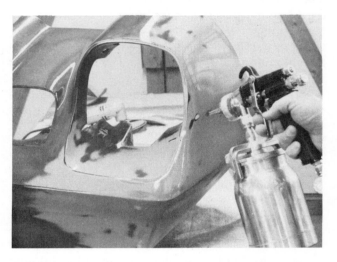

FIGURE 12-16   The bumper after the topcoat has been applied. *(Courtesy of Urethane Supply Co.)*

proximately 5 minutes after application, then apply a clear coat.

6. Follow the dry time recommended by the manufacturer.

A summary of repainting procedures of urethane can be found in Table 12-5.

PAINTING EXTERIOR VINYL ROOFS

Exterior vinyl roofs can be painted by using either the vinyl system described for interior vinyl parts or the optional procedure of equal parts of acrylic lacquer and vinyl system material. With either method proceed as follows:

1. Wash the old top with a bleach-type detergent, a brush, and plenty of water. Rinse the top and entire car thoroughly in clean water.

2. Clean the top thoroughly with paint finish cleaning solvent or with vinyl prep conditioner.

3. Blow out all gap spacing and crevices around the top and tack-wipe the top as required.

4. Be sure masking is carefully done and cover the entire hood and deck lid. The adhesion property of the vinyl system will make overspray difficult to remove.

5. Start the color application with a banding coat at low air pressure (20 to 25 pounds) and a narrow fan. Spray into drip rails and cracks where windshield and back window molding meet the roof.

6. Then, increase the air pressure to 35 pounds and open the fan to a normal spray pattern. Apply vinyl color, working toward the center.

TABLE 12-5   SUMMARY OF THE REPAINTING STAGES OF A URETHANE BUMPER

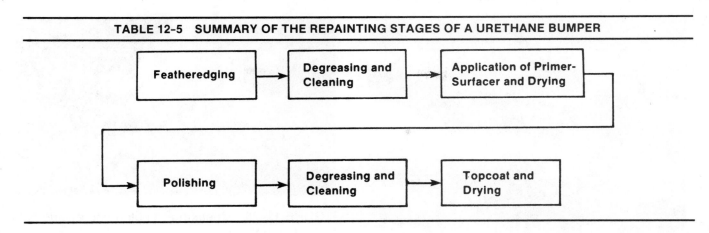

Featheredging → Degreasing and Cleaning → Application of Primer-Surfacer and Drying → Polishing → Degreasing and Cleaning → Topcoat and Drying

7. On the opposite side of the car, start at the center and maintain wet application of the near side. Keep the application wet with a full and uniform 50 to 75 percent stroke overlap. Keep the spray gun as perpendicular to the surface as possible. Control the hose by positioning it over the shoulders and back.

8. Apply a second full wet coat for complete hiding and uniformity of wetness. Adjust gun distance and speed for the desired texture. If streaks or dry spots are present, apply a good acrylic lacquer thinner through the spray gun to wet out the dry spots and even out the spray pattern.

9. For the final coat, many manufacturers recommend an application of one wet coat of 200 percent thinned vinyl lacquer (1 part vinyl color to 2 parts lacquer thinner) over the entire vinyl roof area to obtain a uniform appearance.

10. After 1 hour of drying, remove the masking. Allow to dry a minimum of 4 hours before putting the car into service.

Any vinyl roof repairs should be completed before applying a new finish.

Vinyl Preserver

A clear protective dressing is available for use on vinyl roof tops, upholstery, and other areas covered with vinyl color—floor mats, tires, wires, hoses, and batteries. Its water and dirt repellent film withstands sun, salt, and snow. It is also ideal for spray applications to preclean the engine compartment.

When applying over vinyls, use a thin, even coat of preserver with cellulose sponge or clean soft cloth (Figure 12-17). Dries to the touch in 10 to 20 minutes, is water repellent in 1 hour and detergent resistant in 1 day. Do not thin the preserver; use it at can consistency.

RETEXTURING INTERIOR PLASTIC PARTS

Many different textures or grains are found in the average automobile interior. When retexturing a repaired part, it is important to keep in mind that the existing texture does not have to be duplicated. There is no need to spend time and effort trying to get the retextured area to look exactly like the rest of the piece; a variation in the grain is meaningless. Only the coarseness of the grain must be duplicated in order to achieve professional results (Figure 12-18).

Retexturing can be done one of two ways:

- by blending the new texture out into the old
- by retexturing to a natural break line on the panel

Use a refillable aerosol sprayer; the lower pressure will prevent the material from atomizing, which means a faster texture buildup. To achieve a coarse

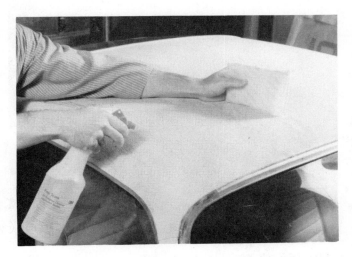

FIGURE 12-17 Applying a vinyl gloss and preserver

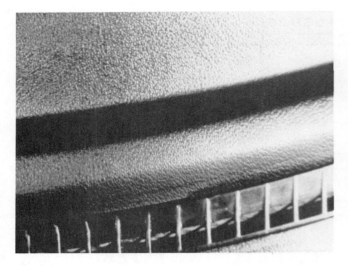

FIGURE 12-18   Retextured plastic surface

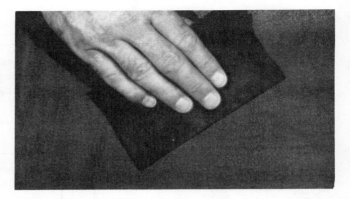

FIGURE 12-20   Checking the blending of original texture with the new

texture, use the material unthinned. For a finer texture, use a small amount of lacquer thinner. A typical retexturing procedure is as follows:

1. Mix the texture material as per the manufacturer's instructions. Direct the first coat toward the repaired area only. Hold the sprayer 18 to 24 inches from the surface (Figure 12-19), and always dry spray the material. Spraying it on wet will destroy the grain effect.
2. Allow flash time between coats. As many as eight to ten light coats might be needed to achieve the required buildup. Remember that this is by no means a one-slot application.

3. When buildup has been achieved, begin blending the texture out and away from the repaired area, similar to a color coat. Force-drying between coats speeds up the process.
4. When the texture material has dried, nib sand with #220 grit paper. This will blend the newly textured area into the original texture of the panel (Figure 12-20).
5. If not satisfied with the texture, apply more light coats of material and repeat the sanding.

After retexturing, the part should be blown dust-free in preparation for the refinishing. Do not use any type of cleaner on a newly retextured area. Since the flexible texture material is usually lacquer based, a conventional interior acrylic lacquer is considered the best final color.

PAINTING INTERIOR VINYL AND SOFT ABS PLASTIC PARTS

The outer cover material of flexible instrument panel cover assemblies is made mostly of ABS plastic modified with PVC or vinyl. The same is true of many padded door trim assemblies. The soft cushion padding under ABS covers is urethane foam plastic.

The most widely used flexible vinyls (polyvinyl chloride) are coated fabrics as used in seat trim, some door trim assemblies, headlinings, and sun visors. Examples of hard vinyls are door and front seat back assist handles, coat hooks, and exterior molding inserts.

The paint system for vinyl as well as for interior ABS plastic involves the use of vinyl lacquer. Originally, this heavy-bodied finish was used over paint-

FIGURE 12-19   Using an aerosol sprayer to apply a new finish to a repaired area

ed steel tops to simulate vinyl fabric tops. By changing reductions and air pressures, the vinyl lacquer will dry to a leather-like texture similar in appearance to a fabric textured vinyl top. Also this product is frequently used to restore faded vinyl tops.

More recently vinyl lacquer has been used as a flat black topcoat to produce accent stripes and nonglare hood trim. Vinyl lacquer is also suggested as a basecoat for duplicating the OEM chip-resistant coating on rocker panels. Once dry, most vinyl lacquer can be recoated with acrylic lacquer or acrylic enamel to match the car color. Vinyl system finishes are also usually available in a wide array of colors.

No primer or other undercoat is required. Also no thinning is necessary since vinyl lacquer or color is usually packaged at the proper spray viscosity. The painting procedure is as follows:

1. Always make sure the panels or parts to be colored are free of soil, oils, waxes, food, and all other debris. Synthetic enamel reducer or a vinyl cleaning and preparation solvent should be used to clean vinyl. Isopropyl alcohol will remove ballpoint pen ink. Do not use wax and grease removing solvents; they evaporate too slowly and can cause poor adhesion and cracking of coatings. If an extremely soiled condition exists, detergent and water can be used for a first washing before the solvents are used. Be sure all moisture has completely evaporated before any coatings are applied. Infrared radiation is the most effective method of evaporation.

2. As soon as the surface dries, apply interior vinyl color in wet coats. Allow flash time between coats according to label directions. Use proper vinyl color shown by interior trim code combination. Apply only enough color for proper hiding to avoid washout of grain effect. Use an air pressure of 20 to 25 pounds.

3. Before color flashes completely, apply one wet double coat of vinyl clear topcoat. Use topcoat with appropriate gloss level to match adjacent similar components. The clear coat is necessary to control the gloss requirement and to prevent crocking (rubbing off) of the color coat after drying. Remember that instrument panel covers require a nonglare final topcoat.

4. Allow to dry according to label directions before installing part or putting the vehicle back in service.

   Optional procedure: Since acrylic lacquers are available for a perfect, or near perfect,

color match to interior surfaces, many painters like to choose the proper acrylic lacquer color then mix it with a proper vinyl system according to the directions on the label. When coloring seats or panels that will be flexed as much as a seat, mix the acrylic lacquer into an equal amount of vinyl system for the proper feel and flexibility. No thinning will be required. If the panels are not as flexible as a seat, such as headliners, trim pads, crash pads, dash panels, kickpanels, and roof coverings, use 3 parts color to 2 parts vinyl system. A little more than a half pint of good acrylic lacquer thinner should be added to this mixture for proper spraying.

Leather interior parts can be refinished in much the same manner as vinyl plastic. It must be remembered that vinyl is not dyed but colored with pigment and coatings. The same is true of leathers used for upholstering vehicles. Leathers are coated in Europe with nitrocellulose lacquers and urethanes. In the United States, leathers are coated with acrylics and urethanes. Vinyl colors are usually used to repaint leather.

 **SHOP TALK** ⎯⎯⎯⎯⎯

American made cars with leather seats use a vinyl impregnated leather. These can be coated with vinyl color. Do not use on leather generally without testing for scratch off on a test piece after 24 hours curing time.

When painting leather, some interesting applications can be achieved. For example, leather can be given a dual tone accent. This is accomplished by using a basecoat to cover the panel and supply the primary color, then a darker color is applied over the base color in a shadowy manner. Some interior colors have metallic flakes to add sparkle, but some colors have a pearlescent pigment.

WOODGRAIN TRANSFER MATERIAL

Woodgrain decals or transfers are subject to repair or replacement, depending on the amount of damage that they have received. It is not necessary to replace the vinyl woodgrain transfer, for example, because of blisters, air bubbles, chips, or scratches.

To repair blisters or air bubbles, pierce the air bubble or blister with a pin. Work the trapped air out of bubble and press the transfer firmly against the sheet metal. It might be necessary to preheat the metal slightly to soften the adhesive.

If the woodgrain transfer (decal) lifts off the sheet metal, check the recessed surface for pinholes. If holes are evident, release the trapped air through the holes and make sure the transfer is adhering to the sheet metal. Then, patch the holes with a small scrap of transfer to create the necessary vacuum to hold the transfer in the depression.

If the transfer has lifted off the sheet metal and holes are not evident, cut a slit approximately 1/4 inch long in the transfer near the edge of the depression (not in the depression or the vacuum will be lost) to release the air and adhere the transfer to the sheet metal.

For chips or scratches, use touch-up paint of the appropriate color or colors to repair the damaged areas.

REPLACEMENT OF WOODGRAIN TRANSFER

Whenever woodgrain overlays are badly damaged, the only solution is replacement. They are available in suitable form from parts depots or service warehouses. When listing a woodgrain overlay replacement, be sure to have the correct body style, model year, car model, and panel name to which it is to be applied.

If the woodgrain transfer (decal) is to be installed on a new sheet metal panel or on a panel that required extensive straightening, remember that refinish operations must be completed **before** the transfer is applied. These transfers are never applied directly over bare metal or only primed metal. However, new transfers can be applied over old transfers if the damaged areas are small, featheredged, and filled in with primer-surfacer or spot putty to bring the surface up to the surrounding level. It is often necessary to remove exterior moldings, handles, and lock cylinders before the transfer can be removed or installed.

To remove the woodgrain decal, use a heat gun to soften the adhesive on the transfer (Figure 12-21). Start at one edge and slowly peel the decal back. Keep the heat working over the area until the sheet is completely off.

After the old decal is removed, repair the damaged metal and prime the repair. With either a new panel or a repaired one, sand the surface smooth (Figure 12-22) and then clean with wax and grease remover.

The first step in the reinstallation of the woodgrain decal is to make a template of the area to be covered. Using a sheet of masking paper, align it with the centerline of the molding attaching clip holes across the top of the panel. Tack-tape the paper in place.

With the template paper securely taped to the panel, mark the centerline of the panel on both the panel and the template. Smooth the paper flush against the panel and mark the front, rear, and bottom edges of the panel. If the woodgrain transfer on adjacent panels has a plank design, mark the top horizontal plank line on the front and rear edges of the panel.

Remove the template from the panel and lay it out in a flat, clean work surface. Measure 3/4 inches out from the panel outline and mark another perimeter line. Oversizing the template this way will allow

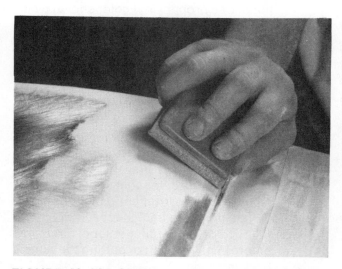

FIGURE 12-21 Removing old transfer (decal) with heat

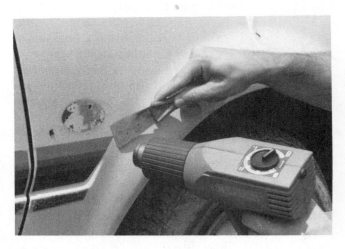

FIGURE 12-22 Sand the surface smooth before applying the transfer material.

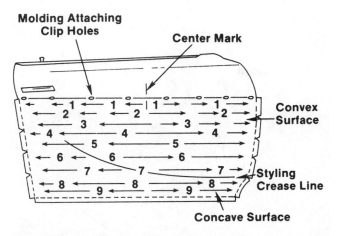

FIGURE 12-23 Transfer installation sequence—right front door shown. *(Courtesy of General Motors Corp.)*

room for fitting the transfer to the panel. With a pair of scissors, cut out the template along the perimeter line. Mark the front edge of the template on the backside of the paper.

Now, roll out a sufficient amount of overlay and cut it to length. Lay the transfer face down on the work surface. Turn the template over and place it face down on the transfer. Make sure that the woodgrain is running left to right and that the horizontal planking lines on the template align with plank lines on the transfer (Figure 12-23). Trace the outline of the template on the transfer backing paper and cut the template to shape with a pair of scissors. Align wood grain as close as possible.

Hold the transfer cutout against the panel again. Carefully position the top edge of the transfer with the centerline of the trim clip holes and mark the centerline of the transfer with the centerline of the panel.

Lay the transfer facedown again on the work surface and peel off the adhesive backing paper. With a sponge and a solution of water and liquid detergent, wet the adhesive side of the woodgrain overlay and the panel.

Align the decal with the clip holes and panel centerline. Lightly press the top of the transfer to the panel, making sure to align any plank lines or grain. With the transfer aligned, squeegee the center 3 or 4 inches of the transfer. Use an upward motion with the squeegee, forcing the liquid solution out along the top. This anchors the transfer in position.

Raise one side of the decal and with short strokes gradually squeegee the top edge of the transfer in place. Make sure the transfer edge stays even with the centerline of the molding clip holes. Then, squeegee the top edge with a long horizontal stroke. Repeat this procedure for the other side top edge. Then raise the transfer and with the squeegee press down another 2 or 3 inches in the center. Use overlapping horizontal strokes to bond another band of decal across the top of the panel. Progressively work down and across the panel in this manner. If the decal gets tacky and sticks to the panel before it is pressed in place, break the grab with a fast firm pull. Periodically, rewet the panel to decrease the tack as well as to make the transfer easier to position.

When reaching the edges of the decal cut 90 degree notches in the corners and V-shaped notches along the edges where necessary to fit the transfer to the panel. Avoid excessive pulling and stretching; the decal can tear.

Apply vinyl trim adhesive to door hem edges. Apply the adhesive sparingly to avoid a lumpy build-up under the transfer. Heat the edges of the door hem flanges and the transfer. Then, wrap the transfer around the flange edge and firmly press it to the backside. Apply heat to any depressions, or hole edges, and firmly press the transfer to ensure a good bond. Cut the excess decal away from panel edges and holes with a razor blade.

Inspect the application from an angle where light reflections will expose any irregularities. Pierce bubbles with a fine needle from an acute angle and press these down firmly. Reinstall all moldings and other hardware (Figure 12-24).

SPECIAL DECORATIVE EFFECTS

In addition to wood grain, other decorative effects can be achieved by using decals. For example,

FIGURE 12-24 Inspecting a finished application for bubbles

FIGURE 12–25 Vans that have been given a special custom treatment

FIGURE 12–27 Using striping tape to achieve a special design

many customers like to personalize their car, truck, or van with stripe designs (Figure 12–25). There are several ways to apply striping.

1. **Freehand Using Sign Painting Equipment.** This method is for only a real craftperson. This method employs paint.
2. **Tape Method.** This method, as explained in Chapter 9, gives a painted-on stripe.
3. **Stripe Guide.** A guide is first applied to the body and then a roller gun glides on the guide (Figure 12–26). As the roller gun

moves along the top of the guide, a paint stripe is painted.

4. **Decal or Transfer Method (Figure 12–27).** Decal professional adhesive striping is available in a variety of colors and in sizes ranging from pinstripe to 6-inch bands. The professional decal stripes have gained

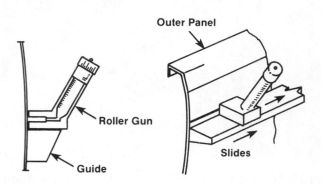

FIGURE 12–26 Paint stripe painting with a roller gun and guide

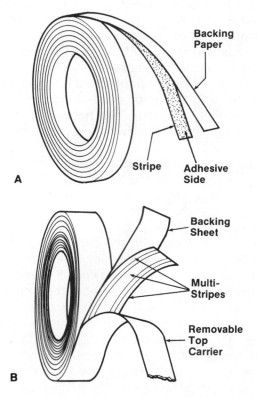

FIGURE 12–28 Two basic types of stripe tape: (A) without removable top carrier and (B) with removal top carrier

popularity in refinishing shops. A clear coat is often used by custom paint shops in overall painting to provide protective cover over murals, lacework, striping, and other customizing decal techniques.

STRIPE DESIGN

The first step is to look over the vehicle and plan a design that takes into account such factors as the vehicle's body lines and customer's personal taste. Most commonly, stripes follow the upper fender line and the lines that run between or just above the wheel wells. It is a good idea to sketch a rough design on paper and obtain the customer's approval before beginning the actual application.

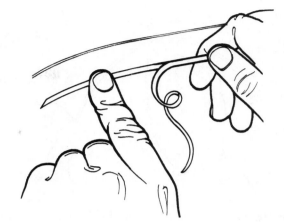

FIGURE 12-29   Applying the first few inches

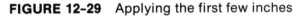 **SHOP TALK** ―――――――

When applying decal striping, be sure to follow these tips for a successful job:

- *Stripe only when the temperature is between 60 and 80 degrees Fahrenheit. Warm weather can cause tape stretching, quick evaporation of the wet solution, and other complications. Cooler weather will affect the flexibility of the stripe and, consequently, the quality of adhesion.*
- *Thoroughly clean the car's surface with a mixture of water and mild liquid detergent. In order for the striping to adhere properly, the surface must be free of dirt, wax, and other contaminants. Use wax or polish remover if necessary.*
- *To remove old stripes, use a hair dryer to soften the adhesive; the stripes should pull off easily. If adhesive residue remains, use a recommended solvent to remove it.*
- *It is wise to allow 24 hours before washing the vehicle.*

There are two basic types of stripe tapes:

- Tape without a removable top carrier (Figure 12-28A)
- Tape with a removable top carrier (Figure 12-28B).

Using a Tape Without a Removable Top Carrier

Follow these procedures when using a striping tape that does not have a removable top carrier.

Straight Lines.   To make straight lines, the tape is applied in the following manner:

1. Measure the amount of striping needed.
2. Unwind and cut a length of tape a few inches longer than the required length.
3. Make sure the surface of the car is clean.
4. Remove the backing paper from the tape and apply the first few inches of striping to the application area (Figure 12-29).
5. Grasp the loose end of the striping tape. Avoid contaminating the adhesive with the fingers. The natural oils in the skin will affect its adhesion qualities.
6. Gently pull the striping taut, but do not stretch it. If the tape is stretched during application, shrinkage will be a problem later.
7. Carefully scan the tape for proper alignment. It is helpful to use the car's body lines as alignment guides.
8. Once the striping is aligned, gently lower the tape to the car's surface. Applying the striping in long lengths ensures straightness; do not apply it in short pieces.
9. Step back to check the alignment. If the line is not straight, gently lift the striping and try again.
10. Burnish the stripe to the car using a squeegee or soft rag.
11. Apply each stripe in this manner. Be sure to stand back and double-check each line before burnishing. For panel ends, such as door openings, use a knife or single-edge razor blade to trim the striping tape 1/8 inch before the panel end. If possible, hold the knife flat against the tape and lift the loose end. When a direct cutting action is necessary, hold the blade flat against the surface to prevent the point from digging in. Remember that a too heavy trim cut can penetrate the vehicle's finish. Trimming

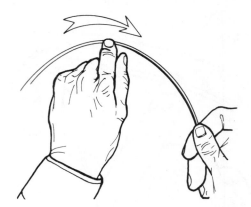

FIGURE 12–30 The right hand establishes the arc.

the tape 1/8 inch from the panel end leaves a flat, uninterrupted surface for adhesion, and also guards against lift when the car is washed. For extra protection, dab the ends of the tape with clear lacquer.

Curves. When applying intricate curves, feel free to use drafting aids (such as french curves) and a marking pen to establish guides. Keep in mind, however that the tape will not stick to these marks. It is probably better to get accustomed to working freehand. To make curve striping designs, proceed as follows:

1. Cut off an ample amount of striping tape.
2. Use the right hand to establish the arc of the curve (Figure 12–30).
3. Use one finger of the left hand to press the tape to the car as the curve is being formed.
4. Do not remove any more backing paper than is necessary. To avoid contaminating the adhesive, leave the backing paper on the tape where your hand is grasping it.
5. Keep both hands moving as the curve is being formed. Some gentle stretching might be required when running curves, but avoid this whenever possible.
6. If the first attempt fails, gently lift the tape and try again. In some awkward situations, it might be easier to apply the striping by switching hand functions.
7. Once the curve is properly applied, burnish the tape for permanent adhesion.

Using Tape with Removable Top Carrier

Striping tape with a removable top carrier is applied in the same manner as tape without a carrier, at least until the stripe has been burnished to the car.

At that point, the top carrier must be removed. Lift it up at the start of the stripe and slowly pull it back in the direction of the remaining stripe, keeping it close to the car. Then burnish the striping again. Trim the tape in the manner already described. When applying around a tight curve, it might be necessary to remove the top carrier first.

Applying Wide Stripes. Striping that is 3 inches wide (or more) is much easier to apply when wet. Use the following procedure:

1. Mix a capful of mild liquid detergent with 1 gallon of water. This solution will make the striping tape more manageable and allow it to be properly positioned before it permanently adheres.
2. Place the solution in a bucket or spray bottle.
3. Measure and cut a piece of tape to the desired length, adding a few inches to allow for errors.
4. Slowly peel away the backing paper, being careful not to let any dirt particles contaminate the adhesive surface.
5. Thoroughly moisten the adhesive side of the tape with the water and detergent solution. This temporarily deactivates the stickiness.
6. Apply liberal amounts of the solution to the vehicle's application area.
7. Position the stripe on the vehicle. The entire piece of tape can be moved freely when the adhesive and body surface are wet.
8. Once the tape is positioned, squeegee the water from beneath it so that it adheres firmly to the surface. To avoid wrinkling the tape, do not squeeze too hard or too fast. Apply just enough pressure to remove all air and water.
9. If applicable, separate the top carrier from the end of the stripe and slowly pull it back toward the other end of the stripe, not out from the body.
10. Trim the edges around the doors and fender wells in the manner described earlier.

End Designs. A variety of end designs can be used to add the finishing touches to the striping job. A popular choice is an arrowhead, which can be done in one of two ways.

Single-Stripe Tape

1. Run a second piece of tape at an angle to form the lower portion of the arrowhead.

FIGURE 12-31   Designing an arrowhead with single-stripe tape

2. Run a third piece of tape in a slight curve to form the backside of the arrowhead (Figure 12-31).
3. Trim the excess tape with a knife or single-edge razor blade.
4. Burnish for permanent adhesion.

Multiple-Stripe Tape

1. Leave an extra length of tape at the ends during the initial application.
2. Once the top carrier is removed (if applicable), separate the stripes and begin to form the backside of the arrowhead with each stripe (Figure 12-32).
3. Take another piece of tape, separate the stripes, and form the actual arrowhead.
4. Trim away excess tape with a knife.
5. Burnish the design. Some multiple-stripe tape kits include precut arrowheads. All that has to be done is trim the end of the stripe square, apply the arrowhead (leaving a 1/8 inch gap between the strips and the arrowhead), then burnish.

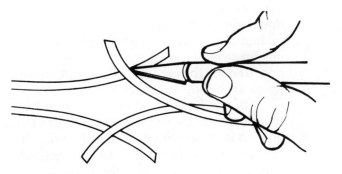

FIGURE 12-32   Designing an arrowhead with multiple-stripe tape

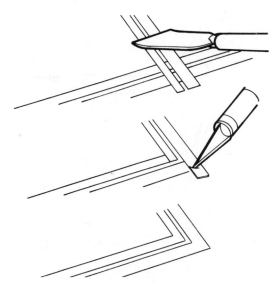

FIGURE 12-33   Standard method of cornering with multiple-color tapes

Panelizing

Applying striping around a panel (such as a door, fender, or pillar) is known as **panelizing.** The procedure is done as follows:

1. Lay stripes around the border of the panel. Leave extra lengths of tape for overlapping.
2. After all the stripes have been applied, trim the ends. In the case of sharp-angled ends, trim bluntly to insure proper adhesion.
3. Check the lines for alignment after the panel is complete.
4. If any adjustments are necessary, lift the tape carefully and reapply.
5. Burnish for proper adhesion.

There are three techniques that can be used to form corners when panelizing with multiple-color tapes. They include:

Standard (Figure 12-33)

1. Remove the top carrier (if applicable) when overlapping the two stripes.
2. Make sure the right colors align (for example, red with red) on the inside angle.
3. Trim away any unnecessary overlapping portion.

Basketweave (Figure 12-34)

1. Remove the top carrier (if applicable) when overlapping the two stripes.
2. Make sure that the same colors do not match up on the inside angle.

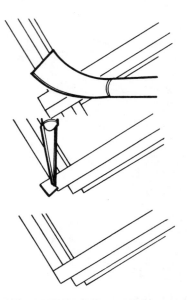

FIGURE 12-34 Basketweave method of cornering with multiple-color tapes

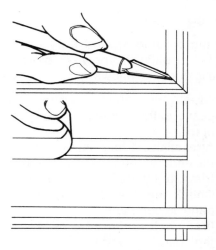

FIGURE 12-35 Reverse method of cornering with multiple-color tapes

3. Cut the stripes at 90 degree corners or angles.

Reverse Corners (Figure 12-35)

1. Apply and burnish the horizontal stripe.
2. Remove the top carrier (if applicable).
3. Apply the vertical stripe so that it overlaps the horizontal stripe to form a 90 degree corner.
4. Make sure that the same colors do not match up at the inside angle.
5. Cut the stripe at a 45 degree angle.
6. Remove the excess tape and the top carrier (if applicable).
7. Burnish for proper adhesion.

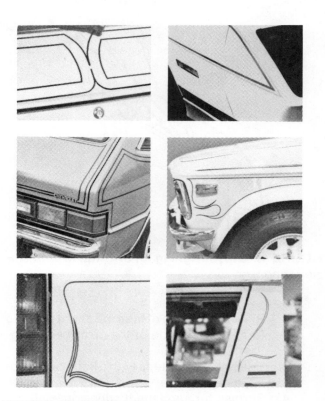

FIGURE 12-36 Creative striping

Some examples of the creative use of the striping procedures just described are shown in Figure 12-36.

ADDING THE FINISHING TOUCHES

Before returning the vehicle to the customer, the refinisher must be constantly aware of all those little things that make a big difference to the customer. These include:

• Vacuum the interior of the car carefully. It should be cleaner than when the customer brought it in. To achieve this it might be necessary to use an automobile fabric reconditioner on interior upholstering and carpet surfaces. Most fabric reconditioners are available in several color tints and a clear shampoo. Reduce the reconditioner solution with water according to the ratio on the label.

After all areas to be reconditioned have been cleaned by either a vacuum or blow gun, apply the reconditioning solution with a soft wire brush to all soiled spots on seats and door panels. Apply a light coat of pre-mixed reconditioner, using a sponge or bristle brush on both front and rear fabric seats, seat belts, carpets, and door panels. No masking is required because leather, vinyl, and metal surfaces are not affected by most reconditioners. (Check manufacturer's instructions.) It is important to saturate stains and water marks thoroughly and brush them with a soft wire brush. When an air gun is used, an air pressure of 60 psi is recommended. Hold the air gun 12 to 18 inches from the surface and direct so that the reconditioner contacts fabric for the best penetration. After an application of the material, use a highly absorbent turkish towel or cloth and with heavy pressure, rub and remove the excess reconditioner from seats, door panels, seat belts, and rugs. Be sure to remove all excess from seat crevices and folds with a dry towel. Heavy toweling removes stains and loosens dirt along with the excess reconditioner. Stubborn stains or water marks remaining after the completion of the application can be removed by brushing an application of an unmixed reconditioner solution. Remove the excess material with an absorbent towel or cloth. Under normal conditions, the entire interior should dry within 12 hours.

- Thoroughly clean all the glass, including windows, mirrors, and lights (Figure 12-37).
- Touch up any overmasked areas and carefully remove any overspray that may have been left on windows or chrome. Touch up overmasking.
- Clean and polish chrome, moldings, and bumpers. Steel wool should not be used to polish chrome because pieces of the wool can easily become embedded in the new paint. Instead, use a commercial chrome polisher.

- Use a brush with soap and water to clean the tires and wheels. Do not let dirty wheels spoil the appearance of an otherwise quality job.
- Use chassis black to blacken wheel openings, the tail pipe, and any other exposed undercarriage parts since overspray often gets on these areas. The customer generally will not notice the time to do this, but it certainly will be noticed if it is not done.
- Replace wipers, moldings, and emblems that were removed before painting. Take the time to clean off old paint that might be on these items and be certain that everything is replaced.
- If the car has a vinyl top, do not forget to wipe it with a damp cloth or a commercial vinyl top cleaner.
- As a finishing touch, most body shops today clean the engine compartment. The easiest way to do this is to spray the engine and engine compartment with a heavy-duty engine cleaner. Flush out the engine compartment with high-pressure water. (Most modern cleaners do not require steam or flammable solutions.) A clean engine and engine compartment usually makes a big impression on the customer.

Finally, inspect the car with a careful eye for all these important details. Make the extra effort. If a window is smeared, clean it again. If a piece of masking tape or paper still remains, remove it. If an emblem is missing, replace it before the customer asks where it is. If the car gets dirty before the customer arrives, wipe it down with a clean cloth (Figure 12-38).

FIGURE 12-37 Clean all glass.

FIGURE 12-38 Always try to send the customer home satisfied.

REVIEW QUESTIONS

1. Which of the following should be applied to a semirigid unpainted plastic material?
   a. primer
   b. primer-surfacer
   c. vinyl washer-primer
   d. none of the above

2. To promote best adhesion to polypropylene plastic parts, Painter A allows primer to flash dry for 10 minutes and then applies interior acrylic lacquer. Painter B applies the acrylic lacquer during the flash period. Who is right?
   a. Painter A
   b. Painter B
   c. Both A and B
   d. Neither A nor B

3. A synthetic primer-surfacer should be applied to rigid plastic parts when _____.
   a. enamel is to be applied
   b. lacquer is to be applied
   c. polyurethane is to be applied
   d. all of the above

4. Painter A does not apply a primer to rigid plastic parts. Painter B does. Who is right?
   a. Painter A
   b. Painter B
   c. Both A and B
   d. Neither A nor B

5. When refinishing a previously painted sheet molded compound with a full panel paint procedure, Painter A does not apply a coat of an adhesion promoter. Painter B applies an adhesion promoter. Who is right?
   a. Painter A
   b. Painter B
   c. Both A and B
   d. Neither A nor B

6. Painter A compounds the surface that has been painted with a topcoat having a flexible additive. Painter B does not compound this type of surface. Who is right?
   a. Painter A
   b. Painter B
   c. Both A and B
   d. Neither A nor B

7. Flexible replacement panels must be _____.
   a. primed with an elastomeric enamel-based primer
   b. solvent cleaned
   c. sanded
   d. all of the above

8. Polypropylene plastic is most commonly used for _____.
   a. fender liners
   b. fenders
   c. bumpers
   d. headlight doors

9. Force drying polypropylene parts above this temperature could result in deformation.
   a. 176 degrees
   b. 185 degrees
   c. 198 degrees
   d. 212 degrees

10. Which of the following is ordinarily used to repaint leather?
    a. vinyl colors
    b. urethanes
    c. acrylics
    d. nitrocellulose lacquers

11. Vinyl preserver withstands which of the following?
    a. sun
    b. salt
    c. snow
    d. all of the above

12. Painter A retextures by blending the new texture out into the old. Painter B retextures to a natural break line on the panel. Who is right?
    a. Painter A
    b. Painter B
    c. Both A and B
    d. Neither A nor B

13. Which of the following is the best final color on a newly retextured area?
    a. acrylic lacquer
    b. acrylic enamel
    c. alkyd enamel
    d. polyurethane

14. It is not necessary to replace the vinyl wood-grain transfer because of _____.
    a. blisters
    b. air bubbles
    c. chips
    d. scratches
    e. all of the above

15. Painter A uses steel wool to clean and polish chrome. Painter B does not. Who is right?
    a. Painter A
    b. Painter B
    c. Both A and B
    d. Neither A nor B

Appendix A
Auto Paint Shop Terms

Abrasive A substance used to wear away a surface by friction.

Accent stripe Any decorative stripe used on an auto body.

Adhesion The ability of one substance to stick to another.

Air drying Allowing paint to dry at ambient (surrounding) temperatures without the aid of an external heat source.

Airless spraying A method of spray application in which atomization is affected by forcing the paint under high pressure through a very small orifice in the spray gun cap. On emerging, the paint instantly expands breaking up into very fine particles.

Alligatoring Term describing lacquer or enamel films in which the finish has cracked into large segments resembling alligator hide. Similar to checking, crazing, and cracking.

Atomize The extent to which the air at the spray gun nozzle breaks up the paint and solvent into fine particles.

Basecoat The coat of paint upon which the final coats will be applied.

Basecoat and clear coat A paint system in which the color effect is given by a highly pigmented basecoat. Gloss and durability are given by a subsequent clear coat. The basecoat **can** be either straight color or metallic.

Binder The ingredient in a paint that holds the pigment particles together.

Bleeding An older color showing through after a new topcoat has been applied.

Blending Mixing together of two or more materials or the gradual shading off from one color to another.

Blistering A bubbling up of the paint film in the form of small blisters.

Body The apparent viscosity of a paint as assessed when stirring it.

Body filler A heavy-bodied plastic material that cures very hard and fills small dents in metal.

Bounce-back Atomized particles of paint that rebound from the surface being sprayed and contribute to overspray.

Buffing compound A soft paste containing fine abrasive in a neutral medium, used to eliminate fine scratches and polish lacquer.

Burnishing To polish or buff a finish by hand or machine using a compound or liquid manufactured for this purpose.

Catalyst A substance that causes or speeds up a chemical reaction when mixed with another substance but does not change by itself.

Chip-resistant The ability to withstand chipping when exposed to normal stone and sand abrasion; and to withstand normal contact with a neighboring car when opening the door in a parking lot.

Chipping A term used to express the condition of the finish flaking off or chipping away from the underneath surface.

Clear coat A top coating on a painted surface that is transparent so that the color coat beneath it is visible.

Closed coat A type of abrasive construction in which the abrasive particles are close to or touch each other.

Coatings Covering material used to protect an area.

Color The visual appearance of a material: red, blue, green, and so on. Colors are seen differently by different people.

Color retention A paint of a certain color, when it is exposed to the elements and does not change, is said to have good color retention.

Compounding The action of using an abrasive material—either by hand or machine—to smooth and bring out the gloss of the applied lacquer topcoat.

Compressor A device used to compress air which in turn is used to spray paint.

Contaminants Foreign substances on the surface to be painted (or in the paint) that would adversely affect the finish.

Conventional reduction Reducing package viscosity material with a solvent according to label directions.

Conversion coating A special metal conditioner or primer used on galvanized and uncoated steel and aluminum to prevent rust.

Corrosion The chemical reaction of air, moisture, or corrosive materials on a metal surface. Usually referred to as rusting or oxidation.

Coverage The area a given amount of paint will cover.

Crawling The action of a finishing material when it appears to creep or crawl away from certain spots and leaves them uncoated.

Crazing Minute interlacing cracks on the surface of a finish.

Cure The process of drying or hardening of a paint film.

Degreasing Cleaning a substrate (usually metallic) by removing greases, oils, and other surface contaminants.

Double coat One single coat followed immediately by a second single coat.

Drier A catalyst added to a paint to speed up the cure or dry.

Drying The process of change of a coat of paint from the liquid to the solid state due to evaporation of solvent, chemical reaction of the binding medium, or a combination of these causes.

Dry spray An imperfect coat, usually caused by spraying too far from the surface being painted or on too hot a surface.

Elastomer A man-made compound with flexible and elastic properties. The resin system of elastomeric enamels and lacquers is made of these elastomeric compounds.

Enamel A type of paint that dries in two stages: first by evaporation of the solvent and then by oxidation of the paint film.

Epoxy A class of resins characterized by good chemical resistance.

Evaporation Solvents in the paint escaping to the air.

Featheredge Tapering the edges of the damaged area with sandpaper or special solvents.

Filler Any body refinishing material used to fill (level) a damaged area.

Film A very thin continuous sheet of material. Paint forms a film on the surface to which it is applied.

Fish-eyes Blemishes in the finish coat usually of a circular and opalescent character.

Flash The first stage of drying where some of the solvents evaporate, which dulls the surface from an exceedingly high gloss to a normal gloss.

Flat Lacking in gloss.

Flood The floating of a pigment to the surface of a coating, giving a changed color to the surface and lack of uniformity in color appearance through the film.

Fog coat A thin, highly atomized coat applied in such a way as to obtain a fast flash off of the thinner and thereby achieve a minimum penetration of the thinner into the old finish.

Force-drying The application of infrared or quartz heat lamps to a painted surface to speed drying. Normally, temperatures up to 180 degrees Fahrenheit, maximum, are safe on cars.

Galvanized Metal coated with zinc.

Gloss The ability of a paint to reflect images when polished.

Grit A measure of the size of particles on sandpaper or discs.

Gumming A condition where the sandpaper becomes clogged by the abraded surface coating. Same as caking.

Haze A degree of cloudiness in an enamel spot repair, particularly around the edges; looks like blushing.

Hardener A curing agent used in plastics.

Hue The characteristic by which one color differs from another, such as red, blue, green, and so on.

Isocyanate Resins This is a principal ingredient in urethane hardeners. Because this ingredient has toxic effects on the painter, the painter is always advised to wear a correct respirator approved by NIOSH.

Lacquer A type of paint that dries by solvent evaporation. Can be rubbed to improve appearance.

Masking Using tape and paper to protect an area that will not be painted.

Metal conditioner A chemical cleaner that removes rust and corrosion from bare metal and helps prevent further rusting.

Metallic paint   Finish-paint colors that contain metallic flakes in addition to pigment.

Mil   A measure of paint film thickness equal to one one-thousandth of an inch.

Miscible   Capable of being mixed

Mist coat   A light spray coat of high-volume solvent for blending and/or gloss production.

Model year   The production period for new motor vehicles or new engines, designated by the calendar year in which the period ends.

OEM   Original Equipment Manufacturer

Opaque   A material is opaque when it is impervious to light. Not transparent.

Original finish   The paint applied at the factory by the vehicle manufacturer.

Overall repainting   A type of refinish repair in which the car is completely repainted.

Overlap   The amount of the spray pattern that covers the previous spray stroke.

Overspray   Paint that falls on the area next to the one being painted.

Oxidation   The combining of oxygen from the air with a paint film. One principal cause of alkyd and acrylic enamel drying.

Paint film   The actual thickness of the paint on a surface.

Paint remover   A mixture of active solvents used to remove paint and varnish coatings.

Peeling   Detachment of a paint film in relatively large pieces.

Pigment   Material in the form of fine powders. Used to impart color, opacity and other effects to paint.

Pinholing   Holes that form in the top coat or undercoat.

Plastic filler   A compound of resin and fiberglass used to fill dents on car bodies.

Polychromatic   A term used by some paint manufacturers for color coats that contain aluminum powder in flake form.

Pot life   The amount of time a painter has to apply a plastic or paint finish to which a catalyst or hardeners was added.

Prime coat   The first coat in a paint system—its main purpose being to impart adhesion.

Primer   An undercoat applied to bare metal to promote adhesion of the topcoat.

Primer-sealer   An undercoat that improves adhesion of the topcoat and seals old painted surfaces that have been sanded.

Primer-surfacer   A high-solids primer that fills small imperfections in the substrate and usually must be sanded.

Putty   A material made for filling small holes or sand scratches.

Reducer   The solvent combination used to thin enamel is usually referred to as a reducer.

Refinish   To remove or seal the old finish and apply a new topcoat; to repaint.

Respirator   A device worn over the mouth to filter particles and fumes out of the air being breathed.

Retarder   A slow evaporating thinner used to retard drying.

Run-sags   When too many or too heavy coats are applied at one time, causing the film to droop under its own weight.

Rust   A form of corrosion in which oxygen combines with metal, causing it to turn brown in color and deteriorate.

Tack cloth   A cheesecloth that has been treated with nondrying varnish to make it tacky. Used to pick up dust and lint from the surface to be painted.

Three-stage   Consist of distinct paint layers that produces a pearlescent appearance: a basecoat, a midcoat, and clearcoat.

Thinner   The solvent combination used to thin lacquers and acrylics to spraying viscosity is usually called thinner.

Tint   A very light color, usually a pastel. To add color to another color or to white.

Tone   A graduation of color, either in hue, a tint, or a shade; as a gray tone.

Topcoat   The last or final color coat.

Toxicity   Pertaining to poisonous effect.

Translucent   Having the property of allowing light to pass through but the objects beyond cannot be clearly distinguished; partly transparent.

Transparent   Having the property of allowing light to pass through so that objects can be identified clearly through it. The opposite of opaque.

Two-part A paint or lacquer supplied in two parts that must be mixed together in the correct proportions before use. The mixture will then remain usable for a limited period only.

Two-stage Consists of two distinct layers of paint: basecoat amd clearcoat.

Undercoat A first coat: primer, sealer, or surfacer.

Vaporization The conversion of solvents into gases during spray painting.

Vehicle The liquid portion of a paint.

Vehicle identification number (VIN) The number assigned to each vehicle by its manufacturer, primarily for registration and identification purposes.

Viscosity Consistency or body of a paint.

Volatile Capable of evaporating easily. That portion which readily vaporizes.

Weathering The change or failure in paint caused by exposure to weather.

Wrinkling The term used when a paint film buckles at its surface, causing a shrivelled appearance.

Index